The Revelation of Restoration

The Revelation of Restoration

Creation's Journey from the Fall to Everlasting Life

DAN SALTER

WIPF & STOCK • Eugene, Oregon

THE REVELATION OF RESTORATION
Creation's Journey from the Fall to Everlasting Life

Copyright © 2025 Dan Salter. All rights reserved. Except for brief quotations in critical publications or reviews, no part of this book may be reproduced in any manner without prior written permission from the publisher. Write: Permissions, Wipf and Stock Publishers, 199 W. 8th Ave., Suite 3, Eugene, OR 97401.

Wipf & Stock
An Imprint of Wipf and Stock Publishers
199 W. 8th Ave., Suite 3
Eugene, OR 97401

www.wipfandstock.com

PAPERBACK ISBN: 979-8-3852-3912-2
HARDCOVER ISBN: 979-8-3852-3913-9
EBOOK ISBN: 979-8-3852-3914-6

02/20/25

Unless otherwise noted, all Scripture quotations are taken from The Holy Bible, New International Version®, NIV®, Copyright © 1973, 1978, 1984, 2011 by Biblica Inc.™ Used by permission. All rights reserved worldwide.

To my mother, whose life and love first showed me the heart of God.

*He who was seated on the throne said,
"I am making everything new!" Then he said,
"Write this down, for these words are trustworthy and true."*

Revelation 21:5 NIV

Contents

Abbreviations   ix
Introduction   xi

PART 1 | GOD'S ACTIVITY IN CREATION'S STORY

1	God Loves	3
2	God Exists	13
3	God Creates	23
4	God Knows	32
5	God Sustains	41
6	God Redeems	49
7	God Gives	59
8	God's Desire	67
9	God Reveals	89
10	God Releases	104

PART 2 | GOD'S IMAGE IN CREATION'S STORY

11	God Imaged in Sonship	115
12	God Imaged in Israel	123
13	God Imaged in Marriage	136
14	God Imaged in Zion	144
15	God Imaged in Suffering	154
16	God Imaged in Blood	160
17	God Imaged in Sacrifice	165
18	God Imaged in Temple	174
19	God Imaged in Warfare	181
20	God Imaged in Sabbath	192

PART 3 | GOD'S RETELLING OF CREATION'S STORY

21	Introducing the Theme (Rev 1)	207
22	Encouraging with Reward (Rev 2–3)	217
23	Forming God's Restoration Plan (Rev 4–5)	230
24	Preparing for Atonement (Rev 6–9)	242
25	Hoping for Redemption (Rev 8–11)	250
26	Explaining the Current Age (Rev 12–13)	265
27	Reaping through Wrath (Rev 14–16)	278
28	Viewing the Fall (Rev 17–19)	288
29	Concluding the Bitter and Sweet (Rev 20)	299
30	Reigning in Rest (Rev 21–22)	308

Appendix: Kinship Theology   319
Bibliography   323

Abbreviations

CSB	Christian Standard Bible
ESV	English Standard Version
HCSB	Holman Christian Standard Bible
KJV	King James Version
KNT	Kingdom New Testament
KT	Kinship Theology
NASB	New American Standard Bible
NET	New English Translation
NIV	New International Version
NT	New Testament
OT	Old Testament
TGB	Truth, Goodness, and Beauty (God's essence)

Introduction

Our little systems have their day;
They have their day and cease to be:
They are but broken lights of thee,
And thou, O Lord, art more than they.

—Alfred, Lord Tennyson, from "In Memoriam"

Guide me in your truth and teach me,
for you are God my Savior,
and my hope is in you all day long.

—Psalm 25:5

I WAS 10 YEARS old when I attended my first prophecy conference. An evangelist known for his dispensationalism came to Greenville, South Carolina—then the buckle of fundamentalism's Bible belt—to stir up excitement with his prophetic teachings of the rapture, tribulation, and Christ's thousand-year reign on earth. He filled his talks at Greenville Memorial Auditorium with fantastic images leaping from the pages of Revelation—all literal, he insisted (that is, at points here and there). He titled one sermon "The Coming War with Russia" and predicted the conflict would break out within five years. That was in 1967. Five years later, he was still preaching the same message though omitting reference to exact timing. His sermon temporized a bit more after the USSR dismantled.

The evangelist's sermons were electrifying. His enthusiasm never waned, even as the prominent "signs" he identified faded into obscurity, forcing him to shift his focus to new events. His dramatic delivery, punctuated by the rapid recitation of dozens of the thousands of Bible verses he'd memorized, mesmerized his audiences. We all left those meetings both anxious about the antichrist and hopeful for Christ's imminent return ("maybe even tonight before this meeting ends!").

But what I remember most vividly isn't what the evangelist said, but how his listeners absorbed every word. Prophecy captivates, especially when brought to life with charts and graphs, highlighted by images of falling stars, sea monsters, and scorpion-stinging demons belched from a bottomless pit. Revelation can be daunting to navigate alone, so preachers who paint these scenes with drama and vibrancy fill seats with seekers eager to be both frightened and fascinated.

By the time I turned 14, however, I had already read George Ladd's *The Blessed Hope*, which tempered my dispensationalism into classic premillennialism. The charts shifted slightly, but surrounded by my fundamentalist community, I found it difficult to question the framework I had inherited. My inquiries remained confined mostly to the *what* rather than advancing to the *why*.

Over time, though, I grew restless with merely identifying events and arranging them in presumed order. Lingering questions about purpose nagged at me. For instance, after dismissing the idea of national Israel as the focal point of Christ's future kingdom, I began to wonder why God would need a thousand-year reign on earth before finally eradicating sin. One evening during my high school years, I asked my dad—the smartest person I knew—about the purpose of the millennium. Though I knew he was given more to philosophy than prophecy, his simple answer, "I don't know," stunned me. He, too, had attended those prophecy conferences and read George Ladd, but his keen adult mind hadn't grasped any clearer conclusions than mine had.

And so began a turbulent journey through various millennial views, interpretive methods, and, of course, many more charts. Oddly enough, when I finally reached solid ground, I found myself on the *un*charted island of amillennialism—a stripped-down, Ockham's razor approach that, despite its simplicity, proved far more satisfying. But more on that later.

Eschatology is the study of last things. The Greek word *eschatos* emphasizes the remoteness of these events, focusing on topics at the uttermost end: judgment, final death, heaven, and hell. Millennial interpretations, especially those of Revelation, often seem to encompass almost everything in our future, much as prophecy did for Old Testament Israel. The unknown future can be frightening, especially when it involves death. Prophecy offers answers that soothe these fears, and that's a large part of its appeal.

But the real source of comfort lies deeper than merely having prophecy explained—it's the assurance that God is guiding us into the future. Consciously or subconsciously, we welcome the arrival of beasts, flying demons, and fire-breathing dragons because we trust that God is our shield and protector. More foundational than the belief that God *can* protect us is our certainty that he *will* protect us. He will shield us because he loves us.

Love relationship with God is the foundation of every aspect of eschatology. I believe the many opposing views of the future exist because we often fail to fully realize how love relationship permeates every dimension of God's eschatological plan. Of course, love extends beyond eschatology. God created the world for the purpose of relational love, making love the compass for any theological study—including eschatology. I've come to call this relational perspective "Kinship theology"—the belief that God interacts with his creation always and only for the purpose of love relationship.

KINSHIP THEOLOGY

Kinship theology (KT) is a concept that runs throughout all Scripture. At its core, KT emphasizes the kindred bond we share with God and his people by our imaging. Just as God exists in a trinitarian structure—three distinct persons united in one essence of infinite truth, goodness, and beauty (TGB)—so we, as humans, reflect this in our own "multiple-in-one" design. We are a multitude of individual persons, yet we share a single essence of physical creation—the air, water, and elements that not only surround us but flow through and constitute our bodies. Each of us, as individuals, possesses a metaphysical aspect, our soul, which relies on an intergrative relationship with this shared essence—the elemental composition of all physical creation. Thus, what we perceive as our individual bodies is essentially an accumulation of this physical essence, sustaining life through continuous interaction.

Our souls, this metaphysical aspect of our being, can also be further divided into two categories: the psyche and the spirit. The psyche encompasses the mind, will, and emotions, while the spirit contains certain intrinsic affections that define our human condition. These include the desire for truth, goodness, and beauty (whether or not we recognize their source in God), the drive toward relationship, and even the longing or hope for life.

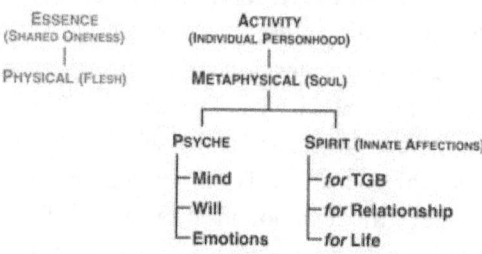

In addition, our souls themselves image God. Through the combination of our psyche and spirit, we *comprehend* through our conceptual intelligence, conscious morality, and critical aesthetic. We *concur* in concluding faith and continuing hope. And we *communicate* that comprehension and concurrence in communal love. Within these imaging qualities, we can understand God (within the broad limits he has set for our finite minds) and enjoy a relationship with him through faith, hope, and love.

God also endowed human souls—our psyches and spirits—with dominion over physical creation—our essence. The fall occurred when our first parents abandoned their authority, choosing to define good and evil by their own essence rather than God's. In this act, they "exchanged the truth about God for a lie, and worshiped and served created things rather than the Creator—who is forever praised. Amen" (Romans 1:25). The holy bodies, misused in idolatry, brought a curse upon all physical creation. The curse reversed the order, giving physical creation dominion over human souls. As slaves to the flesh's sinful desires, humanity continued to sin (to miss the purposed mark for which they had been created—love relationship with God based on his TGB). Romans describes this curse as creation groaning in birth pangs, longing for release from its corruption (Romans 8:21). Consequently, the constant rejection through sin caused by the curse on human essence created a seemingly insurmountable barrier between God and his image bearers.

Yet God planned a rescue for this dire situation, addressing both the need for forgiveness for committed sins and redemption from the curse. While no human soul could overcome the dominion of cursed human essence, Jesus, a Person of the Godhead, took on human essence ("flesh like ours under sin's domain" Romans 8:3, HCSB). He lived without yielding to its sinful control and willingly put that essence to death, only to resurrect it freed from the curse. This redeemed condition of his essence is promised to all who repent of their sins to receive forgiveness and who embrace God's redemptive work through faith in God's rescue and TGB foundation for life.

KT focuses on the three human relationships God established for humans in pre-fall Eden. The first is God's provision for his image bearers, who trusted him for that care. The second is the bond between humanity's souls (psyches and spirits) and their essence (their bodies). The third is the relationship among humans, characterized by mutual self-giving for the benefit of the relationship.

The fall shattered these three relationships. Humanity turned away from God's care, placing trust in themselves. The soul's dominion over the body deteriorated into subjugation to the body's selfish desires. Human relationships also fractured, as seen in Genesis 3's depiction of the struggle for control between husband and wife.

However, God's restoration plan promises renewal for each of these relationships. He restores his bond with humanity through *soteriological* means: our faith in God, who forgives sins and secured, through the atonement, the future redemption of our bodies from the curse. The healing of the rift between soul and essence awaits Christ's return, when he will liberate the physical through resurrection and redemption—our *eschatological* hope. Finally, the discord among humans is resolved through a proper understanding of *ecclesiology*, a spiritual community where God is intricately involved. Recognizing our equal status before God in image and worth, we learn to relate to one another in love, embracing a posture of mutual submission.

These aspects of KT, made possible only through God's restoration plan, are grounded in the triad of faith, hope, and love, by which we embody God's revealed truth, goodness, and beauty. This path of TGB, manifested and embraced through faith, hope, and love, unfolds and develops throughout the Bible, from Genesis to Isaiah, to John, to Romans, and finally to Revelation. The Old Testament was not a preliminary plan or "Plan A" to be discarded in favor of the New Testament's "Plan B." It is the same divine plan, with the same relational elements, growing through revelation as we accept in faith, rest in hope, and act in love.

CREATION'S STORY

While eschatology often brings our thoughts to the book of Revelation, it's important to recognize that the events of the end times have meaning only as the culmination of creation's entire story. This story spans God's purposeful creation, the disruption caused by sin, God's plan of restoration, his gathering of those who seek rescue and relationship with him, the removal of evil, and the ultimate fulfillment of God's purpose in embracing his image bearers.

Which part of this grand narrative does Revelation reveal? It is more than just the conclusion—that final defeat of evil and the everlasting rest that Christians long for. Despite its complex apocalyptic imagery, Revelation marvelously summarizes the full scope of God's redemptive, refining, and restorative work. With this in mind, our study must revisit earlier elements of the story to fully understand the foundation that leads to Revelation's climactic summary.

This book is organized in three parts: (1) God's Activity in Creation's Story, (2) God's Image in Creation's Story, and (3) God's Retelling of Creation's Story. The first part explores certain truths about God, his motivation, and his actions in addressing the problem of the fall. The second part focuses on the images in Scripture that reveal God's purpose and plan. Finally, in part three, we will journey through the book of Revelation to see how John encapsulates this entire narrative.

Each part contains 10 chapters, and they are designed to correlate with one another in perspective. For example, the first chapters of parts one, two, and three (the book's chapters 1, 11, and 21) are linked together thematically. This pattern continues throughout the book, creating a thematic connection among the corresponding chapters of each part (e.g., chapters 2, 12, and 22), as shown below.

Part 1 Activity	Part 2 Imagery	Part 3 Retelling	Perspective
Ch 1	Ch 11	Ch 21	Who God Is (the basis for life)
Ch 2	Ch 12	Ch 22	God's Relationship with His People
Ch 3	Ch 13	Ch 23	God's Glory (seen predominantly in Jesus)
Ch 4	Ch 14	Ch 24	God's Protection (through necessary growing)
Ch 5	Ch 15	Ch 25	Curse Effects
Ch 6	Ch 16	Ch 26	Rescue and Waiting in Hope
Ch 7	Ch 17	Ch 27	How Love Wins
Ch 8	Ch 18	Ch 28	Necessity of Love Relationship
Ch 9	Ch 19	Ch 29	Contrast of Love and Wrath
Ch 10	Ch 20	Ch 30	After Evil Ends

Part 1

God's Activity in Creation's Story

1

God Loves

O love of God, how deep and great!
Far deeper than man's deepest hate;
Self-fed, self-kindled like the light,
Changeless, eternal, infinite.

—Horatius Bonar, from "The Love of God"

And so we know and rely on the love God has for us.
God is love. Whoever lives in love lives in God,
and God in them.

—1 John 4:16

"God is love!" I imagine the beloved disciple pausing after writing those words, overcome once again, even in his old age, by their wonder and hope. He proclaimed them in his first letter not just because they brought him joy, but because they were the culmination of his argument. "God is love" (1 John 4:8) is the conclusion drawn from his starting point: "God is light" (1 John 1:5). Light illuminates and reveals. The psalmist called on God to "send Your light and Your truth; let them lead me" (Psalm 43:3 HCSB). True to his nature as light—where no darkness exists at all (1 John 1:5)—God has indeed revealed himself. We know of God because he has unveiled his truth, goodness, and beauty to us. We know of God because he sent Jesus to be the full revelation of himself. Through Jesus, we discovered that God seeks a loving relationship with us. This reveals something profound: if God desires a relationship of love and intentionally discloses that to us, then the revelation itself—God's light—is also a gift of love.

When John asserts that no darkness exists in God, he means that what God reveals of himself is true, fully consistent with every aspect of his entire being. Embracing that light not only overcomes sin's separation from God but also leads to fellowship with all who embrace God's light (1:7, 9). In chapter 4, John draws the connection between light and love: because God is love (revealed through his light), to know God in relationship is to have his love within us, as we have embraced him through Jesus (4:8–9).

This conclusion is profound, though it may be challenging to grasp how John moves from understanding love as an action to recognizing love as God's very nature. In 1 John 4:8, John emphasizes that God is love, not merely that he loves. While we often refer to love as a noun—whether in expressions like "love is a warm puppy" or "love means never having to say you're sorry"—these typically label a collection of loving actions. However, John's insight goes deeper. Just as Isaiah called God "my salvation" (Isaiah 12:2) because God saves, we might call a generous person "generosity itself" or a hospitable one "hospitality itself." Similarly, John calls our loving God "love itself" because love is the only possible expression of his divine nature, characterized by truth, goodness, and beauty.

Paul discusses this nature and activity of God in Romans 1:20, where he writes that God reveals his eternal power and divine nature. This nature—comprising truth, goodness, and beauty—forms God's very essence. Since power is expressed through activity and activity stems from one's essence, God's actions must align with his essence of truth, goodness, and beauty. Therefore, his eternal power must be love. The Bible's portrayal of love, as summarized by Paul in 1 Corinthians 13, as a derivative of truth, goodness, and beauty, confirms this point. Thus, John's declaration that God is love makes perfect sense.

Yet, this concept can be difficult for both unbelievers and believers to grasp. The problem lies in our tendency to conceptualize God in human terms. We imagine God as the greatest possible human, much like the Romans and Greeks envisioned their gods or how we think of comic book superheroes. We create a god in our image, endowed with noble attributes, rather than recognizing that God *is* truth, goodness, and beauty himself. We think of him as a superman with powers and abilities far beyond those of mortal men. However, the true distinction between God and us is not that he has supercharged versions of our human attributes, but that his eternal power of love is rooted in his divine nature of truth, goodness, and beauty.

The so-called riddle of the heavy stone illustrates this misunderstanding. A common atheist challenge asks whether God can create a rock so heavy that even he cannot lift it. The question is intended to expose a limitation in God's power—whether he cannot create such a rock or cannot lift it. Either answer seems to suggest a limit to his omnipotence, thereby challenging the existence of an all-powerful being.

However, as many have pointed out, the question itself is irrational, and God does not engage in the irrational. Asking whether an infinite being can overpower his infinite power is inherently absurd, akin to asking whether an infinite being can beat himself in a boxing match or be born in 1957. By definition, an infinite being cannot impose limits on himself while remaining unlimited. This is the law of non-contradiction. Yet, even if the atheist acknowledges this and the Christian applauds the answer, they may still miss the deeper point.

God is not merely an enhanced version of humanity with supernatural extensions of our powers. God is infinite in who he is, not in who we are. Thus, even though God is powerful, there are things he cannot do—not because of a lack of power, but because they are contrary to his essence. God cannot use his muscles to lift a rock, whether heavy or light, because he does not have muscles; they are not part of his essence. Similarly, God cannot lie because truth is not just a good idea for him; it is part of who he is. God cannot do evil because goodness is his very being. As Paul tells Timothy, even "if we give up on him, he does not give up—for there's *no way he can be false to himself*" (2 Timothy 2:13, *The Message*; emphasis added). Therefore, in John's first epistle, we learn that because of who God is, love must be the catalyst for all his actions.

WHAT IS LOVE?

What, then, are we trying to say about God? If God is love, what do we mean—what is love? Is it merely an act of kindness? Is it simply the emotional surge of sentimentality? We often speak of tough love. Does God's love encompass that? If so, in what way? Because love is often tied to feelings, many people find it difficult to define. However, we need to look beyond ourselves. We may love at times, but we are not love itself. What are the common aspects of love that exist in God and thus set the boundaries for its definition?

First, love is not merely the wish for another's happiness. Some atheists attempt to disprove God's existence by arguing that if an all-good, all-powerful Creator existed, he would both want to and be able to make his creatures happy. Since humanity is far from universally happy, they reason, an all-good, all-powerful God cannot exist. However, the logic is flawed because it assumes that personal happiness (the goal of humans) is the ultimate goal of a God of truth, goodness, and beauty. But is simply bestowing happiness—or conversely, preventing evil—the greatest gift that the only true, good, and beautiful God could give? Would not a good God, acting in love, resist fulfilling his creatures' immediate desires if the opportunity for growth could lead to a greater good? Wouldn't an all-good God, acting in perfect love, want and *necessarily* allow his image bearers to realize for themselves that same great and satisfying love? I believe he would. And if that's the case, how would this infinitely loving God go about accomplishing that greater good?

We may have to realign our thinking here. The common perception of goodness—and love's activity toward it—is that it provides exclusive benefit for the individual self. But this idea stands in contrast to the New Testament's view, which connects love with *giving*, particularly of oneself. In the Bible's most famous verse, John quotes Jesus explaining the gospel (my paraphrase): "In this way God loved the world: he *gave* his only begotten Son so that all those trusting in him will never be separated from him but rather will join him in everlasting love relationship" (John 3:16).

At the Last Supper discussion, Jesus emphasized the *sacrificial* aspect of love when he told his disciples, "Greater love has no one than this: to lay down one's life for one's friends" (John 15:13). The comparative in his statement implies degrees of love, measured by the cost to oneself. A person's life is the most precious possession (the use of the body [human essence] by the individual's soul), so giving one's life is giving everything. By identifying the giving of one's very life as the pinnacle of love, Jesus reveals that self-giving is the fundamental quality of love.

Earlier that evening, Jesus had washed his disciples' feet. Peter, still thinking in worldly terms, believed what Jesus was doing was utterly wrong. Peter saw Jesus as their leader, their teacher, the Messiah, the Son of God! He shouldn't be the one washing feet! But Jesus's response—that if he didn't wash Peter's feet, Peter would have no part with him—turned

Peter's world upside down because the values of the kingdom of heaven *are* indeed upside down compared to those of this world.

Our Adam-caused curse makes us seek our own promotion in admiration, possession, comfort, and control—and consider it justified for others of worldly importance to claim those same benefits. Peter reasoned that the more important a person was, the *less* that person should *give* of himself or herself. However, Jesus's kingdom "is not of this world" (John 18:36). When Jesus later mentioned the kingdom contrast to Pilate, he explained, "If it were [if his kingdom were of this world], my servants would fight." Jesus was not suggesting that under different circumstances, his servants *would* then fight. Rather, he was arguing that fighting—seeking to gain control over others by force—while typical of every kingdom in this world, did not characterize his. Why? Because the kingdom of God is a kingdom of love—one in which its citizens and even its God *give* of themselves.

The simple lesson of the rich, young ruler illustrates these upside-down values. Matthew tells of a man who approaches Jesus to ask what good he must do to have eternal life (Matthew 19:16). Jesus asks the man why he is concerned with what good to do since the Law already outlines what is good. When the man insists that he already follows the Law, Jesus drives home his point: keeping the commands (not killing, not stealing, not lying, etc.) was not meant to promote self-worth through technical but minimal compliance. Instead, they were meant to demonstrate what an attitude of love for others—love that benefits others—looks like. Not stealing from someone benefits that person who then retains all his possessions. Not lying to someone benefits that person by preserving truth. And certainly not killing someone benefits the one allowed to live. Jesus, therefore, expands the Law's commands from check-off-list activities to an all-encompassing attitude of purpose when he tells the man to sell all he has and give it to the poor. Jesus was not suggesting that the more he gave, the more worthy he would become. Rather, Jesus was advocating a shift in focus—from self to a whole-hearted commitment to relationships with those around him. Jesus later sums up this purpose in Matthew 22:39: "Love your neighbor as yourself." Just as you value your possessions for yourself, love for others should lead you to desire the same benefit for them, causing the internal struggle for exclusive possession to melt away.

But notice another deeper, more fulfilling aspect of love that we can draw from Jesus's comment. When I was young, I wondered why Jesus said, "Love your neighbor *as* yourself." I thought he should have said, "Love your neighbor *more than* yourself," or even "*instead of* yourself." In other words, I confused kindness and sacrifice with love. But they are not the same. Kindness is demonstrated by providing a benefit to another, and sacrifice refers to the cost to the provider. But kindness and sacrifice become *love* when the provider hopes that his or her actions will *benefit a relationship*. The contrasting views of the kingdom of this world and the kingdom of heaven pivot on the desire for benefit: one is focused exclusively on self, and the other is centered on relationships. More than mere kindness, if I love, I desire *mutual* benefit, not only for the other person but also for myself. In love, I recognize the shared aspect of benefit *in a relationship*. And that, I think, is why Jesus said to love your neighbor *as* yourself, rather than *instead of* yourself.

The giving of self, then, is not focused on self-deprivation but on the recognition that love desires relationship, not self-exclusivity. Paul echoes this sentiment. He doesn't contradict Jesus's advice to the rich man to sell all for the poor when he writes in 1 Corinthians 13:3, "If I give all I possess to the poor . . . but do not have love, I gain nothing." Paul notes that the gain comes not merely from kindness and sacrifice but from using them with the hope of fostering a relationship.

In summary, we can define love as the giving of oneself for the benefit of relationship. This definition does not imply a differentiation from the categorical types of love that, for example, C.S. Lewis identifies: affection, friendship, romantic love, and charity.[1] *All* these types of love are rooted in self-giving for the benefit of relationship. Returning to John 3:16, we find these elements of the love we're urged to imitate clearly expressed. Notice particularly that in the opening line (again, of my paraphrase), Jesus leads with "In this way, God loved the world." In other words, Jesus is intent on explaining *how* God loves. And the first aspect of that divine love is self-giving: "he gave his only begotten Son." Jesus concludes with the purpose of God's self-giving: "that all those trusting in him (those who embrace the Son's glory and receive his redemptive love) will never be separated from him but rather will join him in everlasting love relationship."

So why does a good, all-powerful God tolerate the presence of evil? He does so because his essence is expressed in love—a noncoercive giving of self for the benefit of love relationship with his image bearers, who,

---

1. Lewis, *Four Loves*.

in turn, adopt and reflect his truth, goodness, and beauty through his love-infused light.

CAN LOVE HARM?

Any understanding of God's actions that suggests he sometimes sets aside his love to perform some contrary task is both anti-biblical and contrary to the nature of God. While this assertion may seem bold, it is undeniable if we believe in a God of *infinite*—not just occasionally expressed—love. Therefore, Christians who firmly hold that God always acts in love must, at times, pause in their Scripture reading to reconsider and reevaluate the violent depictions of a warrior God. How do we reconcile the judgment passages of Scripture? Don't they depict a God who hurts, harms, and ultimately destroys? Does believing in a God of infinite love mean he never becomes "angry enough to destroy" (Deuteronomy 9:8)? Isn't it true that this God of infinite love has enemies who "at the blast of his anger they are no more" (Job 4:9)? After all, Jesus said, "Whoever rejects the Son will not see life, for God's wrath remains on them" (John 3:36). So how do we harmonize a God who always acts in love with the biblical depictions of his angry violence?

The answer is not simple; it requires deep, reflective thought. In our soundbite-driven generation, where ideas are often reduced to brief, dogmatic statements that can be shouted from a street corner or fit on a bumper sticker or tweet, we risk superficial understanding. But presenting ourselves approved to God usually demands more diligence in our study.

The easy, but incorrect, way to harmonize these ideas is to believe that God sometimes stops loving. If God embodies infinite truth, goodness, and beauty, he cannot cease being those things, even when he assumes a judicial role due to the sinfulness of his creation. Recognizing this, some Christians attempt to redefine love. They reason, "If God truly loves truth, goodness, and beauty, he must oppose all that is contrary to them. Therefore, even his violent actions can be considered expressions of love, as they are directed against evil, which opposes his essence." While this reasoning may initially seem to offer a solution, it overlooks the biblical definition of love as the giving of self for the benefit of relationship.

Our struggle to justify God's seeming violence stems from our habit of ascribing merely super*human* characteristics to him. We assume that if God loves his tri-noble essence, he must hate all that opposes it—and that is true. But we go astray when we assume that God's "hate" manifests in the same way as our human anger.

God created us as his image bearers, but imaging does not mean duplicating. Humans reflect God's structure of one essence and multiple persons. God is one essence of truth, goodness, and beauty expressed in three persons, each with mind, will, and actions. Humans, too, are multiple persons, each with individual mind, will, and action, but our one essence differs from God's. He is infinite and non-physical, while our essence is rooted in physicality—the universe of matter and energy. This physical universe is finite, unlike God's infinite essence. Thus, when we act, we do so according to our physical essence. But when God acts, he does so according to his essence of infinite truth, goodness, and beauty. Therefore, when we love, we express it through physical gestures like a caress, and when we feel anger, we might strike. But when God loves, he embraces with his spirit—his presence—infusing his object of love with life-giving truth, goodness, and beauty. Conversely, when God is angry, his presence is absent—he cannot embrace with his spirit. Paul alludes to this dynamic in Romans 1, contrasting God's embrace in salvation (1:16–17) with his wrath in "giving over" (1:24, 26, 28), which signifies the absence of his presence. This embrace and absence express the eschatological action of God for redemption and justice, already unfolding and culminating when Christ returns. As Ben Witherington III observes, "What differentiates Paul's discourse from the usual Jewish polemics against paganism is that Paul believes that since the Christ-event has transpired the eschatological action of God for both salvation and judgment is already in play."[2]

God is not, as some atheists might imagine, merely a being who arbitrarily makes situations good for individuals, reveals truth, or shines beauty upon them. His actions—whether doing good, revealing truth, or displaying beauty—stem from his loving presence. The greater the opportunity for love, the more his presence enriches relationships with truth, goodness, and beauty. But when love is rejected, his presence diminishes, making it impossible for the individual or situation to reflect his divine essence.

In essence, if God embodies all that is true, good, and beautiful, his absence, is the opposite—falsehood, horror, and ugliness. The question is

---

2. Witherington, *Romans*, 65.

not whether God "can" make a situation good, but whether love relationship can or does still exist. If it does, God is present, and his presence enriches. If love is resisted and the relationship with the Source of life and blessing is rejected, his limited presence means that his essence cannot flourish in that life or situation.

Consider these passages and reflect on God's actions when confronted with evil (all emphases added):

- Deuteronomy 31:17–18 "And in that day I will become angry with them and forsake them; I will hide my face from them, and they will be destroyed. Many disasters and calamities will come on them, and in that day they will ask, 'Have not these disasters come on us because our God is not with us?' And I will certainly *hide my face* in that day because of all their wickedness in turning to other gods."
- Job 13:24 "Why do you *hide your face* and consider me your enemy?"
- Ezekiel 39:24 "I dealt with them according to their uncleanness and their offenses, and I *hid my face* from them."
- 1 Peter 3:12 (quoting Psalm 34:15–16) "For the eyes of the Lord are on the righteous and his ears are attentive to their prayer, but *the face of the Lord is against those* who do evil."
- Revelation 22:3–4 "No longer will there be any curse. The throne of God and of the Lamb will be in the city, and his servants will serve him. They *will see his face*, and his name will be on their foreheads."

Many translations speak of the "face of God" in these passages—hiding his face when people act wickedly and showing his face when they seek him. The "face of God," a prominent concept in Scripture regarding the consequences of actions, symbolizes the blessing of his presence. Where we read that God hides his face, Scripture's intent is to signify the absence of his presence, leading to chaos and destruction.

Thus, when the Bible describes God bringing harm to someone, it should be understood anthropomorphically, much like Isaiah 59:1: "Surely the arm of the Lord is not too short to save, nor his ear too dull to hear." Just as God has no physical arm or ear, he has no physical capacity to harm. Often, when Scripture speaks of harm accompanying God's displeasure, it uses anthropomorphic language to help us grasp the consequences of rejecting him. In reality, pain and destruction stem from the absence of God's presence, which occurs not because God turns away, but because the person turns away from him.

James 1:20 tells us that human anger does not produce God's righteousness. Why? Because human anger leads to violence—a striking out against another. God, however, does not (and cannot) respond in this way. The contrast between God's presence and absence is as stark as day and night when it comes to the good and evil that emerge in any situation.

Understanding the God who loves affects every aspect of Scripture we hold dear. Much more can be said and must be understood to fully grasp this concept. In the following chapters, we will explore the various ways God's love operates in a fallen world. In chapter 2, we will examine his love in seeking relationship, and in chapter 3, how he manifests TGB. Chapter 4 will address how a God of love could create a world knowing the potential for evil. Chapters 5 and 6 will explore how God continues to love within a cursed environment. Chapter 7 will focus on God's love in redemption, while chapter 8 will discuss how adhering to the Bible's definition of love can help us navigate doctrinal extremes. Chapter 9 will delve into the connection between God's light in revelation and his love. Finally, in chapter 10, we will revisit God's wrath to understand how the end does not signify God ceasing to love.

God loves. And our unchanging God always loves. But does our definition of love not require that God give of himself? And doesn't that imply that God, in some way, changes? The transition from not having a love relationship with someone to having one suggests change. How does God's consistent, unchangeable nature interact with a world of process and change? We'll explore that idea next.

2

God Exists

He who binds to himself a joy
Does the winged life destroy;
He who kisses the joy as it flies
Lives in eternity's sunrise.

—WILLIAM BLAKE, FROM "ETERNITY"

Before the mountains were born,
or you brought forth the whole world,
from everlasting to everlasting you are God.

—PSALM 90:2

CAN YOU IMAGINE A world without time? It's almost inconceivable, as existence without any sequential progression defies everything we know. We live by process and understand reality point by point. Even this very paragraph moves from one thought to another! And hope itself implies a future.

All eschatologies must grapple with questions about time.[1] As Christians, we believe we will live forever because our God lives forever, and

---

1. I am using the term *time* to mean sequence of moments, not the measurement of those moments. By this I'm hoping to avoid some of the issues tackled in both the general and special theories of relativity. For deeper discussion along those lines, I recommend William Lane Craig's *Time and Eternity: Exploring God's Relationship to Time*.

he created us for everlasting love relationship. Facing an unending future poses no difficulty for us. But when we consider the past, the perspective shifts. Our finite earthly lives begin at birth, and while we may debate the exact starting point of the human race, most people envision a definite beginning. But let's extend our view further back, beyond the formation of the world and before the initial explosion of creation. Christians generally agree that God, as the First Cause, initiated everything by creating the universe and setting it in motion. But did God, back then—or before then—experience time as we do, with one moment leading to the next? Can such progression stretch eternally into the past, just as we imagine it will into the future? Or did God create time—along with progression and sequence—when he created the universe?

We need a foundational truth to guide our thoughts. As we discussed in chapter 1, love is God's motivation in all activity. With that understanding, I believe we can find a satisfying path through this perplexing question.

REENFORCING OUR DEFINITION OF LOVE

As we discussed in the last chapter, the Bible defines love as the giving of oneself for the benefit of a relationship. This act of giving suggests movement—a reaching out from within to beyond. It involves a form of sacrifice, offering something we possess, whether it's an object, assistance, or simply time. When Jesus said, "Greater love has no one than this: to lay down one's life for one's friends" (John 15:13), he was pointing to the ultimate sacrifice, offering everything we have—our very lives, including all our earthly time. But we must remember the second part of the definition: for the benefit of a relationship. Love is not just about sacrifice; it carries a purpose—for relational benefit. Jesus illustrated this in Matthew 25 when he praised those who fed, gave drink, clothed, and cared for others—for the *benefit* of the king's *brothers*. Acts of kindness become acts of love when they are done with the intent to build and nurture relationships.

Marriage serves as a good example of this understanding of love. Ideally, both husband and wife give of themselves, not just for the other person, but for the well-being of their shared relationship. In Ephesians 5, Paul uses marriage as a metaphor for the kingdom-of-heaven love relationship he encourages among the Ephesians. After urging them to submit to one another in verse 21, Paul illustrates this concept through marriage, instructing wives to give of themselves (as seen in the word "submit" in verses 22 and 24) to their husbands, and husbands to give of themselves (as seen in the word "love" in verse 25) to their wives. These instructions are not different in essence, as if wives don't need to "love" and husbands don't need to "submit." Rather the words are synonyms Paul uses to reflect the same principle: the giving of oneself for the benefit of the relationship.

It's crucial to understand that a love relationship cannot exist unless both parties express love. Love may exist in one partner who gives of self in hopes of building a relationship, but a love relationship becomes real only when love flows in both directions. If only one person loves, the relationship remains an imagined goal of the one lover's desire. Many marriages fail because one partner enters the union with the intent to receive love rather than to offer himself or herself for the relationship's benefit.

In fact, if we adhere strictly to our definition, "unrequited love" is a misnomer. When someone realizes that his or her self-sacrifice does not—and will not—lead to a loving relationship because the other party refuses to reciprocate, what remains is no longer love. Continued giving in this context may be kindness, grace, or compassion, but it cannot be considered love. For an act of self-giving to be classified as love, it must be intended to benefit the relationship.

As we discussed in chapter 1, God's essence is truth, goodness, and beauty. But essence and action—who we are and what we do—are inseparable. God's gift of love to humanity is his essence of truth, goodness, and beauty (TGB); he reveals himself so that we can know him and understand the foundation for our relationship with him.

To emphasize further: who God is—his *essence*—is TGB. What God does—his *actions*—are expressions of his essence for the benefit of our relationship with him. Therefore, all of God's actions align with the definition of love. In every revelation—every interaction—from creation to teaching, from redemption to prophecy, God acts in love, because all he gives is for our relational benefit. This love fueled the creation of the world, embraced Adam and Eve even after they caused the curse, devised the plan of redemption, and triumphed through the cross and resurrection. Love defines all God's actions.

As we delve into the study of biblical eschatology, we must recognize God's divine nature and eternal power in shaping his everlasting kingdom. God's love, empowered by his essence of truth, goodness, and beauty, is not only what God does but also what he desires, expects, and urges us to do. He doesn't encourage love merely because it's good for us or because it seems fitting for a good king to command. He does so because he, just as much as we, desires this shared love relationship. Imagine that! God lives to love, and he directs his love toward us! Our understanding of "things to come" must, therefore, encompass our creator and sustainer's purpose as it flows into the eschaton—through love, and only through love.

Before we return to the topic of God's eternality, one more idea needs reinforcement. We believe in God's immanence and transcendence: God relates to us in our world but transcends us in power, knowledge, goodness, and many other ways. However, God's transcendence does not imply a difference in definition. For example, I've just argued that God acts in love and that love defines his activity. We see this love embodied in Jesus, who perfectly reflects God. Yet some argue that while Jesus commands us to love our enemies, God intends to torment his enemies eternally. When challenged on how a loving God could do such a thing, they sometimes respond, "Well, God's ways are not our ways [Isaiah 55:8], so God's love must look different from ours," as if that somehow justifies the idea. But this argument misrepresents God's transcendence, suggesting that God's love is fundamentally different from ours rather than beyond our capability. Scripture doesn't teach that. Isaiah 55:8 doesn't imply that God's love resembles torture; it reveals that God loves even when our response might be to hate. That is why God's ways are not our ways. We can be confident that the Bible's definition of love applies equally to God as it does to us. Otherwise, his exhortations for us to truly imitate both Jesus and God would be, at best, disingenuous. We must strive to love as God loves.

LOVE EXISTS ETERNALLY

Understanding what love truly is allows us to grasp God's perspective in his interactions with us. The Bible tells us that we are all born into sin, meaning we are brought into a shared essence—our physical reality, our bodies—that is cursed. Originally, our human spirits were given authority over this essence, including our bodies. However, we abdicated that authority, allowing our bodies to dominate us, leading us to satisfy bodily desires. As a result, we live in a state of missing the mark of a genuine love relationship with God, constantly following the lead of our cursed essence and turning away from him. This is the essence of sin, and the fact that everyone succumbs to this cursed nature necessitated God's intervention and rescue.

Now, consider this from God's perspective. God is fully aware that I was born into sin, encased in my cursed physical housing (what Paul refers to as "the flesh"). God knows that I allow this cursed flesh to dictate my actions, and as a result, my soul—particularly, my mind and will—becomes guilty. In short, I am not loving God. Because I do not reciprocate God's love, he cannot have a love relationship with me, as love must be mutual.

But suppose I recognize my sin, repent, and accept that Jesus offers freedom from this curse, and that God will forgive my sin. I pour out my heart to God, seeking forgiveness and freedom—seeking salvation. At that moment, my relationship with God changes. I have entered into a reciprocal love relationship with God. From God's perspective, a significant shift has occurred. My sin no longer stands as a barrier to his embrace; he has cast it as far as the east is from the west (Psalm 103:12).

What I have described is a process, a sequence of events in which God treated me one way at one point in time but then changed to treat me differently at a later time. This sequence of change in our love relationship, from my perspective, was temporal. But importantly, it was also temporal from God's perspective because he transitioned from not having a love relationship with me to having one. This basic example suggests that if God indeed forms relationships, he cannot be entirely unaffected by time.

Some may struggle with this notion, as it seems to suggest that God is mutable, which many Christians find troubling. After all, doesn't the Bible state the opposite? In Malachi 3:6, God explicitly declares, "I the Lord do not change." Similarly, James writes, "Every good and perfect gift is from above, coming down from the Father of the heavenly lights, who does not change like shifting shadows" (James 1:17). However, in these cases, the subject is intrinsic change, not extrinsic change. God's essence—truth, goodness, and beauty—is unchanging. God always, constantly, immutably acts according to his unchanging essence. However, God can experience extrinsic change—change in relation to something outside himself. Thus, when moving from not having a relationship to having one, God undergoes extrinsic change.

Scripture provides additional support for God's changing perspective in time. In Revelation 21, John presents the new creation—the eschatological hope of redemption's fulfillment. Verses 3 and 4 poetically describe the union of the new, or redeemed, creation with God, where heaven declares, "There will be no more death." If God is timeless and unchanging in his perspective, how could death come to an end in God's mind? The closing of Revelation 20 also describes death being thrown into the lake of fire. If God is in a timeless state where everything occurs concurrently, would death still confront him? No, these statements carry real meaning; God's breathed-out word is not a false front.

Similarly, Hebrews 8:12 quotes God's words from Jeremiah 31:34: "For I will forgive their wickedness and will remember their sins no more." Both the Revelation and Hebrews/Jeremiah passages assert that certain things—death and sin—will no longer be in God's view, even though they once were. We cannot dismiss these passages by claiming that they speak only from our perspective. In the Hebrews/Jeremiah passage, God speaks directly about his own perspective on a future state, which can occur only if the past no longer influences his present reality.

Yet, a problem remains. If God is temporal, progressing through sequential moments, how can we avoid concluding that God must have had a beginning? An eternity of past sequential moments is impossible; we could never have reached the present moment if past time were infinite. In other words, if there were no beginning, advancing to the present would be impossible, as it would require crossing an infinite. "Crossing an infinite" means moving past an end point of a series that has no end point, which is obviously incoherent. Infinites, by definition, have no end points. It would be impossible for God to traverse a past duration of time that is infinite. No matter how much we might want to say that God can do anything, crossing an infinite is as incoherent as positing a married bachelor; it is logically impossible.

So where does that leave us? It seems we must choose between two conclusions: (1) God is temporal and therefore must have had a beginning, or (2) God is timeless, making a relationship with him impossible. However, the Bible insists on both—that God is temporal in relation to us and timeless in relation to eternity. Is it possible to embrace both propositions?

What if God were both temporal and timeless at the same time? Some theologians have proposed this dualistic idea, and many Christians subconsciously adhere to it. However, Christian philosopher William

Lane Craig decisively debunks this possibility: "Often laymen, anxious to affirm both God's transcendence (His existing beyond the world) and His immanence (His presence in the world), assert that God is both timeless and temporal. But in the absence of some sort of model or explanation of how this can be the case, this assertion is flatly self-contradictory and so cannot be true."[2] Craig, however, offers an intriguing solution. He suggests that while God cannot be both temporal and atemporal (timeless) simultaneously, he could have been atemporal before his interaction with creation. Then, at the moment of creation—which included the creation of time—God entered into temporality to experience a relationship with his creation. I believe this solution has merit.

All our objections to God's timeless existence stem from the difficulty of reconciling an atemporal God with his relationship to temporal beings. But what about before creation? Without temporal beings to relate to, could God have existed in an atemporal state? As Craig notes, "So long as God exists changelessly, He can, in the absence of a temporal world, exist timelessly."[3]

When I first considered this idea, one major objection persisted. Even before creating the universe and humanity, God was still involved in a relationship—namely, the Trinitarian relationship. I reasoned that any activity, particularly the expression of love within a relationship, would have to involve a temporal process.

I explored ways to resolve this difficulty, and admittedly, my thoughts sometimes strayed from orthodoxy. I wondered whether we could push the atemporal-to-temporal divide back another step from where Craig placed it. What if God had once existed singularly before entering into his Trinitarian state? Could he then have existed atemporally before adjusting himself to the Trinity—and temporality—to begin his interactive and creative process? However, I quickly abandoned this line of thought. As we've seen, love is the motivation by which God acts. To strip any of God's activity of its relational intent would be to sever the connection between his persons and the only legitimate outworking of his essence as truth, goodness, and beauty (TGB). If I pursued this idea further, I believe the apostle John would forcefully hand me his first epistle and tell me to read it more carefully!

---

2. Craig, *Time and Eternity*, 15.
3. Craig, *Time and Eternity*, 219.

Unable to find a defensible adjustment to the atemporal-to-temporal divide, I reconsidered Craig's placement of it at the beginning of creation. I asked myself, could a love relationship possibly exist atemporally within God's Trinitarian nature? I concluded that, yes, it could. To be fair, Craig also addressed this question and answered affirmatively, though I found his defense somewhat underwhelming. He likened Trinitarian love to a couple momentarily mesmerized while gazing into each other's eyes. While there is undoubtedly a love relationship in such a moment, could that really be analogous to the Trinity's eternal, atemporal existence? The feelings of love, however intense, are not love itself. Love, as defined by biblical support, is the giving of oneself for the benefit of the relationship. And "giving" seems to imply a temporal change from a state of not having to one of receiving. However, I believe the shared relationship within the Trinity may function differently.

First, consider that we can understand the function of the Trinity based on what we know about humans. After all, humans are created in the image of God, so our construct of shared physical essence by individual souls within that shared essence may reflect how we should view the Trinity. Of course, humans are not exact duplicates but rather image bearers, so differences remain. One key difference is that our essence is physical, while God's essence is TGB. We live within our essence and relate to it, albeit in a limited fashion, while the persons of the Godhead live within their TGB essence and relate to it infinitely.

Despite these differences, we can still draw parallels between how God created us to relate to our essence and how the Trinity functions. Each person of the Trinity engages fully and equally with the shared essence of TGB, but their relational interactions amplify this shared essence in unique ways. These distinct interactions do not divide or partition TGB but express the mutual love relationship between the persons of the Trinity. One Person, traditionally called the "Father," may be better understood as the Enactor, initiating purposeful ideas and plans that reflect the shared essence. The Word (traditionally the Son) brings these ideas into action, giving form and coherence to Truth, Goodness, and Beauty. The Breath (traditionally the Holy Spirit) animates and sustains these expressions, infusing relational energy and harmony into all they accomplish. Together, they act in perfect unity, revealing the fullness of their shared essence through love.

Now, consider this in the context of atemporality. Obviously, movement and change occur as love is expressed between God and us, his creation. But within the perfect nature and existence of the Trinity, the members (Enactor, Word, and Breath) continually share their common essence in TGB, constantly giving of that shared essence for their shared relationship. This infinite giving and receiving within the Trinity does not involve progression or sequence; it is a perfect and unchanging dynamic. What might seem to us like a process is, in fact, constant and eternal. God's essence, being shared, does not alter; likewise, the offering of each person to the relationship remains unchanged as it is infinitely given. Nothing ever changes, and "nothing ever changing" is the definition of atemporality. In this way, we can affirm the possibility of perfect relationship within the Trinity existing in an atemporal state.

I, therefore, agree with Craig that God must have been atemporal before his creative activity. God must have eternally existed in that timeless state. But God chose to create. This choice did not develop over time, as time did not exist in God's atemporal reality. Instead, out of his eternal, timeless love, God acted in creation. The beginning of creation marked the beginning of time. In this temporal existence that God created, he invested himself to ensure that his primary, preeminent activity—his love, the giving of himself for the benefit of relationship—would permeate all his creation.

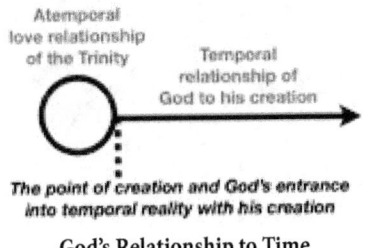

God's Relationship to Time

This book is about eschatology, but truly understanding where we're headed requires grasping the nature of the timeless God who created us for relationship and entered into the temporal world to establish a perfect love relationship with his creatures. For me, there is no other way for all the philosophy, theology, and psychology to come together than in this fulfilling view of our Creator—a God who lovingly creates and lovingly engages to realize an everlasting love relationship that encircles him and his image-bearers. Eschatology is not merely about future events; it is about transformation—of our souls through minds set on God, and of our bodies through redemption from the curse. This entire process, from creation to love's rescue, applying revelation, repentance, and restoration, is rooted in God's essence, poured out through love. It is truly overwhelming!

To continue organizing our thoughts—loving God with all our minds—we must know the God whom we serve and trust. We need to understand his perspective not only on time but also on knowledge, revelation, activity, and even anticipation. What does God know? How does God reveal? How does God decide on matters of life and death? The concept of things to come is daunting, whether or not we admit it, and that fear stems from what we've discussed in this chapter. As theologian Nelson Pike aptly states, "The position that a theologian takes on the topic of divine eternity has a kind of controlling effect on the general shape and texture of his broad theological view about the nature of God." These words are telling. This book is based on certain logical and theological positions regarding God, and it's essential that we examine and categorize them as we move forward.

3

God Creates

God preaches, a noted Clergyman—
And the sermon is never long,
So instead of getting to Heaven, at last—I'm going, all along.
    —Emily Dickinson, from "Some Keep the Sabbath Going to Church"

You are worthy, our Lord and God,
to receive glory and honor and power,
for you created all things,
and by your will they were created and have their being.
    —Revelation 4:11

Question 1 of the Westminster Shorter Catechism asks, "What is the chief end of man?" In other words, it inquires about purpose: What are we doing here? Why were we created? The given answer is, "Man's chief end is to glorify God and to enjoy him forever." But doesn't that response feel somewhat incomplete? The second half of the answer leaves something to be desired. In our chapter 1 discussion, we defined love as the giving of self to benefit relationship. When love is realized, that benefit is shared among all parties involved. Therefore, the answer should at least acknowledge that God also enjoys us, and ideally, it would include our enjoyment of one another. While this complete relationship must, of course, be grounded in God—on who he is (TGB)—if God created us for love relationship, then any discussion of our purpose cannot omit the mutual enjoyment of all parties within that relationship.

However, it's the first part of the catechism's answer that's truly challenging. Few Christians would dispute that humanity's chief end is to glorify God. But when pressed, how do we explain what it means to glorify God? Is it simply a matter of praising him? While praise is certainly part of it, the full answer depends on why we are praising him in the first place.

GLORY AND GLORIFYING

Of course, God is worthy of our praise. He created us. He loves us. He redeemed us. We should be thankful and offer praise for all God's loving actions toward us. But beyond mere praise and thankfulness, to glorify carries additional perspective. Many books have been written on the subject of glory, but the best concise definition (specifically, of God's glory) I've encountered comes from popular author and speaker John Piper, who describes glory as "the infinite worth of God made manifest."[1] This definition aligns well with biblical references, particularly Romans 3:23: "For all have sinned and fall short of the glory of God." We fall short of God's infinite worth, especially in relation to who God is. As we've discussed, God's essence is truth, goodness, and beauty. He is the very definition and foundation for TGB; that is his worth. So his glory is his TGB *made manifest*—revealed, expressed, and reflected in love.

While God's expression of his TGB worth is his *glory*, to *glorify* him implies that we acknowledge, accept, adore, and *adopt* that glory. "Adopt" does not mean that his worth becomes ours. Rather, we become the means through which God manifests his worth; in other words, by reflecting God's worth, we become his glory. God *is* TGB—TGB is the essence of God—and therefore, it is *his* worth. We, as humans, can act in accordance with the virtuous reality of TGB, but it is not our essence, nor can it ever be. God alone is TGB.

Moving forward from who God is, we consider his glory, the *manifestation* of that essential worth. God's worth is made manifest—or reflected and expressed—in creation (Romans 1:20) and most perfectly in the begotten life of Jesus. When Jesus says in John 12:45, "The one who looks at me is seeing the one who sent me," and in John 14:9, "Anyone who has seen me has seen the Father," he is not claiming deity, as some

---

1. Piper, "Rebuilding the Basics."

may suppose. Though Jesus is God, in these passages, he is emphasizing that the world's distorted perspective is not God's perspective. Instead, Jesus's right-side-up perspective, which reflects TGB through love, is the true *manifestation* of who God is. Hebrews 1:3 affirms this: "The Son is the radiance of God's glory and the exact representation of his being." Thus, Jesus, *as a human*, perfectly reflects God's glory. And we, called to be like Jesus, also become God's glory when we reflect who he is in and to this dying world.

CREATED FOR LOVE RELATIONSHIP

Only God is TGB, but we can comprehend him and recognize his worth. When we align our lives with that understanding, we live according to who God is for the sake of relationship with him. Although we do not become TGB, in our pursuit, trust, and enjoyment of it, we reflect it. And that, in fact, is why God created us—to establish a love relationship based on his essence. God reveals his glory, and we glorify him by embracing a relationship founded on his worth.

Consider Job 7:17–18. Here, Job speaks out of frustration, but even in his struggle, he asserts a profound truth about God. Grumbling against God's heavy hand, Job says, "What is mankind that you make so much of them, that you give them so much attention, that you examine them every morning and test them every moment?" Though Job protests the constant attention, as seen in his verse 16 cry, "Let me alone," he still acknowledges God's meticulous care. But why is God so interested? The reason ties directly to the purpose we just discussed.

Throughout both testaments, God's focus is on relationship. In the Old Testament, God calls Israel not just his servant or subject, nor merely a student or assistant, but his wife, illustrating his desire for an intimate love relationship. The delight in the Song of Songs and the heartache in Hosea both reflect this intended relationship of joy and glory. Time and again, God pleads with Israel to draw near, promising to dwell with them. He reveals himself not as an unapproachable, disinterested chieftain, but as a caring friend willing to share knowledge of himself: "For I desire mercy, not sacrifice, and acknowledgment of God rather than burnt offerings." (Hosea 6:6).

Christ enters the world as Immanuel—God with us. Once again, Jesus emphasizes the intimate knowledge that elevates us from servanthood to friendship: "You are my friends if you do what I command you. I no longer call you servants, because a servant doesn't know his master's business. Instead, I have called you friends, for everything that I learned from my Father I have made known to you" (John 15:14–15). He further prays that "all of them may be one, Father, just as you are in me and I am in you. May they also be in us so that the world may believe that you have sent me" (John 17:21). Just as Christ embraces us now, throughout history, God has embraced those of faith as friends (James 2:23).

Paul identifies the true Israel of God as all those joined with him in faithful relationship, which is the direction of his thought in Galatians, concluding, "All who walk by this standard are the true Israel of God—his chosen people. Peace and mercy on them!" (Galatians 6:16 *The Message*). This true Israel of God is Christ's bride, symbolizing the intimate relationship that we, free from sin, will share with God forever in joy and glory (Revelation 21:9). This is the ultimate purpose of reconciliation, to which the whole Bible points—the very purpose of creation itself. Humanity's chief end and God's eternal purpose in creation converge: to rejoice in everlasting love as we glorify our worthy God, who is the foundation of that relationship through his infinite essence of truth, beauty, and goodness.

OUR PRIDEFUL(?) GOD

We thrill at an exquisite singing voice, our jaws drop at a gravity-defying football catch, and we admire the quick wit of a gifted debater. We marvel at the artist's masterpiece and the artisan's skill. We even admire those who do nothing but merely look amazing. But if any of those people were to utter one word in boast about their appearance or ability, we would sneer instantly at their arrogance. We don't like arrogant people; everyone agrees. Even the Bible warns against pride (Jeremiah 13:15), noting that it leads to destruction (Proverbs 16:18).

So why does God demand praise? Why, as the catechism suggests, did he create us to glorify him? In Matthew 4:10, Jesus quotes the Old Testament, telling Satan, "Worship the Lord your God, and serve him only." Similarly, in John 4:24, Jesus tells the Samaritan woman, "God is spirit, and his worshipers must worship in the Spirit and in truth." In both cases, "to worship" means to revere or bow down. But how can God demand praise and yet tell us it is sinful to demand the same, especially when we are called to imitate him?

A common answer is that God demands praise because he alone truly deserves it, but this response doesn't fully address the question. The issue isn't about worth but about the demand. Even if an artisan's skill is the best among humans, it's not the talent we reject; it's the arrogance in demanding praise that repels us. No matter how exceptional someone is, our admiration often grows in proportion to his or her humility.

To resolve this, we can explore two key thoughts. First, God's urging us to praise him is essential for our satisfaction and our relationship with him. Second, even in his demand for praise, God remains a God of humility. Let's start with the first point.

What is worthy of praise? We could list many virtues, but philosophers have long grouped all virtues into three broad categories: truth, goodness, and beauty. These are called transcendentals because they are universal realities that transcend the physical world and our experience of it. For Christians, these transcendentals are not merely virtues to value and pursue. We are drawn to them by both God and our innate desire because they extend beyond mere concepts to the very nature of God himself. They exist as the one divine essence shared equally and infinitely by the three persons of the Trinity. As we discussed in Chapter 1, where God is present, truth, goodness, and beauty shine; where he is absent, they are denied.

Since these transcendentals exist only in and from God, any praise, worship, or recognition of TGB must ultimately be directed toward God. We seek the good because we admire it, and in admiring the good, we worship God. With humans, we can admire what they do while disapproving of who they are. With God, admiring his good works means admiring him, for he is goodness itself. God's call for us to praise and worship him, then, is not arrogance; it is the only way to genuinely promote TGB.

Yet, even though he demands praise, God remains humble. Humility is a virtue, primarily associated with goodness but also connected to beauty. It involves giving up something, allowing oneself to become vulnerable, for the greater good of a relationship. And God does exactly that. His mere presence is necessary to sustain creation; if he turned away, life and creation would cease. But despite being infinite TGB, he cares enough to form relationships with us, who are finite, and endures our ill will for the sake of that relationship. This effort is humility in action, even as he draws us to himself—the true, good, and beautiful one.

GOD'S WRATH IS NOT HIS GLORY

I've argued that God's essence as TGB compels him to act only and always in love. But doesn't God ever get angry? Yes, he does. The Bible, in both the Old and New Testaments, recounts numerous instances of God's anger, which cannot be dismissed simply as the result of the writers' limited understanding. God becomes angry with any part of his creation that drives events or others away from TGB—essentially, toward the destruction of relationship with him. The question, then, is whether this God, who loves infinitely but can become angry, ever *acts* in anger. As we've already discussed, the short answer is no.

In chapter 1, we explored certain things God cannot do, noting them as absurdities. For example, God cannot create a rock so heavy he can't lift it, defeat himself in a boxing match, or make himself come into existence in 1957. These are limitations to infiniteness, and a God who is infinite cannot simultaneously be limited. I also mentioned that it is absurd to imagine God lifting, in the human sense, any rock because he doesn't have a physical body with arms and muscles designed for lifting. Similarly, God could never punch someone in the face because he has no fist or arm to swing.

So when God feels angry and frustrated, does he experience a desire to punch something, as a human may? The answer must be no. Humans may feel like punching or expressing their anger through other bodily actions—such as angry words, facial expressions, body language, hand gestures, or manipulative behaviors—because our essence is physical. When humans are angered, the emotion triggers physiological changes: adrenaline in the bloodstream, heart rates increase, muscles tense, and so on. In this way, anger manifests through the body. If someone encourages the angry person to calm down—calming that includes slowing breathing and heart rate and relaxing muscles—that person begins to feel less angry. While the realization of the injustice remains, the body becomes less reactive.

Unlike humans, whose essence is physical, God's essence is TGB. Since emotions are expressed through essence, God's anger would have to be expressed through his essence of TGB. But if TGB cannot source the *demonstration* of anger, the only way God can express anger is by *not* extending TGB. As mentioned earlier, the greater the opportunity for love, the more present God is. Conversely, when sin promotes action that diminishes love, God's presence is less involved in that life or situation.

However, we must be careful not to say that God actively withholds his TGB out of anger, ill will, or even indifference. Such motives cannot align with TGB, and since God is TGB, it is impossible for him to act based on those motives. God does not "withhold" TGB in these situations, as that would imply an active prevention of expression; rather, he simply cannot express TGB in circumstances that contradict his essence. God expresses TGB in every instance where he can, but where he cannot (based on his essence), he does not.

Naturally, when his presence is not fully involved, the horrors that result from the absence of TGB to any degree manifest. In later chapters, we will explore more about how God's actions and inactions present themselves in the world, but for now, let's return to the consideration of God's glory.

Some popular writers and preachers within the Reformed tradition, including John Piper, have argued that God's wrath is actually part of his glory. They suggest that God determined not to rescue some people because he wanted to manifest the full spectrum of his glory, which includes wrath. However, this perspective confuses the definitions of glory and essence. As I've previously stated, based on Piper's own definition, glory is the manifestation of worth. God's worth is his essence—the infinite TGB that constitutes the entirety of who God is. Therefore, if wrath is not part of God's essence (and it is not, since wrath does not exist in the absence of sin), God's glory does not—cannot—include wrath as part of his worth.

Moreover, God does not act in violence. He expresses himself through his essence, which is truth, goodness, and beauty—not as separate qualities, but as a harmonious whole. Why was the cross the epicenter, as Greg Boyd would say, of God's glory? It is because it revealed his worth—his TGB—through the extremes of his vulnerability and love for the sake of relationship with his creation. The cross also demonstrated God's wrath, not by inflicting harm, but by not extending his TGB to the physical form that Jesus surrendered to death.

WHY CREATE CONSIDERING THE COST?

Jesus himself taught us, "Enter through the narrow gate. For wide is the gate and broad is the road that leads to destruction, and many enter through it. But small is the gate and narrow the road that leads to life, and only a few find it" (Matthew 7:13-14). Given that so many—the majority—bypass the narrow gate, wouldn't it have been more consistent for a loving God to simply not create at all? This question might seem confrontational, as if it challenges God's decision. Should Christians dare to wonder about such things? Yes, we should. We do not serve a mere chieftain god whose pride demands blind trust at the expense of understanding. God reveals himself so we may comprehend him; he reveals his plan so we may understand his direction; and all that God reveals is intended to build our trust based on that understanding. To "love the Lord your God . . . with all your mind" (Matthew 22:37) is a commandment, not an option to dismiss in false piety. Wondering, questioning, and growing are essential to our relationship with him—our chief purpose. At the end of Jesus's ministry, after his disciples had wondered, questioned, and grown through his teaching, he told them, "I no longer call you servants, because a servant doesn't know his master's business. Instead, I have called you friends, for everything that I learned from my Father I have made known to you" (John 15:15). We should not, therefore, suppress our thoughts and questions about why God does what he does.

Certainly, God has not revealed everything, but that shouldn't deter us from seeking greater understanding. Often, our limited knowledge leads to embrace a plan—or even a theology—that results in logical inconsistencies. When we encounter these inconsistencies, rather than questioning the foundations of that theology, we may find it easier to dismiss the conflict by saying, "We see through a glass darkly," and assume, "The logical inconsistencies will be resolved when we see Jesus." For example, a Calvinist might respond to the question of why God would create knowing that the majority would head for everlasting destruction, as John Piper did, "We are not in a good position to pass judgment on the wisdom of God given the limits of our minds and the weakness of our hearts. We do well to humble ourselves with trembling."[2] While this posture may appeal to those who prefer to cling to their theological system rather than adjust it for the sake of biblical consistency, it can also hinder deeper exploration.

Adherents of Kinship theology, however, offer a different perspective. They argue that God creates to foster love relationships because these relationships manifest his TGB worth. The manifestation of his TGB worth through love relationships is not only the greatest good but

---

2. Piper, "Would God have Been More Loving?"

also a necessary expression of his nature. Therefore, while the possibility of rejecting a love relationship—and the consequent destruction of the rejector—exists, God's infinite love will not deny his glorious purpose. In other words, the glory of God, as perfectly manifested in love relationships that reflect his TGB worth, surpasses all else, even the possibility that some beings, through their rejection, will face destruction.

But can we narrow the question of creation a bit further? Instead of asking why God created at all, could we ask why he created those he knew would ultimately face destruction? Did he create them solely to destroy them? This question presumes that God knows the future perfectly—fixed in his mind like a completed movie reel. But is this truly how God knows the future?

4

God Knows

And I know that the way leadeth homeward,
To the land of the pure and the blest;
To the country of ever fair summer,
To the city of peace and of rest;
And there shall be healing for sickness,
And fountains life's fever to slake.
What matter beside? I go onward,
"He knoweth the way that I take."
—Emma E. Goodrich, from "He Knoweth the Way"

This is how we know that we belong to the truth
and how we set our hearts at rest in his presence:
If our hearts condemn us, we know that God is greater than our hearts,
and he knows everything.
—1 John 3:19–20

Despite my deep appreciation for Paul's letters, the apostle John is quickly becoming my favorite New Testament writer. He gave us the world's most recognized verse—John 3:16—and in his letters, he emphasizes that God always acts in love because God is love. In this current book, we will explore his great apocalyptic work, Revelation, which details God's rescue plan, particularly during the interadvental age. John's writings offer us so much to consider, including his reminder that God *knows everything*.

But what does it mean to *know everything*? Obviously, we need to limit the idea to everything that can be known. In the discussion of power in chapter 1, we realized that the skeptic's favorite argument—whether God can create a rock so big he cannot lift it—was incoherent because it asks whether unlimited power includes the power to limit that being's own unlimited power. Regarding power, we can think of many similar self-contradictory absurdities God cannot do: God cannot make a lie the truth; God cannot make a round triangle; God cannot create a married bachelor. The fact that God cannot do the absurd does not undermine the idea of a God with limitless power.

These impossibilities extend to omniscience as well. Not only can God not create a married bachelor, but he also cannot *know* what a married bachelor thinks. The thoughts of a married bachelor do not and cannot exist because a married bachelor does not exist. The key point is that God lacks knowledge in such an instance, not due to any limitation, but because the absurdity is not real and, therefore, not knowable. God's knowledge encompasses only reality or possible reality, and this understanding must guide our study of eschatology.

Eschatology is the study of things to come—the future. Does God know the future? Before we hastily answer, "Yes, John said he knows everything!" we need to consider whether the future is real—whether it falls into the category of what can be known. The question here is not whether God is omniscient; we have already established his omniscience biblically. The question concerns the nature of the future—whether it is real and can be included in the "everything" that can be known by God.

In chapter 2, we discussed that in relation to creation, God is temporal (functions sequentially), experiencing and interacting with us in a progression of changing, successive moments. To truly engage in a love relationship with temporal creatures requires temporality for the engaging person. We reached that conclusion by comparing our past (sinful) relationship with God to our present (converted and loving) relationship with him. Both relationships could not exist simultaneously from God's perspective any more than from ours because they require opposing interactions. Even for God, one relationship must give way to the next, and that progression or change makes the present the only real relationship.

We can apply that same logic to evaluate the future. Let's say that John Doe has recently become a Christian. A year earlier, on the same month and day, John had not yet entered into a love relationship with God; at that point, the relationship was still in the future for both John and God. As of that prior moment, even from God's perspective, no love relationship between them existed because John's point of conversion was still future—it was not yet a reality. Therefore, in both our views, past and future, the only reality at any given moment is the present moment. While God does indeed know everything, the future is not part of the reality that can be known.

God knows the past because the past was real at one point. Therefore, God's knowledge of the past depends on the time when it was the present—when it had been reality. God knew it as real then, just as we know the past as real because we experienced those moments when each was momentarily present. Thus, present memory of the past is real and can be known. The future, however, is not real now, nor has it ever been real. Because knowledge is based on reality, the future remains beyond the scope of knowledge.

Does this conclusion leave God hopelessly blind regarding things to come? What about prophecy? What about security? How can God have confidence in his rescue plan? How can we have confidence in such a God? Our unease at the idea of God not knowing the future arises only because we fail to grasp what it means for God truly to know everything now.

KNOWLEDGE OF POSSIBILITIES

Earlier, I mentioned that God's knowledge encompasses both actual and possible realities. Possible reality simply means that something could happen. Before we delve into this idea, some background is helpful. We understand God's desire for a love relationship not only from the clear statements and examples in Scripture but also from the very fact that we know anything about God at all. Our knowledge of God comes through his revelation, and he reveals himself because he desires a relationship. Any relationship requires mutual knowledge between the parties involved. God's act of revealing his essence and activity for the sake of a relationship with us is an expression of his love. Since love cannot be coerced, we humans can either accept or reject God's love. What we should also realize is that our response—whether we embrace or reject his love—triggers a corresponding response from God. When we embrace the revelation he's given, God provides more revelation. If we reject it, he respects our choice, which increases our distance from him and his revelation. But here's an additional thought: just as the increased revelation to those who embrace his love is gradual, so too is the withdrawal from those who reject it. This ongoing exchange of revelation and response is the dance of life.

I call this interaction with God his "revelation-response approach" to building his kingdom. We see God's initial revelation described in Romans 1:20. If we respond positively to him, he will act exactly as James 4:8a describes: "Come near to God and he will come near to you." In terms of soteriology, this process of God revealing himself and our embracing that revelation ultimately leads to salvation, while our rejection of it leads to everlasting death (separation). This revelation-response pattern meaningfully describes our interaction as the future continues to unfold into the present.

Yet, we are still capable of expecting and imagining future moments just beyond the border of actual reality. We use our knowledge of the past (former present moments) along with the present (current reality) to plan for those moments when the future becomes the present. In other words, we adjust our current actions in anticipation of future outcomes. This is what we call planning. For instance, I may hope to buy bread at the store in the future, so I take the present step of getting into my car, planning further steps of driving to the store, walking in, selecting the bread, and paying for it—a series of future events that I envision to achieve my goal.

This kind of planning is routine, and we do it multiple times a day, often without even consciously thinking about it. These same principles apply when we consider eschatology and prophecy. The fact that the Bible includes prophecy does not mean that God exhaustively determines the future or that the future is a fixed reality that can be fully known. Instead, it shows that our present reality (and therefore our present knowledge) includes a range of possibilities that can be planned for. If I, with my limited understanding, can imagine future possibilities and plan for them, how much more does the omniscient mind of God anticipate and direct his actions based on countless possibilities? Could anything that happens escape God's anticipation?

From his absolute, all-encompassing knowledge of every move, thought, and choice we freely make in each present moment, God knows and anticipates every possible move, thought, and choice we could make. Moreover, he fully understands the likelihood of those possibilities actually occurring. As an example, when I play chess, I usually think one or two moves ahead, considering the possible and probable responses of my opponent and how I might react. Anyone familiar with chess knows that while this approach may help me compete with a novice, it wouldn't suffice against an expert, let alone a grandmaster who can think 20 moves ahead. But even as we marvel at a grandmaster's ability to think so far ahead, how much more would we be in awe of a player who could think 50 or 100 moves ahead? How confident would we be in a player who could anticipate 1,000 moves ahead for every possible movement of their opponent? Of course, chess games rarely last 1,000 moves, but you get the point: could we seriously doubt the skill of a master who could foresee and plan for every possibility in a chess game before the first pawn was even moved? Imagining such a capability is challenging, but it doesn't begin to capture the depth of God's knowledge and ability. Even if we imagine a chessboard expanded from 64 squares to 64 million, with 16 million pieces per side, we would only scratch the surface of an analogy to God's mastery.

Thus, although God faces an unknown future, he is not as limited as we might first imagine. His comprehensive knowledge of possibilities provides us with the security that God has prepared his plan to navigate every future outcome. So, if God knows all possibilities, does he simply ordain one path through this maze to force things to conclude as he desires? The answer is not a straightforward yes or no—it's a bit of both.

The chess analogy, like all analogies, has its limitations, but it's useful enough to illustrate the point. The imagined grandmaster, who knows every possible move, does not force his opponent's hand toward one move or another. Both players make their own choices. The master responds to each move to steer the game toward the desired outcome. Along the way, the master might be surprised by an opponent's poor or improbable choice—one that differs from the more likely possibilities. But while the choice may surprise or disappoint him, it could never confound the master, who is fully prepared with a response to even the least likely move.

God has said, "I am God, and there is no other; I am God, and there is none like me. I make known the end from the beginning, from ancient times, what is still to come. I say, 'My purpose will stand, and I will do all that I please.'" (Isaiah 46:9b–10). His declaration sounds both determined and determinative. Yet, like the chess master, God's approach shifts based on the responses of his image-bearers: "And if at another time I announce that a nation or kingdom is to be built up and planted, and if it does evil in my sight and does not obey me, then, *I will reconsider the good I had intended to do for it.*" (Jeremiah 18:9-10, emphasis added).

We may wonder why God responds to human actions rather than simply charting a fixed course. A God of all power could easily impose his will on his creation. After all, he isn't just playing a game of chess. But the chess analogy doesn't capture everything. The principles of God's essence and activity support the balance he maintains between his power over creation and his love for it. God is love. His purpose in creation was to establish an everlasting love relationship with us. And love cannot be coerced; the act of relinquishing oneself for the sake of a relationship cannot be forced. Just as we would condemn a manipulator who brainwashes someone into "loving" him or her, we could not excuse God if he used mind-control tricks to make us love him. An omniscient manipulator would always recognize the deficiency in a relationship founded on trickery and hostility toward the other person's will. If God desires a love relationship, he cannot force his image-bearers to love him; he must risk their rejection as he reveals himself for their consideration, as recounted in Romans 1.

God's loving embrace of the world is central to the yes-and-no answer to the question of whether God determines a fixed path. We, as his image-bearers, are the ones with whom God intended to have love relationship. And God fully knows every way we might respond. With that knowledge, he charts his course, but he does not trample the possibility of genuine love while ensuring that his will is accomplished.

Kinship theology (KT) navigates a middle path between the extremes of open theism (the idea that since the future is not yet reality, God cannot know what may occur) and Calvinism's view of God's total control (determining every detail of the future). Insisting on either full openism or rigid determinism presents a false dichotomy. Instead, we should consider a both-and approach—a balance of both perspectives. God's love propels him to take risks for the sake of a true love relationship, while at the same time, his love drives him to ensure the future he intends. So, the answer is both yes and no: God partially determines and partially remains open. Greg Boyd sums it up well:

> The distinct claim of Open Theism is that we have biblical, experiential and philosophical reasons for believing that God did in fact create a world in which some "might and might

not" propositions are *true*. Which is to say, he created a world in which the future is partially open, comprised of possibilities rather than settled facts. And God did this, in our view, precisely because he didn't want to unilaterally determine all that comes to pass.... God rather wanted to populate this cosmos with free agents, thereby creating the possibility of genuine love, adventure, and yes, the risk of sin and evil.[1]

God may also change course in response to human actions. As we saw in the Jeremiah 18 passage, God adjusts his plan based on the evil actions of people. However, God also promises to respond to the prayers of the righteous (James 5:16). Sometimes, God changes course simply because he foresees that continuing along a particular path may lead to more harm than good. Consider the story of the Tower of Babel.

Genesis 11 records the descendants of Noah uniting to build a tower that symbolized their social and engineering accomplishments. God perceived that nothing they planned to do would be impossible for them, so he confused their language, causing them to scatter and form different societies across the earth.

The most memorable part of this story is God confusing their language. While the exact method remains unclear—whether it happened instantly or gradually as like-minded people formed groups that eventually erected barriers to broader communal efforts—the specifics are less important than understanding what God was thinking. The significance of the story lies in understanding why God wanted it included, beyond simply explaining the origin of languages.

We are told that the people all shared the same language. The passage gives examples of their discussions: "Come, let's make bricks and bake them thoroughly," and "Come, let us build ourselves a city, with a tower that reaches to the heavens, so that we may make a name for ourselves; otherwise we will be scattered over the face of the whole earth." These statements reveal their intent to unite and achieve great things together. At first glance, this might seem unproblematic—after all, didn't God create us for relationships? Isn't the eschatological vision a single heavenly community on earth? So why was God concerned that "nothing they plan to do will be impossible for them" (Genesis 11:6b)?

This story unfolds shortly after the flood. The lead-up to the flood followed a similar pattern: the community of those who followed God (the lineage of Seth) had separated from those more focused on themselves

---

1. Boyd, "Molinism and Open Theism."

(the lineage of Cain). Although other communities may have existed, the narrative in chapters 4 and 5 highlights the division between the God-loving and the self-loving. However, by the beginning of chapter 6, these separate groups began to intermarry (Genesis 6:1–2). This integration led to a societal identity rooted in evil—"powerful" people (Nephilim) whose "wickedness was widespread on the earth and [whose] every scheme his mind thought of was nothing but evil all the time" (Genesis 6:5 HCSB). The word *Nephilim* in verse 4 literally means "giants," as translated in the KJV. However, they were giants, not in a physical sense but rather in their capacity for evil. As this group turned away from God, the resulting chaos allowed the floodwaters to destroy the corrupted creation, as no hope remained.[2]

Thus, God did not confuse the language at Babel because he felt threatened by the tower. Instead, he saw the very real possibility that their feelings of self-sufficiency would lead to the same deadly spiral that had destroyed the pre-flood community. Acting to preserve the possibility of love relationships, God divided his image-bearers into multiple communities. He did this to encourage communities that would depend on him, to fulfill his promise never again to allow an earth-destroying flood, and to ensure his restoration plan continued.

Reflecting on this story, we should realize that if God had merely determined everything unilaterally, he wouldn't have needed to intervene as he did. Instead of fostering the development of multiple communities, he could have simply changed the hearts of some or all of them to continue his restoration plan culminating in Christ. However, he encouraged the spread of communities to create the potential for multiple possibilities, because he does not coerce hearts but interacts to offer future possibilities aligned with his purpose of love relationships.

Given all we've discussed about God's knowledge and activity, we may need to rethink our view of prophecy. Prophecy is not just about God knowing what will happen and passively watching us act out preordained roles. Rather, God's prophecy involves outmaneuvering the world and its evil intentions with his anticipatory knowledge.

When examining any text cited as proof that God knows the future as if it were a film reel, we should question whether it truly forces that conclusion. I believe these passages affirm God's knowledge of possibilities

---

2. We will discuss the lack of hope in chapter 10 of this book.

and his power of loving influence. Isaiah 44:6–8 is a good example, as it reflects God's determined stance:

> This is what the Lord says—
> Israel's King and Redeemer, the Lord Almighty:
> I am the first and I am the last;
> apart from me there is no God.
> Who then is like me? Let him proclaim it.
> Let him declare and lay out before me
> What has happened since I established my ancient people,
> and what is yet to come—
> yes, let them foretell what will come.
> Do not tremble, do not be afraid.
> Did I not proclaim this and foretell it long ago?
> You are my witnesses. Is there any God besides me?
> No, there is no other Rock; I know not one.

In these verses, God indeed claims the ability to announce the future. But notice that he isn't simply boasting about knowing something others don't. His bold declaration that he can reveal "what is yet to come" becomes truly impressive when we consider God as one who shapes and influences the future by his power, rather than merely foreseeing a predetermined course. God asserts that no one else can impose his or her will on the future as he can. To support this claim, he points to the people he chose and established to represent him to the world. God redeemed Israel from the clutches of Egypt, placed them in the land he promised, and brought forth the hope of the world through them. He didn't just foresee these events—he made them happen. In the realm of possibilities, God is the one who turns potential into reality.

Returning to the chess analogy, no one marvels at a computer playing another computer according to a single, programmed pattern. Similarly, our God is not awe-inspiring because he happens to know a fixed future. The true wonder lies in a God so knowledgeable that he anticipates every possibility, so powerful that he can guide the future according to his progressively revealed plan, and so loving that he does all this without trampling on our free will to force the responses he desires. That's the glory! That's our God! *He does know everything!*

5

God Sustains

Earth trembl'd from her entrails, as again
In pangs, and Nature gave a second groan,
Skie lowr'd and muttering Thunder, som sad drops
Wept at compleating of the mortal Sin Original;
—John Milton, from "Paradise Lost" Book 9 (1674 version)

He is before all things,
and in him all things hold together
—Colossians 1:17

"Death ... comes for us all," reflects Thomas More in the climactic scene of Robert Bolt's *A Man for All Seasons*. Yet Jesus said, "And whoever lives by believing in me will never die." Neither More nor Jesus is wrong, but these truths require explanation.

Understanding death involves more than a simple division between the physical and spiritual. We've already touched on the concept of death in this book's earlier chapters, and Revelation 20 introduces the idea of a second death. However, death in various forms permeates much of Scripture, influencing key theological concepts from the fall to the atonement and ultimately to the eschaton. To grasp the nature of death—especially its role in the eschaton, where it both appears and disappears—we must first ensure we understand the foundational elements associated with it.

DEATH'S DEFINITION

Death, in its simplest form, is separation from life. To grasp this concept, we first need a biblical definition of life. The New Testament uses three Greek words often translated as "life." The term *bios* refers to physical life, as seen in 1 Timothy 2:2, where Paul encourages prayers for authorities so that we may lead peaceful lives. However, the life that transcends the physical is more complex. The Greek word *psyche* often signifies the life-force, as in 1 Corinthians 15:45, where it is translated as "living being" in the NIV. More specifically, *psyche* refers to that aspect of the soul encompassing mind, emotions, and will. Paul uses it to describe emotions and will in 2 Corinthians 2:13, where he was troubled in spirit. He also uses it to describe the mind, as in 2 Corinthians 1:23, where it relates to his decision-making, and in Philippians 1:27, where it refers to the collective mindset of a group. Thus, *psyche* seems to encapsulate much of our metaphysical essence.

But there's more. The word *pneuma*, often translated as "spirit," can indicate life-force, as in Romans 1:9 and 12:11, but it also points to something deeper. *Pneuma* often refers to our innate desires—our longing for truth, goodness, beauty, relationships, and life itself. For example, an unregenerate person, driven by self-interest, may seek truth, goodness, and beauty, but only as they relate to the physical world and personal gain. In contrast, believers, transformed by the Holy Spirit, "serve in the newness of the spirit [*pneuma*]" (Romans 7:6) because they have received "the spirit ... from God" (1 Corinthians 2:12).

Bringing these metaphysical concepts together with the physical, we arrive at the Greek word *zoe*, which typically indicates the fullness of life—encompassing both the essential and the ethical. This term is often paired with "eternal" or "everlasting," as in John 3:16. Life, in its broadest sense, is the sum of our being and existence. When we consider humanity's ultimate purpose—enjoying relational love in God's glory among God and his people—we must conclude that the most comprehensive biblical definition of life is a whole person in a love relationship with God. Therefore, death, or separation from life, is the departure from this love relationship with God.

While each human is an individual, we are also connected by a shared essence. As mentioned in the introduction to this book, God's Trinitarian nature involves one essence, which I describe as truth, goodness, and beauty (TGB)—a shorthand for what might also be called transcendental virtue or cosmic value. Intertwined with God's essence is his activity, expressed through the actions of his three persons in faith, hope, and love, motivated by this one essence.

God created us for everlasting love relationships with him and with one another. To facilitate this, he made us in his image, reflecting his multi-personal nature in a single essence. Unlike God's essence of TGB, our shared essence is our physical creation—the elements and energy that constitute our bodies and sustain our physical life. We share this physical essence through a continuous exchange of matter and energy, just as God's multiple persons share his essence.

Yet, as with God, our individual souls (*psyche* and *pneuma*) are drawn to and comprehend God's TGB essence. God gave us the ability to think conceptually, understand morality, and appreciate beauty, enabling us to recognize and respond to him as he reveals himself in love. While we cannot possess God's TGB essence as he does, we can respond to it in our souls: (1) by exercising faith to accept or reject what we comprehend, (2) by pursuing it with hope if we accept it, and (3) by sharing God's revealed TGB with others, driven by the same love that he has shown us.

Thus, when we talk about what it means to be human, we cannot separate the intertwined aspects of essence and activity. Together, they define what it means to be human. We are not merely souls temporarily housed in flesh; each human is a unity of body and soul. Just as God cannot be Father or Son without his TGB essence, we cannot be human without our physical essence.

This understanding of our shared physical essence and individual souls must inform our view of life and death. In creating humanity, God gave us life—a relationship with him. But what happens in death? Does separation from God affect the individual soul, the shared essence of all humanity, or both? To answer this, we must first consider how death entered God's creation.

THE ENTRANCE OF DEATH

The question of how death came about is crucial for Christianity because its central doctrine is the atonement—the overcoming of death. To address this, we must first consider whether death was part of God's initial plan for creation.

The rise of evolutionary theory has led many Christians to sidestep this question and its implications. Most Christians are not scientists, and most scientists who are Christians are not theologians. This divide has often left the defense of a young earth and the direct act of creation to non-scientific Christian literalists, who argue that the "days" in Genesis 1 must be literal 24-hour periods because of the plain meaning of the Hebrew word *yom*—despite its use in other senses throughout the Old Testament. Confronted with the scientific plausibility of evolution, Christian scientists who lack theological training might find it easy to accept. Similarly, non-scientist Christians, overwhelmed by the complexities of evolutionary evidence, may reinterpret Genesis 1 as a literary device—a poetic or condensed version of ages of development.

However, the real question isn't whether evolutionary theory is plausible or whether Genesis 1 is a literary device. Instead, it's whether God included death in his original creation blueprint. If death was not part of God's plan and entered the picture only later with the advent of humans, then theologically, the ages of evolution—which depend on death's existence—may be ruled out.

BioLogos, an organization that advocates for a Christ-centered faith while affirming modern science, argues that evolution does not conflict with the Bible's teachings. In an article titled "Did God Intend Death?" Bethany Sollereder concludes that physical death was probably in God's plan from the beginning and that only spiritual death was introduced by sin. I disagree with this view.

The argument for physical death as part of God's original plan is often based on observing current conditions. While it's undeniable that physical death and biological dependence exist in today's world, this does not mean they existed before sin. To conclude otherwise requires two assumptions: (1) that God intended parts of creation (and possibly humans) to die physically before sin, and (2) that sin's entrance did not have as catastrophic an effect on creation as the Bible suggests.

Our definition of human death—separation from a love relationship with God—guides our thinking here. Humans are not just metaphysical souls; we are body-soul amalgamations, each part depending on the other for existence. The mind processes thoughts through the physical brain, and if the brain dies, so does the mind's ability to think. This cessation of thought is a departure from a love relationship with God. Therefore, if physical death was part of God's original plan, it would imply that separation from God's love was also part of that plan—an impossibility for a God of infinite love. If God promises an eschaton free of death, it is illogical to believe that he originally intended for death.

Regarding sin's impact on creation, Genesis 1 reveals that God gave humans dominion over physical creation. After they sinned (missed God's mark of relationship) by trusting in physical creation over God, the resulting curse affected all creation, as detailed in Genesis 3:14–19.[1]

Thus, death came about because of our first parents' sin in the garden. Eve, deceived, ate the forbidden fruit, leading to separation from God. A conversation and explanation may have corrected Eve's thinking, leading her to repent, which God, in his mercy, would likely have accepted. But Adam, perhaps unaware of God's ready forgiveness, chose to cling to Eve rather than to God, thereby opening the door to death and its curse.

SUSTAINING IN SEPARATION

The Bible teaches that God sustains all things, and for us, that sustaining influence is life (Job 33:4; Colossians 1:17). But this raises an important question: if God told Adam and Eve that trusting anything other than him for truth, goodness, and beauty would result in death—defined as separation from a love relationship with him—how could God continue to sustain their lives after they departed from that relationship? The answer lies in understanding the nature of love, death, and God's sustaining power.

Love is the giving of oneself for the sake of a love relationship. We've argued that this expression of love can persist not only in a realized relationship but also in the hope of one. So, even though Adam and Eve experienced spiritual death by leaving their love relationship with God, he could still extend his love to them by sustaining their lives while hoping for their restoration.

I used the phrase "to a certain extent" to describe God's extended love, which might seem contradictory given that God's love is infinite. However, I was not implying that God withholds his love. Rather, God's love is always infinite, but it can be received only to the extent that a person is willing to accept it. A person who limits his or her acceptance will experience less of God's unchanging and inexhaustible love. God does

---

1. Interestingly, among these physical effects resulting from sin is the well-known phrase of dust returning to dust, which speaks of physical death, confirming that the curse of sin, not God's original plan, brought in physical death.

not force his love upon us; as James 4:8 says, "Come near to God and he will come near to you." This idea isn't about God choosing whether to come close—God is omnipresent—but rather it is about our movement toward or away from accepting his love, which determines how much of his love we experience.

This understanding dispels questions like, "How is it right for God to allow evil to continue when he could simply withhold his sustaining hand and end it?" Such a question misunderstands the nature of God's love. Satan himself accused God of unrighteousness by suggesting that sustaining evil people without a foreseen purpose for good was itself an evil act. Satan's accusations, seen in Job, Revelation, and Romans, imply that God's support of sinful beings without an ongoing love relationship is wrong. However, these accusations were made before the atonement. Through the atonement, God vindicated his righteousness by making redemption and the restoration of love possible.

Paul explains this in Romans 3:25: "God presented Christ as a sacrifice of atonement, through the shedding of his blood—to be received by faith. He did this to demonstrate his righteousness, because in his forbearance he had left the sins committed beforehand unpunished." The Greek word *hilasterion* is translated in the NIV as "sacrifice of atonement," but other translations use "propitiation," meaning satisfaction. The intent here is to show that Christ's work satisfied God's covenant obligation to create for everlasting love, not simply to appease wrath. God's decision to pass over previous sins and continue sustaining life, despite the active antagonism to love brought about by the curse, was proven righteous by the atoning victory of Jesus, which made the restoration of the love relationship possible again.

EXISTENCE IN PHYSICAL DEATH

But what happens at physical death? Revelation 20–22 informs us that the final disposition of all humans will occur following Jesus's return for redemption and judgment. Chapters 21 through 22:5 describe the everlasting, glorious reign of those who are God-focused. However, chapter 20 addresses the fate of the curse-focused. After discussing the "first resurrection," which brings God-focused humans to life during this age, verse 5 reveals that "the rest of the dead did not come to life until the 1,000 years were completed." In other words, the unsaved remain in their state until the end of this age at Christ's return. My point is that before Christ's return, both the saved and the unsaved retain their human status (an amalgamation of body and soul) as they await their final disposition at that time.

But *how* does this happen? I have argued that to be human means possessing both human essence (physical creation) and soul (the metaphysical aspect that we identify as personhood). We observe the interaction between essence and soul in various functions. If our souls desire to move, we coordinate our minds with our bodies to make that change. If our souls are overcome with drowsiness, we understand that our bodies need rest. In all matters of conscious thought, the mind of the soul works within the confines of the body's brain to think.

However, when we physically die, this interaction ceases. Our souls no longer engage our bodies: we cannot move, speak, or eat. We lose all manipulative control of the soul over the body. Consequently, because thought arises from the interaction between mind and brain, it follows that, at physical death, humans can no longer think.[2]

Now, let's consider those who were curse-focused (those who rejected God as rescuer) among the physically dead before the atonement. After physical death, without direct, active interaction between soul and body, how could these "humans" retain their definition of humanity? Jehovah's Witnesses argue that they don't; these spirits are annihilated after physical death, only to be somehow recreated at the future judgment resurrection. However, this position is logically untenable because God could not justifiably impute sin guilt to newly recreated spirits. Therefore, for the pre-atonement God-rejecting dead, there must be a connection—albeit an unconscious one—between their spirits and their shared physical essence as a whole. The specifics of this connection or the location of these spirits remain questions unanswered by revelation, and reason offers little additional insight. Nevertheless, this state of unconscious dormancy, with the soul in a mix with physical creation, must describe the pre-atonement, curse-focused dead. By extension, the state of the pre-atonement God-focused would likely be no different.

---

2. Certain OT and Gospel-era stories seem to counter the idea of cessation of thought at physical death (e.g., 1 Samuel 28 and Luke 16:19–31), but the latter is a parable, and the former includes elements opposed to God's order as interpreted through the lens of Christ (see chapter 9). Thus, the purpose for these stories is to teach lessons rather than to communicate history.

As for the post-atonement God rejecters, there seems to be no reason to imagine any difference. Although the atonement revealed to them, while they were alive, God's means of rescue through Jesus, their rejection of that rescue leaves them in the same condition of unconscious dormancy after physical death, with the soul somehow inhabiting or being tied to physical creation.

However, the condition of the post-atonement God-focused differs from that of the curse-focused, and this difference is because of Christ and his redemption. We will explore this further in the next chapter.

6

God Redeems

Death, be not proud, though some have called thee
Mighty and dreadful, for thou art not so;
For those whom thou think'st thou dost overthrow
Die not, poor Death, nor yet canst thou kill me.

—JOHN DONNE, FROM "HOLY SONNET 10"

Not only so, but we ourselves, who have the firstfruits of the Spirit,
groan inwardly as we wait eagerly for our adoption to sonship,
the redemption of our bodies.

—ROMANS 8:23

IN THE PREVIOUS CHAPTER, we learned that God sustains all things. He does this despite the fall and the resulting curse, because of the hope found in the atonement. God sustains both the cursed human essence (physical creation) and even the souls of those who oppose him, all for the sake of love—for the hope, the possibility, of love relationship with all who will come to him.

PURPOSE FOR PHYSICAL DEATH

If the possibility of a loving relationship allows God to sustain life with his hand, why does physical death exist at all? Why not sustain physical life as long as hope remains? And why not sustain physical life for those who have already embraced a loving relationship with him? Why must they die physically at all? The fact that both the saved and the unsaved continue to experience death in the same way, despite the atonement, offers a clue to the answer. While God does sustain life for both those who lack a relationship with him and those who are in relationship with him, he cannot simply disregard the curse to perpetuate life. If he could, the atonement would not have been necessary. For life to continue everlastingly, the curse must be defeated. God's redemption plan will ultimately remove the curse from the world—all physical creation—when Jesus returns. But until that time, the world remains enslaved to the curse; decay and death still hold a grip on our shared essence.

However, the hope realized in Christ's atonement changes everything. In his first advent, Jesus—God who became the Son—came to accomplish the redemption of the flesh he assumed, securing the right to the future redemption of all physical creation. Let's now delve into the discussion of Jesus's first advent.

CHRISTOLOGY—BACKGROUND

Essence and activity—or, as Paul refers to them in Romans 1:20, nature and power—are crucial in qualifying Jesus as the redeemer.[1] In one sense, only God could qualify as the redeemer because his spirit would have to resist the sin influence of the cursed human essence—something human spirits, in their enslavement, are powerless to do. Yet, the redeemer also had to be human in order to be personally associated with the cursed essence, to defeat it by putting it to death and resurrecting it without the curse. In Jesus, we see God take on humanity without relinquishing his deity, thus qualifying on both accounts. But how was this accomplished? How could one person be both God and human, given that the essences are different?

The early church grappled with this question. The necessity for both humanity and deity in the redeemer easily refuted early ideas like those of the Ebionites, who denied Jesus's deity, and the Docetists, who denied his humanity. These conclusions also counter the arguments of the Arians (modern-day Jehovah's Witnesses), who argued more sophisticatedly

---

1. Christians, for the most part, form this book's audience. Therefore, I will assume the idea that Jesus is God without presenting a defense.

that Jesus was merely the first and highest created being. However, the debate becomes more complex and intriguing when considering those who acknowledged both the deity and humanity of Jesus but questioned how they were united—such as the arguments presented by the Apollinarians, Nestorians, and Eutychians.

Apollinarius taught that while Jesus had a human body, only the divine psyche (mind and will) could save; therefore, Jesus did not have a human psyche, with the divine psyche replacing the human one within his body. Nestorius argued that the two natures were merely morally united but not actually (or organically) united, resulting in two persons—a human and a divine—within Jesus's one body. Eutychius believed the union to be a true, integrated mix, creating a third type of nature distinct from both the human and the divine—*tertium quid*.

While several councils denounced one or more of these six views, the Council of Chalcedon in AD 451, convened specifically to address the Eutychian heresy, ultimately delivered the final word by defining the "orthodox" view in its developed Chalcedonian Creed:

> We, then, following the holy fathers, all with one consent teach men to confess one and the same Son, our Lord Jesus Christ, the same perfect in Godhead and also perfect in manhood; truly God and truly man, of a rational soul and body; coessential with the Father according to the Godhead, and consubstantial with us according to the manhood; in all things like unto us, without sin; begotten before all ages of the Father according to the Godhead, and in these latter days, for us and for our salvation, born of the Virgin Mary, the mother of God, according to the manhood; one and the same Christ, Son, Lord, Only-begotten, to be acknowledged in two natures, without confusion, without change, without division, without separation; the distinction of natures being by no means taken away by the union, but rather the property of each nature being preserved, and concurring in one person and one subsistence, not parted or divided into two persons, but one and the same Son, and only begotten, God the Word, the Lord Jesus Christ; as the prophets from the beginning have declared concerning Him, and the Lord Jesus Christ Himself has taught us, and the creed of the holy fathers has handed down to us.

The creed sought to refute both Apollinarianism and Eutychianism by insisting on the two distinct natures of Christ. It also rejected Nestorianism by affirming that these two natures were united without separation. This led to the concept of the hypostatic union—a union that is partly conjoined and partly distinct, often described as a mystery. As a result, the idea of the God-man Jesus became solidified in a somewhat undefined way. Today, traditional thinkers are quick to label opposing views as heresy, even though they may struggle to clearly articulate what the orthodox understanding of Jesus as both God and man truly entails.

INCARNATIONAL SONSHIP

The Chalcedonian Creed closely aligns with what I profess, but it contains a concept I find erroneous and another that misunderstands the nature of the divine and human "natures." The concept I consider false is the idea that Jesus is "begotten before all ages of the Father," a notion echoed from the Nicene Creed, which describes his preincarnate being as "the only Son of God, eternally begotten of the Father, God from God, Light from Light, true God from true God, begotten, not made." What does it actually mean to be "eternally begotten"? I've heard more about what it doesn't mean than what it does. Proponents of this idea insist it does not imply that the preincarnate Jesus was either born or created.

If that is the case, what is meant by the descriptors "Father" and "Son," since those terms universally imply that one precedes the other? Some who uphold an eternal Father-Son relationship suggest that "Son" means "in the likeness of," and I would agree that likeness is indeed a significant aspect. This idea is reflected in the genealogical lists of both the Old and New Testaments. However, likeness is not the only implication, and this is evident by the fact that we never reverse the order. Seth was in the likeness of his father Adam, which means Adam was also like Seth. But we never say that Adam was the son of Seth, because, in addition to likeness, the father-son relationship indicates that Adam preceded Seth. If the father-son relationship meant only "likeness," we should be able to use the phrase in both directions, e.g., "The Son is begotten of (like) the Father, and the Father is begotten of (like) the Son." But proponents of the eternally begotten Son would not make such a claim.

Advocates of this view deny the natural precedence implied by a father-son relationship by insisting that divine begetting is different. They argue that the generation of the Son by the Father is an eternal activity, with no point in time where one preceded the other. However, describing the eternal relationship between two necessarily equal members of the

Godhead as one "eternally generating" the other introduces a dependency: the Father, being unbegotten, needs no other, while the Son, however, derives his very being—his personal existence—from the Father's continuous generating activity. To claim that the Godhead involves necessary equality while also admitting that one depends on the other for existence is stunningly bizarre. Dependency inherently implies subordination. As William Lane Craig puts it, "This doctrine of the generation of the Logos from the Father cannot, despite assurances to the contrary, but diminish the status of the Son because he becomes an effect contingent upon the Father."[2]

Rather than disrupting the balance of the Trinity, we should understand the Father-Son relationship only in the context of Jesus's post-incarnation but pre-resurrection life. The Greek word for "only begotten" is *monogenes*. The first part, *mono*, means "one" or "only one," emphasizing his uniqueness. The second part, *genes*, relates to "generate." Thus, the "only begotten Son," the uniquely generated Son, was unique because no human born into this world mirrored his divine nature. The God-man Jesus was truly Immanuel, God with us.

A simple test for these two views of "only begotten" can be found in the interpretation of John 3:16. Consider how the verses are altered by different interpretations:

> For God loved the world in this way: he gave his *eternally-generated-of-the-Father* Son, so that everyone who believes in him will not perish but have eternal life.

Now, why would Jesus, in his discussion with Nicodemus in John 3, feel the need to introduce the idea that his existence was made possible only through the eternal generation activity of the Father? The truth is, he wouldn't, and he doesn't. Their entire conversation centers on the necessity of being born again through faith in the redemption that Jesus would provide. This understanding aligns much more naturally with the following interpretation:

> For God loved the world in this way: he gave his *uniquely-born-as-both-God-and-human* Son, so that everyone who believes in him will not perish but have eternal life.

Nicodemus, to whom Jesus spoke, needed to be born again. This rebirth was possible only through the God-man Jesus, who, because he was

---

2. Craig, "Is God the Son Begotten?"

both God and man, could withstand the temptation of sin, lay down his human body in death, and take it up again in redemption, free from the curse. That was Jesus's central point. To ignore this and suggest that Jesus was introducing an argument for a subordinate preincarnate relationship within the Godhead is not only categorically wrong but also contextually nonsensical.

Advocates of the eternally begotten Son often point to passages that say "the Father sent his Son" (e.g., Galatians 4:4), arguing that if God sent his Son, then Jesus must have been the "Son" before being sent. However, this presumed logic does not hold. A passage that counters this idea is 2 Samuel 24:15, where it is written, "So the Lord sent a plague on Israel from that morning until the appointed time." In this case, the plague did not exist in heaven with God in its "plagueness" before God sent it. Similarly, one can imagine many things being sent that do not become what they are until after they are sent. For example, if I send my son to Hawaii to teach high school, I can tell his students, "I sent you your teacher," even though he was not their teacher when I sent him. In the same way, God did send Jesus as his Son, but Jesus became the Son as a result of the sending, not as a condition prior to the sending.

Beyond the ideas of likeness and precedence, the father-son relationship also conveys care—a loving, intentional giving by the one with greater ability to the one more vulnerable. Fathers assist sons in their development; sons depend on fathers for instruction and guidance. This is the point Paul makes in 1 Corinthians 11:3 when he says that God is the head of Christ. The Father, with greater ability, gives of himself to help the Son, who is more vulnerable. This attitude characterized Jesus's life, as he depended on the Father and was led by him in all things. However, this dynamic would not apply to the preincarnate Christ, who had equal access to the divine nature.

TWO NATURES, ONE PERSON

The other Christological concept that the Chalcedonian Creed complicates concerns the divine and human nature of Jesus. Here is what I believe: Jesus had a divine nature and a human nature, and he was one person with a unified soul—mind, emotions, will, and desire. At first glance, this seems to align with the Chalcedonian Creed. However, given what that council and its creed aimed to define and protect against, further clarification is needed.

For instance, when the creed speaks of "our Lord Jesus Christ," it describes him as "perfect in Godhead." The term "perfect" implies completeness. Therefore, if one aspect of the Godhead is omniscience, Jesus must, according to the creed, be perfect (complete) in omniscience. Yet, in reference to his return, Jesus says, "But about that day and hour no one knows, not even the angels in heaven, nor the Son, but only the Father" (Matthew 24:36). There are other biblical examples, but this one suffices: if the Godhead includes perfect (complete) omniscience and the Son does not know something that the Father does, how can the Son be perfect in Godhead?

Nevertheless, I do believe that Jesus possessed the fullness of God, and this requires further explanation.

Earlier in this chapter, we discussed both human nature (or essence) and God's essence. In his essence, God is TGB (True, Good, Beautiful) to an infinite and absolute degree. However, Paul tells us in Philippians 2:5–7 that there was an emptying of God's attributes in Jesus:

> In your relationships with one another, have the same mindset as Christ Jesus: Who, being in very nature God, did not consider equality with God something to be used to his own advantage; rather, he *made himself nothing* by taking the very nature of a servant, being made in human likeness.

The NIV translates the phrase as "made himself nothing," while many other translations render it as "emptied himself." The Greek word used is *kenoo*, which literally means "to empty." Kenoticism, or kenotic Christology, argues that Jesus relinquished certain attributes of his deity to become human. This interpretation is difficult to dispute, given the Philippians passage and the portrayal of Jesus in the Gospels. For instance, we've already mentioned Jesus's apparent lack of infinite knowledge. Similarly, he was not omnipresent, as he was only present where his body was. However, to strictly adhere to the idea that Jesus gave up or emptied himself of divine attributes would imply that he was less than fully God.

Commentaries often try to mitigate the impact of this concept by arguing that the text doesn't say Jesus emptied himself of divine attributes, but rather that he emptied himself to take on human form. In other words, they suggest the emptying was an act of selflessness that serves as an example for us. However, this explanation doesn't address the apparent loss of omniscience, a divine attribute, in Jesus.

The most satisfying resolution I've encountered, which maintains the idea of Jesus's full deity while acknowledging the limitations of his human essence, is found in William Lane Craig and J.P. Moreland's *Philosophical Foundations for a Christian Worldview*. The authors propose that certain divine attributes were largely subliminal in Jesus. In other words, "the human consciousness of Jesus was underlain by a divine subconsciousness."[3] I would further suggest that the Father controlled the release of this divine knowledge into Jesus's human consciousness. For example, Jesus could know what Nathanael (John 1) and Mary (John 2) were thinking or experiencing based on God's selective release of that divine knowledge to him. Similarly, Jesus could be led into the wilderness by the Spirit without necessarily knowing why or how long he would be there.

One other challenging aspect of this concept is the view of Apollinarius, who argued that the divine psyche (person) of Jesus was the single mind and will of Jesus, replacing any human psyche. However, this specification seems unnecessary. The preincarnate psyche of Jesus was indeed the psyche of the incarnate Jesus, but it didn't "replace" a human psyche because rational mind and will are not inherently only divine or only human. As Craig and Moreland explain, "It is one's nature, not one's person, that determines one's deity."[4]

JESUS—UNIQUELY BORN TO CONQUER THE CURSE

Many Christians, perhaps unknowingly, hold ideas about Jesus's death on the cross that undermine the concept of a united God. God necessarily exists as a Trinity. If the persons of the Trinity were separated by essence (nature), the Trinity—and therefore God—could not exist. One such problematic idea is that Jesus took on the guilt for humanity's sins and, as a result, God the Father turned away from Jesus—his person, his soul—on the cross. But how could such a state be imagined?

If Jesus, as a person, were guilty of sin, he could not be God. By definition, God acts in person according to his singular nature (essence) of TGB (True, Good, Beautiful). If guilt were attributed to Jesus's person,

---

3. Craig and Moreland, *Philosophical Foundations*, 610.
4. Craig and Moreland, *Philosophical Foundations*, 606.

he would lack the unity of nature (TGB) and person required to be God. Consequently, he could not be God. However, if Jesus did not bear the guilt of our sins in his person—if he was not being punished in his person for sin and was not separated from God in death—then why did Jesus have to die, and what exactly died in Jesus?[5]

On the cross, Jesus's human essence—his body—died. This human essence was never part of the Godhead, so its death did not affect the Godhead. However, the death of his human essence was necessary so that Jesus, in conjunction with his divine essence, could reclaim that material essence from the grave without its curse. Only in this way could humanity be redeemed by God without compromising the very God upon whom we depend.

Notice how all aspects fit together seamlessly. Two reasons support the fact that no mere human could have died to bring redemption. First, all human spirits are enslaved to their cursed physical essence, leading them to succumb to its lusts and fall into idolatry. Romans 1 describes this threefold inability: verse 28 speaks of degraded minds (inability in truth); verse 26 of degraded passions (inability in goodness); and verse 24 of degraded bodies, particularly sexuality (inability in beauty). Thus, all human souls are guilty of sin: "For all have sinned and fall short of the glory of God" (Romans 3:23). But Jesus, the only begotten Son—the uniquely born God-man—never succumbed to the sin temptations of human physical essence, and therefore, he qualified as Redeemer.

Second, upon the death of the body, a mere human loses control of the metaphysical, as human consciousness requires the active union of soul with body. The human soul, dependent on physical functioning for conscious thought (through interaction with the physical brain), becomes an unconscious, non-functioning entity upon death. However, Jesus did not possess only a human essence. Upon the death of his human essence,

---

5. Jesus's cry from the cross, "My God, my God, why have you forsaken me?" (Matthew 27:46; Psalm 22:1), mirrors David's own words in Psalm 22. While David expressed a sense of abandonment, we know from God's assurance in 2 Samuel 7:15—"My faithful love will never leave him"—and the triumphant conclusion of the psalm itself, that David was never truly forsaken. Similarly, Jesus, fully aware of the Father's continual presence, did not utter these words in despair but for the sake of those watching. By quoting this psalm, he invited his listeners to reflect on its entirety, which transitions from anguish to praise and ends in a vision of God's ultimate victory: "All the ends of the earth will remember and turn to the Lord" (Psalm 22:27). Thus, Jesus's words pointed to the promised rescue and affirmed the unbroken bond between himself and the Father, offering hope and comfort to those who felt abandoned in that moment.

Jesus, retaining his divine essence, remained consciously active and was thus able to reclaim his human physical essence without its curse.

PHYSICAL DEATH IN CHRIST

Significant and purposeful change occurs as a result of the atonement. Jesus's effective redemption removes the curse from his own body—his portion of human essence. With that victory, and because of the unity of human essence, Jesus holds the authority to redeem all human essence. However, he delays this full redemption, tolerating the continued cursed condition of human essence, in order to rescue as many as possible from this and future generations who will come to him.

Despite the delay in redeeming the rest of creation, Jesus's own body has already become the firstfruits of realized redemption (1 Corinthians 15:20); his body is now free from the curse. Remember, to be human is to possess both a soul and physical essence. Therefore, the souls of the God-focused who died before the atonement, as well as those who die afterward, can be brought into human consciousness in association with redeemed creation through Christ's own body. This is why Jesus could confidently tell the thief on the cross, "Today you will be with me in paradise" (Luke 23:43), and Paul could express his longing: "I am torn between the two: I desire to depart and be with Christ, which is better by far; but it is more necessary for you that I remain in the body" (Philippians 1:23–24). Then, at Christ's return, all who have died in him will be brought with him to rise in their new, redeemed (curse-free) bodies (1 Thessalonians 4:14, 16).

7

God Gives

Overwhelm me, from above,
Daily, with thy boundless love.
—William Cowper, from "Gratitude and Love to God"

Every good and perfect gift is from above,
coming down from the Father of the heavenly lights,
who does not change like shifting shadows.
—James 1:17

I began this book with a chapter titled "God Loves," where I defined love as "the giving of oneself for the benefit of relationship." So, why is there a need for a chapter called "God Gives" if giving is inherently part of loving? Haven't we already addressed this? In a sense, yes. However, while nearly all Christians agree that God is love, many struggle with its application. In this chapter and the next, I want to explore the views of two groups that, in my opinion, consistently misunderstand and therefore misrepresent the idea that God is love. First, we'll discuss the Reformed tradition.

Before diving into specifics, I want to clarify that I regard most individuals within the Reformed tradition as true brothers and sisters in Christ. From the Reformed writers and preachers I've encountered, I sense a genuine love for God and for their fellow human beings. However,

I believe certain principles they hold lead to a confusion and distortion of the true meaning of love. By carefully examining their stated beliefs, we will uncover viewpoints that, philosophically dissected, reveal themselves to be distinctly unloving. How, then, can I sense love from the Reformed yet find their beliefs unloving? The paradox resolves when we understand that true love exists in relationship, not in doctrinal formulation.

Consider this: I could write a thesis on why I love my wife, and in doing so, I might omit key concepts or include ideas that lead to logical absurdities or indefensible conclusions. But even if the thesis is flawed, it doesn't necessarily mean I don't love my wife. The truth of my love lies in the relationship, while the thesis is merely a representation. Similarly, in our relationship with God, we may misarticulate or misunderstand certain doctrinal points, but this doesn't negate the reality of the love we experience. I believe this is the case with many Reformed believers, whose faulty representations of salvation and what it means to have a relationship with God do not cancel the love they may genuinely experience.

The two aspects of Reformed theology that I find most misaligned with biblical teaching are (1) the idea that God allows relationship with his people only through coercive determinism, and (2) the belief that God does not love the majority of humanity who remain estranged from him.

I refer to these points as biblically "off-center." However, I will approach them philosophically, supported by biblical evidence. Philosophy is necessary because merely pointing to verses doesn't suffice. Everyone interprets scripture based on a philosophical foundation. For example, Calvinists might argue that the most obvious reading of Romans 9 suggests that God chooses some to love and others to hate based on arbitrary whim. In contrast, faith electionists[1] reject this notion, grounded in 1 John 4:8, which affirms that God is love and always acts out of love. Faith electionists, therefore, interpret Romans 9 as emphasizing that God's choices to fulfill his plan are based on love, rather than ethnic or moral qualifications. Thus, philosophical perspectives influence scriptural interpretation.

Even though Calvinists may advocate for the "most obvious" reading of Romans 9, they often prefer more complex interpretations of other passages. For instance, when considering John 3:16, faith electionists typically argue for the plain, straightforward understanding that God

---

1. Faith electionism, a soteriological concept within Kinship theology, expresses the belief that salvation is granted by God based on the faith of the individual. In this sense, faith electionism plays a central role in the soteriology of Kinship theology, much as Calvinism does in Reformed theology.

offers eternal life to every individual ("the world"). Calvinists, however, often qualify "world" to mean either (1) the entirety of ethnic or national groups, signifying that God's offer is not exclusive to one group, (2) only the elect, or (3) a qualitative term, indicating that although the world is fallen, God loved it enough to send his Son, albeit for a select few.[2]

My point here is that faith electionists advocate for a simple interpretation of John 3:16, while Calvinists argue for deeper consideration. Conversely, Calvinists advocate for a simple interpretation of Romans 9, while faith electionists insist on a more nuanced approach. Ultimately, the interpreter's philosophical viewpoint determines his or her interpretation. The challenge is to find the interpretation that not only has fewer ambiguities but also remains consistent with the entirety of God's revealed character and plan.

With this foundation, let's explore the two key difficulties in Reformed theology I mentioned, both philosophically and biblically. These issues are not new. One common critique of Calvinist soteriology is the claim that God irresistibly forces salvation upon those he chooses. The other is the notion that God arbitrarily saves some and not others. I contend that a correct understanding of the love of God undermines both of these ideas.

BACKGROUND: WHAT IS JUSTICE?

As we've discussed, 1 John 4:8 tells us that God is love—a truth that no one in the Reformed tradition disputes. In fact, they often proclaim it with great enthusiasm. However, this declaration often comes when love is considered in isolation. When concepts like justice or sovereignty are introduced, it seems, based on my observations, that God's love is often relegated to a secondary position, almost like a tagalong sibling. Many Calvinists I've encountered tend to first emphasize love intensely and emotionally, perhaps as a conscious or subconscious effort to disarm it as a potential challenge. Yet, in the heat of defending Calvinism, the emphasis on love often fades in favor of what are perceived as the more demanding doctrines of justice and sovereignty. But theology cannot afford to be selective in its defense or promotion. Love must shine just as brightly alongside justice, and justice must be as radiant next to love. To diminish one in the proclamation of the other is to risk distortion.

2. Warfield, "God's Immeasurable Love."

The first step in any meaningful debate is the definition of terms. We've already defined love in chapter 1 as "the giving of oneself for the benefit of relationship." Now, let's turn our attention to justice. Simply and biblically put, justice is right relationship. In most New Testament translations, the Greek word *dikaios* is rendered as "just," "righteous," or "right," and its derivative *dikaiosyne* is almost always translated as "righteousness." Paul frequently uses these terms in Romans to explain covenant faithfulness and right relationship with God.

Consider Paul's use of these words in Romans 3:26 (KNT), where he speaks of God's divine forbearance in passing over sins previously committed. This was done "to demonstrate his [God's] covenant justice in the present time: that is, that he himself is in the right, and that he declares to be in the right everyone who trusts in the faithfulness of Jesus." This verse highlights the interchangeability of "just" and "righteous" (and their derivatives). While most translations use "righteousness" instead of the KNT's "covenant justice," and "just" instead of "right," the core idea remains the same. More importantly, the justice referred to here is relational—the one who trusts in the faithfulness of Jesus is counted as "right" or "just" in relationship with God. Thus, justice is realized through faith in Jesus, precisely because it establishes right relationship.

Jesus forgave the sins of everyone who sought a right relationship with him. Take, for example, the woman caught in adultery in John 8. She did not need to pay any penalty or make reparations to receive God's forgiveness; her faith alone was sufficient for Jesus to lovingly embrace her. This concept is consistent throughout both the Old and New Testaments. Even Nineveh, despite its many atrocities, did not have to offer reparations to God or Israel; God forgave them simply because they repented following Jonah's preaching. Ephesians 4:32 further reinforces this idea: "Be kind and compassionate to one another, forgiving each other, just as in Christ God forgave you." We are not instructed to forgive only after punishment is administered. Rather, we are to forgive as God forgives—upon repentance, not payment. God's forgiveness flows from his embrace of a restored relationship, a relationship grounded in his true goodness and beauty. That right relationship is justice—biblical justice.

Biblical justice does not demand punishment; it demands right relationship. If a relationship is rejected, justice cannot exist, and God cannot embrace. The result—whether we call it consequence, punishment, or judgment—is separation. And in that separation, without a relationship with God, life is lost.

CALVINISM'S FAULT #1: GOD REQUIRES COERCIVE RELATIONSHIP WITH HIS IMAGE BEARERS

Given our definitions—love as the giving of oneself for the benefit of relationship, and justice as the realization of right relationship—how do we understand the ways in which people either find salvation or leave this life without it? Kinship theology argues that God reveals himself to all. Those who embrace his relational TGB in faith are saved, while those who reject that relationship cannot be coerced into a loving embrace.

Reformed theology begins similarly to Kinship theology: all who face eternal death do so by their own willful rejection. However, the Reformed position diverges significantly on the matter of desire. According to the Reformed view, for those God chooses to save, he unilaterally alters their wills to incline them toward a loving relationship with him. The Westminster Longer Catechism, in response to question 67, defines effectual calling:

> "Effectual calling is the work of God's almighty power and grace, whereby (out of his *free and special love* to his elect, and from nothing in them moving him thereunto) he doth, in his accepted time, invite and draw them to Jesus Christ, by his Word and Spirit; savingly enlightening their minds, renewing and powerfully *determining their wills*, so as they (although in themselves dead in sin) are hereby *made willing* and able freely to answer his call, and to accept and embrace the grace offered and conveyed therein" [emphasis added].

Thus, the Reformed belief, according to the catechism, is that for those whom God chooses to save, he determines (or controls) their wills, aligning them to willingly accept his call. Conversely, for those whom God does not choose to save, he withholds this "free and special love," leaving their wills unaltered and unable to respond to his call. In other words, to the elect, God offers a salvation they cannot refuse; to the non-elect, he offers a salvation they cannot accept.

Certain Calvinists argue that ensuring salvation is more important than preserving human free will. Consider this perspective from R.C. Sproul, Jr.:

> The idea that God chooses not to save everybody is horrifying to some. The idea that He wants to save everybody and would save everybody but His desire for such is trumped by a deeper desire to leave room for free will is horrifying to me. I have a hard time

imagining the damned complaining about the heat but finding some consolation in the blessings of their free will. God has the power to save all people. The value of the suffering of Christ is sufficient to cover all the sins of all God's people. Protecting man's free will is not something the Bible says God has the least interest in.[3]

Sproul's argument, however, overlooks the true significance of free will. He reduces it to mere control—the exercise of self-determined desire. If that were all free will entailed, I might agree that rescuing someone from destruction is more valuable than preserving their autonomy. But salvation is not about escaping destruction to enjoy luxury by simply adhering to a set of doctrines. Salvation is about entering into a loving relationship with God. And love, which is the giving of oneself for the sake of relationship, is the only way—not one of the ways, but the only way—that salvation can be attained.

God does not grant us free will so we can feel in control or make decisions independently. Rather, God cannot manipulate the wills of his creatures for two reasons. First, he is a God of love, which means he gives of himself for the sake of relationship. Because of who he is, he cannot act otherwise. Second, even if God could manipulate wills, he could not compel love, because love, by its nature, cannot be forced. We established in chapter 1 that God does not engage in absurdities. The very idea of manipulating or coercing someone into love contradicts the essence of what it means to give of oneself. Therefore, love, which inherently involves self-giving, cannot exist through any form of coercion or determinism. C.S. Lewis captured this idea well: "Free will, though it makes evil possible, is also the only thing that makes possible any love or goodness or joy worth having."[4]

CALVINISM'S FAULT #2: GOD FAILS TO LOVE CERTAIN OF HIS IMAGE BEARERS

Calvinist author and pastor Sam Storms acknowledges that God loves infinitely, but he attempts to resolve the problem of God not extending salvific love (as described in the Calvinist doctrine of effectual calling) to certain individuals, the non-elect, by distinguishing between different

---

3. Sproul, "Why Doesn't God Save Everybody?"
4. Lewis, *Mere Christianity*, 48.

kinds of love. Storms argues that there are five types of divine love: (1) the love of God for his Son and Jesus's love for the Father, which is untainted by sin; (2) God's love for his creation, evident in the sun and rain falling on both the good and the evil; (3) God's love for the sinful, fallen world, as expressed in John 3:16, where "world" refers not to the quantity of those loved but to the moral nature of his image bearers; (4) God's love for the nation of Israel, as seen in Deuteronomy 7 and 10; and (5) God's love for his elect, redeemed people—a love that "goes beyond merely providing physical blessings." According to Storms, God fulfills his role as a God of love by loving everyone, but only the elect receive the salvific love of effectual calling.

The problem, which Storms seems to overlook, is that calling certain blessings "love" when the intention is ultimately to destroy the person receiving them cannot truly be considered love. True love, as we've defined it, involves vulnerability for the sake of relationship. Jesus highlights this distinction when he asks, "What good will it be for someone to gain the whole world, yet forfeit their soul?" (Matthew 16:26a). To "love" his fallen image bearers in any way short of providing the possibility of salvation is not love at all. Referring to the provision of sun and rain as "love" for those destined for doom feels hollow and meaningless. True love seeks relationship.

What Storms tries to categorize as different types of love are actually just varying degrees of beneficence. According to this view, God grants some people enough blessings to provide temporary physical comfort but not enough to offer them salvation. In other words, the so-called God of infinite love arbitrarily limits, curtails, and eventually stops his love. This notion severely distorts the biblical portrayal of God's infinite love.

As we briefly discussed in the last chapter, the phrase "son of" in the Bible, while often suggesting a genealogical link, frequently conveys the idea of image-bearing. Angels are sometimes called "sons of God" because they reflect his glory. Similarly, in John 8, when Jesus says to the Jews questioning him, "You belong to your father, the devil," he isn't referring to a genealogical link but rather to a likeness in behavior. Paul uses the same concept in Acts 13:10 when he calls Bar-Jesus (literally, "son of Jesus") a "son of the Devil" (HCSB). Paul's play on words emphasizes that the sorcerer, despite his name, was not reflecting Jesus but was instead displaying the traits of the devil.

This idea of likeness also permeates the genealogical list in Genesis 5. Verse 1 mentions that Adam was made in the likeness of God, and verse 3 notes that Adam fathered a son, Seth, "in his likeness, according to his image" (HCSB). Although Adam already had a son, Cain, who did evil and was unrepentant, Seth, a godly man, was more like his father Adam and is included in the line leading to Noah.

In Matthew 5, Jesus begins the Sermon on the Mount. Toward the end of the chapter, he urges us to love our enemies so that we may be "sons of [our] Father in heaven." Here, Jesus is not giving an entry qualification for salvation. He isn't saying that loving our enemies will secure us a place in heaven regardless of what we believe about God, faith, or repentance. When Jesus tells us to love our enemies to be "sons of God," he is urging us to love them to be like God, because God loves his enemies. The example Jesus gives is that of providing sun and rain—blessings—not only to the righteous but also to the unrighteous. Through this illustration, Jesus teaches us that there are no different levels or types of God's love. John said, "God is love," not because God changes with circumstances, but because God expresses his nature by love. God doesn't evaluate individuals to decide how to react; he simply loves. And God does not limit his love. Jesus doesn't say, "Love only this much." He tells us to love as God does, and God loves infinitely.

The realization that God never stops his love has led some Christians to wonder whether everyone may eventually be drawn into a full, relational embrace with God. How could there be everlasting destruction if God's love is infinite and everlasting? How could anyone ultimately resist the overwhelming glory of our God of infinite truth, goodness, and beauty? Who could withstand the splendor of such majesty? We will explore these questions next.

8

God's Desire

The world is charged with the grandeur of God.
It will flame out, like shining from shook foil;
It gathers to a greatness, like the ooze of oil
Crushed. Why do men then now not reck his rod?
Generations have trod, have trod, have trod;
And all is seared with trade; bleared, smeared with toil;
And wears man's smudge and shares man's smell: the soil
Is bare now, nor can foot feel, being shod.

And for all this, nature is never spent;
There lives the dearest freshness deep down things;
And though the last lights off the black West went
Oh, morning, at the brown brink eastward, springs —
Because the Holy Ghost over the bent
World broods with warm breast and with ah! bright wings.

—GERARD MANLEY HOPKINS, FROM "GOD'S GRANDEUR"

Our God is in heaven
he does whatever pleases him.

—PSALM 115:3

IN THE CHAPTERS SO far, I have explored how Yahweh—the I AM, the only existent God—created all things with his love purpose in mind. I have argued that this eternal God ventured from his timeless realm to engage with his creation in a new relational bliss. I have agreed with the apostle John that this all-seeing God knows everything, not just calling each star by name or counting each hair on every head, but also holding the entire universe of possibilities within his mind. I've likened our omniscient God to the perfect chess grandmaster, anticipating and preparing for every move his limited opponent might make, even by accident. For such a God—infinitely loving, truly all-powerful, and undeniably all-knowing—could anything he desires be denied? Proponents of Reformed theology would answer no. Universalists would ultimately agree. But proponents of Kinship theology must answer yes.

In the previous chapter, I discussed some of the difficulties Kinship theology (KT) faces with Reformed theology. The conclusion—that God does not manipulate the direction or intensity of his love—often leads us to consider whether limited humankind truly has the ability to resist the overwhelming force of God's love and thus choose to embrace the darkness and horror of life without him. We must, therefore, examine the finer points of this idea and its connection to eschatology, particularly in relation to universalism.

Universalism, simply put, is the doctrine of universal salvation—the belief that every person who has ever lived will eventually realize his or her full actualization as a child of God. Historically, the orthodox traditions of Reformed, Lutheran, Catholic, and even the less organized Anabaptists have often treated universalists with disdain. However, one would think that every Christian should long for universalism's central idea, not only because it aligns with the love we are called to bear and the joy of communion with God, but also because it reflects God's desire that none should perish and that all should come to repentance. Could God's purpose be thwarted? Can God be denied?

On the surface, universalism seems to have strong biblical support, despite numerous passages that speak of the destruction of unbelievers. For example, in 1 Corinthians 15:22, Paul writes, "For as in Adam all die, so also in Christ *all* will be made alive." Paul also tells the church in Colossae, "For God was pleased to have all his fullness dwell in [Christ], and through him to reconcile to himself *all* things, whether on earth or in heaven, by making peace through his blood, shed on the cross" (Colossians 1:19–20). Similarly, in Romans, Paul declares, "Consequently, just as one trespass resulted in condemnation for all people, so also one righteous act resulted in justification and life for *all* people" (Romans 5:18), and "For God has bound everyone to disobedience so that he may have mercy on them *all*" (Romans 11:32). These verses are just a few of the many that universalists interpret in their favor.

Of course, non-universalists seek to diminish the impact of these verses in various ways. For example, they argue that when Paul refers to "all," he is often speaking of those who have faith—the group he has already identified earlier in the passages—or that "all" refers to the possibility of inclusion rather than its actuality. On the other hand, universalists also dismiss the "proof" verses that speak of the destruction of unbelievers. For instance, 2 Thessalonians 1:9 seems particularly strong: those who don't know God "will pay the penalty of eternal destruction from the Lord's presence and from His glorious strength" (HCSB). Universalists point out that the Greek word translated as "eternal" could also mean "a certain age" or another specific time period, such as a lifetime. Classical Greek uses the word in both ways. Therefore, universalists urge us to "interpret Scripture in light of Scripture," concluding that the "eternal" in 2 Thessalonians 1:9 refers only to a finite period. Clearly, merely aligning *proof* texts on either side of the argument will not *prove* anything.

I deeply feel the allure of universalism's dream. However, I characterize it as a "dream" rather than a "hope" because it conflicts with the foundational concepts of Kinship theology, especially in relation to image-based atonement. Universalism envisions a conclusion that, while involving a loving relationship, overlooks the love-defined basis of that relationship

God did intend creation for everlasting love relationships. As previously noted, God's essence—his very being—is truth, goodness, and beauty (TGB). God acts in love by revealing his TGB. The unity of God's essence and the multiplicity of his persons in activity serve as the pattern for the image-bearing nature of humans. We, too, are one in essence (comprising the physical elements of our universe, including our bodies) and multiple in persons (the individual souls that share this one physical essence). But although we share this model with God, our relationship with him depends on basing our actions on God's essence of virtue, rather than on the impulses of our own physical nature.

Therefore, God created us with the capacity to comprehend his TGB, to agree with it after evaluation, and then, once comprehended and agreed upon, to communicate it in love, just as he does. The point I want to emphasize here is that God *made* us this way—capable of desiring TGB to fuel our image-bearing qualities of comprehension, concurrence, and communication. The universalist agrees that God formed us with this innate love for TGB and argues that when confronted with the full revelation of the TGB found in God, our innate desire for it will not just possibly, but inevitably, lead to concurrence and communication—faith, hope, and love.

I cannot fault this conclusion. The human with a fully mature relational understanding that TGB, sourced in God, alone provides perfect satisfaction is indeed the persuasion that will keep us forever in God's embrace in the eschaton. But I believe universalists, in their eagerness to reach this philosophical end, overlook other crucial points along the way.

LOVE'S LIBERTY

In both chapters 1 and 7, I argued that love cannot be coerced because love, by its very nature, involves the giving of oneself for the benefit of a relationship. For an action to truly be love, the act of giving must be controlled solely by the one who is giving. This principle holds true even though God created us with an innate desire for truth, goodness, and beauty (TGB), because that desire exists whether we seek its fulfillment without God or through a relationship with him.

Understanding that love cannot be coerced means we cannot simply compare coerced love to uncoerced love, as if the latter is merely a better version of the former. Coerced love is not love at all. The very idea of "coerced love" is as nonsensical as a married bachelor or a square triangle. Just as God cannot create a square triangle, he cannot coerce love.

The Universalist's Misunderstanding of Salvation

A clear grasp of the definition of love helps us avoid misconceptions about salvation. Consider a statement by universalist Gregory MacDonald:[1]:

> There is an objection that applies to all freewill theists' attempts to justify a traditional doctrine of hell that is worth making at this stage. It could be argued that an all-loving God will try all that he can to elicit freely a positive response to the gospel: but, if all else fails, he would be justified in not leaving people free

---

1. Gregory MacDonald is the pseudonym of author Robin Parry.

in a libertarian sense *with respect to their salvation*" (emphasis added).[2]

MacDonald's mistake lies in treating salvation as merely the object of a choice. We do not simply choose "salvation"; rather, salvation is the entry into a love relationship with God. God created us for love relationship, and salvation—forgiveness and redemption—restores that relationship. Only love can lead to a love relationship. God does not act unilaterally to pull someone out of a pit; there is no pit!

Many Christians envision hell as a physical place or a set of dire consequences, like a ravine with a collapsed bridge, with God desperately trying to warn us of the danger. But this imagery misses the point. There is no bridge, cliff, or external peril. There is only love relationship or the absence of it. Embracing God in love relationship brings the fullness of his TGB into our lives. Rejecting God, on the other hand, means losing all the TGB of his embrace.

Salvation is not about being rescued from some external danger that God can intervene to prevent through unilateral goodwill. He cannot simply infuse faith or increase revelation to make us love him. Love is, by definition, a voluntary giving of oneself for the benefit of a relationship. This mutual embrace is what salvation truly is.

The Universalist's Misunderstanding of Human Freedom

When discussing the freedom to choose love, some universalists, including Eastern Orthodox scholar David Bentley Hart, describe freedom as "a being's power to flourish as what it naturally is, to become ever more fully what it is." Hart compares this to the freedom of an oak seed growing uninterrupted into an oak tree. In this analogy, God removes obstacles—like rocks or foraging animals—that might hinder the oak tree's natural growth to its full potential. However, this analogy falls short when applied to the growth of a human being designed for everlasting love relationship with God. Unlike an oak tree, our path to freedom is obstructed not just by external factors, but also by our internal choices. Human freedom, therefore, must encompass more than just the potential for fulfillment; it must also include the choice to either follow or obstruct that path.

God certainly assists us—in fact, he takes the first step. God reveals himself to us, and embracing and growing into the love relationship

---

2. MacDonald, *Evangelical Universalist*, 23.

he offers is the natural course for which we were made, much like an oak tree naturally grows from its seed. But unlike an oak tree, human liberty includes the freedom to say no. We all—universalists and non-universalists alike—acknowledge this truth. Adam's sin was not a natural part of growth toward fulfillment; it was an abnormal, selfish, God-rejecting decision that interrupted the glorious course of growing into a God-embracing relationship. Our response to God's revelation depends on our limited understanding—what we, at any given moment, perceive to be the best path to satisfy our desire for truth, goodness, and beauty. Often, when faced with God's revelation, people choose wrongly, rejecting what God reveals. This wrong choice does not leave them in a neutral state, ready for the next revelation. Both the creature and the Creator are affected. When a person rejects God's revelation, God cannot offer greater revelation. The person's withdrawal from God creates an imposed distance—not because God rejects the person, but because the person rejects God. As Romans 1 puts it, God must "deliver them over" to their delusion. He does so not out of anger or wounded pride, but because of the inherent limits on how he can interact with those who reject TGB. The creature, too, is changed by this rejection. The refusal hardens the heart of the God-rejecter and does real intrinsic damage to his or her spirit, like an oak seed damaged before it can grow.

The story of Adam and Eve in Genesis is not just an account of how it all began; it illustrates exactly what we are discussing here—how God intended to bring us to relational maturity and how his image bearers chose wrongly. The Genesis 2 and 3 narrative provides the foundation for understanding the rest of Scripture as God's restoration plan. Why did God become man? The story of the garden answers that. What did the atonement accomplish? The fall in the garden provides the explanation. How can we be reunited with God? The events in the garden chart the course.

God created Adam and Eve and placed them in Eden, the garden of his pleasure. He revealed his TGB: "God made all kinds of trees grow from the ground, trees beautiful to look at and good to eat. The tree of life was in the middle of the garden, along with the tree of the knowledge of good and evil" (Genesis 2:9). As image bearers, Adam and Eve were given responsibility for this good physical creation (Genesis 1:26–28), with one stipulation: they were commanded not to eat from the tree of the knowledge of good and evil (Genesis 2:17).

First, we should consider what it meant for God to give Adam and Eve responsibility over creation. Did they truly sustain creation by their word of power? Of course not. God created all things and sustains all things. However, God gave Adam and Eve responsibility over the direction of their own essence, not just to highlight an image-bearing trait or to teach them accountability, but because their relationship with him had to be based on the TGB of his essence. For their relationship to flourish—for them to grow into the fully realized love partnership God intended—they had to exercise control over their essence, ensuring it did not usurp the place of God's essence in their TGB-desiring focus.

Importantly, this responsibility over their essence was not a mere illusion. God wasn't secretly pulling the strings while letting Adam and Eve believe they were in control. No, they truly had the authority to make decisions about physical creation, whether for self-satisfaction or for sacrifice.

A second key aspect of the Eden story is the command not to eat from the tree. The tree itself was not evil, nor was the knowledge it represented solely evil; it held the knowledge of both good and evil. So why would God want to prevent his image bearers from gaining this knowledge, especially since they were meant to reflect him? In fact, didn't they already have some knowledge of what was good, as evidenced by the garden itself, which proclaimed God's goodness?

God's command was not intended to prevent knowledge but to metaphorically show Adam and Eve that they were to gain knowledge by depending on its source—God—not by relying on the physical creation, which they were meant to rule. God intended for human dominion over creation and the command about the tree to work together as a process of relational growth. What we learn from this arrangement is true of any relationship: as partners gain knowledge of each other, their relationship deepens and matures. While God fully knew his created image bearers, they had to learn to know him. Genesis 3 explains how they failed in that relationship-building process by their own choice. Their failure to follow the natural course of development into fully mature relational creatures with God had consequences far more severe than a simple teachable moment followed by an apology and forgiveness. Their sin shook the world.

The fall would not have been so devastating if its only consequence had been guilt because of sin. God could have forgiven Adam and Eve for their sin as easily as he forgave Israel in the Old Testament (Leviticus 19:22; Psalm 85:2). But Adam's sin fundamentally altered the basis for their relationship with God, shifting it from dependence on God and his essence (TGB) to dependence on physical creation—Adam's own essence, for which he was responsible. God had warned Adam that eating from the tree would result in death, which is separation from God. Without reliance on God's TGB, the relationship died.

By embracing their own essence as their idol, Adam and Eve relinquished their rule over physical creation and became subject to it. This change corrupted the image bearers, distorting the image and damaging the path to fulfilling God's design. In other words, they—the rulers—removed physical creation from its purpose under God and subjected it to the false, anti-God purpose of idolatry. To devote something that has been dedicated to holy use to unholy use is to curse it—what the New Testament calls "anathema," meaning devoted to destruction. Consequently, physical creation, including Adam and Eve's very bodies, became separated from God and destined for death and destruction.

Here's where the conversation diverges between Kinship theology and universalism. Adam and Eve's very essence became the disruptor of God's design—the foraging animal that unearthed the oak seed, preventing its growth. Because of this, God could no longer continue his charted course for full love revelation in TGB. For greater revelation to be given, there first must be greater relational development. Universalists believe that every soul, when fully exposed to the divine glory for which all things were made, will eventually embrace that freedom. But this belief overlooks the necessary path of development required to fully expose that divine glory. Adam and Eve, and all humans since, obstruct their path to freedom and relational wholeness with God by their free decision to pursue TGB from their own cursed, separated essence.

The Universalist's Misunderstanding of God's Revelation Process

Throughout the Bible, the necessity of a developmental process toward relational maturity is consistently emphasized. This process was the purpose behind God's command to Adam and Eve not to eat from the tree of the knowledge of good and evil. It is evident in the faith journey God led Abraham on and in the lives of many other Old Testament figures. Even Jesus experienced this growth, as Luke tells us: "Jesus increased in wisdom and stature, and in favor with God and with people" (Luke 2:52). Consider that! Jesus "matured, growing up in both body and spirit" (The

Message). He had to do so because genuine relationship demands development. By the time Jesus was led by the Holy Spirit into the wilderness, he had reached a level of relational maturity that enabled him to resist the temptations Satan offered. Jesus achieved this maturity by consistently choosing dependence on God's TGB essence throughout his life.

We often compare the temptation scenes of Jesus in the wilderness and Adam in the garden, highlighting how Jesus succeeded where Adam failed. However, this comparison is flawed if we view it as two equals making opposite choices. Instead, these scenes contrast the choice of one person fully mature in relational freedom with that of a novice just beginning the journey toward maturity. The key takeaway is that if Adam and Eve, who were "for one restraint, Lords of the World besides,"[3] could choose evil in the garden, then any human, short of mature realization of God's TGB provision, always has the possibility of choosing evil throughout his or her life. The ability to choose against God's revelation remains unless God imposes his will to the contrary—something he *cannot* do as a being of love.

Hart seems to misunderstand this argument about freedom of choice. He argues that "there is no such thing as perfect freedom in this life, or perfect understanding, and it is sheer nonsense to suggest that we possess limitless or unqualified liberty." However, the liberty-to-choose position does not claim "perfect freedom in this life" or that we are completely, or even mostly, free creatures. The freedom at issue pertains only to what God cannot directly coerce without destroying its essence—love. Hart's critique misses the point by attacking a strawman of full and perfect freedom in all things. Indeed, humans are influenced in countless ways, with our wills pulled in multiple directions. We cannot claim perfect freedom from these influences. Yet God, with his grandmaster ability to anticipate, works all things for good, creating the clearest opportunity for each individual to choose love when confronted with that choice. Still, he will not coerce.

Adam and Eve chose wrongly, as did Cain later. Just as good can be compounded by an ever-increasing positive response to God's revelation, so too can evil be compounded in a downward spiral of negative responses. Genesis 4 illustrates this degradation. Even the omnipotent and omniscient love of God cannot simply sweep aside the cursed condition without simultaneously sweeping away love in its self-giving nature.

---

3. Milton, *Paradise Lost*, I:27–32.

God constantly provides revelation—as much as he is able. But he cannot offer full relational revelation to those who have not matured in their relational development. James did not say, "Draw away from God, and he will nevertheless draw near to you." This necessity for revelational growth is echoed in the Old Testament's repeated notion that seeing God would result in death. In Exodus 33, when Moses asked to see God's "glory," God responded that while Moses could recognize his goodness and know his name, he could not see God's face and live. Instead, God said he would show Moses his back. This conversation seems strange, as God has no physical face or back. What is God telling Moses?

Moses asked to see God's glory, which represents the manifestation of God's essence. For humans, a face reveals the person most fully. Seeing a back, by contrast, is only a partial view, not fully satisfying our desire to see and know the person. To see God's "face" would be to see his essence in full, which is what Moses sought. But God explained that Moses could not handle the fullness of his essence; he could see only part of it (his "back"). The reason given is that seeing God's full essence would kill him.

Why would God's essence be fatal to Moses? It is not that lightning bolts would shoot out from God's essence. Rather, it is that the full revelation of God's TGB would overwhelm a person still immature spiritually and deeply entangled in the curse of his own essence, leading to a spiritual rejection rather than an embrace of God. That is what death means—separation. Moses, like all humankind, needed to be brought along in a relational growth process until he could say, as John did in his Gospel, "We have seen his glory, the glory of the one and only Son, who came from the Father, full of grace and truth" (John 1:14b).

The necessity of relational growth for full love relationship is evident in the garden of Eden, through the history of Israel, in Jesus's own growth to maturity, and in the development of the disciples. Love relationship cannot emerge by overwhelming force, nor can it flourish when someone's rejection of God distances them from the very source of TGB revelation. In a final, fully established separation in death, what remains for a rejecting, TGB-separated, destruction-bound sinner might be a desire for personal relief, but that could never be mistaken for a decision to love.

The Universalist's Misunderstanding of Determinism

We all agree that God is perfect. However, when defining that perfection, many Christians tend to rely on ancient Greek philosophy. Without realizing it, we, like Plato and Aristotle, often assume that perfection must include determinism in every outcome. This assumption is evident in Reformed theology—and surprisingly, also in universalism, despite its anti-Reformed stance. I'm not referring to determinism in the sense that every event is the result of prior influences. Rather, I'm speaking specifically of God determining certain outcomes that he irresistibly causes to happen. While I believe God can intervene in certain areas without denying himself, I also maintain that he cannot determine the love choice of his image bearers without undermining his very purpose in creation.

The vision of universalism is indeed compelling, but in pursuit of this ideal, universalism sacrifices coherence by demanding a deterministic form of love. Consider what David Bentley Hart writes:

> As far as I am concerned, anyone who hopes for the universal reconciliation of creatures with God must already believe that this would be the best possible ending to the Christian story; and such a person has then no excuse for imagining that God could bring any but the best possible ending to pass without thereby being in some sense a failed creator.[4]

Hart envisions a creator who would override his creatures' free will to achieve a predetermined state of reconciliation—an idea reminiscent of the Reformed doctrine he opposes. To insist that "love wins" while ignoring the self-giving nature of love reveals a fundamental inconsistency. Hart continues:

> In the end of all things is their beginning, and only from the perspective of the end can one know what they are, why they have been made, and who the God is who has called them forth from nothingness. Anything willingly done is done toward an end; and anything done toward an end is defined by that end.[5]

and

> Precisely because God in himself is absolute—'absolved,' that is, of every pathos of the contingent, every 'affect' of the sort that a

---

4. Hart, *That All*, 66.
5. Hart, *That All*, 68.

finite substance has the power to visit upon another—his moral 'venture' in creating is infinite.[6]

But Hart's arguments are pure determinism. In love, the "giving of self" inherently involves relinquishing control. Love requires a willingness to become vulnerable, to risk for the sake of relationship. As Clark Pinnock, an openness theologian, explains, "God does not risk for risk's sake, but for love's sake."[7] C. S. Lewis echoes this sentiment: "To love is to be vulnerable."[8] John Sanders further elaborates: God "does not get everything he desires,"[9] and "Love takes risks and is willing to wait and try again if need be," but "success is not guaranteed."[10] Sanders concludes that the relationship God offers is "not one of control and domination but rather one of powerful love and vulnerability."[11]

So while God's motivation in creation was surely for all to enjoy an everlasting love relationship, the fact that not all do does not redefine God or his original purpose. The nature of love necessarily involves risk, and God created a world of love possibilities because the glory of God is the glory of love! A world whose Maker loves and elevates love, regardless of the consequences, demonstrates not a rigid commitment to determinism, but rather a profound wellspring of vulnerability.

Herein lies the tension. Universalism asserts that, in the end, God will force his way toward a deterministic outcome, regardless of his creatures' contrary choices. This reasoning implies, first, that God values the dream of a love relationship more than the love relationship itself. Dietrich Bonhoeffer's insight on Christian community applies here: "Those who love their dream of a Christian community more than they love the Christian community itself become destroyers of that Christian community." This is because love necessarily involves vulnerability—the risk of loss.

A second significant issue arises. If God were to achieve final victory through dynamic influence, why does he not employ this influence to protect his creatures—designed and destined for glory—in the meantime? The fact that God allows pain and horror without immediately intervening with his supposedly irresistible revelation is as indefensible

---

6. Hart, *That All*, 70.
7. Pinnock, *Most Moved*, 52.
8. Lewis, *Four Loves*, 78.
9. Sanders, *Risks*, 207.
10. Sanders, *Risks*, 179.
11. Sanders, *Risks*, 71.

as the Calvinist notion of God selectively saving some while permitting others to perish.

If God has no qualms about interfering with human freedom for the greater good, why does he not do so to prevent the hellish birth of a drug addict's baby? Why does he not stop volcanoes from burning people alive? Why does he not prevent the torture of countless vulnerable people groups? What about cases of intentional maiming, rape, and pedophilia, or unintentional but horrific accidents? If God can justify interference in some cases for the greater good, what justification can he offer for not intervening in the overwhelming pain and suffering that has plagued the world throughout history? This line of thinking paints God as monstrous rather than loving.

In contrast to the universalists' lack of a satisfying answer, Kinship theology offers a more coherent explanation. God's refusal to force his revelation is not due to a temporary limitation of his love. Instead, God *cannot* advance his revelation or force his love when the intended partner in that love relationship turns away. While human resistance could not thwart the efforts of a deterministic God, a creature designed for love must be able to choose not to love. Ultimately, while God created his image bearers with a desire for TGB, he did not create them without the ability to give of themselves—the absolute prerequisite for love.

This is a crucial point that we cannot ignore without diminishing our understanding of the Creator. If perfect love requires the giving of self, then God could not create his potential partners fully inclined toward that choice. Claiming that God must do so to avoid being labeled a "failed creator" reduces God's purpose to something less than love. But God's love is infinite. He created in love—giving of himself, making himself vulnerable to rejection—so that love could shine in its ultimate brilliance.

Thus, despite its embrace of the concept of love, universalism ultimately oversteps the bounds of love's definition and denies love in its purest form. But that is not its only problem.

LOVE'S RESCUE

Universalists often struggle to provide persuasive interpretations of many New Testament texts because they misunderstand the atonement. Atonement theories can generally be classified into three categories: (1) specific payment for sin (e.g., ransom, satisfaction, penal substitution),

(2) mimetic demonstration (e.g., Christus Victor, moral influence, governmental), and (3) image-based atonement. I contend that the third category is the only fully viable option. Theories in the first category largely fail because they offer no legitimate means for transferring sin guilt from the sinner to Christ. Theories in the second category fail because they provide no legitimate mechanism for transferring Christ's victory to the sinner. Only the third category, which separates sin-guilt from curse and, consequently, forgiveness from redemption, adequately accounts for all aspects of representation and deliverance.

In Colossians, Paul begins with a hymn celebrating Christ as God the Redeemer, emphasizing redemption as the reclaiming of our unified essence in physical creation. The entire letter counters Gnostic ideas that exalt spirit and diminish the importance of the flesh. Paul counters these Gnostic ideas emphatically by declaring that we are indeed the "body of Christ"—a unity of creation redeemed through the cross.

Many universalists, however, conflate redemption with the forgiveness of sin-guilt, leading them to interpret passages like Colossians 1 through this distorted lens. When image-based atonement is disregarded, Paul's references to "flesh" and "redemption" are often misapplied to the soul. For instance, regarding Colossians 1, universalist Gregory MacDonald claims, "The context also makes it abundantly clear that Paul sees Christ as effecting the salvation of all creation."[12] However, the context of Colossians 1 does not mention salvation; it focuses on the redemption of all creation. When the correct atonement theory is applied, these passages come alive with profound meaning!

Salvation—entering into a love relationship with God—requires (1) atonement for the curse, (2) sin-guilt forgiveness for the repentant, and (3) an individual's loving response to God's offer of relationship. The first point, atonement, is indeed a universal concept, encompassing all of physical creation and accomplished unilaterally by God through Jesus. However, the universality of atonement does not extend to sin-guilt forgiveness or the birth of love. Atonement pertains to redemption, and redemption concerns physical essence. This redemption of physical essence is the true subject of Colossians. Conflating the forgiveness of sin-guilt and the birth of love with Jesus's atonement mission distorts the interpretation of these passages.

---

12. MacDonald, *Evangelical Universalist*, 46.

Similarly, universalist interpretations of Romans 5 and 1 Corinthians 15 exhibit the same misunderstanding. Romans 5:18 states, "So then, as through one trespass there is condemnation for everyone, so also through one righteous act there is life-giving justification for everyone." The one trespass resulted in the curse on physical creation—the reason we share in Adam's failure. The one righteous act was the redemption secured at the cross, which will remove the curse at Christ's return. This verse is not discussing the forgiveness of sin-guilt or entering into a love relationship with God, no matter how much universalists emphasize the word "everyone."

In 1 Corinthians 15:22, Paul writes, "For as in Adam all die, so in Christ all will be made alive." Consider this from the perspective of image-based atonement without defaulting to penal substitution. What did Jesus accomplish for us? Did he pay for our individual sin-guilt on the cross? No. He died to secure redemption for all physical creation. So, when Paul speaks of resurrection in the likeness of Jesus, how does verse 22 imply that the entire world's sin-guilt will be forgiven? It doesn't! That conclusion misses the point. Jesus brought about redemption for the whole world—for our shared essence. The next verse clarifies that when physical creation's redemption is realized (at his coming), only "those who belong to Christ" will benefit from that universal redemption.

Ephesians provides another example. MacDonald refers to the "apparent universalism of Ephesians 1:10." However, this claim overlooks the context of Paul's discussion. The adoption in verse 5, the redemption in verse 7, and the mystery in verse 9 all lead to the culmination of Christ's work in verse 10, which is not about the forgiveness of sin-guilt but rather the removal of the curse. By removing the curse on physical creation, Jesus succeeded in bringing "everything together in the Messiah, both things in heaven and things on earth." This verse does not speak of individual soul salvation and, therefore, has nothing to do with universalism.

LOVE'S TIMING

Universalism relies on time—time for unbelievers to reconsider, to abandon their pursuit of TGB apart from God, and to ultimately repent and embrace the true satisfaction that comes from its source. The universalist envisions that, given enough time and complete revelatory knowledge, even the fallen and hopeless will turn to God. But how much time does each person actually have?

Till Christ Returns

Paul's statement in 1 Corinthians 15:17 is crucial: "And if Christ has not been raised, your faith is futile; you are still in your sins." The necessity of the body's redemption for the removal of the curse highlights the inseparable connection between our souls and our shared physical essence.

If God could simply extract our souls from our bodies, destroy the cursed physical creation, recreate it ex nihilo, and then insert our forgiven souls into the new creation, the problem of sin and curse could have been resolved without the cross. However, God cannot do that. A human being is an integrated body-soul combination. As I've mentioned, our souls are inherently tied to our physical essence, making survival of the soul apart from the body impossible. This is why the death-and-resurrection plan of God, embodied in Jesus, was necessary. God had to redeem this physical creation; otherwise, our humanity would be lost.

Christ's work on the cross and his resurrection did not remove the guilt of sin but rather redeemed our essence—our physical creation, which includes all matter and energy, including our very bodies. Without this understanding, the concept of Jesus as the firstfruits lacks a clear connection to the rest of creation.

At Christ's return, what happened to him at his resurrection—the cleansing and redemption of his body to its uncursed, firstfruits condition—will happen to the rest of creation. Paul describes this in 1 Corinthians 15:20-23:

> But Christ has indeed been raised from the dead, the firstfruits of those who have fallen asleep. For since death came through a man, the resurrection of the dead comes also through a man. For as in Adam all die, so in Christ all will be made alive. But each in turn: Christ, the firstfruits; then, when he comes, those who belong to him.

Paul also emphasizes that all physical creation will be redeemed when we are resurrected, which occurs at Christ's return:

> For the creation waits in eager expectation for the children of God to be revealed. For the creation was subjected to frustration, not by its own choice, but by the will of the one who subjected it,

in hope that the creation itself will be liberated from its bondage to decay and brought into the freedom and glory of the children of God. (Romans 8:19–21)

Therefore, if all physical creation is redeemed at Christ's return—cleansed, with its curse removed—and since the soul is tied to its physical essence, unbelievers cannot continue to exist beyond that point. They cannot receive the redemption benefits of the cross without faith. As C. S. Lewis points out, a bodiless soul could no longer be considered human. Thus, the opportunity for entering into a love relationship with God ends at Christ's return.

Till Death Do Us Part

What happens to a person at physical death? As discussed earlier (and in chapter 6), a person is a physical-spiritual amalgamation. At physical death, the soul does not simply depart to unknown realms. To be human—to truly exist as human—a soul must remain connected to physical creation. However, at death, the soul loses its ability to control or function cognitively within its individual portion of physical essence—its body. For example, when my soul wants to move, it engages my body to walk. When my soul wants to see, it uses my eyes to take in information. If my eyes fail or my legs don't work, I cannot see or walk. Therefore, when my entire body ceases to function, my soul—though still connected to physical creation—can no longer engage with it.

In other words, even though the soul of a physically dead person still exists, it cannot think because it no longer has a brain to process thoughts. The only exception to this is for the Christian, who, after physical death, is united with Jesus, the firstfruits of redeemed physical creation.

Jesus, as both God and human, was the sinless spirit of God residing in a cursed physical essence (Romans 8:3). His death on the cross was not a spiritual death; it was a physical death to put an end to that portion of shared physical essence over which his individual soul had personal responsibility. The astounding glory of his resurrection lies in the fact that, because he is God, his soul could think independently of physical creation. And because of his sinlessness, he could reclaim control over physical creation after death. Ordinary humans cannot do this because physical death fully subjects them to the essence they had idolized.

At Christ's return, Jesus will redeem all physical creation. The removal of the curse from all physical creation signals that unbelieving souls cannot continue beyond that point. An unrepentant soul, resistant to a love relationship with God, cannot be granted redeemed flesh.

Physical death perfectly illustrates our souls' enslavement to the curse. The Bible repeatedly suggests that death gains victory through its absolute control over the soul at the moment of physical death. Jesus's resurrection shattered that power—the power that would otherwise permanently enslave the human soul in rebellion against God.

LOVE'S SATISFACTION

Gregory MacDonald suggests that "supremely worthwhile happiness" can exist only when a person is filled with love for others. However, if annihilation is true, then at the moment of annihilation—just before God-rejecters cease to exist—God would supposedly have to limit his "infinite" love as they depart from his sustaining hand.

But, properly understood, God's love is never limited. Love, by definition, is the giving of oneself for the sake of a love relationship. As we discussed in chapter 1, a love relationship cannot exist unless both parties express love. However, legitimate love can exist even without a realized relationship, as long as the hope for one remains. Love gives of oneself for the benefit of a love relationship, anticipating and hoping for its fulfillment. If a person rejects God's offer of relationship and, due to that rejection, enters a downward spiral of heart-hardening, a point may be reached where the heart becomes so hardened that any response to TGB is impossible. (The story of the flood illustrates this lesson, showing the only condition by which God could be justified in ending an age—a subject we will explore in chapter 10.)

Here's the key point: while God does not know the future in the deterministic sense, he knows all possibilities exhaustively. Therefore, God can know with absolute certainty if and when a person reaches a state where pursuing TGB in love is no longer possible. If such a state occurs, it becomes impossible for God to love that person. This impossibility arises because love is defined as the giving of oneself in hope of a relationship. If no hope for such a relationship exists, and God knows this with certainty, then love, by definition, cannot exist for that person. It's not that God chooses to stop loving; rather, God cannot love if the rejecter becomes absolute in his or her rejection.

Even so, the emotional weight of losing someone we love who ends up outside God's embrace is profound. Can we truly experience "supremely worthwhile happiness" while knowing that someone we loved was annihilated? MacDonald emphasizes the capacity of rational beings to reach correct conclusions when they are "fully informed." If, in heaven, we are fully informed and fully convinced by God of the impossibility of a love relationship with someone we once loved, no rational feeling of kindness would lead us to wish that person back into existence to endure torment. In fact, to wish them back would be akin to desiring eternal conscious torment for someone we supposedly loved. Non-existence is not suffering. We wouldn't lament their discomfort because they would no longer exist to experience discomfort.

For those who still insist, "No, it would lessen the joy of heaven for me," I would argue that universalism already embraces a similar idea. Consider those in heaven who have experienced their children being brutally tortured and murdered in this life. Could those memories ever fade? Even for the universalist, those memories would persist. Yet, in heaven, those memories wouldn't torture us because they represent a sadness that, at that heavenly point, is no longer actual reality. The same is true for annihilation. In both cases, the sadness is tied to a memory that no longer reflects the present reality.

A universalist friend of mine once said, "I just can't get past the idea that if one of my children were unsaved at death, I'd never manage to be truly happy in eternity without him. How would I ever get over the loss? More importantly, how would God? And if justice is making things truly right, how could God not deliver justice to all his children?" I understand and sympathize with these concerns, but I believe they stem from a misunderstanding of both justice and the resolution for those who have rejected relationship.

God's interaction with Nineveh offers a valuable perspective on justice. The book of Jonah ends with Nineveh repenting and seeking relationship with God. In response, God did not punish, scorn, or demand reparation; he willingly forgave. However, years later, when Nineveh rejected God and refused to repent, God did not force love, repentance, or obedience. The point is that he could not. Doing so would undermine his purpose for creation—love. God could not compromise his infinitely loving purpose. He simply could not pursue a withdrawn Nineveh, and so Nineveh was destroyed. This absolute forbearance by God—remaining true to his love purpose even when love is denied—demonstrates that God doesn't change because others refuse to love. For God to do so would mean abandoning the love he treasures.

Both of God's responses—in embracing the repentant Nineveh and in releasing the defiant Nineveh—exemplify justice. As noted in the previous chapter, the goal of justice is to restore the community to a state of righteousness, which is faithfulness to covenant purpose and obligations. Justice is achieved in only two ways: through the guilty one's repentance or their removal. God will ensure that justice is accomplished; this is an unchangeable aspect of his nature, based on who he is, not merely on what he chooses to do. But the manner in which justice is realized depends on the violator, not God—it comes through their repentance or their refusal.

When considering our own children, we must first reflect on how God views his children. While God created all humans, and in that sense, all people are his children, the Bible repeatedly narrows the definition of God's children to those who truly enter into a relational bond with him. I believe this understanding will hold true for us as well. While a non-Christian child may have some semblance of a love relationship with a Christian parent, deep down, their foundation is one of self-serving, antichristian motives. As that spirit increasingly rejects God's call, what is TGB loses its sustaining power, leaving only the self to self-destruct. Consequently, the relationship, even with a parent, must necessarily degrade. And even Christian parents, confronted with their child's unrepentant, ever-hardening opposition to love, must eventually recognize that it is a merciful outcome for such a soul to be left to its own destruction. I do not doubt the pain this causes the parent—or God—but I also do not doubt that this resolution is better than hopeless, perpetual wickedness.

I realize this sounds harsh, and we may struggle to imagine such a state. But this is precisely what Revelation 19's pronouncement of destruction and Revelation 20's depiction of the lake of fire reveal. It is not a torture chamber where God, in anger, casts those who missed their chance. The flames into which they rush are of their own making, fueled by their rejection of God. And God—mercifully and necessarily—does not impede their path, sparing them from continuing in a state of constant, painful depravity.

As we stand at the Great White Throne in Revelation 20, with a full understanding of God's heart, a complete grasp of his TGB, and a clear recognition of those—even our own children—who have twisted their hearts in irredeemable hatred, we will acknowledge that there will be tears, both from our eyes and from God's. But as creatures destined for love, we will not wish for them to continue in such a state.

CONCLUSION

This chapter has been lengthy, but necessarily so. It outlines the crucial sequence of creative purpose, human dominion over the soul, the need for God to become flesh, and the redemption from cursed existence. God created humans for the purpose of everlasting love relationship, but love requires the free giving of oneself. To enable this, God entrusted humans with dominion over their physical essence, allowing them to choose to give themselves for the sake of relationship with him. In his dominion, Adam chose his own essence over God's, a decision that brought about the curse—a distortion that severed humanity from God's creative purpose. We are no longer merely creatures designed for and moving toward the fulfillment of love; we are cursed, separated from God's full embrace.

What could God do? The only way for God to enact redemption was to reclaim dominion. But humans, who held sovereign control over their physical essence, had surrendered it, and as a result, no human could escape enslavement to that cursed existence. So God became human. He had to join humanity in order to exercise dominion over its physical essence. He put that essence to death in his own body and, through the purity of his soul, took it back to life and relationship.

Through his victory, he will reclaim all human essence—all of physical creation. But regarding that resurrection, each human soul now faces the same decision Adam faced. Each must choose between God's essence and human essence, between giving of oneself for the benefit of relationship or clinging to self in defeat. We have an advantage over Adam in that we possess the full revelation of God in Christ Jesus. However, we are also disadvantaged by our enslavement to sin and the increasing distortion and hardness that result from repeatedly choosing self over God. If Adam could choose wrongly, so can we. Physical death marks the final threshold, where we lose any further opportunity to choose God.

For all its admirable desire for universal reconciliation, universalism cannot be true. It reduces the Bible's many warnings of destruction to mere scare tactics. If God could overcome human resistance with his revelation but chooses not to intensify it, then he is not acting in love. Conversely, if God were to intensify it and thereby force humans into his embrace, he still would not be acting in love. Contrary to the premise of universalism, God walks the path of a true lover—open, vulnerable, and willing to risk for the sake of the only genuine relationship love can create.

God's love calls, pleads, opens its arms, and embraces whosoever believes. But love cannot force. On the other side, the turn away from God is real. It represents a rejection of God's presence, a rejection that—despite God's persistent revelation—can spiral into ever-deepening darkness. This is the darkness that moved our Lord to weep over Jerusalem, grieving not just over a delay in their return to God, but over the profound loss of their rejection.

9

God Reveals

*If we, dear, know we know no more
Than they about the Law,
If I no more than you
Know what we should and should not do
Except that all agree
Gladly or miserably
That the Law is
And that all know this
If therefore thinking it absurd
To identify Law with some other word,
Unlike so many men
I cannot say Law is again.*

—W. H. Auden, from "Law, Like Love"

"You have heard that it was said, 'Eye for eye, and tooth for tooth.'
But I tell you, do not resist an evil person.
If anyone slaps you on the right cheek,
Turn to them the other cheek also."

—Matthew 5:38–39

IMAGINE THE HEART OF a Jew exiled to Babylon. Years earlier, after a series of arrogance-driven foreign-policy blunders by Jewish leaders, King Nebuchadnezzar of Babylon had sacked Jerusalem. He broke down the walls, burned the city, destroyed Solomon's temple, seized its sacred contents, starved the inhabitants, brutally killed men, women, and children, and carried off tens of thousands of Jews—about an eighth to a quarter of Judah's population—to Babylon. In this foreign land, the exiled Jews were ridiculed and ostracized, living in misery for many years.

You can imagine the despair in their hearts. What if we were in their place? What if we had witnessed friends, neighbors, family, loved ones, our own children being raped, tortured, torn apart, burned alive—how would we feel toward those captors, toward those new neighbors whose daily scorn and ridicule persisted for years?

Psalm 137 confronts us with a reality starkly different from the typically pastoral and idyllic tone we expect from many of the psalms. This psalmist, one of the Jewish exiles in Babylon, had experienced the heartache of violence against his family, friends, and nation. The psalm speaks of how the Babylonians mocked them, urging them to sing of their captured, destroyed homeland.

We should not maintain psychological distance from these words to avoid their disturbing bite. The psalmist evokes the anguish and frustration of the captured Jews. Lamenting their slavery, he works himself into a frenzy of anger and burning hatred for the Babylonians, wishing the same tragedy upon them. With restraint cast aside, his emotions cry out near the psalm's end: "Happy is the one who repays you according to what you have done to us." And in a final, vengeful declaration, he concludes, "Happy is the one who seizes your infants and dashes them against the rocks."

Pause to let that sink in. Read the verse again. Consider the motivation, the pain, the heart behind those words. They are staggering. We can feel the despair. And yet . . . can we possibly justify the intent behind them: "Happy is the one who seizes your infants and dashes them against the rocks"?

One commentator, inviting us to recognize how badly the Jews had been treated, tries to sympathize with the exiled Jew to justify these words, despite acknowledging the shocking violence of the sentiment:

> The psalmist here is wishing not for vengeance in human terms. He is praying for God's justice. He is putting his trust in God's promise to repay the Babylonians for what they had done. He

GOD REVEALS 91

is trusting that God will deliver his people, as God had promised. Throughout this psalm, he calls the people to remember. Remember Jerusalem in your grief—and remember the Lord's promise of deliverance. *This is what he calls us to do as well.*[1] (Emphasis added.)

Another commentator similarly attempts to accept the psalmist's scandalous cry as God's righteousness:

> This prayer for vengeance also speaks of the hope and trust that the people placed in Yahweh that he would not allow injustice to remain unpunished. The cry for vengeance should thus be understood as a cry for justice. Those who captured the people of God should know that the God of the captured would not remain angry with them indefinitely. They must know that the God of Israel is the only true and living God who will not allow the aggressors to get away with it. This violent prayer thus affirms the integrity of Yahweh, which might otherwise have seemed in doubt.[2]

Both commentators attempt to justify the psalmist's violent plea, but both are mistaken. In their odd defenses, they obscure God's image. Could we imagine Jesus spewing the same hate as the psalmist? Could Jesus have wished for babies to be smashed on rocks? No. We might apply Jesus's admonition to these commentators: "Leave them alone! They are blind guides. And if the blind guide the blind, both will fall into a pit" (Matthew 15:14). But seriously, if this psalm does not reflect God's heart, what is it doing in his inspired book?

While we can sympathize with the psalmist's suffering, we cannot excuse the wrong turn his heart takes. The New Testament is replete with exhortations on how to respond to evil, even in the face of overwhelming struggle and pain. Paul tells us that vengeance is God's and to overcome evil with good. Peter encourages us to cast our care on God. Jesus commands us to love our enemies and turn the other cheek. But wait, we might protest, what about the hurt? What about what those enemies did? What about their violence?

Jesus did not qualify his "love your enemies" command with "unless, of course, what they did was really bad." Moreover, Jesus told us that in loving our enemies—even in the face of their violent evil—we would

---

1. Armstrong, "Psalm 137."
2. Mare, "Psalm 137."

be like God! Before returning to Psalm 137, let's think some more along with Jesus.

JESUS, THE STANDARD FOR SCRIPTURAL INTERPRETATION

Imagine hearing Jesus teach in person. Have you ever envisioned that? Have you wondered what it would be like to sit on that hillside near the Sea of Galilee, listening to Jesus explain the blessedness of the meek? Would you have smiled in appreciation? Do you imagine his words refreshing you like a gentle breeze, or your thoughts settling into contentment as he urged you to let your light shine? In one sense, it's hard to picture the experience any other way. But then I wonder—if I had truly been a Galilean of that time, wouldn't all those beatitudes and what followed have actually jarred me? Matthew records the essence of Jesus's Sermon on the Mount not merely to present him as a kind and gentle teacher (although he was) but to show Jesus as one who aimed to redirect the distorted trajectory of Jewish thinking.

The Jews were indeed thinking wrongly. Paul had to dismantle their conviction that they were the only community God cared for. And Jesus challenged their long-held interpretations of the Sabbath and vengeance. They were mistaken, but their twisted ideas didn't come from reading ancient Greek philosophy. Instead, their confused thinking emerged from a misguided study of their own God-given Scriptures.

Back on that hillside, Jesus distinctly taught about love. In the sermon, he highlighted the humble, the caring, the gentle, the covenant-keeping, the merciful, the pure in heart, the peacemakers, and the persecuted, saying they would receive God's loving care. He then identified this very group as the salt of the earth and the light of the world. Notice that he doesn't refer to all Jews, his disciples, or even all Christians and proselytes; he specifically points out that it is the gentle, merciful, and loving who are the true salt and light. These ideas likely startled his original audience because of their fresh perspective—a fitting beginning to the Sermon on the Mount, where his teachings on love were novel, at least to the Jews who had been interpreting the Scriptures through the lens of worldly values.

This sermon begins in chapter 5 of Matthew's Gospel. Just before, in chapter 4, Jesus had gone to John to be baptized. John, recognizing

Jesus as the Messiah, hesitated, aware of the purity of Jesus's heart. But Jesus insisted that he baptize him for the sake of righteousness—fulfilling the covenant. Jesus demonstrated through his baptism at the start of his ministry what would be accomplished at its end—the putting to death of his body and taking it up again, renewed. That's what baptism symbolizes (Romans 6:4), that's what Jesus gave to us (2 Corinthians 5:17), and that's the hope of ultimate renewal (Revelation 21:5).

In the Sermon on the Mount, Jesus emphasizes this shift—a change in thinking to illuminate God's ways—because Jesus is the ultimate revelation of God. We recognize this revelatory fulfillment through the testimony of the Scripture writers:

- Hebrews 1:3 "The Son is the *radiance of God's glory* and the *exact expression of His nature*, sustaining all things by His powerful word."
- Colossians 2:9 "For the *entire fullness of God's nature* dwells bodily in Christ."
- John 14:9b "The one who has seen Me *has seen the Father*." (All three quotations are from HCSB.)

So Jesus—the *exact expression* of God's nature—came to correct the misunderstandings the Jews had developed in their reading of Scripture. He stated, "Don't suppose for a minute that I have come to demolish the Scriptures—either God's Law or the Prophets. I'm not here to demolish but to complete" (Matthew 5:17).

But why does Jesus accuse them of "supposing"? Specifically, why would he think the Jews had assumed he came to destroy the Law or the Prophets? After all, he had just opened his message with what we consider to be wonderful words of kindness, care, and love. How could Jesus imagine that people would hear those words and conclude that he intended to destroy the Law? The answer lies in the fact that Jesus was preaching a change from what they believed the Law and Prophets dictated. However, Jesus clarified that he was not altering the Law but rather fulfilling it, along with the prophetic word, by revealing their true purpose. The Jews had spent centuries harboring hatred for the Babylonians—and for the Persians, the Greeks, and the Romans. But Jesus reoriented their understanding of the Law and Prophets, preaching with authority that God's love must form the heart's foundation for the life of God's community, the kingdom of heaven.

Jesus spends the rest of chapter 5 correcting their distorted understanding of God's ways. This distortion arose because they emphasized the letter of the Law rather than its spirit, and the spirit's motivation was love—the foundation of creation, the basis for relationship, and the perfect activity of God. Jesus underscores the spirit by linking attitude to action: the attitude of hatred to the act of murder (verses 21–26), lust to adultery (verses 27–30), self-concern to divorce (verses 31–32), untrustworthiness to breaking oaths (verses 33–37), and vengefulness to lawbreaking (verses 38–42). This progression culminates in the most radical shift they could imagine: he urges them to love even their enemies.

At first glance, this command might not seem like love, because earlier we defined love as the giving of oneself for the benefit of a relationship. Since no love relationship exists with an enemy, how is it possible to love that enemy? However, the definition does not require that a love relationship already exists. Rather, simply having the motivation to foster a future love relationship turns the giving of self into love, even if that relationship is only a possibility. God's love is rooted in his relational hope. We see this purpose in other passages, such as when he is described as "not wanting anyone to perish, but everyone to come to repentance" (2 Peter 3:9). Therefore, Jesus calls us not merely to be nice or kind to our enemies; he elevates our attitude toward enemies to the point of hoping for a future relationship.

By claiming to fulfill the Law and Prophets and urging his listeners to act in love beyond the Law's limits, Jesus reveals God's motivation and the Law's purpose—*love!* With that understanding, how should we interpret the attitude of the Psalm 137 writer? We must conclude that the psalmist's attitude was misguided. If Jesus, who is the exact expression of God, teaches us to love even our enemies, then God is teaching us to love our enemies. The psalmist, in expressing hate and violence toward his enemies, wrote from an attitude of *error* within the context of God's Word.

STUDY TO SHOW YOURSELF APPROVED

How do we proceed with Scripture now? The psalmist provides no indication that his attitude was wrong. There's no divine footnote warning us that we're reading an expression of error. No prophet later in the Bible mentions that Psalm 137 contains ideas outside the desire of God. The violent attitude of hate simply remains there, in a chapter of our Holy

Scriptures. How, then, can we trust anything in the Old Testament if we identify the attitude in this uncorrected passage as error? Can we still call this the "Word of God" if an attitude contains error?

The Neo-Orthodox say no, arguing that the Bible is not the "Word of God." They insist that humans wrote Scripture, not God. Therefore, in their view, Scripture is not the revelation of God but merely a witness to that revelation. To the Neo-Orthodox, calling Scripture the Word of God, when Scripture itself identifies Jesus as the Word of God (John 1:1, 14), causes confusion. Paul Tillich described it like this:

> In some church services the minister concludes his reading of the Bible with the sentence, "May God bless this reading of His holy Word." For a thoughtful congregation, nothing could be more misleading than this sentence, for it identifies the "Word of God" with the Scripture. It reduces the different meanings of "Word of God" to one, and it blurs the difference between the divine Word given to the prophets and apostles in their state of inspiration and the human words in which they expressed their ecstatic experience. The Biblical words are human words....[3]

According to Tillich, the human witness could be wrong, just as a preacher could be wrong while sincerely attempting to convey God's word.

This idea has some merit. If God had wanted to convey his exact words, he could have carved them into stone tablets, just as he did with the Ten Commandments—but he didn't. Humans directly wrote Scripture, and humans are limited, error-prone beings. Therefore, even the "Thus says the Lord" passages were spoken by human prophets trying to remember and repeat (and perhaps embellish for emphasis) what God had said.

However, the Neo-Orthodox view doesn't fully capture the concept of inspiration. The apostle Paul tells us that Scripture is *theopneustos*, or God-breathed (2 Timothy 3:16). While inspiration is not a mechanical dictation of exact words, Paul, through his choice of Greek word and surrounding context, indicates that God's breathing out Scripture involves a more interactive process with human effort. This God-breathed quality connects to the breath God breathed into Adam to give him life (Genesis 2:7) and understanding (Job 32:8). Paul deliberately associates that breath of God with the Scriptures themselves—not just the authors. That

---

3. Tillich, "Word of God," 122–123.

God-breathed quality in written Scripture should give us a level of trust, even as our conclusion about Psalm 137 requires us to carefully define that trust.

Many conservatives use belief in the inerrancy of the Bible as a litmus test to determine the suitability of a person or organization for Christian fellowship. But this standard faces issues of consistency and clarity. For instance, the Bible sometimes rounds off numbers (e.g., contrast Genesis 15:13 with Exodus 12:40). Well, 430 is not exactly 400, but am I wrong if I say the children of Israel remained in Egypt for 400 years? I'm just rounding off. But can I still argue adamantly for "inerrancy," a term that—technically—means the absence of any error? Perhaps I could qualify my belief: I believe in inerrancy, with the caveat that the Bible may round off numbers. Safe now? Well, another issue is that grammatical irregularities appear in Scripture (e.g., Ephesians 3:1–2). So, I believe in inerrancy with the qualifications that numbers may be rounded and grammatical irregularities may occur. But then what about figures of speech, historical precision, the New Testament's misquoting of the Old Testament, and the differences among the Gospels concerning Jesus's words? Inerrantists often find themselves compiling a long list of qualifications, to the point where the term "inerrancy" loses much of its meaning. And then how do we address the psalmist's hateful anger in Psalm 137? If we include that outburst in our definition of inerrancy, we need a defense much broader than that of mere technical anomaly.

Perhaps it's time to stop trying to defend our notion of inerrancy. However, if we let the term (with its notebook full of qualifiers) fall by the wayside, does that threaten the Bible's trustworthiness? I would argue that it doesn't. In fact, dismissing such feeble standards calls us to a more diligent regard for Scripture. In his second epistle to Timothy, Paul urges him:

> 2:14 Keep reminding God's people of these things. Warn them before God against quarreling about words; it is of no value, and only ruins those who listen.

Well, Paul, what then should we do instead?

> 2:15 Do your best to present yourself to God as one approved, a worker who does not need to be ashamed and who correctly handles the word of truth.

And we should do so for this reason:

> 3:16, 17 All Scripture is God-breathed and is useful for teaching, rebuking, correcting and training in righteousness, so that the servant of God may be thoroughly equipped for every good work.

Here we find the balance. Fallible humans wrote the entire Bible, and at times they may have misspoken. But we must never lose sight of the fact that God's breathed-out quality makes even their errors profitable for study. These errors set up a contrast with the truth that comes from God's heart—the full revelation of Christ. Yes, the psalmist of Psalm 137 had the wrong attitude, but God included his error in this inspired book because even that, when viewed in light of Jesus's revelation, shows us the error and profits us in our prayerful study. God-breathed means that everything in Scripture—every story, law, discussion, and reflection—belongs there, infused with purpose because God not only reveals but invites us to join in the struggle for the truths he wants us to know through revelation and reason, not mere memorization.

GOD'S IMPERFECT PROPHET

When we view Scripture from this perspective, we may need to adjust our interpretation of certain stories in the biblical record. Remember, all Scripture is God-breathed and teaches us truth—but sometimes God teaches truth by showing us what not to do. A striking example of this can be found in the ministry of Elijah.

Perhaps we know Elijah best from the story of his challenge to the prophets of Baal on Mt. Carmel. In 1 Kings 18, the Baal prophets fail to summon fire from their god to consume their sacrifice. But God answers Elijah's prayer, sending fire that burns both the sacrifice and the altar Elijah had built. God granted Elijah dominion over physical creation to perform this miracle in a spectacular and glorious fashion.

A lesser-known story appears in 2 Kings 1:1–15, where Elijah again calls down fire from heaven. After King Ahaziah of Israel was injured in an accident, he sent messengers to consult the prophets of Baal about his recovery. Elijah intercepted these messengers, questioning why they were seeking guidance from the Philistine god instead of Israel's true God. Elijah told them to inform the king that because of his faith in other gods, he would die.

Angered by Elijah's message, Ahaziah sent a captain and his 50 men to bring Elijah to him. The captain addressed Elijah as "Man of God" (perhaps mockingly) and ordered him to come along. Elijah responded, "If I am a man of God, may fire come down from heaven and consume you and your 50 men." Fire indeed came down, killing the captain and his soldiers. Ahaziah sent another captain with 50 more men, and the same deadly outcome ensued.

When a third captain and his 50 men arrived, the captain knelt before Elijah, pleading for their lives to be spared. God then instructed Elijah not to be afraid but to go with them. Elijah did so and delivered the same message to the king, who soon died as predicted. But the question we must grapple with is whether Elijah acted in godly righteousness when he caused the deaths of the previous 102 soldiers.

Inerrantists often don't struggle much with this question. For example, one commentator remarks, "Elijah must have rejoiced at this captain's humility, which made it *unnecessary* to destroy him."[4] This implies that it was somehow necessary for the first 100+ soldiers to burn to death. But what could justify such a brutal and agonizing loss of life? Was it merely the captains' lack of humility? How can one not struggle with this passage? Did Jesus command us to love our enemies only if they were sufficiently humble?

We cannot imagine Jesus setting people on fire. And if we cannot imagine Jesus doing so, we should not imagine God doing so. Jesus perfectly and completely reflects God's attitude. Flushed with the success at Mt. Carmel, it was Elijah—driven by a mix of fear and arrogance—who demanded the deaths of these men, just as he had demanded the deaths of the Baal prophets in 1 Kings 18. The stories only mention God specifically acting or intervening twice: first, the fire that consumed the altar sacrifice in 1 Kings 18 is identified as *God's* fire, and second, in 2 Kings 1, we learn that an angel of *God* urged Elijah to go to Ahaziah. That's it. We are not told that the other actions were done at God's direction. The killing of the Baal prophets and the soldiers were Elijah's decisions. Elijah's destructive attitude here mirrors the psalmist's attitude in Psalm 137.

Not once in the Gospels do we see Jesus calling down fire to destroy people, not even when faced with the arrogant Pharisees. In fact, in Luke 9, Jesus confirms the wickedness of Elijah's actions by countering an attitude that mirrored Elijah's fiery judgment. On his way to Jerusalem,

---

4. Neal, "Elijah," 19.

Jesus and his disciples passed through Samaria, near the very place where Elijah had called down fire on his enemies. When the Samaritans did not welcome them, James and John, recalling Elijah's story, asked, "Lord, do you want us to call down fire from heaven to consume them?" (Luke 9:54 HCSB). Jesus immediately rebuked them, and some manuscripts include the rebuke, "You don't know what kind of spirit you belong to!"—a rebuke similar to "Get behind me, Satan!" that Jesus would later direct at Peter (Matthew 16:23 HCSB). Jesus then said, "For the Son of Man did not come to destroy people's lives but to save them." Surely, Christ's words make it clear that if God did not intend to destroy people's lives in Jesus's time, he would not have acted in vengeful, violent destruction in Elijah's time either. Because Jesus demonstrates his loving power by refraining from prideful punishment, we can conclude that God was not complicit in Elijah's calling down fire to consume the soldiers. Nevertheless, Elijah's wrongful actions are recorded in God's breathed-out Scripture, not for us to imitate or honor, but to recognize the contrast with Jesus's attitude and to commit ourselves to following Jesus's teaching of love.

We might wonder, "But God did give Elijah the power to call down fire. Why would God do that if he didn't want the soldiers burned alive?" The same question could be asked about why God made Adam and Eve rulers over physical creation. They were given dominion for relationship-learning reasons but failed to exercise it properly, resulting in the curse on creation. Scripture shows other examples of God granting control, with outcomes varying between good and bad. Samson's misuse of his supernatural strength is a negative example, while Paul healing the sick is a positive one. Peter walking on water has elements of both success and failure. So yes, Elijah was given control over physical elements, but in God's consistent non-coercive manner, Elijah was allowed to choose whether to act according to God's kingdom principles. In this instance, Elijah failed. And there are multiple stories of such failures, especially in the Old Testament.

FOLLOWING GOD WITHOUT VIOLENCE

The Old Testament is filled with violent stories where God is portrayed as either directly destroying armies or commanding Israel to do so. However, when we align these stories with the revelation of Jesus, it becomes clear that such actions do not reflect God's true character. While God chose to include these depictions in his breathed-out word, we should recognize that certain actions in these stories—those that do not align with Jesus's teaching and example—are meant to show us what to turn away from, not emulate. Yet, scattered throughout the Bible, God provides clear examples of how his upside-down kingdom truly triumphs.

One such example is found in 2 Chronicles 20:1–20. A multinational force consisting of Edom, Moab, and Ammon threatened God's people, and God promised to help when Judah prayed for deliverance. God's help came in the form of no longer sustaining these three nations, which rejected him. Without God's presence, darkness prevailed, and Edom suddenly attacked Moab and Ammon. Moab and Ammon then turned on each other, leading to mutual destruction. When Judah's people finally arrived at the valley where these armies had gathered, they found only dead bodies strewn across the battlefield. With no hope for relationship, God allowed evil to consume itself, resulting in its own violent end.

This lesson of nonviolent trust in God is not an isolated incident. In 2 Kings 6, we find two separate events (6:8–23 and 6:24–7:7) in which God protects Israel without resorting to violence. In the first incident, the king of Aram becomes frustrated by his failed attempts to ambush Israel and suspects a spy among his advisors. However, they inform him that Elisha, the prophet of God, seems to know his secret strategies and reports them to Israel's king. So the king of Aram sends a contingent to Dothan to capture Elisha. Elisha's servant is terrified, but Elisha prays for his eyes to be opened, revealing God's armies of horses and chariots of fire covering the mountains—an angelic force that symbolizes God's unstoppable power and might.

Here's the key point: Instead of praying for this angelic force to destroy the Aramean contingent, Elisha (guided by God's Spirit) prays for God to temporarily blind the Arameans. God grants this request, and Elisha leads the blinded soldiers straight to Israel's capital, where they are surrounded by the full strength of Israel's army. When their sight is restored, they realize they are prisoners. The king of Israel, elated, asks Elisha if he should kill the Arameans, but Elisha stops him. Rather than killing them (as we might expect Elijah to do), Elisha instructs the king to prepare a feast for the captives. After eating and drinking, the Arameans are sent back to their own country, and the raiders, struck by this unexpected kindness, never return.

This entire nonviolent episode mirrors the wisdom of Proverbs 25:21–22: "If your enemy is hungry, give him food to eat; if he is thirsty, give him water to drink. In doing this, you will heap burning coals on his head, and the Lord will reward you." Whether the phrase "heaping coals" is interpreted as causing conviction or providing an extra measure of needed coals to a neighbor, the overall picture aligns with Jesus's New Testament teaching. The Spirit-led action that Elisha proposes reveals God's victory, not through worldly violence, but through the love and mercy of the kingdom of heaven.

Following this story, another event unfolds where the Arameans again attack, this time laying siege to Samaria, Israel's capital. The prolonged siege leads to extreme scarcity of food, driving the city to desperation. One day, as the king walks along the city wall, a woman cries out to him, telling a horrifying tale. She and another woman, starving, had agreed to kill and eat her son, planning to do the same with the other woman's son the next day. However, after eating the first child, the second woman hid her son, and the first woman now seeks justice. The king, horrified, tears his clothes and vows to kill Elisha, whom he blames for the calamity befalling Israel.

The king's messenger repeats the king's words to Elisha: "This disaster is from the Lord. Why should I wait for the Lord any longer?" (6:33b). The king reveals that he had been holding his army back from violent defense based on Elisha's prophetic word from God, but now, in his desperation, he questions whether he should continue to wait for the Lord's deliverance.

Elisha, however, does not share the king's despair. He doesn't concede that the Lord has abandoned them or suggest a change in strategy. Instead, he prophesies that the Lord's victory is imminent, and the economic turmoil caused by the siege will soon be reversed. Food, currently scarce and highly valued, will become abundant and affordable.

The story concludes with a group of diseased outcasts from Israel, who, facing starvation, decide to approach the Aramean camp to beg for food. Expecting death, they find the camp deserted. The Lord had caused the Arameans to hear the sound of a vast army approaching, leading them to believe that Israel had allied with the Hittites and Egyptians to destroy them. In their panic, the Arameans fled, leaving all their supplies behind. The outcasts return to Samaria with the news, and the famine is ended by the abundance of the spoil.

In all three of these stories, God demonstrates that his provision and power are sufficient if his people will trust him rather than relying on their own violent strength. The Ammonites, Moabites, and Edomites were left to their own evil, which consumed them. In the second story, the enemy became confused when God directed them to be treated with love and mercy. Finally, he allowed the self-serving fears of those who rejected him to drive them to defeat, losing not only the battle but also their supplies. In each case, these enemies within Israel's or Judah's borders were removed without a single sword being wielded by Israel or Judah.

Could God have removed the Canaanites from the Promised Land without the bloodshed caused by Joshua and his armies? Of course! Joshua and his armies should have appealed to and trusted in God for that very outcome. But God's breathed-out Scripture includes these stories to teach us about the knowledge of good and evil and to reveal how God operates in love. These stories ultimately direct us to the full revelation of God and his kingdom as revealed in Christ.

CONCLUSION

The Bible is God's revelation, but it is not meant to be a reference book of commands simply to be memorized and followed. Rather, God worked through the lives and spirits of its writers to infuse their writings with his purpose. Although the words are theirs, the inspiration is divine. This process is unique to Scripture and has a distinct effect in the Old Testament compared to the New Testament.

Before the full revelation of God in Jesus, God's guidance was only partially revealed, limited by the sin-cursed influence of the world. In the Old Testament, God included the flawed efforts of his maturing followers as they struggled to understand the path to the coming Messiah. This was done not only for their instruction but for ours as well. Recognizing that Scripture was shaped in this way doesn't give us the freedom to dismiss or reject passages based on personal preference. We are constantly urged throughout Scripture to study, understand, and interpret wisely. And in all this, Jesus is the light that illuminates our understanding.

As the New Testament unfolds, we see a significant shift. While the Gospels and Acts continue the storytelling tradition of the Old Testament, they now reveal Jesus, the perfect "image of the invisible God" (Colossians 1:15). From this culmination, God's inspiration extends to the doctrinal clarity found in the epistles. Yes, the New Testament writers were also human, but we cannot discount the indwelling Spirit and God's guiding hand in preserving his truth within this book, his gift to us.

The testaments differ in that the Old Testament contains the flawed actions and testimonies of a people just beginning to grasp God's ways, while the New Testament presents the more complete revelation that God carefully guards through his Spirit. It would be a mistake to assume that this progression in Scripture is haphazard. Both the Old and New Testaments are "useful one way or another—showing us truth, exposing our rebellion, correcting our mistakes, training us to live God's way" (2 Timothy 3:16–17, The Message).

10

God Releases

Bring me an axe and spade,
Bring me a winding sheet;
When I my grave have made,
Let winds and tempests beat:
Then down I lie, as cold as clay.
True love doth pass away!

—William Blake from "Bring Me an Axe and Spade . . ."

But the day of the Lord will come like a thief.
The heavens will disappear with a roar;
The elements will be destroyed by fire,
and the earth and everything done in it will be laid bare.

—2 Peter 3:10

Few of us enjoy waiting. We wait at the grocery checkout, at the doctor's office, at the restaurant. We wait for the elevator, for the light to change, for pizza delivery. We want the concert to start, the commercial to be over, the dawn to break on those restless nights. I don't like waiting! Apparently, the apostle John felt the same. After Jesus assured him, "Yes, I'm coming soon." John urgently responded, "Amen. Come, Lord Jesus!" (Revelation 22:20). But here we are, 2,000 years later, still waiting. So what exactly is God waiting for? God waits because he refuses to limit his love (2 Peter 3:9).

TRUE LOVE WAYS

Prophecy often attracts those eager to know the future, regardless of their eschatological beliefs. While only some dispensationalists envision literal horned beasts and seas of blood, most Christians recognize the real terror of evil and find solace in the prophetic promise of safety. This security comes from knowing that, through love, God will redeem all creation and overcome Satan and his forces.

But what does it mean for God to defeat Satan and evil? Do God's angels engage in swordplay or hand-to-hand combat, wielding weapons like Thor's hammer or Poseidon's trident? Daniel 10:13 presents a curious image: Gabriel's arrival[1] to Daniel was delayed by a conflict with the "prince of the kingdom of Persia" (likely a high-ranking demon). After three weeks of struggle, the archangel Michael intervened. Was it a battle? The text suggests angelic conflict, but why would such a struggle last three weeks? Why can't God's angels swiftly defeat his foes? And doesn't God help at all? Surely, with his assistance, these demons would be squashed like bugs!

When considering spiritual and cosmic battles, particularly in the context of a future Armageddon, we often let our imaginations run wild, detached from biblical restraint. Many Christians find it more just, fitting, and even satisfying to imagine Christ pummeling those who have historically threatened us. We envision ourselves as spectators in a cosmic arena, watching angels and demons clash. But as we project our desire for vengeance onto God's motivations, do we ever consider that Scripture may chart a completely different path to victory?

The Bible champions love as central to God's activity—indeed, as the very essence of God. We Christians celebrate God's love when we consider our own rescue. However, we must remember that before our rescue, we were not the "good guys" held captive by evil tormentors. We were the ones who were evil—our motivations corrupt, our very essence cursed. Our Savior overcame the evil in us through love (Romans 5:8). Though Satan and death were cast aside, Christ achieved this not "by

---

1. The text doesn't specifically identify the angel in chapter 10, but from previous introduction (Daniel 8:16 and 9:21), it seems likely Gabriel appears in this scene as well.

strength or by might, but by [God's] Spirit" (Zechariah 4:6 HCSB), and God's Spirit is love (1 John 4:8). At the cross, Jesus confronted death but then turned from it to life, overcoming death through love—the most powerful force the universe has ever known.

It's perplexing that some Christians dismiss love as a watered-down version of the gospel. An article on the "Christian Today" website titled "3 Ways We Water the Gospel Down" touches on this concern. Without openly scoffing, the author warns against focusing too much on love: "Our sin deserved God's wrath—and what a wrath it is! If we keep focusing only on God's love and fail to balance it with God's righteous anger against our sin, we will dilute the very reason Christ had to die on the cross."[2] Many might wonder why I find this statement problematic. Doesn't God's wrath apply to evil? Yes, God's wrath represents the reality that evil cannot exist without God's sustaining presence. However, tempering our view of God's love with a hefty dose of wrath distorts rather than balances.

In chapter 1, we discussed the primacy of love as the expression of God's nature. Love is not only primary; wrath has no place as an attribute of God's nature. In God's existence before creation, alone in his Trinitarian self, wrath had no target and, therefore, did not exist. So when considering God's wondrous rescue of his image-bearers, we must acknowledge that even in God's ultimate and necessary separation from evil, it is love that demands our full attention.

We might think of God's love and wrath as we do light and dark. Darkness is defined only by the absence of light. In the brilliance of sunshine, we marvel at the beauty of the day without needing to "balance" it against darkness. We know that the absence of light brings gloom and darkness, but in the full radiance of the sun, we spend our time dancing! And so it should be in the embrace of God.

Nevertheless, the Bible does speak of God's anger. This anger, however, is not God striking out. Rather, Scripture reveals God's wrath as the natural consequence of separation from his sustaining presence (Deuteronomy 23:14; 2 Kings 17:18; Jeremiah 7:15; Psalm 78:59–60)—often described in the Old Testament as God "hiding his face." Emotionally, God remains true to his nature, and in his love activity, even amid anti-love activities, God does not set aside his love; infinite love cannot be disrupted. Instead, God's recognition of rejection results in the separation

---

2. Cachila, "3 Ways."

often described as his "hiding his face." Therefore, love is not something God turns on or off; darkness floods in only as light is rejected. And "light departing" reflects the reality of separation from God's sustaining presence. In sum, God does not and cannot carry with him a "balance" of love and wrath.

Imagine in our new-earth home, Gabriel blows his horn every Friday night to assemble us to watch a video of the terrors of sin—just so we can maintain a balance of wrath and love to fully appreciate the glories of heaven. Can you picture such a scenario? Of course not. We will live that triumphant life in the same glory that secured it for us, not through physical prowess but in relational love. Jesus secured our redemption through love by laying down his life for us.

Love does contain the strength—indeed, it is the strength—that wins the victory. This was Asaph's exact meaning when he exclaimed, "My flesh and my heart may fail, but God is the strength of my heart, my portion forever" (Psalm 73:26 HCSB). Consider Hebrews 2:14-15 (HCSB):

> Now since the children have flesh and blood in common, Jesus also shared in these, so that through His death He might destroy the one holding the power of death—that is, the Devil—and free those who were held in slavery all their lives by the fear of death.

Notice first that through his death, Jesus won this victory. Was Jesus's death planned in love, motivated by love, and accomplished in love? The question is not difficult. The answer emanates from all of Scripture, concentrated in the most well-known verse of all—John 3:16. So, yes, this love of God—giving himself in death for our relational benefit—won the victory. No flaming swords were swung, and no fireballs were hurled. Love conquers. Love wins the victory. That love is God's strength, and it is our strength as well.

It's interesting that many Christians see no conflict in accepting God's constant exhortations to love our enemies (Proverbs 24:17; 25:21; Matthew 5:44; Luke 6:27-36; Romans 12:14, 20; 1 Peter 3:9) while assigning to God a vicious desire to defeat his own enemies through physical assault. When their hatred and anger reach a boiling point, some even try to justify their feelings by labeling them righteous anger: "We must love our enemies, but we can hate God's enemies!" Veiled in Christian piety, they live out the curse of the flesh.

But they have it all wrong. God doesn't seek to maim, scar, or batter his enemies while urging us to love ours. Our God, whose very essence is love, does not abandon his nature to take offense at those who reject a love relationship with him. His commands to love flow from a consistent heart. While he becomes angry at anything that seeks to destroy love, he never descends into active rage or exhibits violence. Rather, he allows separation for that which is contrary to relationship, as it cannot exist within his sustaining presence.

Believing that God acts only in love does not equate to sappy sentimentality. Those who champion shallow emotionalism may unbiblically believe that God overlooks the heinousness of sin in favor of benign tolerance, but God's very nature disallows such a notion. Sin, which is anything that misses the mark of love, violently assaults God's essence and activity. To maintain the integrity of God's nature, sin cannot be sustained indefinitely within his presence; when no hope for love relationship remains, God cannot continue to uphold what fully rejects his essence. He cannot continue to pursue a love relationship with those who have closed themselves off to every possibility for love.

Part of the problem with accepting a God who is consistently loving is that it conflicts with our idea of winning. In wars, battles, and struggles, we fight against our enemies, often envisioning victory as standing over our opponents, crushed beneath us. Mel Gibson's portrayal of William Wallace in *Braveheart*, gloating over the dead bodies of his enemies at the Battle of Stirling, is a scene where the survivors let loose a victory yell, a cry that accentuates their pride, satisfaction, and thrill in destruction. But this kind of violence that we often savor does not align with biblical values.

When you read the Sermon on the Mount, how does "Love your enemies" (Matthew 5:44) strike you? Do you feel the need to rein in your desire for victory? Do you presume Jesus is urging you to be passive, to relinquish any chance to triumph? If we think that's what God is endorsing, we need to reevaluate the activity of love. Love is no sleepy surrender; in fact, it is by love that God conquers. Consider these passages:

- John 16:33b "But take heart! I have overcome the world."
- 1 Corinthians 1:18 (HCSB) "For the word of the cross is foolishness to those who are perishing, but it is the power of God to us who are being saved."
- Hebrews 2:14 (HCSB) Jesus shared in flesh and blood "so that through his death he might destroy the one holding the power of death—that is, the devil."

The Bible consistently links Christ's work on the cross to the conquering power of God. And Jesus himself describes that work as a work of love (John 15:13). Moreover, Scripture reveals that we too become conquerors in the power of God's love:

- Romans 8:35-37 (HCSB) "Who can separate us from the love of Christ? Can affliction or distress or persecution or famine or nakedness or danger or sword? As it is written: 'Because of you we are being put to death all day long; we are counted as sheep to be slaughtered.' No, in all these things we are more than *conquerors* through him who loved us."
- 2 Corinthians 12:10b (HCSB) "For when I am weak, then I am *strong*."
- Philippians 3:10 (HCSB) "My goal is to know him and the *power* of his resurrection and the fellowship of his sufferings, being conformed to his death."
- Revelation 12:11 Speaking of the defeat of Satan, the heavenly voice said, "They triumphed over him by the blood of the Lamb."

A favorite passage of mine is Romans 8:35-37, not only for the confidence Paul inspires but also for how it opens our eyes to God's Old Testament teaching. In that passage, Paul refers to Psalm 44, a maskil of the sons of Korah. Through the psalm's 26 verses, we learn of Israel's misunderstanding. The Israelites begin by recounting victories of war attributed to God (1-3). They continue with praise for God's destructive arm (4-8). Then they describe their current condition of defeat and humiliation (9-16), which they object to as unfair because of their own faithfulness (17-19). They protest that they could understand their condition if they had been unfaithful (20-21). Their complaint culminates in verse 22: they are being killed! They conclude that God, as he did in the past, should rescue them by crushing their enemies now. "Wake up, Lord!" they plead. "Why do you sleep? Rouse yourself! Do not reject us forever.... Rise up and help us; rescue us because of your unfailing love" (23-26).

Some Christians, pondering why God was waiting, suggest Israel misunderstood the true cost of their original unfaithfulness. They fault the chosen nation for not being as righteous as they should have been. Others believe Israel may have been faithful but misunderstood that God's followers might need to suffer to refine and steel their faith.

Both interpretations fall short. Paul responds, "No!" not to their declaration of faithfulness in verses 17-19, but to their summary complaint in verse 22—their attitude of impoverishment and defeat. Romans 8:35–37 argues that affliction and persecution do not mean defeat, and escaping physical persecution does not mean victory. "None of this," Paul declares. "In all these things [even in the suffering of affliction] we are more than conquerors through him who loved us." Reversing persecution to harm those who harm us should not constitute victory in our eyes. Victory comes through love and the giving of our essence for the sake of both our enemies and ourselves.

As discussed, Kinship theology views God as interacting with his creation always and only for the purpose of love relationship. Foundational to this theology is that God's very purpose in creation was for everlasting love relationship. So even when the fall came and sin tore apart relationship, allowing evil to abound, grace abounded more. Grace brought love, and "in this way did God love the world: he gave his Son, the only human born of his nature, so that all those trusting in him will never be separated from him but rather will join him in everlasting love relationship" (my paraphrase of John 3:16).

If love motivated creation, if love defines how God acts, and if love powers the conquering of the world, why would we ever think of setting love aside when envisioning Christ's return and the new heaven and new earth? We cannot believe that God would abandon his own covenant of creative purpose in a display of power based on physical violence. Our God will remain righteous—faithful to his activity of love.

This understanding should also shape our conception of angelic battles. God does not send angels to fight his battles violently. He doesn't dispatch them to physically battle so he doesn't have to. His angels, no doubt, fight as he fights—in view, impression, and exaltation of God's love. The angelic battle may last weeks because love cannot be coerced. But God, through his angels, ensures opportunity.

And so God waits; he waits in love. Our God, who knows all possibilities, will wait as long as any possibility remains for extending love because he truly does not want any to perish. But a time will come when waiting no longer serves a purpose.

THE WAITING DONE

In chapter 4, I referenced the flood story to illustrate the world's evil course and God's necessary response. The downward spiral took time, but the multiplied rejection made destruction inevitable. The relatively small world population at the time reduced the opportunity to turn back from faithlessness. So when the "sons of God" (representing the community of God-followers) began to entwine their lives with the "daughters of men" (those who rejected God), hopelessness became pervasive. This reached a point where "every inclination of the thoughts of the human heart was only evil all the time" (Genesis 6:5). This was the tipping point—the condition where God's continued interaction would lose its definition as love. If love means giving of self for the benefit of relationship, and no possibility exists for relationship, then "giving of self" ceases to be love. And if it is not love, God does not continue doing it because he acts only in love.

The flood story illustrates the coming end of our current age—the rescue of God's people (represented by Noah and his family), the judgment of the rejecters, and the renewal or redemption of the earth. Note that God's hand does not lash out to destroy. Consistent with our earlier discussion, destruction arises when hope for relationship ceases, preventing God from acting for their benefit. Currently, God sustains the world for his loving purpose. But in the world's ultimate departure, violence erupts like a flood.

Genesis 6:5 provides the criterion for this violent end: when no possible path remains for anyone who does not know God to come to him. At that point, the waiting will be over, and Christ will return. How could God know that eventually no single path would lead to more souls embracing his love? As discussed in chapter 2, God knows everything that can be known, including all possibilities.

At the end of the flood story, God places a rainbow in the sky, symbolizing a covenant in which he vows never to destroy the earth again by flood. This promise holds significance. By it, God assures us that he will not take a hands-off approach and simply allow the natural (and cursed) world to run its course toward inevitable death. This Noahic covenant does not differ inherently from God's previous approach. God has always worked in the affairs of his image-bearers to position them favorably to respond to his revelation. But now he assures us of two things: (1) the possibilities he foresaw at the flood's end provide hope through the cross, and (2) for the sake of love, he will involve himself in our activity to ensure the opportunity for everyone to come to him. The tower of Babel story that follows the flood illustrates this point. The people were on another downward trajectory into death. God interposed himself to ensure that opportunity continued.

Thus, a loving God will end the world—not in vindictiveness and not without concern for those who will perish. But when it is impossible for any new love relationship to begin, the God of love will extend his efforts only toward those who have embraced him in love. Then, and only then, does love truly win.

Part 2

God's Image in Creation's Story

11

God Imaged in Sonship

By Thee my prayers acceptance gain,
Although with sin defiled;
Satan accuses me in vain,
And I am own'd a child."
—John Newton, from "Out of the Depths"

And it will be in the place where they were told,
You are not My people, there they will be called
sons of the living God.
—Romans 9:26 HCSB

Imagine being in a formal gathering where a respected Christian leader, whom you admire, is being introduced to the governor of your state. At the same event, a notorious spiritualist is also presented. Now, imagine this false teacher encouraging the governor to adopt his practices of sorcery-related divination. Suddenly, your admired preacher interrupts, shouting, "You son of the Devil! Stop perverting the truth!" Would you be shocked? Would you feel awkward, uncomfortable, or even disconcerted that this respected Christian leader would speak such harsh words, publicly calling another person a "son of the Devil" right in front of the governor? You might even think, "That's not how Christians should act." Yet, this very scenario is recorded in our Bible—Acts 13:10. Paul, standing before Sergius Paulus, the pro-consul of Cyprus, directly addresses another man (who is identified as a false prophet) and exclaims, "You son of the Devil!" (HCSB).

It's important to remember that just because Paul said something, it doesn't automatically make it the right thing to do. Paul was a limited, fallible human, just like the rest of us. In this case, I'll explain why Paul used such strong language, even if we may not entirely defend the offense in how he expressed it.

"SON OF" IS LIKENESS

We briefly touched on the reason behind Paul's words in chapter 7. When someone is referred to as a "son of" another person, unless it's specifically indicating a bloodline relationship (the primary usage of "son of"), it often points to a resemblance or similarity. In the Acts 13 passage, the sorcerer is named "Bar-Jesus," with "bar" meaning "son of" in Aramaic, indicating that the man's father was named Jesus. However, Paul, thinking of the Lord Jesus and recognizing that "son of" often indicates likeness, concluded that the sorcerer's name was misleading—this man was nothing like the Lord Jesus. Paul's verbal attack was intended to make it clear that this man was not like Jesus but rather like Satan. So, he shouted, "You son of the Devil!" I imagine Paul might have even used the Aramaic form alongside the Greek, saying, "You are no Bar-Jesus but rather Bar-Diabolos!"

Understanding that "son of" indicates likeness, we can better appreciate Jesus's titles "son of God" and "son of man." Consider Matthew 16:13–18 (KNT):

> Jesus came to Caesarea Philippi. There he put this question to his disciples: "Who do people say that the son of man is?"
> "John the Baptist," they replied. "Others say Elijah. Others say Jeremiah, or one of the prophets."
> "What about you?" he asked them. "Who do you say I am?"
> Simon Peter answered. "You're the Messiah," he said. "You're the son of the living God!"
> "God's blessing on you, Simon, son of John!" answered Jesus. "Flesh and blood didn't reveal that to you; it was my father in heaven.

"And I've got something to tell you, too: you are Peter, the rock, and on this rock I will build my church, and the gates of hell won't overpower it."

Notice how Jesus begins by asking who people say he is, using the term "son of man" to describe himself. Since "son of" implies likeness, we see Jesus referring to himself as someone in the "likeness of man." In other words, this title actually affirms his deity—he is God, but he took on the likeness of man.

Peter's response shifts this concept of "likeness" slightly. He declares, "You're the son of the living God." In other words, Peter recognized Jesus as a man in the "likeness of God." Jesus is pleased with Peter's response because it shows that Peter correctly understood that Jesus manifested God, embodying the revelation God intended through him. Jesus revealed to them (and to us) who God is through his perfect imaging.

Jesus continues this emphasis on imaging by first addressing his disciple as "Simon, son of John," and then quickly giving him the name "Peter," meaning "a specific rock." This name change involves a wordplay that links Peter to the foundational role he would play in building the church on the large rock or bedrock of Jesus's manifestation of God. In other words, Peter (and the other disciples) would, like Jesus, act in the likeness of God as they worked to build the kingdom. Just as a specific rock resembles the larger bedrock of which it is a part, Peter's (and our) efforts to manifest God's likeness are tied to Jesus's perfect imaging. While Peter's or any disciple's (or our) manifestation of likeness doesn't shine as brightly as Jesus's due to his perfection, Jesus uses the "son of" expression and other "likeness" phrases to emphasize the continuity of the kingdom mission.

This passage makes it clear that God's intent from creation was for us to bear his image, and now, with redemption revealed in Christ, our imaging aligns with the upside-down kingdom of God as disciples of Jesus. In chapter 1, we learned that God is love, and, as we explored in chapter 5, he created and designed us for a loving relationship with him. As the unique God-human, Jesus's purpose in imaging God during his earthly life was twofold, encompassing both his titles as "son of God" and "son of man": (1) to perfectly image God for us so that we might know him, and (2) by his active imaging, to teach us how a perfect human should relate to God in a life of love relationship—the kingdom of God life. Jesus didn't just give us an example; he also taught us the way—through his discipleship program.

Unfortunately, because we know Jesus is God, we often emphasize his deity when reading the Gospels—that he is God and that everything he does reflects his divine nature. However, many of the stories in the Gospels are intended to show Jesus as a man, not just as God. We read with reverence that John and the others saw "his glory, the glory of the one and only Son, who came from the Father, full of grace and truth" (John 1:14). But note that this glory is related to his "begottenness"—his entrance into human form and activity. John begins by saying, "The Word became flesh and made his dwelling among us"—that's his humanness. His glory, then—his manifestation of worth—is seen in his utter dependence as a human on God for direction, activity, thought, and word, just as all worthy humans should do. But of course, imaging perfect humanity for us requires us to first seek God's rescue.

BECOMING A CHRISTIAN

Certainly, God desires for us to enter into a loving relationship with him. This relationship is initiated through a profound transformation of mind and heart, which involves three key elements: (1) repentance of sin, (2) embracing who God is, and (3) trusting in God's rescue.

Repentance is more than simply recognizing wrongdoing and offering an apology. It goes deeper. Many Christian teachers suggest that repentance involves a turning away from sin, which is a step in the right direction, but the concept needs further exploration.

God created us with a natural longing for truth, goodness, and beauty (TGB), and this desire was meant to serve the purpose of a loving relationship with him. However, sin begins with the belief that the fulfillment of these desires—TGB—can be manipulated for selfish gain. This is not just a matter of some people being more selfish than others; it's a universal human condition that stems from the curse introduced by Adam. God intended our desire for TGB to benefit the community, but sin distorts this desire into a self-centered pursuit, regardless of the harm or loss it may cause to others. This sinful condition drives us to satisfy our own desires, even when we know they are wrong, and sometimes despite other conflicting needs and desires.

To better understand this, consider extreme examples of sin that we all recognize as terrible. For instance, a drug addict seeks satisfaction regardless of the harm or loss to others—that is sin. But the depth of the sin condition—the curse—is evident when the addict continues to pursue the drug despite reasoned intervention and awareness of the self-harm involved, even to the point of death. This cursed condition enslaves the mind and will to immediate, craving desires. As Paul states in Romans 1: "They exchanged the truth about God for a lie, and worshiped and served created things rather than the Creator—who is forever praised. Amen" (Romans 1:24b-25).

The situation becomes more subtle—and just as controlling—when the pursuit involves actions that are not as overtly harmful. Even telling inconsequential lies to improve self-image carries the same curse-related significance. In our natural state, even when we morally or reasonably reject such minor lies, our motives often remain rooted in a perceived benefit to ourselves, with little regard for the good of the community. We might wonder, "Is that so bad?" Compared to drug addiction, murder, or rape, the answer may seem to be no; it doesn't have the same immediate destructive impact. Yet, this self-centeredness—though not always noticeable—underlies much of the world's disharmony, struggle, and tension, where everyone is vying for personal satisfaction. This is not the kingdom-of-God life, and it cannot be reconciled with a God of love, despite his desire to rescue those who are entrapped by it.

Repentance, then, is not merely a decision to avoid certain harmful actions. It is a turning away from self-centered motivations, realizing that our desires are based on something—ourselves—that cannot truly satisfy TGB. When we make this turn, God forgives.

However, repentance—the recognition and rejection of a self-centered foundation for life—must be accompanied by a replacement for that foundation. This is where faith comes in. In his truth, goodness, and beauty, God provides the true foundation for life's satisfaction. God's TGB is expressed through love—the giving of oneself for the benefit of relationship. Thus, repentance, the turning away from a self-centered foundation, and faith, the embracing of God's love-centered foundation, mark the beginning of our conversion.

The final step in this conversion is trust in God's rescue. We may repent of self. We may embrace God as the foundation of life. But does that guarantee we will be with God forever? What about the cursed state in which we once lived? Will that not always be a barrier to our relationship with God? No. Through Jesus, God redeemed humankind by taking on the curse himself, putting it to death, and then reclaiming life—redeeming it—without the curse.

BECOMING A DISCIPLE

The repentance, embrace, and trust that bring us into a loving relationship with God mark a critical transition, ensuring our eternal life with him. But the essence of kingdom life is not merely about securing our future; it's about experiencing the full, multifaceted satisfaction that comes from immersing ourselves in truth, dancing in goodness, and delighting in beauty within a community of love. Yet, many Christians seem to choose a more static approach—praying for rescue to secure their future but continuing to pursue selfish goals, much like those of the old world's kingdom. This paradox is common, driven by the narrow perception that salvation is primarily about getting into heaven when you die. Once that ticket is punched, the mindset suggests, there's little need to deepen the relationship beyond a Sunday church appearance and a cursory prayer before meals.

However, Jesus called us to more than just joining a club; he called us to discipleship. The Greek word for disciple, *mathetes*, can best be understood as apprentice. Think of an apprentice, especially in historical contexts, who would live with a master craftsman to learn a trade. First, the apprentice spent time with the master, gaining knowledge simply by being in the master's presence—learning, contemplating, asking questions, and listening. Next, the apprentice had the opportunity to become like the master. This process was not merely about replicating the master's work. Instead, it involved adopting the master's habits, appreciating the love the master had for the craft, and developing a parallel desire and esteem for it. Only then, with this foundation, did the apprentice truly begin to do what the master did. Similarly, as true disciples of Jesus, we follow those three essential steps: (1) be with Jesus, (2) become like Jesus, and then (3) do what Jesus did.[1]

But why should we care so deeply about being disciples—apprentices—of Jesus? Isn't this just adding more obligations, leading to eventual burnout? Not if we approach it correctly. In fact, when we focus on fulfillment rather than merely avoiding burnout, the desire to be disciples

---

1. Comer, "Apprentice."

becomes life-giving. Two important considerations frame our desire to be disciples of Jesus.

First, following Jesus as a disciple provides full satisfaction in life. God created us for relationship, and true relationship is grounded in God's truth, goodness, and beauty. The illusion of our fallen state, with our flesh in control, tempts us to believe that selfish indulgence is the path to happiness and satisfaction. But we were made to be image bearers, and only by reflecting God can we find true fulfillment.

How do we know what to reflect of God? As discussed in chapter 9, God reveals himself through Jesus, who is "the image of the invisible God" (Colossians 1:15). Not only is Jesus the exact expression of God's nature (Hebrews 1:3), but he also embodies the fullness of it (Colossians 2:9). Therefore, as disciples—by being with Jesus, becoming like Jesus, and doing what he did—we imitate God, cultivating a perfect, satisfying relationship.

The second key to avoiding burnout in our discipleship journey is ensuring we follow the apprenticeship steps in the right order. Although a disciple learns to do what Jesus did, jumping straight into action without first spending time with Jesus and becoming like him is the quickest route to burnout.

Jesus often retreated to solitary or remote places. The New Testament frequently translates the Greek word used here as "wilderness" or "desert," but it could simply refer to any out-of-the-way place where Jesus could be alone to pray. Luke 5:16 tells us that he often withdrew to these isolated places to pray, knowing he needed to be with God. Similarly, we need solitary time—time away from the busyness, even if that busyness involves important work. As apprentices, our journey begins by being with Jesus. We spend time in prayer and contemplation, listening for God's voice in our lives. We allow the Spirit to fill us, finding a peace that becomes the foundation of our Christian lives, not just a temporary respite from them.

Then we focus on becoming like Jesus by cultivating a love for what God loves. We won't succeed in long-term kingdom-building work if the activity hasn't captured our hearts, imaginations, and desires as it did for Jesus. In other words, our efforts in evangelism and care should not rely on temporary, stirred-up energy or sheer willpower. The mission should flow naturally from who we are—who we've become—as we grow into the fullness of Christ (Ephesians 4:13).

Chapter 1 introduced love as the way of life that permeates everything God does. God created us to be image bearers—sons of God—reflecting his love. Jesus, the perfect Son and the perfect image bearer, shows us how to live in love and calls us to be his disciples. This pattern, lost in a world marred by curse and sin, is central to God's plan to renew all creation—physical and spiritual—in perfect harmony, rooted in a loving relationship based on God's truth, goodness, and beauty.

12

God Imaged in Israel

Come, O Thou Traveler unknown,
Whom still I hold, but cannot see;
My company before is gone,
And I am left alone with Thee.
With Thee all night I mean to stay
And wrestle till the break of day.

—Charles Wesley, from "Wrestling Jacob"

Neither circumcision nor uncircumcision means anything;
what counts is the new creation.
Peace and mercy to all who follow this rule—
to the Israel of God!

—Galatians 6:15–16

When you hear the word "Israel," where does your mind go? It might immediately jump to the current political situation in the Middle East, but biblically speaking, what comes to mind? You might think of Jacob, whose name was changed to Israel, or his children, who formed the biblical nation of Israel. Another possibility is Jesus, whom Matthew and other New Testament books link to the fulfillment of Israel's purpose, making him the true Israel. In Galatians 6:16, Paul refers to all those born of Jesus as the "Israel of God," which includes God's people as depicted in Revelation's portrayal of the current age. To understand this concept fully, it's important to consider the Bible's various references to Israel, as they all work together and build on one another.

ISRAEL—JACOB'S NEW NAME

Names in biblical times carried significant meaning. For example, Sarah laughed when she heard she would have a child in her old age, so Abraham named their son Isaac, which means "laughter." When Isaac's twins were born, the Bible describes the first as being covered in what appeared to be a hairy garment. As a result, he was named Esau, meaning "hairy." His brother was born holding onto Esau's heel, leading to the name Jacob, meaning "supplanter."

Jacob lived up to his name, scheming to usurp both the birthright and blessing from his slightly older twin brother. Because of this stolen blessing, Esau's anger burned toward Jacob, and he vowed to kill him as soon as their father died. Rebekah, their mother, learned of Esau's intent and encouraged Jacob to leave and visit her brother Laban. In that patriarchal society, Isaac, the head of the family, would need to approve the move. So Rebekah, concealing the true reason, urged Isaac to send Jacob away to find a wife. Both Rebekah and Isaac had been displeased with the Hittite wives Esau had chosen (Genesis 26:34–35), so Rebekah convinced Isaac that Jacob should find a wife from her family, not from the Canaanites. Isaac agreed and sent Jacob to Laban, Rebekah's brother.

During one night on his journey, Jacob had a dream of a ladder extending from earth to heaven, with angels ascending and descending. Through this dream, God assured Jacob that he would be involved in his life and care for him. God specifically promised Jacob the same blessings given to his grandfather Abraham and his father Isaac: land, offspring, and blessings for the world through him.

This dream had a profound impact on Jacob. The text does not indicate that God gave this dream because Jacob was seeking him, his ways, or his blessings. But the Bible does record that the ladder vision deeply shook Jacob. Overcome with awe, he named the place Bethel, meaning "house of God." He set up a stone marker or altar, pouring out a drink offering and anointing the stone with oil. Jacob's response to the dream was one of exuberance, describing the place as "awesome" and "the gate of heaven." Note the vow Jacob made that morning:

> If God will be with me and watch over me on this journey I am taking and will give me food to eat and clothing to wear so that I return safely to my father's household, then the Lord will be my God. (Genesis 28:20–21)

Jacob's vow reflects not a bargaining with God but rather a deep sense of certainty that God's care and provision would sustain him. In other words, Jacob placed himself entirely in God's hands.

Jacob eventually arrived at Laban's land, where Laban welcomed him. Interestingly, and perhaps as a bit of comic relief, Genesis 29:13–14 tells us that Jacob explained to Laban everything that had happened to him, likely including more than just the journey itself. It seems Jacob recounted the entire purpose of the trip, including his trickery in securing the birthright and blessing from his brother. Laban responded with a chuckle, saying, "You are my own flesh and blood" (Genesis 29:14). In modern terms, Laban's reply might be akin to saying, "I can see we're related—you act just like I do!" This should have been a warning to Jacob, as Laban's admiration of Jacob's deceitful behavior hinted at his own similar tendencies. Jacob should have realized that Laban's promises were unreliable. But instead, he trusted Laban, who then tricked Jacob into additional years of service while securing both his daughters' futures. Yet, it's important to note that Jacob's departure from Laban's household was no longer an act of fleeing but was directed by God.

As Jacob journeyed back to his homeland, his fears of Esau's murderous anger resurfaced. To soften Esau's heart, Jacob prepared gifts and sent representatives ahead, but he also turned to God in prayer.

One evening, Jacob sent his wives, children, and possessions across the Jabbok stream, leaving himself alone. While the text doesn't explicitly state his motivation, many commentators suggest that Jacob wanted to be alone to think and pray. As he did, a man suddenly appeared and wrestled with him until daybreak. The abruptness of the encounter is startling, likely intended to reflect Jacob's own shock in the narrative. Jacob, fearing for his life and anticipating an attack from Esau, may have initially thought this man was his brother.

Instead, we learn that the man was God in human form. They wrestled, but God, appearing as a man, did not prevail. When God saw he could not overcome Jacob, he struck Jacob on the thigh, dislocating his hip and leaving him with a lifelong limp. This story raises many questions: Why did God appear as a man? Why did he wrestle with Jacob without any prior conversation? Why couldn't he prevail? How did Jacob recognize this man as God? And why did God cause him permanent physical harm? While not all these questions have clear answers, viewing the story through a Christocentric lens reveals its deeper significance. Jacob's night of wrestling with God, filled with fear and struggle, mirrors the Gethsemane scene where Jesus wrestles with God over his impending death. This episode teaches us several important lessons about our relationship with God.

- God, as the wrestling man, demonstrates that he engages with humankind not simply in the spirit but through our own essence, our flesh. God's revelation to us is from his essence of TGB, through his persons acting in love, to our essence (our physical connection), and it is comprehended by our persons—our souls. So regarding relationship with him, God does not use his God-power to overcome, although he certainly does make every attempt for us to see and accept.

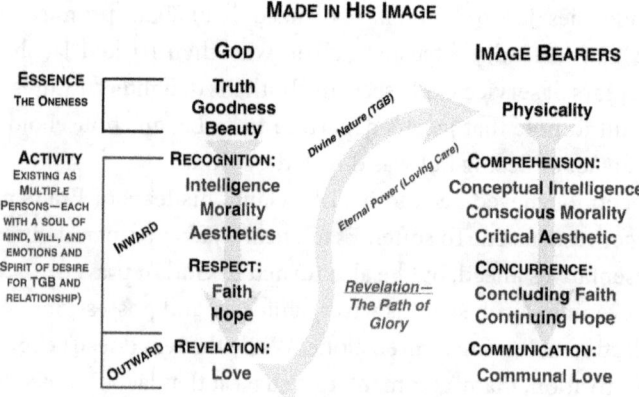

- During the struggle, Jacob comes to realize that the one he is wrestling is not Esau or some unknown attacker; he recognizes that he is striving with God. His focus shifts immediately from defending his life to holding on in pursuit of a blessing. We see a similar shift in the Gethsemane scene, where Jesus, though naturally averse to the prospect of losing his physical essence, turns away from thoughts of self-preservation and centers his mind on the greater glory found in dependence on God and his TGB essence.

- As Jacob clings to God in human form, dawn approaches, and God tells Jacob to let go. Those who worship their physical essence as an idol will ultimately lose their lives. But those who deny their physical essence—even to the point of death—to hold onto God's TGB essence will gain life. Jacob risks death for the sake of the blessing, realizing that without God and his TGB blessing, life is meaningless. When daylight comes, Jacob sees the face of the man, but because of his changed attitude, he lives and names the place Peniel, saying, "For I have seen God face to face, and I have been delivered."

- God then changes Jacob's name to Israel, meaning "striving with God." From both Jacob's and Jesus's wrestling, we learn that striving with God is neither about opposing him nor simply working alongside him. The struggle occurs in the space between, beginning with our instinct to defend and dominate. Our spirits bear the weight of craving to satisfy our essence. However, a relationship with God requires us to bring our desires into alignment with his. We don't just turn away from self; we reorder our desires, with God's essence as the foundation for a life-giving relationship. In this way, the name "Israel" embodies the fulfillment of God's counsel to Cain in Genesis 4:7: "It desires to have you, but you must rule over it." Jacob began the wrestling match seeking to protect and satisfy his physical self, but he ended by risking self for the greater good of God's relational blessing.

ISRAEL—JESUS AS FULFILLMENT

The blessings of God's covenant with Abraham include a blend of temporal and eternal promises, which can be confusing if not categorized correctly. Initially, in Genesis 12, God promises Abram general blessings of land, offspring, and a blessing to all the nations of the earth through him. As the covenant becomes more formalized in Genesis 15, God's specific assurances regarding land and offspring highlight his original creation intent for a loving relationship with the literal land and descendants of his creation. However, the entrance of sin altered God's plan to one of rescue. In Genesis 17, God reveals his everlasting intent by changing

Abram's name, meaning "exalted father," to Abraham, "father of many nations." With this name change, God's promises to Abraham transition from the temporal to the everlasting.

This shift is the reason Paul emphasizes Jesus as the fulfillment of the covenant (Galatians 3:16). The Galatian Christians were struggling to understand the requirements of Jesus's Messianic mission. Jesus was a Jew, so they questioned whether the "new" religion was merely an extension of Judaism to the Gentiles. If that were the case, they reasoned, Gentiles should follow all Jewish laws, such as circumcision, dietary restrictions, and the rest of the Law. Paul's letter counters this notion, arguing not just that the Law doesn't apply to Gentiles, but that the entire purpose of the Abrahamic Covenant's everlasting promises presupposed the one offspring, Jesus, who would fulfill those promises for the world. The physical descendants of Abraham, Isaac, and Jacob served as a precursor to Jesus's actual fulfillment.

Jesus did not come to earth to be king solely over the physical descendants of Jacob. Nor did he alter his plan to become king of the Gentiles when the Jews rejected him. Believers in Jesus, the Church, were not a replacement group for the rejecting Jews. Instead, Jesus was the fulfillment of God's original and only plan to restore creation to its intended purpose of an everlasting love relationship. Jacob and his children symbolized that plan, and Jesus and his followers fulfilled it.

The grouping of the patriarchs—Abraham, Isaac, and Jacob—was meant to reflect the Trinitarian structure in the restoration of creation. Abraham represents the Father, symbolizing the immutability of purpose. Isaac, connecting Abraham to Jacob, mirrors the Spirit, emerging from that unchanging purpose to guide Jesus. For example, Isaac directed Jacob's path to Laban, despite the hardships involved, which ultimately strengthened Jacob's worship of God as he pursued the covenant blessing. Isaac's guidance foreshadows the Holy Spirit leading Jesus through the wilderness and its temptations (Matthew 4:1). Through Jacob, the illustrative promises of land and offspring were fulfilled, just as the everlasting promises were realized through Jesus in his redemption of the children of faith.

Paul concludes his explanation with the discussion of the two covenants in Galatians 4:21–31. Interestingly, Paul links the covenant made at Mount Sinai with the physical descendants of Sarah to the covenant with Hagar. He argues that the covenant with Hagar's offspring corresponds to the current Jerusalem—a physical city of physical descendants who had made their cursed essence, their physicality, the defining mark of their relationship with God. But Paul asserts that the Jerusalem (and therefore the Israel) of God is from above, born of the Spirit (represented by Isaac) into redemption. Thus, the Bible strongly supports the idea that those who are born of Jesus are the true Israel of God.

ISRAEL—70 WEEKS TO TRANSITION

In Daniel 9, we read that Daniel, through his study of Jeremiah (25:11–12), discerns that Babylon/Persia will be defeated 70 years after Judah's capture. Recognizing that the time is near, Daniel prays for the Jews and Jerusalem (Daniel 9:4–19). In response to his prayer, God sends the angel Gabriel to explain two things: (1) the timing of God's restoration plan, and (2) that the restoration concerns more than just Jerusalem and the Jews, the physical descendants of Jacob.

God sent this dual-purposed prophecy because Daniel was beloved. Daniel had prayed for Jerusalem and the Jews—those who were indeed called by God's name. In showing his favor, God clears up a misunderstanding Daniel had—that the physical descendants and the physical city of Jerusalem were who God considered his people and city to be. God's answer revealed the birth of the true Israel through the redemption of physical essence. He would conclude his direct interaction with the physical nation of Israel, which had only ever been an illustration of the true Israel.

We generally refer to this dual-purposed prophecy as "Daniel's 70 weeks" because the English translation of Daniel 9:24 mentions seventy weeks. However, seventy weeks amounts to only 490 days, a period far too short to contain the redemptive blessings described in Daniel 9. The solution lies in understanding that the Hebrew word for "week" (*shebuah*), though typically referring to a period of seven days, literally means something "sevened" or multiplied by seven. Therefore, the term could denote a period of seven days, but it could just as easily refer to a period of seven months or seven years. In this context, the first two words of verse 24, literally meaning "seventy periods of seven," should be understood as seventy periods of seven years, or a total of 490 years.

Verse 24 outlines the purposes of this 70-week, or 490-year, period. First, it states that God decrees this time for "your people" (the Jews) and "your holy city" (Jerusalem). Since the nation served as a representation of the Israel of God, the time period seems to indicate how long it will be until the image gives way to reality. Therefore, the next six phrases, or fulfillments, must support this idea. In other words, the accomplishments listed refer to the results symbolized by Jacob's descendants but realized by Jesus and his followers. These six fulfillments can be understood as two main accomplishments with two subpoints for each:

1. To finish transgression
   a. To put an end to sin
   b. To atone for wickedness
2. To bring in everlasting righteousness
   a. To seal up vision and prophecy
   b. To anoint the Most Holy Place

The first fulfillment of the prophecy brought an end to the transgression. But what was this transgression? It refers to the human rebellion that began in the garden, which caused our estrangement from God. Verse 24 immediately outlines two key consequences—two subpoints—of how God would address this transgression. First, God would "put an end to sin" through the forgiveness of the guilt of the repentant. Second, God would "atone for wickedness" by redeeming human essence from its curse. Through Christ's work on the cross and his resurrection, God removed both the curse on our physical essence and the final guilt associated with it. Hebrews 9:26 states, "He has appeared once for all at the end of the ages to do away with sin by the sacrifice of himself."

The second fulfillment, "to bring in everlasting righteousness," is also tied to Christ's first coming. John 3:16 teaches us that whoever believes in Christ has everlasting life, and by having this everlasting life, we secure covenantal faithfulness—what is defined as righteousness. More specifically, this fulfillment marks the beginning of the Holy Spirit's work within us, based on Jesus's accomplished atonement. The Holy Spirit seals Jesus, who came to fulfill the prophecy: "For on him God the Father has placed his seal of approval" (John 6:27). And because we belong to Christ, we too are sealed. As Paul writes of the Holy Spirit, we are sealed "for the day of redemption" (Ephesians 4:30).

The second subpoint, "to anoint the Most Holy Place," initially refers to Jesus's anointing. In Luke 4:18, Jesus reads from Isaiah 61:1 and applies

GOD IMAGED IN ISRAEL   131

the Scripture to himself: "The Spirit of the Lord is on me, because he has anointed me to proclaim good news to the poor." In Acts 4:27, after Peter and John's testimony before the chief priests and elders, the early believers recognized God's anointing of Jesus. When Peter first preached the gospel to the Gentiles, he said to Cornelius, "You know what has happened throughout the province of Judea, beginning in Galilee after the baptism that John preached—how God anointed Jesus of Nazareth with the Holy Spirit and power" (Acts 10:37–38).

The foundation of our relationship with God is his essence—his TGB. But since God has clothed our souls in physical bodies, this relationship with God takes place within our physical essence. The Old Testament promised that God would dwell in the midst of his people (Numbers 14:14; 35:34; Deuteronomy 23:15; Psalm 46:5), and the tabernacle served as the image of this dwelling. God met with the High Priest within the Most Holy Place. However, as the shadow gave way to the reality, Jesus came to dwell among his people as the Most Holy One (Matthew 1:23) so that we, in turn, might dwell in him (2 Corinthians 5:17; Galatians 3:27).

This anointing of Jesus by the Holy Spirit extends to those who are born of Jesus: "Now it is God who makes both us and you stand firm in Christ. He anointed us, set his seal of ownership on us, and put his Spirit in our hearts as a deposit, guaranteeing what is to come" (2 Corinthians 1:21–22).

Thus, all the purposes outlined in Daniel 9:24 regarding the 70 weeks prophecy find their fulfillment in Jesus and his atonement. Accordingly, the 70 weeks—the 490 years—should logically conclude with Jesus's first advent.

Verse 25 of Daniel 9 tells us that the 70 weeks would begin with a decree to restore and rebuild Jerusalem. From that point, seven weeks (49 years) would pass, followed by another 62 weeks (434 years), leading up to the events described in verses 26 and 27. In total, 69 of the 70 weeks (483 years) bring us to the final, or 70th, week (seven years) when the fulfillment of the atonement occurs.

When was the decree to restore and rebuild Jerusalem issued? The Bible records that Cyrus, the Persian king, delivered the decree. Four decrees are noted during the Persian era concerning the rebuilding of Jerusalem. The first was by Cyrus in 538 BC, the second by Darius I around 516 BC regarding the financing and completion of the temple, and the last two by Artaxerxes: one in 458 BC, sending Ezra back to Jerusalem, and another in 445 BC, when Nehemiah returned to continue building the wall. At first glance, the first decree by Artaxerxes in 458 BC seems to fit the timeline best, as 483 years from that decree brings us to AD 26, close to the start of Jesus's earthly ministry.

However, several factors suggest that the decree by Artaxerxes may not be the intended reference. First, the prophecy to Daniel was given during the time of Cyrus, making it unlikely that God would tell Daniel that 490 years remained for Israel but that the countdown wouldn't begin for another 80 years. Second, it was Cyrus himself who issued a decree around that time, allowing the Jews to return to their homeland to rebuild. In fact, Isaiah prophesied over 200 years earlier that Cyrus would issue this decree. In Isaiah 45:13, God declares of Cyrus, "I will raise up Cyrus in my righteousness: I will make all his ways straight. He will rebuild my city and set my exiles free."

Although many biblical scholars discount Cyrus's decree because it is recorded in Ezra 1 as focusing on the temple rather than the city, the historian Josephus records a letter from Cyrus to other kings stating, "King Cyrus to Sisinnes and Sathrabuzanes, sendeth greeting. I have given leave to as many of the Jews that dwell in my country as please to return to their own country, and to rebuild their city, and to build the temple of God at Jerusalem, on the same place where it was before."[1] This suggests that Cyrus did, indeed, order the rebuilding of the city as well as the temple.

Most Persian records were destroyed during Alexander the Great's invasion, leaving Ptolemy, when constructing his calendar—used to assign the accepted Persian dates—to rely on correlating traditions with lunar eclipses and other archaeological findings. This process resulted in Cyrus's decree being dated approximately 82 years earlier (538 BC) than the timeline that aligns with Jesus's ministry beginning in AD 28. Martin Anstey, an early 20th-century scholar, argued in his work *The Romance of Bible Chronology* that the Ptolemaic calendar was indeed misaligned by 82 years. Anstey's conclusions support Isaiah's prophecy, suggesting that Cyrus's decree marked the start of the 70 weeks prophecy.[2]

Since the publication of Anstey's work, several theologians have supported his dating, including C. I. Scofield. Although Scofield's reference Bible uses the Ptolemaic dates, he later acknowledged the importance

---

1. Josephus, *Antiquities*, III:99.
2. Anstey, *Romance of Bible Chronology*.

of biblical chronology as presented by Anstey: "Whatever confusion has existed at this point has been due to following the Ptolemaic instead of the biblical chronology, as Anstey in his *Romance of Bible Chronology*."[3] G. Campbell Morgan also endorsed Anstey's work, writing the preface for his book. In a 1998 article, Ernest L. Martin wrote:

> Anstey with great dexterity demonstrated that accepting Ptolemy in a dogmatic way was a very precarious and dangerous procedure. Adopting the opinions of this Egyptian astronomer (whose first business was that of being an astrologer) as being the sole authority for understanding the chronology of the Neo-Babylonian and Persian periods was seen by Anstey as a reckless endeavor. Anstey was right! Yet, the whole secular world of the scholars (and sadly, even those who held the Scriptures in esteem) went over to accept Ptolemy's opinions in an infallible sense. Very few even questioned the conclusions of this early astronomer/astrologer. And today, when you look at any historical work or encyclopedia concerning the dates of years within the Neo-Babylonian periods, you will see the opinions of Ptolemy in full evidence and with a rank of infallibility surrounding the dates he indicated.[4]

Thus, our conclusion must be that Daniel's prophesied 70 weeks (490 years) began with Cyrus's decree around 456 BC (rather than 538 BC). The first seven weeks (49 years) conclude with the completion of the temple, and the next 62 weeks (434 years) culminate in the arrival of "the Anointed One" (identified in Daniel 9:25). The final two verses of Daniel 9 describe the last week (the last seven years) of the 70 weeks.

God divides the 70 weeks into three periods: (1) seven weeks to rebuild the temple, (2) 62 weeks to wait for the Messiah, and (3) one final week concerning the Messiah. This final week is the focus of verses 26 and 27 (HCSB):

> After those 62 weeks, the Messiah will be cut off and will have nothing. The people of the coming prince will destroy the city and the sanctuary. The end will come with a flood, and until the end there will be war; desolations are decreed. He will make a firm covenant with many for one week, but in the middle of the week he will put a stop to sacrifice and offering. And the

---

3. Scofield, *What Do the Prophets Say?*, 142.
4. Martin, "Chronological Falsehoods."

abomination of desolation will be on a wing of the temple until the decreed destruction is poured out on the desolator.

These verses describe exactly what Christ accomplished in his ministry. Within the 70th week, Jesus is cut off by his crucifixion—his life is ended, and it appears he has nothing. The next sentence tells us that "the people of the coming prince will destroy the city and the sanctuary." Jesus is that coming prince.

Note that the Messiah is the only person in this entire passage referred to as a prince (in verse 25). So who destroys the city and sanctuary? Ostensibly, the Romans carry out the destruction, but that's not the main point. The true cause lies with the Jews—the people of the Messiah. In Matthew 23:37–38, Jesus laments over Jerusalem, identifying their rejection of God in Christ as the ultimate reason for the temple's desolation.

Back in Daniel 9, verse 27 provides more detail. Jesus established a covenant through his earthly ministry, known as the New Covenant. In the middle of the week (i.e., after three and a half years), the Messiah puts a stop to sacrifice and offering by making the ultimate sin-destroying sacrifice—himself.

Yet, the people continued with their burnt offerings and sacrifices, ignoring the finality of Jesus's sacrifice. Because of these abominations, desolations occurred until the final desolation "is poured out on the desolator." Since the "desolator" refers to the group that caused the desolation, which was the Jewish people of Jerusalem, that final desolation occurred later, as the "until" in the verse implies. The 70 weeks were "decreed about your people" (the Jews) and were meant to "bring the rebellion to an end" and "bring in everlasting righteousness." This scope concluded with Christ's victory three and a half years into the final week and the gospel's outreach to the Gentiles three and a half years later with the conversion of Paul, the "apostle to the Gentiles" (Romans 11:13). The desolation, not part of the 70 weeks, occurred when the Romans ultimately destroyed Jerusalem about 35 years later in AD 70.

THE ISRAEL OF GOD

Jesus is the true Israel, to whom Jacob pointed. Just as Jacob's descendants fulfilled God's promises in illustration, so do Jesus's followers fulfill those promises as the actual recipients of God's promise of restoration. In Galatians, Paul argues that those who have faith in Jesus are the one people of God. This is especially clear in chapter 3, where Paul traces the path from justification through faith to the fulfillment of the promises given to Abraham (verses 6–9) and ultimately to Christ's fulfillment. Paul concludes the chapter with a powerful summary (verses 25–29), dismissing all divisions that could separate us, and declaring that we, who are founded in faith in Christ Jesus, are the promised offspring, the heirs, and, as he later states in Galatians 6:16, the Israel of God.

As believers in Christ Jesus, we are those who strive with God throughout this age. Drawn by the still-cursed flesh and its desires, we often pull against the yoke that binds us in spirit with God. Yet, it is through our union of soul with God that we put to death our physical essence—dying daily, as Paul says in 1 Corinthians 15:31—and wrap ourselves in the resurrected body of our Lord. The Bible portrays this struggle throughout much of the book of Revelation. As we strive with God, we also find divine encouragement that helps us overcome this cursed nature until love ultimately prevails.

13

God Imaged in Marriage

Given in Marriage unto Thee
Oh thou Celestial Host—
Bride of the Father and the Son
Bride of the Holy Ghost.

Other Betrothal shall dissolve—
Wedlock of Will, decay—
Only the Keeper of this Ring
Conquer Mortality—

—Emily Dickinson; from "Given in Marriage unto Thee"

Let us rejoice and be glad
and give him glory!
For the wedding of the Lamb has come,
and his bride has made herself ready.

—Revelation 19:7

The opening poem and verse of this chapter highlight two significant but distinct aspects of the marriage metaphor. Dickinson's poem reflects the spiritual union—our souls joining with God's, fulfilling Jesus's prayer at the Last Supper (John 17:21). While this image is indeed emphasized in Scripture, the more prevalent marriage metaphor is found in Revelation 19. Here, the realization of redemption is depicted as a moment when we essentially become the echo of Adam's declaration, "bone of my bones and flesh of my flesh" (Genesis 2:23). Revelation 19:7 portrays not just a victory, but a triumph specifically of love—marking a return to creation's original purpose. Love, understood as the giving of oneself for the sake of relationship, is embodied in the wedding announcement of Revelation 19. The groom, known as "the Lamb," is glorified for his sacrifice—the offering of his body to redeem the bride, which perfectly portrays the marriage image. As author Mike Mason observes, "In the marriage union, the reflection of divine love is not merely symbolic but sacramental, revealing God's covenantal faithfulness."[1] The bride, representing the faithful of God, has "made herself ready" through trust and patience, submitting her soul—her mind, her will, her emotions, and her spirit all centered on his presence. In return, she fully reflects God, having received the complete revelation of his very essence—the sole source of truth, goodness, and beauty.

This image is deeply significant. Throughout his progressive revelation, God uses marriage as a symbol of relational purpose. It establishes the framework of relationships at creation's inception, underpins the plan of redemption, and culminates in celebration in the renewed heavens and earth of the age to come. Scripture consistently employs the husband-wife relationship to illustrate essential qualities necessary for living within the kingdom community, particularly in the dynamics between God and Israel and between Christ and those who accept his redemptive revelation. But the story begins with Adam and Eve, where God first introduces the husband-wife relationship. So, let's start by examining their story.

MARRIAGE IMPLICATIONS IN ADAM AND EVE'S STORY

"God created [adam] in his own image" (Genesis 1:27). The word "adam" is Hebrew for human—not specifically male, though the word is masculine in gender. Genesis 1:27 poetically elaborates, stating that God "created him in the image of God; he created them male and female" (HCSB). The shift from "him" to "them" is significant, establishing that both male and female are one human race, albeit with distinct differences. Genesis 5:1–2 reinforces this connection: "On the day that God created [adam], he made

---

1. Mason, *Mystery of Marriage*, 119.

him in the likeness of God; he created them male and female" (HCSB). The change in pronouns from "him" to "them" in both Genesis 1:27 and 5:2 emphasizes that human beings are created in God's image, just as God shifts from "us" and "our" in Genesis 1:26 to "he" and "his" in Genesis 1:27. These singular and plural pronoun changes highlight the structural likeness between God and humankind. God has a single essence—his infinite truth, goodness, and beauty; humanity shares a singular essence—physicality, the matter and energy of all creation. God exists as multiple persons (the three of the Trinity); similarly, humankind exists as multiple persons (each individual soul, encompassing the psyche and spirit).[2]

This image-bearing foundation supports the Genesis 2 account of our first parents' relationship, which is not just a love story about two hearts and minds joining, but also a formative story about the whole of humanity bearing God's image—our unified essence of physicality and our multiplicity of souls.

The story begins with the creation of the *adam* from the dust of the ground (Genesis 2:7). It's noteworthy how the emphasis on formation "from the ground" recurs, as seen in Genesis 2:9: "The Lord God caused to grow *out of the ground*" all the trees of the garden, and Genesis 2:19: "So the Lord God formed *out of the ground*" every living creature. "The ground," both here in Genesis 2 and in the curse of Genesis 3, symbolizes all of physical creation—the essence of humankind.

In verse 18, God reveals that it isn't good—thus, it wasn't his intent—for the *adam* to be alone. Yet, a suitable partner—another image bearer—cannot be found among the rest of God's creation. The domains of sky, sea, and land, with their inhabitants of birds, fish, and animals, do not offer the multiplicity of soul (or personhood) that matches the *adam*'s capacity for comprehension (using conceptual intelligence, conscious morality, and critical aesthetic), for concurrence (employing concluding faith and continuing hope), and for communication (offering communal love). So, God parades the animals before the *adam*, helping him realize his solitary condition as the sole human at that time.

This solitude deeply affects the *adam*. Humans were made for relationship because we are images of God, who exists within the community of the Trinity; therefore, our reflection should also exist in, and long for, community. God then fashions a partner for the *adam*, but notice the method. God doesn't scoop out more earth to create another human

---

2. See the related discussion of human essence in the introduction to this book and touched on briefly in chapters 5, 6, and 12.)

(although he could have). Instead, teaching an important lesson, God creates another from the *adam*'s own body. The Hebrew hints at more than just a rib, as often believed—the Hebrew text indicates that God took from the *adam*'s side, essentially dividing the *adam* from one into two. Suddenly, we have male and female, both emerging from what had formerly been a single human, likely without a specific male or female identity before this act.[3]

A crop of "why" questions emerges from this account of human creation. Foremost among them is why, if soul companionship was the goal, didn't God simply create two similar *adams*—why create a male and a female instead? The easy but insufficient answer is that this allowed for reproduction through normal biological means. But it didn't have to be that way. God could have designed humans so that any individual could give birth. Thus, the "why" question extends beyond reproduction: why did God create males and females if his primary concern was a community of soul companions?

I believe the Bible's progressive revelation shows that God intends human community to mirror the Trinitarian community. As discussed in chapter 2, Father, Son, and Spirit give of themselves for the benefit of their relationship. The Father, as I suggested, gives of himself as the lens through which both Son and Spirit access the Truth of their shared essence. The Son provides the Father and Spirit with perfect access to the Goodness of their shared essence. And the Spirit grants perfect access to the others regarding Beauty. Each person gives according to his abilities to support the vulnerabilities of the others.

This general description of Trinitarian interaction (giving abilities to support the vulnerabilities of others) serves as God's instruction for humanity, from the days of Old Testament Israel through the teachings of Peter, Paul, and Jesus. Israel's leaders are criticized for failing to relieve the poor (Proverbs 28:27; Amos 5:11–12; Isaiah 1:17). Peter urges us to use our gifts to serve others (1 Peter 4:10). Hebrews encourages us not to neglect doing good and sharing what we have (Hebrews 13:16). And Paul, most notably, emphasizes using our gifts in love (1 Corinthians 12–13). His letter to the Ephesians culminates in chapter 5, urging us to submit to one another in reverence for Christ (Ephesians 5:21). This submission, giving, and sharing is how we support the love relationship community,

---

3. This understanding may be new to many a contemporary American Christian churchgoer, but it originated back in Hebrew scholarship hundreds (technically, thousands) of years ago.

ensuring that no one lacks—so that we may be "perfect [complete], therefore, as [our] heavenly Father is perfect" (Matthew 5:48). In the parables of the talents and the sheep and the goats in Matthew 25, Jesus reiterates his Sermon on the Mount message to care for one another. This message is central to God's instruction for us. Because of its importance for kingdom life, God provided a model to help us understand love relationships and consistently remind us of how they work: he gave us the marriage image.

For this marriage image, God created two sexes: male and female. He made them different precisely to highlight the relational principle of giving one's abilities to meet the other's vulnerabilities. These differences are most evident in the body—the generally larger bone structure and muscular system of males and the gestational uniqueness of females. These attributes are intended as abilities that each may use in serving the other.

When God presents Eve to Adam after their division, we can imagine Adam's breath being taken away as he exclaims, "At last! Bone of my bone and flesh of my flesh!" (Genesis 2:23, HCSB). But notice something in that exclamation that may initially seem unrelated to the passage. God had paraded all the animals before the *adam* to demonstrate their inadequacy as a human partner, which we typically understand as their inability to relate in mind and heart. Yet, when Adam sees Eve, his awe is not expressed as "At last! Mind of my mind and heart of my heart!" While Adam undoubtedly recognized the cognitive relationship they would share, he marvels that, though now two individuals, they are united in physical essence, fitting together—even in the imagery of the sexual union, which is immediately confirmed in the next verse regarding the "one flesh" (sexual) rejoining.

The sexual aspect of this imagery is crucial, but it cannot be separated from the broader relational unity Adam recognized in Eve. Humans and animals share the same physical essence—this universe of matter and energy—and animals also engage in sexual activity. However, Adam's exclamation transcends the mere physicality of sex. It isn't solely about the oneness of essence he shares with Eve, nor is it only about their similar cognitive abilities. Rather, it celebrates the profound unity of their whole being—mind, heart, and body. Their sexual union, unlike that of animals, is an act of deep communion, a shared giving of self that brings their oneness into tangible expression. This union satisfies not just their intellect and emotions but their entire physical essence as image-bearers of God. In their sexual relationship, Adam and Eve experience a "one flesh" unity that uniquely embodies the relational images found in the creation story:

God's Trinitarian love, God's (and Christ's) covenant relationship with us, and the dynamic interplay of abilities and vulnerabilities in human relationships. Together, these elements make their union a reflection of divine harmony, something no animal could ever achieve.

FAITHFULNESS SHOWN IN SEXUAL INTIMACY

God uses the image of marriage—particularly the faithfulness expressed through sexual intimacy—to describe his relationship with Israel in the Old Testament, especially in the context of Israel's unfaithfulness. Throughout Jeremiah, Ezekiel, and Hosea, God laments Israel's adultery, highlighting the breakdown of the God-with-human relational embrace, which is also the basis for relationship among the members of the kingdom-of-God community.

The violation of this image occurs not only through the lack of committed relationships but also by disregarding the intended male-and-female union in marriage. In Romans 1:26–27, Paul describes the abandonment of "natural sexual relations" as a consequence of the sexual impurity and bodily degradation mentioned earlier in 1:24–25. Here, "natural" refers not to what feels natural to an individual, but rather to the design God intended for his image-bearers. Additionally, translating verse 21 closer to the Greek's meaning, we'd conclude with the KJV on "natural use" (meaning, natural sexual use). This translation moves us away from mere feelings to design, and the natural design for use, as revealed in Genesis 2, is for male-female sexual intimacy.

Jesus emphasizes the importance of this sexual imagery within marriage. In Matthew 19, some Pharisees attempt to trap Jesus with a legal question: is it lawful for a man to divorce his wife for any reason? Their goal is to catch Jesus in a contradiction—if he says yes, they can counter with passages against divorce; if he says no, they'll reference the certificate of divorce Moses permitted.

Jesus's response upholds the sanctity of the marriage image. He begins by stating that God made them male and female (Matthew 19:4). Why does he start a discussion on marriage and divorce with the fact that there are two sexes? Jesus does this to emphasize that marriage should be understood not as a matter of personal feeling but as a reflection of the divine image God intended. He recounts the Genesis account of male and female becoming one, not merely as a history lesson, but as a divine command. Jesus highlights this image by explaining that male and female will unite as one flesh (Matthew 19:5). Only after establishing this foundation does he advocate for the commitment to remain together without separation (Matthew 19:6), emphasizing that this commitment is rooted in the one flesh—the physical essence of male-female union through sexual intercourse.

As expected, the Pharisees, dissatisfied with his answer, quickly point out that Moses allowed divorce. Jesus acknowledges this but explains that Moses permitted it only because of the hardness of their hearts (Matthew 19:8)—because they failed to live within marriage according to God's intention of mutual self-giving in body, mind, and heart. He then concludes by stating, "Anyone who divorces his wife, except for sexual immorality, and marries another woman commits adultery" (Matthew 19:9).

To truly understand Jesus's teaching, it's essential to view marriage as a symbolic relationship, reflecting both divine connection within the Trinity and human relationships. Jesus doesn't condone staying in situations of mistreatment simply because sexual fidelity remains intact, nor does he insist on enduring hostility or contempt as long as there is no sexual betrayal. Rather, his focus is on discouraging impulsive, reactionary responses to life's hardships from damaging the marriage bond, which serves as a model of divine unity and community harmony. By undermining relational loyalty, we risk losing sight of the love that defines God's purpose and our own existence. Jesus calls for a commitment to repair and reconciliation, emphasizing that the core of a marriage—the fidelity symbolized by sexual unity—defines when a bond might reach a point beyond restoration.

His disciples are astonished, essentially asking, "Is marriage really that important?" The entire Bible responds with a resounding "Yes! Absolutely!" Marriage is an image that cannot be treated lightly.

The Old Testament provides numerous examples of Israel's unfaithfulness, likened to the unfaithfulness of a wife. In the New Testament, we see the restoration of this brokenness through a new covenant and a new hope. Jesus, the uniquely born God as human ("only begotten"), brings his ability to provide for our vulnerabilities. He presents himself as a groom to his bride, giving of himself to achieve redemption: "Christ loved the church and gave himself up for her to make her holy, cleansing her by the washing with water through the word, and to present her to himself as a radiant church, without stain or wrinkle or any other blemish, but holy and blameless. In this same way, husbands ought to love their wives as their own bodies" (Ephesians 5:25b–28a). Notice the connection Paul makes between Christ's sacrificial act and the love for a wife's body. Harold Hoehner underscores this, observing that "the love of Christ for the church serves as the model for all marriages, showing a love that is sacrificial and redemptive."[4] Redemption is not just about the forgiveness of sin; it is also about rescuing the essence—the body—from death.

Wives, too, are called to "submit yourselves to your own husbands as you do to the Lord. For the husband is the head [the source of bodily protection in the marriage image] of the wife as Christ is the head [the source of bodily protection] of the church, his body, of which he is the Savior" (Ephesians 5:22–23).

The culmination of all relationships—between humans, between humans and God, and within the Godhead—is the perfection of those relationships in love. Love is "the giving of self for the benefit of relationship." The Bible uses the imagery of marriage—the soul commitment of a man and a woman united into one body through sexual union—to remind us that true satisfaction and contentment, perfect peace, can be found only in this oneness of heart and mind with one another and with God.

"For we were all baptized by one Spirit so as to form one body—whether Jews or Gentiles, slave or free, male or female [black or white, republican or democrat, reformed or kinship]—and we were all given the one Spirit to drink" (1 Corinthians 12:13).

---

4. Hoehner, *Ephesians*, 742.

14

God Imaged in Zion

The swallow stopt as he hunted the bee,
The snake slipt under a spray,
The hawk stood with the down on his beak
And stared, with his foot on the prey
And the nightingale thought, "I have sung many songs,
But never a one so gay,"
For he sings of what the world will be
When the years have died away.

—Alfred, Lord Tennyson; from "The Poet's Song"

I have installed my king on Zion,
my holy mountain.

—Psalm 2:6

Zion is a word many Christians know and sing about, yet its meaning often remains unclear. What does God intend for us to recognize in Zion? Our first encounter with it comes in 2 Samuel 5, where David, after becoming king of all Israel, captures the small city of Jebus, perched on a rocky outcrop rising steeply from the surrounding valleys. David may have renamed the city Jerusalem (meaning "city of peace"), or that name could have predated the Jebusites. Israel, as a nation, also referred to it as the city of David, as he made it his capital. The name Zion, meaning "fortress," technically referred to the mountain on which David's city stood. This might lead us to wonder if Zion should be considered separate from the city—as merely its mountain or stronghold. However, although it could be interpreted that way (finding lessons of trust in God as our foundation), the Bible does not exclusively support this view. Instead, I believe the references to Zion bind the city and its mountain foundation together, making it difficult to separate the two. This interpretation aligns with its first biblical mention: "Yet David did capture the stronghold of Zion, that is, the city of David" (2 Samuel 5:7).

Linking the city to its foundation metaphorically connects activity to its purpose. For example, Hebrews 11:10 reinforces this idea by highlighting Abraham's faithfulness to God's call: he sought not just a piece of land, but a "city with foundations, whose architect and builder is God." This city in Hebrews emphasizes a spiritual reality—a representation of God's people living in communion with him. While Abraham may have been journeying toward a new physical land with cities to build, his true motivation was a deep relationship with God. Hebrews 12:22 further connects the physical location with an eternal purpose: "But you have come to Mount Zion, to the city of the living God." Biblical scholar T. Desmond Alexander captures this connection, observing that "Zion represents not only a physical location but the spiritual home of God's people—a symbol of divine protection, covenant relationship, and ultimate peace."[1]

Even though some biblical references shift between a figurative mountain fortress and the actual foundation of Jerusalem, the spiritual reality links Zion to the city of God, which is the New Jerusalem. This New Jerusalem represents all of God's people, from the Old Testament believers to the New Covenant believers resting in the embrace of Jesus. Given these layers of meaning, it's understandable that the intent behind Zion may sometimes seem blurred.

The old city of Jerusalem, as it was when David first captured it, stood on a ridge bordered by the Hinnom valley to the south, the Kidron valley to the east, and a lesser Tyropoeon valley to the west. By the time of Christ, Jerusalem had expanded westward through the Tyropoeon valley and up the western ridge, which became known as "upper Jerusalem," where Caiaphas's house and the upper room of the Last Supper were located.

---

1. Alexander, *City of God*, 123.

At the top of the hill of old Jerusalem was the peak of Zion, followed immediately along the ridge to the north by the peak of Moriah. Moriah was where Abraham was prepared to sacrifice Isaac before God intervened, and it was also where Solomon's temple was built. The expansion of the second temple courtyard during Herod the Great's reign connected these twin peaks into one temple mount. Thus, the slope on which Jerusalem was originally built was the southern slope of Mount Zion.[2]

The connection between the mount and the city directly leads to the figurative meaning of Zion. Just as no city exists without its foundation, so too the people of God (represented by the city) cannot exist without their purpose—the Zion purpose—supporting them. Returning to Hebrews with this idea in mind, we see Abraham's hope in the city tied securely to the foundation "whose architect and builder is God." Here, Zion's foundation is not God himself; rather, it is a foundation crafted by God.

So, what is it that supports God's people (the city of God) in their relationship with him? It is the New Covenant relationship that forms the basis of our dwelling with him. Jesus secured this relationship through the redemption won by his atoning work. The Old Testament is filled with symbolism of God as rock (Psalm 95:1), mountain (Psalm 24:3), and fortress (Psalm 91:2)—and in combination (Psalm 31:2). Yet, the Zion image specifically identifies the covenant relationship as the support that enables us to live with God.

ISAIAH'S IMAGING FOCUS

We know God didn't breathe out Scripture merely for us to use as a reference for the inspirational and motivational posters we hang in our offices. God gave us stories, poetry, examples, and philosophy woven together to teach us about the kingdom of heaven, which may seem upside-down to our distorted view but is actually right-side up. This broken world, which often feels normal and comfortable, is what's truly upside-down. The concepts and imagery we've been discussing are deeply integrated with biblical instruction, so a cursory skim does little to correct our thinking.

---

2. Josephus identified the mount just to the west of the old city of David as Mt. Zion and many (though not the majority) since then have considered it to be the Mt. Zion of biblical reference. However, that mount (upon which "upper" Jerusalem was built) would have been outside the ancient city, making it doubtful as Zion connected with Jerusalem. Further, Psalm 48 mentions Zion being on the north side of Jerusalem, which would not match that western hill.

We need to immerse ourselves in it, cleanse our minds with its purifying stream, and soak in its healing balm. Only then does the fog lift, revealing the crooked made straight.

Isaiah engages the Zion metaphor extensively. The book begins with an old covenant address (chapters 1 through 39) and then shifts to a new covenant context (chapters 40 through 66). The old covenant portion speaks of failure and enslavement, while the new covenant section highlights rescue and glory.

Chapter 40 marks this transition with the voice of one we recognize as John the Baptist, crying out in the wilderness to prepare the way of the Lord (Isaiah 40:3 and John 1:23). Part of this message insists, "The glory of the Lord will appear, and all humanity together will see it" (Isaiah 40:5). Glory is the manifestation of worth, so the glory of the Lord is the manifestation of his worth—his essence of truth, goodness, and beauty. Since this wilderness voice is linked to John the Baptist's message, the manifestation of glory isn't postponed until Christ's second coming. Rather, Christ's first advent reveals the fullness of God, as Paul affirms in Colossians 2:9: "For the entire fullness of God's nature dwells bodily in Christ."

Isaiah 40 breathes hope into the transition from enslavement to rescue, emphasizing that God himself will provide the way. Some readers might miss the profundity of this passage, focusing only on the thrill of God's revealed glory and the contrast between God's greatness and human frailty. But the text centers on God's motivation and fulfillment in rescue. Verses 6 through 8 prepare us for this: humanity is like grass and flowers that wither and fade, but the word of God remains forever. What is this "word of God" that endures?

We shouldn't interpret this passage as a competition, where humans fade while God lasts forever. That's not the point. The passage explores purpose and resolution. Humanity withers and fades like grass, but the text seems to ask whether, left to itself, humanity's fading would threaten God's covenant of everlasting love. "But no!" the preparatory voice declares, "God's purpose, God's covenant, God's word remains forever!" He will rescue the withering grass and accomplish the restoration of love. This message is proclaimed in the new covenant portion of Isaiah.

How does God accomplish this purpose? How does he rescue? How does he reclaim the cursed essence of humanity from its chosen separation? God accomplishes this by becoming human in Jesus, putting the flesh to death and reclaiming it from death's separation to life without curse. In doing so, Jesus offers the truth, goodness, and beauty of God through redemption to all humanity. Those who renounce the idolatry of their own essence and set their affection on God and his essence become children of God, part of the city of God, resting on the foundation of the redemptive covenant won by Christ. This unity—humanity in communion with God through Christ's redemption—is the Zion image.

Isaiah 49:14–26 links the Zion name to this image. Verse 14 personifies the covenant relationship (Zion), questioning whether God has abandoned it. The previous chapter (especially verses 19 and 22) explains the reason for this doubt: because of Jacob's (Israel's) evil, God's old covenant would end. So Zion wonders if the end of the relationship with physical Jacob means the end of God's relationship with humanity. But God answers in Isaiah 49:15–16, assuring that he will not forget his purpose. He likens himself to a mother who could never forget her child. God has inscribed his purpose on his hands, signifying that every action he takes is directed toward fulfilling his Zion covenant.

The thought continues: Zion feels deprived of children, yet suddenly they abound. They multiply so much that Zion begins to wonder who "fathered" them. The answer becomes clear—God, in his plan, has provided.

From verse 22 onward, God emphasizes that these children are not only the faithful remnant of Judah, but also come from the nations (Isaiah 49:22), from kings and queens (Isaiah 49:23), and even from fearsome captors (Isaiah 49:24–25).

ZION SHINES WITH GOD'S GLORY

Isaiah's presentation of Zion gains additional depth in chapters 60 through 62. In these chapters, particularly in 60 and 62, God speaks to Zion not as synonymous with the Jews but as a personification of his covenant relationship with humanity. Zion represents God's Immanuel ("God with us") purpose. When we read about Zion being bereft of children, we should understand it as a threat to God's covenant purpose. Conversely, when Zion is depicted as receiving sons and daughters, we should see this as the fulfillment of that covenant. These chapters illustrate Zion's restoration, depicted as receiving God's glory in chapter 60, as the object of God's Messiah rescue in chapter 61, and as the focus of righteous pursuit in chapter 62.

Chapter 60 begins with a call to Zion to arise and shine. The earth had been cloaked in darkness by sin and the curse, but God promises light. It's important to remember that God is speaking of (and to) Zion—his covenant purpose for an everlasting love relationship with his created image-bearers. Therefore, the images of darkness and light do not refer to specific good or bad deeds. Darkness represents the absence of relationship, while light symbolizes covenant relationship.

As God calls Zion to rise and shine, the shining symbolizes the gathering of people from around the world into a relationship with God—the central theme of the chapter. God confidently declares the coming fulfillment of his Zion purpose, assuring that he will take the necessary steps to make it happen, though he does not yet explain how.

Zion gains sons and daughters during this age of the kingdom of heaven, even as the corrupted world continues to exist. As verse 3 reveals, all the world may approach the light. God specifically mentions nations (or people groups) rather than individuals, emphasizing that the gathering will come from all over the world, not just from Israel. In verse 4, Zion sees her children as the fulfillment of God's original creation purpose—now the restoration purpose—of image-bearers in an everlasting relationship.

Verses 6 and 7 further verify this covenant fulfillment by mentioning five people groups, the same ones listed in Genesis 25 as descendants of Abraham. Midian was Abraham's son by Keturah, and Ephah was Midian's son. Sheba's father was a grandson of Abraham by Keturah. Kedar and Nebaioth were sons of Ishmael, Abraham's son by Hagar. By naming these groups, God draws a contrast between Jacob's line (the covenant nation of God) and Abraham's other descendants. Remember, God is speaking to Zion—the covenant purpose itself—not to the Jews. If he were speaking to the Jews, these other nations would be offering gifts to the Jews while remaining outside the covenant people of God. Instead, the gifts and offerings (symbolizing children) brought by these other nations are given to the covenant relationship. Verses 8 and 9 extend this covenant-fulfilling activity even beyond the non-Israelite descendants of Abraham to the farthest reaches of the world. The mention of islands denotes distant lands. Tarshish, in Spain, was at the far end of the Mediterranean world. Yet God draws all these people groups fully and purposefully, like "clouds" and "doves," to fulfill the covenant purpose.

Chapter 60 also includes additional insights worth considering. In verse 10, God says he struck "you" in his wrath—not Israel or Judah, as if he were speaking of specific national punishment. The "you" refers to Zion, his everlasting relationship purpose, indicating that a significant threat had emerged. Isaiah often discusses God's wrath, especially in chapters 4, 5, and 8, where God's wrath is expressed by allowing evildoers to follow their own path. In Jeremiah 7:20, God says, "Look, my anger—my burning wrath—is about to be poured out on this place." But verse 29 reveals that God's wrath is expressed as his uncoerced allowance for those who choose to be left to their own selfish concerns. Psalm 78:59–60 supports this idea, using the Hebrew word *natas* (to let alone) to describe God's action. The Bible teaches that God's wrath is his letting go of rebels and rejecters, allowing them to follow their own way.

When Adam and Eve brought sin into the world, cursing their essence, God had to let them go their way, which threatened his Zion purpose. He had to do this because a relationship with God must be founded on his truth, goodness, and beauty. Isaiah 60:10 rightly describes God's release of his image-bearers from Zion's purpose as striking it in wrath, though no physical weapon is implied. God's wrath—his removal of truth, goodness, and beauty—results in darkness and death. However, as verse 10 continues, God's plan includes reconnection to his Zion purpose through mercy and favor. Again, he does not yet explain how, but he declares that it will happen.

In verse 11, God explains that Zion's gates will always be open. This idea should not be confused with God's desire for a relationship with those who, beyond hope, refuse him—as if he leaves the gates open just in case. That's not the point of this chapter, which describes Zion's realization. Verses 11 and 12 should be read together. The ever-open gates symbolize the ongoing nature of God's covenant embrace in relationship with those who have come—the everlasting aspect of the Zion image. Verse 12 presents a sobering truth: the nation or kingdom that does not embrace the Zion purpose "will perish; it will be utterly ruined." Though this stark point might seem out of place amid the rejoicing over Zion's fulfillment, it serves to contrast the blessing of community and relational giving with the self-centeredness of those who reject God.

Verse 16 emphasizes that God himself is the savior and redeemer. The "Mighty One of Jacob" belongs to Jacob not only because he watches over him, but also because he comes from Jacob in the necessary human condition required for redemption.

The chapter's final verses (60:19–22) again shine a light on God's covenant purpose. Verse 19 emphasizes that God, rather than the sun and moon, will be the source of light. We should be careful not to interpret this literally. The sun and moon will not disappear; that's not the point.

The passage assumes the same representation of light and dark as it did at the chapter's beginning. God and his truth, goodness, and beauty are the foundation of the Zion purpose and community. The darkened world searched for these qualities within its own physical essence (symbolized here by the sun and moon), but true fulfillment comes only from God.

As chapter 60 closes, there is a shift in perspective. Up to this point, we've been reading about the glory of the Zion purpose that will come to pass. But how? Who will bring it about? God promises at the chapter's end, "I am Yahweh; I will accomplish it quickly in its time."

GOD RESCUES FOR THE ZION PURPOSE

Isaiah 61 overflows with the purpose of Zion. Jesus chose to read the beginning of this chapter to introduce his ministry in Luke 4:16-21, intrinsically linking his mission with the Zion purpose. In that passage, Jesus enters a synagogue in Nazareth and reads aloud Isaiah 61:1-2a. He then tells the listeners that he fulfills this prophecy, declaring himself to be the Anointed One—the Messiah. As N.T. Wright observes, "Jesus, by announcing the 'year of the Lord's favor,' situates Zion's redemption within his mission—bridging the promises of the old covenant with the fulfillment in his life and work."[3] However, as many commentators note, Jesus stops reading in the middle of verse 2. The Messiah brings good news, healing, and liberty, but he does not proclaim "the day of God's vengeance" at that time. As Paul later teaches, this condemnation will come at Christ's second advent (2 Thessalonians 1:5-10).

The Messiah's message in Isaiah 61 is directed at those who are poor and mournful. Appropriately, in the first two beatitudes, Jesus promises comfort and kingdom blessings to the poor in spirit and those who mourn. These concepts are closely tied to the Zion image. The poor in spirit and the mourners are not merely those who are unfortunate in a harsh, competitive world. These captives are broken-hearted because they recognize that truth, goodness, and beauty come only from God, and they lament their outcast state caused by the curse. They mourn as those without hope. To them, the Messiah proclaims beauty instead of ashes, oil of joy instead of mourning, and garments of praise instead of a spirit of despair. These gifts lead to righteousness, which is the Messiah's mission—to redeem

---

3. Wright, *Victory of God*, 191.

humanity from the brokenness of the Covenant of Life and restore them to covenant faithfulness, which defines righteousness.

The central portion of Isaiah 61 may seem confusing at first. It describes not a literal event but rather a union of purpose between Jews and Gentiles, addressing the call for unity found in Paul's letter to the Ephesians. Where hostility once prevailed, Zion now finds cooperation. Where disgrace and shame were once imposed, Zion now experiences abundant joy. The Messiah fulfills the old priestly role assigned at Sinai, drawing the world to God.

Verses 8 and 9 further emphasize the Zion purpose. Justice, in this context, can be defined as living in covenant faithfulness—a righteousness rooted in God's TGB. God loves justice. Broken justice can be rectified in only two ways: either God forgives the covenant breaker who repents and seeks to return to covenant faithfulness, or God allows the unrepentant covenant breaker to separate from the covenant community. However, forgiveness for the repentant can be fully realized only when their status is changed from cursed idol worshipper to redeemed inheritor of the Messiah's curse-free essence. The chapter concludes with this righteous image, achieved through the Messiah's work and made possible by God's enabling power.

THE ZION-PURPOSE RESTORER

In Isaiah 60, we caught a glimpse of Zion's glory. In Isaiah 61, we learned that Zion would be secured by God's design through his Messiah. Now, in Isaiah 62, God exhorts those who cherish the vision of Zion to actively pursue it. The chapter opens with the Messiah speaking, expressing his desire to see Zion shine, echoing the theme that began in chapter 60. Once again, he addresses the Zion purpose. Understanding the second-person "you" in this chapter as referring to the Jews themselves can lead to confusion. For instance, when God speaks of Zion marrying and says, "Your sons will marry you," it would be incoherent if "you" referred to the Jews, implying their sons would marry them. Instead, "your sons will marry you" suggests that the Jews will embrace the Zion image, symbolizing union with God. Only by recognizing Zion as representing God's covenant purpose can we make sense of this passage.

Verses 6 and 7 offer an exciting depth of hope. God appoints watchmen for Zion, who are undoubtedly us—Christ's "righteous trees" (Isaiah

61:3)—the children of Zion who, as Paul described, look forward to our blessed hope of final and ultimate relationship with God (Titus 2:11–14).

In verses 8 and 9, the speaker seamlessly shifts from the Messiah to God the Restorer. The chapter concludes with a promise of Zion's coming salvation, symbolized by the gift of people—children fulfilling the Covenant of Life's hope for an everlasting relationship with God and among his people.

The final three verses of this chapter introduce another familiar image: the building of a highway. This road, this bridge, represents the path by which people return to a right relationship with God. This imagery first appears in Isaiah 11:16, reappears in Isaiah 35:8, and is seen again in Isaiah 40:3 and Isaiah 57:14, where God urges, "Build it up, build it up." All these references to the highway find their fulfillment in John the Baptist's message of preparing "a straight highway for our God." Notably, this fulfillment begins with John the Baptist, indicating that Isaiah's prophecies regarding Zion's realization find their fulfillment in Christ's first advent. The road that leads nations to Zion exists now in this interadvental age. While we eagerly anticipate Zion's full beauty when sin, evil, and death are forever abolished, we already experience its fulfillment through Christ's work and God's forgiveness in our spirits.

15

God Imaged in Suffering

The "Man of Sorrows" we adore,
And own His sufferings real;
But suffered He as God before;
For God can sorrow feel.

—Joseph Horatio Chant; from "A Suffering God"

Surely he took up our pain and bore our suffering.
—Isaiah 53:4a

Once a central matter of debate, the question of whether God suffers now flickers only occasionally among other theological discussions. The long-standing belief, held for nearly two thousand years, that God is impassible has largely been replaced over the past century. Theologians like Barth, Moltmann, Pannenberg, Torrance, and others argue that God indeed experiences emotions—ranging from joy to grief—and therefore must also experience suffering. I agree with this view. Moltmann wrote, "Were God incapable of suffering in any respect, and therefore in an absolute sense, then he would also be incapable of love."[1] This statement captures the foundational understanding of why God suffers: because God loves—or more precisely, because God loves us.

---

1. Moltmann, *The Crucified God*, 230.

We must distinguish between God's love for us and the broader fact that God loves. The Trinity has always shared love among its members without suffering. However, love directed toward a hoped-for relationship with free-will creatures carries risk, most significantly, the risk of rejection. In our case, that risk was compounded into a curse—a curse brought about by humanity's worship of the created rather than the Creator, enslaving us to our own lusts. This leaves God vulnerable, and in that vulnerability—in the realization of the falseness, badness, and ugliness chosen by his beloved—grief abounds. But this chapter is not solely about God's suffering; it also seeks to connect our suffering with his, to understand it as a reflection of his image. How, then, do we image God in suffering?

GOD DEMONSTRATING HIS RIGHTEOUSNESS

It may seem paradoxical to speak of us imaging God in suffering. Isn't God's suffering caused by us? Yes, but first, we must understand the nature of this suffering; after all, there are various kinds of suffering, all of which are caused by the curse on our physical creation. The curse on our essence distorts our attention from truth, goodness, and beauty, redirecting it toward self-interest. Although we were created with a shared essence, the curse prompts us to reject our relational unity, leading to individual gain at the expense of others and resulting in various forms of suffering. All specific sorrows stem from our distancing ourselves from the source of TGB.

God has not abandoned us, yet he cannot fully engage with us because of our cursed state. The result of this human-imposed distancing is evident in our experience with all that is not TGB—natural disasters, diseases, and other destructive forces that bombard human life. These forms of violence cause physical suffering.

In addition to natural and accidental suffering, there is suffering intentionally inflicted by humans on one another. From wars to personal conflicts, people often harm others out of selfish motives, leading to further suffering. Even unintended consequences, such as a drug addict's pursuit of a high, can result in temporary or permanent harm.

While all this physical suffering results from the curse and our distancing from God, we find in God a different kind of suffering, one that is deeply personal. Though caused by the curse, God's suffering is that of a parent grieving over lost children. Since God is the source of TGB, separation from him, in the ultimate sense, is the absolute absence of any TGB. And if God, the sustainer of all, is absent, nothing can exist. The Bible describes this as destruction—the end of life in every sense. Yet, the continued existence of the world and universe argues that, despite the curse, God continues to involve himself—continues to love—even amid our broken affection. He does so because he is determined to rescue us if possible and realize his hoped-for love relationship.

God's continued love for cursed creatures may seem to challenge his righteousness. How can he maintain a spotless reputation while interacting with a cursed creation that refuses to acknowledge his TGB? Ultimately, the answer is that God cannot deny himself. He cannot remain in partnership with the antithesis of TGB if it were to continue perpetually. But as we discussed in chapter 5, God can and does continue to love (and therefore, continue to sustain) as long as there is a possibility of life—a possibility of a love relationship with his image bearers.

God is justified in sustaining a cursed creation because his purpose is love. He has sustained creation since the fall so that, through Christ, he could rescue it, destroying the curse with the triumph of love. Paul emphasizes this justification in Romans 3:25–26, HCSB: "God presented [Christ] as a propitiation, through faith in His blood, to demonstrate His righteousness, because in His restraint God passed over the sins previously committed. God presented him to demonstrate His righteousness at the present time, so that He would be righteous and declare righteous the one who has faith in Jesus."

Thus, God continues to sustain creation solely for the sake of love. He gives of himself for the hoped-for relationship he can enjoy with us if we repent of our cursed state and rely on him for rescue. However, and this brings us back to our discussion, by sustaining what is cursed, God suffers in grief. He suffers because of the tragedy of his image bearers' fall; he suffers because of the conflicts and catastrophes they endure in their selfish pursuits; he suffers because of those who will not, despite every opportunity, embrace his offered TGB. That suffering—God's grief over his fallen image bearers, created for love—originates in his loving TGB essence. We reflect that suffering only when we recognize the continued curse after receiving his rescue, releasing our dependency on our essence in favor of basing our lives on his.

SUFFERING FOR CHRIST

Of course, our suffering isn't limited to grief over broken relationships; we also bear it in our very essence—and in this, we image him as well. He took on flesh like ours, sharing in our common essence, and bore the physical suffering inflicted on him by those driven by the curse against God's ideal.

Let's pause to consider this further. God entering our world as a human meant that he had to take on the curse—not the guilt of sin, but our physical essence, cursed as a result of Adam's transgression. He had to inhabit cursed flesh so that he could put it to death and redeem it, bringing it to newness of life, free from the curse. The redemption he achieved in his own body is the firstfruits of redemption for all creation. "Christ has indeed been raised from the dead, the firstfruits of those who have fallen asleep" (1 Corinthians 15:20). And in that resurrection, we find hope: "For as in Adam all die, so in Christ all will be made alive. But each in turn: Christ, the firstfruits; then, when he comes, those who belong to him" (1 Corinthians 15:22–23).[2]

Paul speaks directly about Jesus's cursed body in Romans 8:3, saying, "[God] condemned sin in the flesh by sending his own Son *in the likeness of sinful flesh* as a sin offering. And so he condemned sin in the flesh." (Emphasis added.) The phrase "in the likeness of sinful flesh" is translated in the HCSB as "in flesh like ours under sin's domain." This "likeness" or "like ours" indicates sameness, as the word is used in Romans 6:5: "For if we have been united with him in a death *like* his, we will certainly also be united with him in a resurrection *like* his." Paul's point is that our bodies' experience of physical death mirrors Jesus's—in other words, not merely "similar to but somehow different" but rather "just the same as."

Returning to our discussion, Jesus endured the mental and emotional abuse of rejection alongside the physical abuse inflicted by those focused on the curse. This image of God is the one we, who know him and

---

2. As discussed in chapter 8, the "all" in this passage does not refer to every individual person, as Universalists often assert. Instead, the structure links the "all" from Adam's particular case to Christ's resurrection. Paul is not merely referencing Adam's physical death at the end of his life. Rather, the connection points to the curse Adam introduced, which led to estrangement from God for "all" physical creation. Christ's mission was to put to death that cursed physical creation so that "all" of it could be redeemed—of which his body is the firstfruits. By the end of verse 23, the focus shifts to those individuals who will inherit the renewed physical creation "when he comes," specifically limiting it to "those who belong to him."

live according to his redemption, take on. God promises that we will face the same rejection and potential physical abuse—not as a test or development, but simply because we continue to live in our own cursed essence.

On the night before his crucifixion, Jesus told his disciples (and, by extension, us), "Remember what I told you: 'A servant is not greater than his master.' If they persecuted me, they will persecute you also" (John 15:20a). He added that they "will treat you this way because of my name, for they do not know the one who sent me." Thus, our suffering images God, even in the physical sense.

Paul echoed this point: "For it has been granted to you on behalf of Christ not only to believe in him, but also to suffer for him" (Philippians 1:29). Paul's wording is striking. At first glance, it may seem as if Paul is saying that God grants us faith to believe and, in the same way, grants us suffering. But we know that God doesn't cause our suffering. We suffer because of those focused on the curse, who cause suffering precisely because "they do not know the one who sent [Jesus]." They inflict physical suffering on us because we do know Jesus's name, God's name, and the essence of God by which we should live. They target us for our connection with God. Generally speaking, the more our lives align with God's communal ideal, the more we can expect to be attacked and the more suffering we will endure. Just as our belief strengthens as the Holy Spirit's communication with our souls increases, so too does our suffering increase as our knowledge of God deepens within our minds and hearts.

In chapter 10, we discussed that God will not end the world simply because a heavenly alarm clock has gone off. The end will come only when no hope remains. Until then, we endure. This time of cursed living, even though Jesus has won the victory of redemption, continues because God is patient with us, "not wanting anyone to perish, but everyone to come to repentance" (2 Peter 3:9). So we endure, and in that enduring, we suffer. "Everyone who wants to live a godly life in Christ Jesus will be persecuted" (2 Timothy 3:12).

How then should we pray—especially when attacked by those focused on the curse or when overwhelmed by the mere curse of our essence, with its cancers, accidents, and calamities? God will certainly give us the strength to endure. He promises that. His Spirit will speak to our souls, and we can find peace in the midst of the storm. We may also pray to God for relief from our circumstances, and God, who loves us infinitely, will provide that relief . . . if and as he can. However, God cannot violate the love commitment—the love covenant—that is the purpose of creation. That love covenant requires uncoerced freedom for image-bearers to choose the directional basis for their souls.

Chaos theory suggests that a butterfly flapping its wings in China can change the weather in New York. This illustrates the interrelated complexity of all things. Only God has the mind for such maneuvering without destroying the freedom that his love relationship requires. Therefore, he will not deny himself (2 Timothy 2:13). God is love, and love means giving of self. So we pray in distress, but we pray knowing that God does all things well. Whether the circumstances of our physical condition are relieved or we must continue to endure, we know God works together with those who love him and are called to his purpose, bringing all things to good (Romans 8:28). We are patient, as he is patient. We suffer, as he suffers. And in the end, suffering will cease, and our joy will be full.

16

God Imaged in Blood

There is a fountain filled with blood
Drawn from Immanuel's veins;
And sinners, plunged beneath that flood,
Lose all their guilty stains.

—WILLIAM COWPER; FROM "PRAISE FOR THE FOUNTAIN OPENED"

For the life of a creature is in the blood.

—LEVITICUS 17:11

IN SCRIPTURE, WE ARE told multiple times that the life of a creature is in its blood. Moses recorded this in the Law (Leviticus 17, Deuteronomy 12), but centuries earlier, God made the same connection between life and blood when he instructed Noah and his sons not to eat "meat that has its lifeblood" (Genesis 9:4). The NIV translates "lifeblood" as a compound of two separate Hebrew words. One is "soul" or "life" (derived from the Hebrew *nepes*), and the other is "blood" (from *dam*). I emphasize these words separately, as they are in the original, to show that while their meanings are distinct, the text demonstrates an intimate connection: the blood mirrors the soul or life it contains. Blood, then, becomes a symbol of the soul or life it reflects. Thus, in the passages—Genesis, as well as in Leviticus and Deuteronomy—we hear the command, "don't consume the flesh along with the soul." But why? What are we meant to understand from this imagery, and why was God instructing the Israelites (and those before them) not to consume both the flesh and the soul of their food?

As with many spiritual questions, the answer begins with the atonement—the central doctrine of Christianity, which touches on all aspects of creation's story, including the body and soul of humanity. The atonement, God's means of restoring a love relationship with his image-bearers, was not solely about forgiving sins. God had already been forgiving the sins of the repentant long before Jesus went to the cross (e.g., Leviticus 19:22; Psalm 32:1, 85:2; Matthew 9:2; Luke 7:48). The cross and resurrection were about more than forgiveness; they were about putting our cursed physical nature to death and reviving life without the curse. The atonement was redemption—a reclamation of physical creation from the separation brought about by the curse Adam introduced. To be in right relationship with God, humans need both forgiveness and redemption. The repentant believer receives both: forgiveness to cleanse the soul from sin's guilt and redemption to rescue the body from the curse and its resultant death.

This forgiveness and redemption come not only through Jesus's death but even more through his life. Some Christians emphasize that Jesus was born to die, and while that is true, it is only part of the story—half the accomplishment, half the victory. Jesus took on human flesh—this cursed physical nature of ours—to put it to death, but not to pay for sins. If the focus were only on punishment and payment for sins, his death alone would have sufficed. Yet Paul argues in 1 Corinthians 15:17 that "if Christ has not been raised, your faith is futile; you are still in your sins." How can this be? If Christ had not reclaimed his body from death to a life free from the curse and restored his relationship with God, there would be no hope for the redemption of our physical essence. His resurrection is the victory over the curse. His death removes the curse; his life redeems. And his life is symbolized by his blood.

This concept may seem challenging, especially in light of certain atonement theories like penal substitution, which focuses primarily on death as the punishment for sin. In that theory, forgiveness (the cancellation of an unpaid debt) is often overshadowed, even if given lip service. Yet even during Jesus's death, it is his shedding of blood that is emphasized. He is whipped, and he sheds blood. A crown of thorns is pressed on his brow, and he sheds blood. His hands and feet are pierced, and he sheds blood. His side is cut open, and he sheds blood. The shedding of blood represents the release of life from cursed flesh because "the life of a creature is in the blood."

Hebrews 9:22 reminds us "the law requires that nearly everything be cleansed with blood, and without the shedding of blood there is no forgiveness." The Greek word translated as "forgiveness" is *aphesis*, which more specifically means "release." Forgiveness, a kind of release from the imprisonment of sin, is why translators chose the word "forgiveness," though they may have misunderstood the focus. The imagery of sacrifice is not just about God forgiving sin but about the soul being released from the cursed body of sin. Human life is in the blood; blood is life, and life is relationship with God. Releasing the blood from its cursed prison is necessary for full life—full relationship with God. While it may seem counterintuitive to say that "the release of blood means full life," since it leads to physical death, in spiritual terms, the release of the soul from cursed flesh brings the hope of full life in relationship with God.

The Old Testament supports this idea. When God confronts Cain after the first human death, he asks, "What have you done? Listen! Your brother's blood cries out to me from the ground" (Genesis 4:10). This question is not just about the heinousness of Cain's crime but is meant to make him (and us) reflect on the consequences of his actions. Abel's blood—Abel's life—cries out to God. When Adam sinned, the ground—symbolizing human essence—was cursed. But in creation of the human, God had breathed into that essence a living soul—a being of psyche (mind, will, emotions) and spirit (the lifeforce desire to live and realize TGB). Part of the curse was that the human would return to the ground (Genesis 3:19), and that meant a loss of the functioning of the soul—both psyche and spirit no longer able to operate yet still wrapped in existence with (but in total subjection to) the cursed ground.

God impressed upon Cain the significance of physical death because humans were under a curse headed for destruction. The only hope was to turn to God, trusting in him for rescue, repenting of self-focus, recognizing that truth, goodness, and beauty are sourced in God alone. And our minds, wills, and emotions must be functional for us to turn to God, but physical death removes that ability, leaving us subject to the curse. In Abel's case, his hope for restoration appears to have existed prior to his physical death. But that is really not our judgment call, and neither was it Cain's. Cain's sin in ending Abel's life, and any act of murder, cuts short a person's opportunity to respond to God.

The Bible shows a progression of violence stemming from Cain's sin. Lamech, a descendant of Cain, also commits murder and seeks protection from retribution. Even the godly line of Seth (Genesis 5) turns to "only evil all the time" (Genesis 6:5), leading to the destruction of all but Noah's family. After the flood, as the creation story is reintroduced, God tells Noah, "Whoever sheds human blood, by humans shall their blood be shed; for in the image of God has God made mankind" (Genesis 9:6).

God's command may seem harsh, given his love for enemies and his call for us to do the same (Matthew 5:43–45). Yet, God also accommodates human evil, hoping to lead people back to restoration. For example, though divorce is destructive to relationships, God allowed it in Moses's Law because prohibiting it would have caused greater harm (Matthew 19:8).

In an ideal world, murder would not exist, but in the chaos of the curse, it does. Murder terminates the opportunity for a love relationship with God, the very reason he sustains creation. Murderers, who cut off that possibility for others, must be removed from society. While prisons may achieve this in modern times, they did not in Noah's day. As Greg Boyd notes, "God's will is his awareness of the greatest good achievable in a nonideal situation."[1]

Throughout the Bible, blood is repeatedly identified as the image of life, which is synonymous with relationship with God. We see this most clearly in Jesus's use of body and blood imagery during the Last Supper. In Luke 22, he calls the bread his body, broken and given for them. They are to take it in, identifying with his death, as Paul later instructs (Romans 6:11). Then, they are to drink the wine, which Jesus calls his blood. For Jews who had long avoided consuming blood, this was a shocking command. Why was Jesus's blood different? Because his soul was different—pure and not enslaved to the curse. His soul was set on the truth, goodness, and beauty of God. His soul, therefore, could and should be taken in by those who believe.

At the atonement, the life released—Jesus's blood—was God himself. Jesus, not merely human, did not lose function or awareness upon his death. As God, he maintained full personhood and, in that metaphysical state, redeemed his body, bringing it to life free from the curse. We submit to him by symbolically consuming his sacrificed body and receiving his life, transforming us into new creatures. As Paul states in

---

1. Boyd, *Is God to Blame?*, 136.

1 Corinthians 11:26, we proclaim his death until he returns, when all cursed creation will die and be made alive by his resurrection, providing us with new, unstained bodies.

So why were the Israelites commanded not to eat flesh with its life-blood? Because the life of this creation is enslaved to the curse—it seeks after itself and dismisses the source of all truth, goodness, and beauty. But in Christ, God took on this cursed creation. His soul is pure, and we are to drink that in. In Revelation 19, Jesus is depicted with a robe dipped in blood—not the blood of his enemies, but his own. His triumph in coming is marked by life, not death.

> Jesus said to them, "Very truly I tell you, unless you eat the flesh of the Son of Man and drink his blood, you have no life in you. Whoever eats my flesh and drinks my blood has eternal life, and I will raise them up at the last day. For my flesh is real food and my blood is real drink. Whoever eats my flesh and drinks my blood remains in me, and I in them. Just as the living Father sent me and I live because of the Father, so the one who feeds on me will live because of me. This is the bread that that came down from heaven. Your ancestors ate manna and died, but whoever feeds on this bread will live forever. —*John 6:53–48*

17

God Imaged in Sacrifice

So sits the earth's great curse in Adam's fall
Upon my head: so I remove it all
From th' earth unto my brows, and bear the thrall:
Was ever grief like mine?

—George Herbert, from "The Sacrifice"

'What are all your sacrifices to Me?' asks the Lord.
'I have had enough of burnt offerings and rams and the fat of well-fed cattle;
I have no desire for the blood of bulls, lambs, or male goats.
When you come to appear before Me,
who requires this from you—this trampling of My courts?
Stop bringing useless offerings!

—Isaiah 1:11–13a

Understanding the Bible begins and ends with the revelation of Jesus Christ: the revelation *about* Jesus—fully God, fully man, the appointed Savior, Lord of Creation—and the revelation *by* Jesus—his testimony of love displaying God, God's kingdom, and God's rescue. These images intertwine harmoniously, building toward the exciting climax of God's redemptive purpose in Jesus, outlined in this God-breathed book. However, many Christians—even scholars—miss or have become desensitized to this core illuminating truth. Jesus himself expressed frustration with the Emmaus disciples in Luke 24:25: "How foolish and slow you are to believe all that the prophets have spoken!" They had not been reading the Old Testament with minds attuned to love and redemption. Only when Jesus corrected their focus—"Beginning with Moses and all the Prophets, he interpreted for them the things concerning himself in all the Scriptures" (v. 27)—did their hearts "burn" within them (v. 32).

While most of us understand this unifying concept, when our focus shifts from the big picture to the details, we can easily lose ourselves among the trees. Do we truly believe all Scripture—both the Old and New Testaments—centers on Jesus? Do we allow that truth to shape our minds and hearts as we wrestle with difficult passages? Our interpretive goal should always be positioned on how each passage reveals him.

We must also adhere to the principle established in chapter 9: as God-breathed, the whole Bible is profitable for teaching, but the lessons we draw are beneficial only as they relate to Jesus, whether through emulation or avoidance. Only through Christ's life and teaching does God reveal how to interpret other passages: "The one who has seen me has seen the Father" (John 14:9). The Bible consistently reinforces this focus. Second Corinthians 4:6 affirms, "For God who said, 'Let light shine out of darkness,' has shone in our hearts to give the light of the knowledge of God's glory in the face of Jesus Christ." Christ alone reveals the fullness of God (Hebrews 1:3; Colossians 2:9).

The Bible is both map and treasure. It guides us in our search for knowledge of God, essential for cultivating relationship, as it reveals the ongoing search of his people throughout history. As we engage with their search, we, too, discover treasure. From the beginning, God intended to teach his image-bearers the knowledge of good and evil. However, as Adam and Eve should have recognized, that knowledge is rooted in him, not in human wisdom or action. This is why human activities recorded in Scripture are insufficient unless viewed through the perfect lens of Jesus.

Thus, we cannot discard the Old Testament simply because its authors had limited understanding. We still gain wisdom from those God-breathed pages, illuminated by Jesus, even in what Old Testament writers misunderstood. A telling example appears in Deuteronomy 19, where Moses, writing the Law as he understood it from God, instructs the Israelites on how to determine guilt and innocence in legal matters. Consider verses 18–21:

> The judges are to make a careful investigation, and if the witness turns out to be a liar who has falsely accused his brother, you must do to him as he intended to do to his brother. You must purge the evil from you. Then everyone else will hear and be afraid, and they will never again do anything evil like this among you. You must not show pity: life for life, eye for eye, tooth for tooth, hand for hand, and foot for foot.

This passage, part of the God-breathed Old Testament Law attributed to Moses, may strike us as harsh: "Wow, that's tough. It seems extreme for God to insist on no pity. But there it is—God said 'eye for eye,' and we must obey." However, stopping there leaves us in the same place as the Emmaus disciples Jesus rebuked.

To fully understand, we must consider Jesus. In the Sermon on the Mount, Jesus says:

> You have heard that it was said, An eye for an eye and a tooth for a tooth [*notice these are the exact words of Moses in the OT Law*]. But I tell you, don't resist an evildoer. On the contrary, if anyone slaps you on your right cheek, turn the other to him also." (Matthew 5:38–39)

Is Jesus really saying, "Ignore what the Law of Moses instructs"? Not at all. Such a rigid interpretation misses the heart of Jesus's message. Craig Keener argues that Jesus is not contradicting the Law but instead raising the bar, calling for a higher standard. According to Keener, Jesus advocates mercy over retribution, urging people not to take vengeance into their own hands but to rely on the courts to administer justice.[1] However, I believe it goes further than that. The Law mandated strict punishment ("eye for eye"), and Jesus affirms that the Jews were to uphold the Law (Matthew 5:18). But this isn't about merely refraining from personal vengeance so the courts can do it for you. Jesus goes beyond that, revealing that God's heart wants to forgive, and therefore, we too are called to forgive. The legal system in Israel was essential to prevent chaos and violence—after all, we are a cursed race, something Jesus acknowledges. So he makes it clear that he didn't come to abolish the Law but to show the true intent behind it: God's response is not one of vengeance, but one of love, always seeking opportunities to forgive. While the Law was necessary due to sin, Jesus calls for mercy, demonstrating in his own life the way God desires us to respond.

---

1. Keener, *Matthew*, 196–7.

Jesus continues in Matthew 5, instructing his followers to love not only their neighbors but also their enemies, "so that you may be sons of your Father in heaven" (v. 45). To be a "son of" implies likeness to one's parent. Jesus argues that we should love our enemies to become *like* God. He points out that God "causes the sun to rise on the evil and the good and sends rain on the righteous and the unrighteous" (v. 45b). In other words, God doesn't withhold from the bad and reward the good—he offers to all, extending opportunities for relationship. If God acts this way, so should we. Jesus's message is clear: the Old Testament law of "eye for eye" is not how God operates. A God of love and mercy does not command "Show no pity!" and require retribution without compassion. To be like God, as Jesus argues, we must show mercy.

What does this mean for our understanding of Scripture? Moses's law of "eye for eye" was necessary to accommodate the cursed environment in which God's people lived, but it does not reflect God's ideal for righteous living. This is similar to what Jesus taught about divorce, as discussed in our chapter "God Imaged in Marriage." Jesus explained that the Law permitted divorce due to humanity's fallen condition, but this was not God's original intention. Likewise, while Moses, influenced by his upbringing in Pharaoh's court, established a legal system he believed aligned with God's principles, Jesus reveals that Moses fell short of true righteousness. Through Jesus's perfect reflection of God, we see that Moses's law did not convey the full picture of God's heart.

This doesn't mean we discard the Old Testament. These passages still teach us about good, evil, and, ultimately, the love and mercy of God. God breathed out these Scriptures for our learning, so that by viewing them through the lens of Jesus's life and teaching, we may know God more intimately. Consider the laments and imprecations of the psalmists. These writers cried out in personal agony and national distress, expressing real pain. But preachers sometimes use these psalms to justify anger in us. God, however, doesn't present these outbursts for us to imitate. He wants us to see such suffering in light of Jesus, who responded to similar anguish with grace and dependence on the Father. In reflecting on the psalmists' reactions, we can be certain that God calls us to respond differently—by imitating Christ.

THE SACRIFICED REDEEMER

As we consider sacrifice—a dominant theme in both the Old and New Testaments that helps shape our eschatological understanding—we must reinforce the notion of how Scripture teaches right and wrong: by our examining through the lens of Jesus. We need that concept engrained in and at the forefront of our minds. Some practices and beliefs about sacrifice related in Scripture are not correct. We will figure out the right and wrong about sacrifice by viewing it through the lens of Jesus.

After the messages to the churches in Revelation 2 and 3, John introduces Jesus in chapter 5 as the foundation for the rest of the book. In Revelation 5, God holds a scroll while Jesus comes forward as the only one worthy to open it. Part 3 of this book will explore this passage in more depth, but for now, it's important to highlight the description of Jesus in that scene. He appears as a slaughtered lamb with seven horns and seven eyes, symbolizing three aspects of the Redeemer: (1) Jesus's power, (2) his care, and (3) his victory through his humanity.

The horns represent power. Imagery in Revelation often draws from the Old Testament, and John uses these symbols so his audience can grasp their meaning. One of the Old Testament books John references heavily is Daniel, where horns in chapters 7 and 8 symbolize strength. Likewise, in Revelation, Jesus's image consistently portrays his overcoming power—his ability to fulfill his purpose.

The seven eyes symbolize knowledge but also reflect Jesus's care—his watchful attention over his people. Psalm 34:15 says, "The eyes of the Lord are on the righteous," reinforcing the message of faithfulness and the protection promised amid the trials of this interadvental age.

The third aspect is victory in humanity, achieved through sacrifice. Jesus is depicted as a slain lamb, a reminder of the Passover offering. This image, meant to evoke the cross and resurrection, is foundational to the rest of Revelation. Without Jesus's sacrificial victory, the struggles of the age would be meaningless. His death and resurrection signify the defeat of humanity's cursed physical essence, which was put to death by the only human who was not enslaved by sin.

This defeat of the physical nature (through death and redemption to life) defines both Jesus's atoning sacrifice and the deeper meaning of sacrifice throughout Scripture. Without this understanding, we risk getting lost among the many perspectives and purposes for sacrifice seen both in pagan cultures and even among the misunderstandings of God's people.

LEVITICUS SACRIFICES

The concept of sacrifice has existed since the exit from Eden, as seen in the story of Abel and Cain, but its development and refinement are clarified in Leviticus as the Sinai experience shapes the children of Israel into a nation.

Leviticus introduces five categories of sacrifices, or offerings: the burnt offering for general sin, the grain offering as a symbol of devotion to God, the peace offering for thanksgiving or communion, the sin offering for specific and unintentional sins, and the guilt offering for restitution. Each of these offerings carries figurative meanings, not just in their general purpose but also in the specific details of how they were performed. In all but the grain offering, animals were killed. Since both the burnt and sin offerings focused on atonement for sin, we'll examine them more closely.

In these sacrifices, the offeror presented the animal at the entrance of the tabernacle, laying hands on it as a means of identification—the animal represented the offeror. This act did not transfer sins to the animal; in fact, Scripture tells us that sins were passed only through the high priest's laying hands on the scapegoat during the Day of Atonement (Leviticus 16:21). In other cases, the offeror's act signified delight in atonement being made through the animal's representation.

For burnt offerings, the animal was completely burned on the altar. For sin offerings, the fat from the innermost parts of the animal—the entrails, including the kidneys and liver—was burned on the altar, while the rest of the body was burned outside the camp.

The most significant aspect of the sacrifice was the separation of the animal's blood from its body. The priest would sprinkle the blood on the altar, in front of the veil, on the altar's horns, or at its base, depending on who was making the offering. On the Day of Atonement, the high priest sprinkled the blood on the mercy seat.

This separation of blood from the body underscores the two-part nature of human beings: we are individuals as souls, but we share a common physical essence. Our souls' choice to sin, by pursuing TGB (truth, goodness, and beauty) as if it were sourced in physical creation, results in guilt. God forgives our guilt through repentance and faith of our minds and wills (the psyche, or part of the soul), but we remain sinful because of our cursed physical nature—our bodies, our flesh.

As discussed in the previous chapter, blood represents the soul. Leviticus 17:11 states, "For the life of a creature is in the blood, and I have appointed it to you to make atonement on the altar for your lives, since it is the lifeblood that makes atonement." These sacrifices symbolically depict the soul (blood) leaving the cursed flesh, which is put to death (burned). Paul encourages us to adopt the mindset represented by this sacrificial example: "Now if Christ is in you, the body is dead because of sin, but the Spirit is life because of righteousness" (Romans 8:10).

The burning of the innermost fat during the sin offering reinforces the same theme. What we call "heart" in terms of our deepest desires and hopes, the ancient world referred to as the "bowels," symbolizing the deepest parts of a person. Burning the bowels on the altar reflected the idea that these desires were no longer set on the body but on God's essence—his truth, goodness, and beauty.

SACRIFICES—THE RIGHT AND WRONG

If we maintain a clear understanding that sacrifices were never meant as physical gifts to satisfy God for his own benefit, we can avoid many misconceptions about offerings. A burned bull does not appease God. A slaughtered lamb does not motivate him to grant victory in battle. God is not pleased by the blood of a goat in exchange for rain. Nor does he savor the "pleasing aroma" of roasted flesh because he craves a meal. God is metaphysical and does not sustain himself through physical means. Burned animals do not become "God food," and even the fat of the entrails was not intended as sustenance for him. (Although Scripture says, "All fat belongs to the Lord," this should not be understood literally.) The fat is burned—destroyed. What we call the "hearts" of the worshippers are God's—not our physical hearts or an animal's fatty entrails.

Thus, sacrifices were never physical offerings meant to charm God, as was thought with the gods of Egypt, Canaan, and Babylon. Instead, sacrifices served two purposes: (1) to teach that the physical world is cursed and in need of redemption, and (2) to demonstrate dependence on God's truth, goodness, and beauty (TGB) as the foundation of relationship with him.

Because God's concern was with the spiritual meaning behind the sacrifices, he rejected those who misused them—not for any technical errors in the ritual, but for the people's corrupt attitudes. Sacrifices became a waste of life and a mockery of their redemptive purpose, no matter how many animals were slaughtered. At one point, God rebukes this disingenuous display of worship:

> Hear the word of the Lord, you rulers of Sodom! Listen to the instruction of our God, you people of Gomorrah! "The multitude of your sacrifices—what are they to me?" says the Lord. "I have more than enough of burnt offerings, of rams and the fat of fattened animals; I have no pleasure in the blood of bulls and lambs and goats. When you come to appear before me, who has asked this of you, this trampling of my courts? Stop bringing meaningless offerings!" (Isaiah 1:10–13a)

So, what does God want?

> With what shall I come before the Lord and bow down before the exalted God? Shall I come before him with burnt offerings, with calves a year old? Will the Lord be pleased with thousands of rams, with ten thousand rivers of olive oil? Shall I offer my firstborn for my transgression, the fruit of my body for the sin of my soul? He has shown you, O mortal, what is good. And what does the Lord require of you? To act justly and to love mercy and to walk humbly with your God. (Micah 6:6–8)

First, Micah seems to question whether sacrifices can serve as payment for sin: "Should I give my firstborn for my transgression, the child of my body for my own sin?" While God never commands child sacrifice, this question reflects the people's confusion about the nature of offerings. Second, the passage addresses the deeper issue. Judah had sinned by disobeying God, relying on their own strength, and seeking peace and satisfaction apart from him. In response, God did what he always does—he let them go their chosen way. Judah's rebellion led to their downfall, and in their desperation, they wondered if sacrifices could placate God and restore peace.

Micah gives voice to their thoughts: "Shall I come before him with burnt offerings?" Would that atone for their sins? The implied answer is no. "Will the Lord be pleased with thousands of rams, with ten thousand rivers of olive oil?" Again, the answer is no. "Shall I offer my firstborn for my transgression?" The answer is a firm no. None of these things can remove sin. What God truly requires is repentance—returning to justice, mercy, and humility in alignment with his TGB.

My point is that, while the Old Testament congregation sometimes seems to equate sacrifice with paying for sin, passages like this in Micah correct that misconception. They emphasize that sacrifice was never about paying for individual guilt, but about pointing to the need for Jesus's ultimate sacrifice, which took away the curse of sin. With that curse removed, repentance and faith are all God requires for a restored relationship.

It's possible that Moses developed the sacrificial system, in part, as a way to encourage devotion to God, similar to practices in other nations. However, Moses wasn't trying to deceive anyone, though at times he may have emphasized ritual more than relational intent. But if we view the sacrifices through the lens of Jesus, we can see how God used the system to point to the necessity of atonement. And that's what Revelation reveals, with Jesus presented as the slaughtered lamb, gathering to himself all whose hearts rest in him.

18

God Imaged in Temple

Listen! the mighty Being is awake,
And doth with his eternal motion make
A sound like thunder—everlastingly.
Dear child! dear Girl! that walkest with me here,
If thou appear untouched by solemn thought,
Thy nature is not therefore less divine:
Thou liest in Abraham's bosom all the year;
And worshipp'st at the Temple's inner shrine,
God being with thee when we know it not.

—William Wordsworth, from "It is a Beauteous Evening, Calm and Free"

I did not see a temple in the city,
because the Lord God Almighty and the Lamb are its temple!

—Revelation 21:22

At the start of our Revelation discussion, I will assert that the major scroll scenes provide a framework for understanding the rest of the book. The scroll in chapter 5 represents God's restoration plan to redeem his image-bearers, who were separated by the curse. Jesus alone is worthy to take hold of this plan. However, the scroll is sealed with seven seals, and these must be removed before the scroll can be opened. The breaking of the seals, while the scroll remains closed, signals a preparatory period prior to the redemption revealed by the open scroll in chapters 8 and 10. The final appearance of the open scroll occurs in chapter 20, where the names of the rescued are read from it.

Each of these scroll scenes—its presentation, opening, and reading—occurs before the throne or altar of God. These are figurative elements, as there is no literal throne or altar where God physically interacts. John uses these descriptions to communicate God's presence, and this presence—God dwelling among his image-bearers—is central to the concept of the temple. The Hebrew word *miskan* (tabernacle) and the Greek *naos* (temple) both denote a dwelling place, often specifically referring to the dwelling place of God on Earth.

Yet God does not physically inhabit these structures. As Stephen preached, "The Most High does not live in houses made by human hands" (Acts 7:48). God is pure spirit, wholly present everywhere. This raises a paradox: why did God instruct Israel to build a dwelling place for him, while also asserting that he does not dwell in physical creation? As always, the answer points back to the atonement.

THE ROLE OF OUR ESSENCE IN RELATIONSHIP WITH GOD

The atonement rescues humanity by removing the curse, which originated when Adam elevated physical creation above God, subjecting himself in psyche and spirit to it instead of ruling over it as intended (Genesis 1:26-28). While God forgives the guilt of individual sins for those who repent, removing the curse on all creation required a redeemer. Jesus lived as a human without being enslaved to physical essence, put that essence to death, and resurrected it with the curse removed.

Human essence—physical creation—stands in stark contrast to God's essence, which is truth, goodness, and beauty (TGB). God's essence forms the foundation of love relationship. To exist in harmony with God, his essence must be central to our experience, worshipped, embraced, and held as our focus. If we exalt our own physical essence over God's TGB—succumbing to the lusts of the flesh, lusts of the eyes, and the pride of this physical life—we lose hope for continued life with him. This was the essential lesson God sought to teach Adam and Eve in the garden.

Why did God create the garden for our first parents? As discussed earlier, the garden was given amid a newly created good Earth, allowing them to recognize God's loving provision of TGB. While his essence flowed into creation, only God is the true source of TGB. Creation may reflect his TGB, but he alone *is* TGB. As long as his image-bearers acknowledged this foundation for love and relationship, they could have thrived in communion with him as he sustained them. The garden, then, was a temple—a dwelling place where Adam and Eve could meet with God, sustained by his essence. When sin entered, when trust in God was severed and they sought TGB from their own essence apart from him, they lost their communion with God—their garden temple.

This image is complex. God dwelled with his image-bearers *within* the garden-temple, even though it consisted of human essence. Yet, on another level, the relationship was still grounded *within* God's essence. This same concept is found in Jesus's priestly prayer at the Last Supper: "that they all may be one, Father, just as you are in me and I am in you. May they also be in us so that the world may believe that you have sent me." Jesus, in his role as the human Son of God, prayed that our relationship with God would mirror his—God dwelling in us while we dwell in him. This is the temple image: a dwelling place for God (for his soul—psyche and spirit) in us (our physical essence) while our souls remain in him (his divine essence).

Despite God's attempt to teach this to Adam and Eve, they failed—or perhaps refused—to understand. By choosing sin, they left the secure relationship of being in God, and God illustrated their choice by expelling them from the garden-temple of his presence.

EFFECT OF CURSE ON ESSENCE

And yet, even after their expulsion, God continued to pursue his image-bearers and teach them about right relational understanding—that life is possible and complete only with God in us and us in God. I believe those lessons began before Adam and Eve even left the garden. We are told, almost in passing, that God "made garments of skin for Adam and his wife and clothed them" (Genesis 3:21). Before their sin—before leaving God—they had been "naked and unashamed" (Genesis 2:25). But after sinning, "the eyes of both of them were opened, and they realized they were naked" (Genesis 3:7). Adam later admits to God, "I was afraid because I was naked; so I hid" (Genesis 3:10).

Their new understanding of nakedness was a result of their self-awareness after moving away from God. Their bodies became the focus of idolatry. As Paul explains in Romans 1:

> For although they knew God, they neither glorified him as God nor gave thanks to him, but their thinking became futile and their foolish hearts were darkened. Although they claimed to be wise, they became fools and exchanged the glory of the immortal God for images made to look like a mortal human being and birds and animals and reptiles. Therefore, God gave them over in the sinful desires of their hearts to sexual impurity for the degrading of their bodies with one another. They exchanged the truth about God for a lie, and worshiped and served created things rather than the Creator—who is forever praised. Amen. (Romans 1:21–25)

With an overwhelming shift of spiritual desire toward their own essence—particularly their bodies—Adam and Eve became consumed with its worship. This was not a worship of hymns or formal praise but a deep, complete submission to a new master: their physical essence, which now commanded all their passions. In this state, especially before God, they were ashamed of their nakedness, as it exposed their self-serving idolatry.

Yet, despite their fallen condition, God provided help for their embarrassment. He clothed them, covering their now-cursed physical essence, though they were still in need of a miraculous rescue. God sacrificed an animal, part of their physical essence surrounding them, and used its skin to cover their nakedness. This act was more than practical—it symbolized a profound spiritual truth. The sacrifice released life through the shedding of blood, signifying the cursed essence's forfeiture of control over life. Though a simple image, this act laid the foundation for the entire sacrificial system.

This is why God later accepted Abel's animal sacrifice but rejected Cain's offering of vegetables. Cain's gift, devoid of life's release from physical essence, turned the sacrificial meaning upside down. He assumed that the material food he valued and offered was of value to God. But God said no. It wasn't Cain's cursed essence that God desired but his soul.

The Israelite Law reinforced this connection through the Day of Atonement sacrifice. The lifeblood released from the unblemished goat was sprinkled in the temple's Holy of Holies, serving as the purifying agent for the meeting place with God. This act foreshadowed the lifeblood of Jesus, which in reality purified this cursed creation—humanity's physical essence—as the new meeting place with God. Initially, this was fulfilled in the firstfruits of Jesus's own body, but eventually, it will extend to all of creation.

For this reason, Jesus is Immanuel—God with us. Not only was he both God and man, but through his humanity, he removed the curse, becoming our temple. In him, we meet God.

REDEMPTION OF ESSENCE—RESTORATION OF TEMPLE

In the hope of becoming like Jesus in our redeemed bodies, even in our current "already but not yet" existence, those of us who have embraced God and his rescue are temples because we are in Jesus. Paul writes in 1 Corinthians 3:16–17:

> Don't you know that you yourselves are God's temple and that God's Spirit dwells in your midst? If anyone destroys God's temple, God will destroy that person; for God's temple is sacred, and you together are that temple.

God's Spirit dwells within us not merely because we've prayed for forgiveness of sins. We pray "in Jesus's name" because his human essence is freed from the curse, and through him, we meet, dwell, and rejoice. This defines what Paul refers to in verse 17, which must not be destroyed. Together, as a Christian community, we become the body of Christ. The "building up" that Paul describes reflects our grasp on a vision of curse-free, temple-functioning essence—Jesus's literal body, which also forms the figurative body of Christ in us.

In 1 Corinthians 6:15–20, Paul expands on this:

> Do you not know that your bodies are members of Christ himself? Shall I then take the members of Christ and unite them with a prostitute? Never! Do you not know that he who unites himself with a prostitute is one with her in body? For it is said, "The two will become one flesh." But whoever is united with the Lord is one with him in spirit. Flee from sexual immorality. All other sins a person commits are outside the body, but whoever sins sexually, sins against their own body. Do you not know that your bodies are temples of the Holy Spirit, who is in you, whom

you have received from God? You are not your own; you were bought at a price. Therefore honor God with your bodies.

The image of marriage is strongly present here, reaffirming that even in this New Covenant age, God insists we value it. In our hope of redemption, we cannot elevate our cursed bodies to fulfill their desires, whether deviant lusts or even what may seem like natural urges. We often think of sin as something obvious and grotesque, but sin can also present itself subtly, making us ask (as Barbara Mandrell sang), "How can this be wrong when it feels so right?" But trusting our bodies for truth, goodness, and beauty is the very sin that led to the fall. Paul reinforces this in Ephesians 2:19–22:

> Consequently, you are no longer foreigners and strangers, but fellow citizens with God's people and also members of his household, built on the foundation of the apostles and prophets, with Christ Jesus himself as the chief cornerstone. In him the whole building is joined together and rises to become a holy temple in the Lord. And in him you too are being built together to become a dwelling in which God lives by his Spirit.

Paul emphasizes that the Christian community, as a whole and in its individual parts, becomes the dwelling place of God. Our objective, then, is to treat our relationships with others accordingly. Each of us is not isolated in our relationship with God. Together, we form that "whole-building" temple where God dwells. Peter echoes this sentiment in 1 Peter 2:4–5:

> As you come to him, the living Stone—rejected by humans but chosen by God and precious to him—you also, like living stones, are being built into a spiritual house to be a holy priesthood, offering spiritual sacrifices acceptable to God through Jesus Christ.

The "spiritual sacrifices" Peter refers to involve setting aside those things we may initially believe to be intrinsic desires. But we cannot determine whether our desires are right or good based solely on how we feel, no matter how deep those feelings run. We must evaluate our desires as we would doctrines—by comparing them to Christ. This requires more than a simplistic approach, as almost anything can be justified that way. We must consider the full revelation of Christ, including the Gospels, the New Testament writers, and Revelation's figurative descriptions.

Together, these sources reveal that "spiritual sacrifices" involve releasing our souls from the cursed, natural human state that binds us.

Appropriately, Revelation concludes by explaining that the redeemed Earth will have no temple: "The Lord God Almighty and the Lamb are its temple." This echoes 1 Corinthians 15:28: "When he has done this, then the Son himself will be made subject to him who put everything under him, so that God may be all in all." Our perfect-union relationship is within us, and we are in God.

19

God Imaged in Warfare

Ascribe ye pow'r to God most high
Of humble Isr'el he takes care;
Whose strength, from out the dusky sky,
Darts shining terrors through the air.

—Based on Psalm 68; from "Let God, the God of Battle, Rise"

Your hand will capture all your enemies;
your right hand will seize those who hate you.
You will make them burn like a fiery furnace when you appear;
The Lord will engulf them in his wrath, and fire will devour them.
You will wipe their progeny from the earth
and their offspring from the human race.
Though they intend to harm you and devise a wicked plan,
they will not prevail.
Instead, you will put them to flight
when you ready your bowstrings to shoot at them.
Be exalted, Lord, in your strength; we will sing and praise your might.

—Psalm 21:8–13

IN CHAPTER 9, I explored several examples of God protecting Israel by removing enemies without resorting to violence. But does this mean that

God never acts with vicious force? Throughout the books of the Law, it seems God is frequently engaged in battle. The poetry books, especially the Psalms, vividly depict a warrior God. And in Isaiah and other prophetic books, God appears particularly wrathful, wielding sword and spear in judgment. Can we simply ignore these portrayals to present a more consistently loving image of God? Of course not. We can never dismiss Scripture. As I also emphasized in chapter 9, all Scripture is God-breathed and given for instruction. However, as we engage with Scripture, we must remember to "correctly teach" this word of truth (2 Timothy 2:15), which means interpreting it through the lens of Jesus. When we fully grasp the upside-down perspective of the kingdom of heaven, we'll be able to understand Scripture in its proper light.

THE NEW TESTAMENT'S EXAMPLE

We previously touched on the Beatitudes in Matthew 5, but now let's consider their fuller impact. Jesus begins by blessing the poor in spirit—not meaning listless introverts. We know this because he rewards them with the kingdom of heaven, which represents a relationship with God grounded in truth, goodness, and beauty (TGB). This satisfies them in a way the world cannot. These spirits are poor not due to a lack of passion, but because they haven't filled their hearts and minds with selfish, worldly desires. So Jesus promises them the satisfaction of God's TGB, as described in Isaiah 55. God also promises comfort to those who mourn. The New Testament makes it clear that Christians will suffer, and suffering is far from pleasant. But enduring suffering without harboring vengeful thoughts leads to the reward of comfort, as we will later see in Revelation.

In fact, every one of the Beatitudes reveals nonviolent attitudes triumphing over the hostility of the world, precisely because they don't retaliate. The humble do not one-up the arrogant; through humility, they inherit the earth, redeemed and free from evil. Those who seek righteousness find fulfillment without seeking revenge. The merciful receive mercy without wishing harm on the cruel. The pure in heart see God without casting malice on the impure. The peacemakers are called "sons of God" without justifying violence as "righteous." As we have discussed earlier, to be a "son of" someone means to reflect that person's character, so the nonviolent peacemaker is "like God." The Beatitudes end with a broad promise of inheritance and satisfaction within God's kingdom to all who are persecuted for their faithfulness to this nonviolent covenant relationship with God.

Following this blessing-filled introduction, Jesus urges us to love our enemies—not merely to be kind to them, but to embrace them in the hope of relationship. In essence, Jesus leads us to the unmistakably clear message of the Golden Rule: "Therefore, whatever you want others to do for you, do also the same for them" (Matthew 7:12). When this rule becomes the core of your heart, how could you ever react to others with hatred or a desire to harm? Some Christians mistakenly think Jesus, recognizing our self-interest, imposes this rule to make us at least try to treat others as we would want to be treated. But this thinking overlooks the deeper reward. The Golden Rule is not just about outward behavior; it points to the full meaning of love. Love isn't merely about kindness or giving of yourself for another's benefit. Genuine love seeks relationship, where both the giver and receiver are involved. In God's kingdom, relationship is celebrated, and we are all personally involved in this community. Neither my interests nor another's interests stand alone—the Golden Rule emphasizes mutual benefit. Jesus says this rule "is the Law and the Prophets," meaning this attitude is the essence of the entire Old Testament.

Jesus not only taught nonviolent love but demonstrated it by challenging attitudes that opposed it. He defied Sabbath laws to heal the sick (Mark 3:1-6). He confronted the Pharisees' arrogance when they enforced the letter of the law at the expense of the needy (Matthew 23). He intervened to stop the Pharisees from stoning the woman caught in adultery (John 8:2-11). And he ended Peter's violent defense in Gethsemane on the night of his arrest (John 18:10-11).

The apostle Paul, though often passionate in tone, followed Jesus's teachings. In Romans 12, Paul advises blessing those who persecute you, repaying no one evil for evil, and feeding and giving drink to enemies. Paul also gives us a framework for interpreting the warfare imagery in the Bible, declaring that "the weapons of our warfare are not worldly, but are powerful through God for the demolition of strongholds" (2 Corinthians 10:4). Our weapons include the full armor of God: truth as a belt, righteousness as a breastplate, peace as sandals, faith as a shield, salvation as a helmet, and the sword of the Spirit (Ephesians 6:14-17). Paul clarifies that these weapons are for spiritual warfare, not physical battles. This provides a key to understanding why God inspired the violent imagery in the Old Testament—not to endorse physical force, but as a teaching tool, guiding us toward abandoning malevolent actions and embracing spiritual efforts to build relationships through love.

THE OLD TESTAMENT'S WARFARE IMAGERY

When Jesus spoke about the Law given at Sinai, the focus naturally fell on the Ten Commandments, which even the Pharisees recognized as central. When they asked Jesus which law was the greatest, they likely hoped to trap him by forcing him to prioritize one commandment over the others, as if he might dismiss or downplay those not chosen. But Jesus exposed their misunderstanding—and that of the Jews in general—regarding the purpose of the Law. God did not intend it as a mere personal standard of holiness. The Ten Commandments emphasize relationship, and Jesus demonstrated that they symbolize and seal the central message of the Mosaic covenant: God's ultimate goal of restoring everlasting love relationships.

In response to the Pharisees, Jesus summarized the commandments as being about loving God and loving others. The first commandment, not worshiping other gods, is essential for a relationship with the only God who can supply truth, goodness, and beauty. The second commandment prohibits using physical objects as images of God in worship of him. This speaks to the very act that Aaron and the Israelites were guilty of during the golden calf incident—fashioning a physical image for worshiping Yahweh. The third commandment also emphasizes relationship, as God's name represents his TGB. To take it in vain means to trivialize the foundation of love and relationship.

The fourth commandment begins to turn our focus toward other relationships God has designed. As Jesus said, "The Sabbath was made for man" (Mark 2:27), highlighting that humanity's relationship with creation is meant to reflect God's TGB by ruling over it in a way that sustains that relationship. This purpose was lost on the Pharisees, who instead sought to burden people with Sabbath regulations. The fifth commandment draws attention to the growth in wisdom, which is needed by all and was notably lacking in Adam and Eve. In the context of a loving relationship, children are to honor their parents, who are to guide them in understanding God's TGB.

The remaining five commandments focus on relationships among God's people. Murder (ending relationship), adultery (betraying relationship), stealing, lying, and coveting all disrupt the command to love your neighbor as yourself (Matthew 22:39).

Jesus pointed to the relational intent of the Old Testament when the rich young ruler asked what good he must do to gain eternal life. Jesus essentially responded, "Why ask me about what is good when God, who is good, has already revealed his goodness in the commandments?" (paraphrase of Matthew 19:17).[1] Jesus told him to follow the goodness God had revealed. When the young man asked which commandments specifically, Jesus listed five—all dealing with human relationships. Jesus did this not because loving God is less important, but because the young man, as a Jew, already understood that loving God was foundational. Jesus was emphasizing what it means to love God: applying the love of God's essence—TGB—to all aspects of life. Jesus then revealed the man's lack of love by suggesting he sell his possessions, give to the poor, and follow him. The man's sadness showed his internal struggle between the selfish draw of his physical nature and his desire to orient his spirituality rightly.

Both these Gospel incidents illustrate the importance of the Ten Commandments in our discussion: God expresses himself in the Old Testament, but Jesus highlights the principle of love's relational intent. When we return to the Old Testament, we must discern both the elements that align with Jesus's teaching and those that contrast with it. For example, Deuteronomy 15:7–8 instructs the Israelites to open their hearts and loan generously to a poor Israelite in need. Likewise, Leviticus 19:33–34 says that even a foreigner among them should be treated as a native, to be loved as oneself. But these words of relationship and love were given to a people whose hearts had been hardened by persecution

---

1. The exact wording of Jesus's response in Matthew 19:17 is difficult to discern because of textual differences, which generally were "Why do you *call* me good?" in the Byzantine family and "Why do you *ask* me what is good?" in the Alexandrian. The other Synoptics record the scene as well, and in Mark and Luke, Jesus's question in both manuscript families is "Why do you call me good?" But the Greek word used in both Mark and Luke (translated "call") is *legeis*, which is also the word used in the Byzantine versions of Matthew. That word (and its forms) is normally translated "say," rather than "call." In fact, 1184 times out of its 1343 occurrences in the NT, the word is translated "say" and only 48 times translated "call." It is obviously an argument for Greek scholars, but I bring it up because I think from the Greek involved, Jesus meant to draw a tight loop around the ten commandments, God, and that which is good. And for that reason, I paraphrased Jesus's words as I did.

in Egypt and whose newfound power in entering the promised land led them to project their selfish feelings back onto God.

The discussion in Matthew 19 about divorce is one of the most revealing passages on this topic. It shows how God provides guidance to a people still grappling with the concepts of good and evil. In their relentless and misguided pursuit of superiority, the Pharisees ask Jesus what the law requires for a man who wishes to divorce his wife. Even the average person knew that certain conditions had to be met for a divorce to be lawful. However, the law governing these conditions had been recorded, debated, and modified in countless ways over time. The Pharisees, confident in their legal expertise, likely expected to expose Jesus as ignorant of the Law's complexities.

But Jesus deflects their shallow inquiry by referring to the creation narratives. He explains that divorce violates God's original intention for marriage. The Pharisees are astonished; after all, the Law clearly allowed for divorce, provided the proper conditions were met. They ask why, if divorce is wrong, Moses included provisions for it in the Law. Jesus responds that this was permitted because of the hardness of their hearts.

Consider Jesus's answer carefully. Over the centuries, the Jews had continually modified the law, adding countless amendments to define its letter. But Jesus's statement shifts their focus to the spirit behind the very rules found in Scripture (Deuteronomy 22 and 24). Jesus highlights two seemingly opposing truths: (1) God never intended for them to divorce, and (2) Moses included provisions for divorce in the Law. Does this mean God accommodates sin? Many Christians might react by saying, "No! Sin is evil, and God does not tolerate it." And yet, do we sin, and does God still tolerate us? Did King David sin? Did Abraham, Isaac, and Jacob sin? Did Adam sin? Of course Adam sinned—his sin caused the curse on all of creation. And yet, God still interacts, reveals, loves, and accommodates, meeting his image-bearers where they are and guiding them toward maturity.

This isn't about whether God ignores sin. Sin must be removed through forgiveness and redemption for an everlasting relationship of love, and this is central to God's restoration plan. However, God works with sinners without constantly condemning them for their imperfect lives. He accommodates our weaknesses, leading us through a process of revelation, teaching us good and evil, as we grow in relationship with him. Did God decide that the law of divorce was good? No. But it became part of God-breathed Scripture because God teaches us and guides us even through our mistakes and weaknesses.

As a young boy, David left his duties as a shepherd to deliver supplies to his brothers, who were camped near the Philistines. During his visit, the Philistine giant, Goliath, taunted and challenged the Israelites. David, filled with righteous anger, persuaded Saul to let him face Goliath, proclaiming that God would give him the victory. Armed with just a sling and some stones, David confronted the giant and killed him with a single shot to the forehead.

We often celebrate this story, praising David as a young man of faith who depended on God. Sermons and songs highlight how God guided that stone to the only vulnerable spot on Goliath. We rejoice as the Israelites pursue their enemies, leaving "Philistine bodies strewn all along the Shaaraim road to Gath and Ekron" (1 Samuel 17:52).

But let's pause and consider how this story aligns with Jesus's teachings in the Sermon on the Mount. Reflect on the Beatitudes, where the peacemakers are blessed, where we are told to love our enemies, and where God forgives us as we forgive others. Now, where does our enthusiasm for David's killing of Goliath and the scattering of Philistine bodies fit into these teachings? Does it sit comfortably with Jesus's call for humility and mercy? Could it be reconciled with his command to pray for those who persecute us so that we can be like God?

The bravado of the story doesn't quite fit. Insisting that God intended for us to celebrate these Old Testament actions seems to contradict Christ's message of peace and love, tearing at the integrity of Scripture. The only way to harmonize Jesus's words with David's killing of Goliath is to acknowledge that the act of killing was never God's desire. Instead, imagine the victory David could have achieved for God's way of relational love if, instead of using violence, he had knelt in prayer, asking for God's glory to be revealed. God could have delivered Israel by nonviolent means, just as he did in the examples discussed in chapter 9.

Yes, the biblical writers present David's victory as glorious, and from a human perspective, physical dominance may seem triumphant. But these writers, soldiers, and Israelites were still learning the difference between good and evil. God, in his wisdom, accommodated their limited understanding, guiding them along the difficult path set in motion by Adam and Eve's choice in the garden of Eden. However, we, who know Christ and are privileged to read his words of love in the Gospels, should not think like the Israelites of 3,000 years ago. We have both Jesus's corrective perspective on the Old Testament and his full revelation of God's love, demonstrated in his nonviolent sacrifice.

Throughout the many Old Testament stories about David, God consistently points us toward a correct understanding of kingdom values. He teaches us about David's flaws—not only with Bathsheba but also in his treacherous and violent rise to the throne. Yet, God also highlights the good in David's actions. Take, for instance, David's interaction with Saul. Had David killed Saul in the cave, the Israelites would have likely sung his praises once again. Scripture writers might have celebrated "God's deliverance" of Saul into David's hand. Consider 1 Samuel 24:3-4:

> When Saul came to the sheep pens along the road, a cave was there, and he went in to relieve himself. David and his men were staying in the back of the cave, so they [David's men] said to him [David], "Look, this is the day the Lord told you about: 'I will hand your enemy over to you so you can do to him whatever you desire.'"

By this point, David had grown since his encounter with Goliath. In this instance, he chose to trust God rather than resort to violence to claim the throne. Though David was still far from perfect, this story of David's trust and peace is included in Scripture to highlight the positive aspects of his character. These principles—trust and peace—resonate with the teachings of the Sermon on the Mount when viewed through the lens of Jesus.

Let's also take a closer look at Samson. He was undeniably powerful, possessing extraordinary physical strength that was given to him by God and used against Israel's enemies. But should we interpret Samson's violent actions as divinely intended? If not, how do we reconcile the fact that God specifically gave him this dominating strength?

The biblical account of Samson's life is almost totally negative. He shows little concern for God's will, beginning with his marriage to a Philistine woman. At his wedding, he poses a riddle to the Philistine guests, but when they obtain the answer from his wife, Samson, enraged, kills them and abandons her. Later, when he tries to reclaim his wife, he discovers that her father has given her to another man. Again driven by rage, Samson burns the Philistines' grain fields. In retaliation, the Philistines burn his wife and her father alive. Enraged once more (a pattern we now see), Samson kills those responsible for their deaths. When the Philistines come to capture him, Samson kills a thousand of them with the jawbone of a donkey. His story concludes with Delilah's betrayal, his imprisonment, and his death.

Can we truly call Samson "God's man" in the same way we refer to figures like Joseph, Daniel, or David? There is no record of Samson seeking God's wisdom or living in a way that aligns with the teachings of the Sermon on the Mount. In fact, we see only two direct interactions between Samson and God. After killing 1,000 Philistines, Samson, tired and thirsty, selfishly calls out to God, claiming to have done God a great favor and asking if God will now let him die of thirst. God provides him with water. His second prayer is equally self-centered. Blinded and mocked by the Philistines, Samson prays for strength—not to glorify God but to take revenge for his eyes.[2] Samson's relationship with God appears entirely transactional, focused on what God could do for him. He seems to interpret each death he causes among the Philistines as a service rendered to God.

The story gives us some insight into how God viewed Samson's actions. Samson's life ends with his eyes being plucked out, and the following chapter sets the theme for the book of Judges. In Judges 17:6, it states, "In those days there was no king in Israel; everyone did what was right in his own eyes" (NASB). This phrase is repeated at the book's conclusion (Judges 21:25), and in between are stories filled with theft, rape, and murder. Samson's own death, and the loss of his eyes, symbolize the spiritual blindness that characterized his life—using his God-given gifts for selfish ends.

Now, imagine what could have been if Samson had used his strength for peace instead of violence—just as Jesus, the Almighty, refrained from calling 10,000 angels to destroy his enemies. Jesus showed his true power

---

2. The question of why God seemingly granted Samson the strength to topple the house is similar to the question of how Elijah was able to call down fire for a destructive purpose. On occasion, God has empowered humans with what we might consider superhuman abilities, but not for them to act in ungodly ways. The fact that Samson was given power does not imply that God intended for him to use it out of vengeance or spite. Perhaps the narrative invites us to regret that Samson misused God's gift of power, imagining what might have been if he had used it for the salvation of the Philistines rather than their destruction. This parallels the way we often misuse our own human power. What if Adam and Eve had used their reasoning to choose obedience to God rather than to pursue the forbidden fruit? God grants us choice through the empowerment and circumstances he provides. How we respond—and how God continues to interact with us through accommodation, instruction, and working all things for good—could fill an entire book. Many of these questions are explored in Greg Boyd's two-volume work *Crucifixion of the Warrior God*, which I recommend for further study, as it maintains the essential truth that God always acts in love.

by laying down his life for his friends, and in that, there is victory. Samson, by contrast, leaves a shadow of sadness over the book of Judges. Some biblical scholars, misunderstanding inerrancy, try to attribute the murders, lies, and atrocities in Judges to the will of God. But when viewed through the lens of Jesus, it becomes clear that we cannot interpret their evil actions as good.

THE UPSIDE-DOWN KINGDOM OF HEAVEN

Jesus told Pilate that his kingdom was not of this world (John 18:36). In contrast to the violent and oppressive systems of worldly kingdoms, where rulers focus on control for its own sake, Jesus's kingdom is marked by love and peace. Pilate had been commissioned by Rome to suppress any potential Jewish rebellion that might threaten its authority, but in saying his kingdom was not of this world, Jesus reassured Pilate that he had no intentions of leading a political insurrection. Although he claimed to be a king, the nature of his kingdom was entirely different.

The world craves the power to dominate and control through violence. But Jesus's kingdom began in an act of love, as he laid down his life. His crowning moment came when he—sinless in soul—rose from the dead, reclaiming his physical life. While we often think of God as king from eternity past to the everlasting future, the crowning of Jesus as king in his humanity occurred at the resurrection. In that moment, his body and spirit were free from the curse of sin.

From the beginning, God gave his image-bearers authority over physical creation (Genesis 1:28). However, by worshiping creation rather than ruling it, they became enslaved to it, subjecting themselves to the very thing God intended them to govern. Jesus, in a body like ours under sin's dominion (Romans 8:3), put that cursed creation to death and reclaimed it. He cleansed, subdued, and took dominion over it. The core message of the gospel is that Jesus is Lord—he conquered creation by overcoming the curse. And God promises that one day we will reign with him, which means we will be freed from our enslavement to cursed flesh and will finally exercise dominion over it, as God originally intended.

Reigning over the physical world means that its destructive power—its violence in crushing and killing—will no longer have any hold over us. More importantly, it means that physical force will not be the means by which we gain that reign. Jesus won his victory not by striking the Roman soldiers or using some kind of divine physical force against the devil. Instead, he laid down his life in love, becoming physically vulnerable so that he might rise in spirit, redeeming the flesh from its sinful corruption.

While the Old Testament does depict warfare, it serves as imagery in two key ways. In the context of judgment, it reveals the self-destructive consequences of trusting in oneself and the physical world. But in the context of God's victory, it symbolizes the power of God's ways over the ways of the world. As God declares in Hosea 11:9, "I cannot carry out my fierce anger! I cannot totally destroy Ephraim! Because I am God, and not man—the Holy One among you—I will not come in wrath!" (NET).

This theme of warfare as imagery for love and redemption will ultimately shine in Revelation.

> The weapons of our warfare are not worldly, but are powerful through God for the demolition of strongholds. (2 Corinthians 10:4)

> Death has been swallowed up in victory. Death, where is your victory? Death, where is your sting? Now the sting of death is sin, and the power of sin is the law. But thanks be to God, who gives us the victory through our Lord Jesus Christ! (1 Corinthians 15:54b–57)

20

God Imaged in Sabbath

While pilgrims here we journey on
In this dark vale of sin and gloom,
Through tribulation, hate, and scorn,
Or through the portals of the tomb,
Till our returning king shall come
To take His exile captives home,
O! what can buoy the spirits up?
'Tis this alone the blessed hope.

—Annie Smith, from "I Saw One Weary"

Thus the heavens and the earth were completed in all their vast array. By the seventh day God had finished the work he had been doing; so on the seventh day he rested from all his work. Then God blessed the seventh day and made it holy, because on it he rested from all the work of creating that he had done.

—Genesis 2:1–3

The Sabbath—what is it for? Some may argue that it no longer has any purpose. The Jews were commanded to observe the Sabbath, but we aren't. Paul states, "One person considers one day more sacred than another; another considers every day alike. Each of them should be fully convinced in their own mind" (Romans 14:5). Because Paul seems to treat the matter as arbitrary, we tend to dismiss it. Well . . . maybe not entirely.

Christians generally worship on Sundays—the day of Jesus's resurrection. As a result, Sunday has often been referred to as the Christian Sabbath. In other words, what the Jews celebrated on Saturday, we now observe on Sunday, associating it with the greater revelation of our salvation through Christ. So we go to church on Sunday, sing songs, give offerings, listen to a sermon, and close with prayer. Then we go home, maybe to a meal before football, a stroll in the park, gardening, meeting with friends, working on a hobby, reading a book, or finding some other way to relax before the workweek begins.

However, more recently, I've noticed an emphasis among Christian leaders and organizations on paying closer attention to the Sabbath—whether that's on the traditional Saturday or on Sunday. They suggest that the idea of the Sabbath is more than simply going to church for worship. So, we return to the original question: why did God establish the Sabbath?

The Hebrew word *shabbat* means "to stop," and that's what God did on the seventh day of creation—he stopped; he rested. The Hebrew word *kalah* also means "to cease," and it's used in Genesis 2:1 and 2. The Bible reinforces this cessation, stating then that God "rested" (the root of *shabbat*). Of course, God did not need rest due to exhaustion. Isaiah 40:28a tells us, "The Lord is the everlasting God, the Creator of the ends of the earth. He will not grow tired or weary." Yet Exodus 31:17 insists, "In six days the Lord made the heavens and the earth, and on the seventh day he rested and was refreshed." If this "refreshing" wasn't recovery from weariness, how should we understand it?

As I discuss more fully in my book *The Curse Removed*, I believe the creation week in Genesis 1 is structured in "seven days" to represent the process of forming our universe, particularly our world. Genesis 1:1's declaration that "in the beginning, God created the heavens and the earth" refers to more than just the seven "days" of creation's functional development. It also speaks to the *ex nihilo* creation of material substance, which, as verse 2 describes, was initially formless and empty. After that, the Genesis 1 narrative explains how God took this raw material and shaped it into a functioning world, with distinct domains (light/dark, sky/sea, and land/vegetation) and corresponding inhabitants (sun/moon/stars, birds/fish, animals/humans). These "days" serve more as categorical frameworks rather than indicating literal time periods for creation.

Importantly, the seventh day should be seen as part of this creation framework rather than merely what happened afterward. The creation week presents three days of domain construction, three days of populating those domains, and a final day that adds purpose to the entire process. The rest wasn't God withdrawing to recover from his work, but rather a cessation to reflect on his design. Since God embodies truth, goodness, and beauty (TGB) expressed in love, his creation had to reflect those attributes. Humanity, as the pinnacle of creation, needed this reflection of TGB to grow into a proper relationship of love with God.

Not only were humans to recognize TGB in their environment, but God also placed them in charge of maintaining that reflection (Genesis 1:26–28). They were to imitate God by working (ruling) to sustain TGB, and they were also to pause and appreciate it. As Jesus said, "The Sabbath was made for man, not man for the Sabbath" (Mark 2:27).

The first four verses of Genesis 2 are usually translated as narration, but I believe the Hebrew structure forms a chiasmus. Here is my translation:

verse 1:	A		Thus the heavens and the earth, in all their organized array, were finished, and God finished his work on the seventh day.
verse 2:	—B		On the seventh day, God rested from all his work.
verse 3:	——C		Then God blessed the seventh day and set it apart,
	—B1		because on the seventh day, he rested from all the creating work he had done
verse 4:	A¹		that had come about from the creation of the heavens and the earth when the Lord God made the earth and the heavens.

The middle line (C) emphasizes the sanctification of the seventh day. The surrounding lines explain why it was set apart—the creation of a true, good, and beautiful world was complete. The structure of these verses highlights the good work done, leading to a sanctified Sabbath, whose rest involves reflection on that good work. No wonder Jesus dismissed the rebuke of the legalistic Pharisees, who could see only an imposed rule about not working on the Sabbath. The Sabbath was meant for experiencing and enjoying the blessing of creation, which is exactly what the disciples were doing in Mark 2.

After Jesus says, "The Sabbath was made for man, not man for the Sabbath," he adds, "So the Son of Man is Lord even of the Sabbath." In this final statement, Jesus isn't asserting authority over the Sabbath because he is God. He is saying that, since the Sabbath was made for man, he (as a sinless human in complete submission to God's rule of TGB) is a qualified ruler over the Sabbath, which yields its TGB to him. This was God's plan for humanity before sin disrupted everything. Jesus demonstrates the restoration of what had enslaved humankind. We need to be freed to rule in the rest that Christ offers us.

OLD TESTAMENT PICTURES OF ULTIMATE REST

In Matthew 11:28, Jesus invites us to come to him, and he promises, "I will give you rest." This rest—this Promised Land—is described in Revelation 21 and 22, but it begins in the soul that comes to Christ. Even the Old Testament attempts to depict this age of rest, though it provides "only a reflection as in a mirror" (1 Corinthians 13:12). The images understood by OT saints came before the full and perfect revelation of Jesus.

For instance, Ezekiel 40–48 describes a vision of a new temple. Ezekiel prophesied during the period after Solomon's temple had been destroyed and before the rebuilding of the second temple following the Babylonian captivity. However, this prophecy could not refer to the second temple, as its dimensions and practices differ from what actually occurred. Some dispensationalists suggest that this temple will be constructed during a 1,000-year millennial reign of Christ on earth. Yet Hebrews teaches that blood sacrifices, like those mentioned in Ezekiel, have lost their efficacy since Jesus offered the final atonement (Hebrews 10:1–18). Furthermore, the idea that these sacrifices might be commemorative of Christ's atonement seems unlikely, as Ezekiel explicitly speaks of them as atonement for sin. Moreover, Christ instructed his followers to commemorate his death through the use of bread and wine, not by reverting to animal sacrifices. Additionally, there is no New Testament instruction for Christians to construct a physical temple of wood and stone.

Rather than imagining the Ezekiel temple occurring during some future age related to the still-cursed creation, I believe the temple prophecy in Ezekiel is symbolic of our relationship with Christ. The New Testament refers to believers as "living stones" (1 Peter 2:5), built together "on the foundation of the apostles and prophets, with Christ Jesus himself as the chief cornerstone," forming "a holy temple in the Lord" (Ephesians 2:20–21).

Another Old Testament passage that points to our future rest is Isaiah 60–66. John draws on several phrases from these chapters in writing Revelation 21 and 22. However, chapters 65 and 66 of Isaiah present a challenge because they describe a change from the normal course of this age, yet do not seem to depict the perfection John envisions in the final chapters of Revelation. To begin understanding this section of Isaiah, we must first recognize that chapters 65 and 66 are God's response to Israel's plea found in chapters 63 and 64.

In Isaiah 63 and 64, the speaker voices a familiar argument on behalf of Old Testament Israel: praising God for past help, followed by a plea for him to either remember his people, take notice of their oppressors, or reveal his greatness—all in the hope that God will act decisively to deliver Israel or Judah once again. God's response in chapters 65 and 66 combines both condemnation and restoration, but not in the way the speaker had expected. God reveals that he is not a mere tribal deity. He extends his embrace to all who come to him, while cutting off those who reject him. His response is framed in the structure of a chiasmus.

A   Israel/Judah wanted God in conformity to their own terms (65:1)
—B   Israel/Judah rebelled despite God's open arms (65:2–7)
——C   But Israel/Judah includes a remnant who desire God's ways (65:8–10)
———D   Of Israel/Judah, God rejects rebels but rescues his own (65:11–16)
————E   God's people are restored (65:17–66:2)
———D^1 Of nations, God favors the humble but rejects the rebellious (66:2b–4)
——C^1 God gives birth to Zion—his covenant fulfillment (66:5–14a)
—B^1 Many from the nations of the world will continue to reject God (66:14b–17)
A^1 God gathers from all the world those who give themselves to his TGB (66:18–24)

This remarkable passage reveals the full purpose and plan for Zion. God chose Israel both to bring forth the Messiah and to serve as a nation of priests, representing him to the world. Some in Israel fulfilled this role—the faithful remnant who remained focused on God. Others did not—the rebels who were driven by human-centered motives, even within the chosen nation. God promises to restore the remnant, those focused on him, while rejecting those who rely on human efforts.

The passage also clarifies that God's ultimate purpose has always been to gather people from all nations who trust in him. Israel was chosen for a specific role in this, but not to be a separate people with a distinct reward or relationship. In the central climax (part E of the chiasmus), the text reveals the covenant blessings for all who embrace God, whether from Israel or other nations. This is the fulfillment of Zion's purpose! The clarity of this message becomes even more vivid as we explore each corresponding pair of elements within the chiasmus.

A—Israel/Judah wanted God in conformity to their own terms (65:1)

Isaiah 65:1 refers to Israel and Judah. The verse begins with God saying, "I revealed myself to those who did not ask for me," and continues by describing Israel and Judah as "a nation that did not call on my name." At first glance, we might assume God is addressing foreign nations, since Israel and Judah, as God's people, surely sought him. However, God refers to "a nation," not "nations," indicating that he is speaking about Israel and Judah, who are now in captivity, pleading for deliverance.

This introduction, in response to the pleas of chapters 63 and 64, highlights God's concern for hearts that sincerely pursue him. God would have helped Israel and Judah in their troubles, just as he would have helped them before, had they truly sought him. His priority is that their hearts be devoted to him—focused on his truth, goodness, and beauty (TGB).

The imagery here is clear. Expanding the example of Israel to the entire world, we see that the curse placed on humanity by Adam has imprisoned our souls in our physical essence. We long for release, and God longs to provide it. But we must turn to him willingly; he does not coerce. He desires our hearts, but we must freely offer them.

A1—God gathers from all the world those who give themselves to his TGB (66:18–24)

At the other end of the chiasm, we see a focus on the Gentile nations. In 66:18, God declares, "I am about to come and gather the people of all nations and languages." In verse 23, it says, "All mankind will come and bow down before me." This confirms that the second half of the chiasm, extending from the central point, speaks of the nations.

Verse 18 is striking. Although the Jews had their faults, the Gentile nations showed no interest in living for God, and he knew it. Yet, he reaches out to them with the same emphasis on his glory—the TGB necessary for relationship—that he highlighted with Israel.

Verse 19 includes Tarshish among the cities of witness. Likely located in modern-day Spain, Tarshish represents the farthest reaches of the earth from Jerusalem, along with the "distant islands." From these distant lands, God brings "brothers" (misleadingly translated as "people" in verse 20 of the NIV) to the Jews. This demonstrates that the Gentiles gathered will stand on equal covenant footing with the Jews. They will be presented in "clean" vessels, with some becoming priests and Levites. While Gentiles do not literally become priests and Levites, the image signifies the erasing of boundaries between them and Israel.

Verse 22 speaks of new heavens and a new earth, symbolizing the enduring nature of God's protection and provision. Notice that God extends this promise to "your" name and descendants. Who is the "you" here? Throughout this section, God has referred to the Gentiles in the third person ("they" and "them") while addressing the Jews in the second person ("you"). So, although this passage emphasizes the inclusion of Gentiles in the covenant, God does not forsake the Jews. According to verse 22, they too will endure. Paul echoes this idea in Romans 11, explaining that a partial hardening has come to Israel until the full number of Gentiles enters, and then all Israel will be saved. Paul reassures us that God has not abandoned the Jews; rather, he has brought Gentiles into the covenant, creating one people, the "Israel of God" (Galatians 6:16).

This theme neatly bookends the entire book of Isaiah. In chapter 1, verse 2, there is a call to the heavens and earth concerning the children of God who have rebelled. Here, in 66:22, there is a final appeal to the new heavens and the new earth, promising that God will keep his faithful children forever.

B—Israel/Judah rebelled despite God's open arms (65:2–7)

The first interior point addresses the failures of both Judah and the Gentile nations. Focusing first on Judah, we see that the Jews were rebellious, and their rebellion reflected the universal human tendency to rely on something other than God for provision. They began to view God in the same way other nations viewed their gods—merely as a local or provincial deity. When the Jews saw strength in other nations, they wanted to adopt and worship those nations' gods, hoping for the same fortune. In chapter 65, verses 2 through 5a, God expresses this sentiment, saying that though he reached out with open arms, they responded with, "Keep away!"

God declares that he will repay them for their actions, but notice how he frames this judgment. In verses 6b-7a, he says, "I will repay them fully for your iniquities and the iniquities of your fathers together." Who are "them" and "your" referring to? The text connects the actions of parents to their children. While we are not held guilty for our parents' sins, we often follow their patterns, inheriting their dependencies. As we imitate our parents in their sin, we become guilty for reflecting their image rather than God's. Thus, our guilt accumulates for not breaking from past transgressions. So, the "they" and "you" both refer to the Jews, highlighting a heritage that embraced sin across generations.

B1—Many from the nations of the world will continue to reject God (66:14b-17)

On the opposite side of the chiasm, we see the nations engaging in idolatry as well. Chapter 66, verse 17, contains figurative language that manifests in the literal worship of false religions. God had instructed Israel to dedicate and cleanse themselves, with the Old Testament outlining several rituals to achieve this. However, these rituals were never meant to cleanse sin—only God can do that. Instead, they symbolized the act of putting aside anything that might draw them away from God. Similarly, in the rituals of false religions, worshippers wholly dedicate themselves to false gods through their own cleansing rituals.

The phrase "the one they follow" in verse 17 of the NIV is more accurately translated as "the one in the midst that they follow." This suggests that those engaged in these abominable practices are gathered around a central figure. This imagery seems to depict a leader—possibly the most wicked among them—guiding others in their sinful actions. While it may be tempting to identify this leader as Satan, I don't believe that is the intended meaning here. The reference to gardens in worship practices offers further insight. In Scripture, land often symbolizes provision and security. God frequently uses land—whether a garden, mountain, or promised land—to represent his care and protection. Similarly, false religions place emphasis on worship in groves and gardens, mimicking this sense of provision and security.

In the garden of Eden, two trees stood at the center. One symbolized the reward of a relationship that acknowledged God as the provider, while the other symbolized the consequence of a broken relationship. Adam and Eve chose wrongly. I believe verse 17 subtly references this wrong choice—the choice of "the one in the midst," representing those who choose against God.

C—But Israel/Judah includes a remnant who desire God's ways (65:8–10)

Throughout the first half of Isaiah, even among rebellious Judah, a faithful remnant remained—though sinful, they continued or returned to God, trusting him as their provider. In this final passage, we encounter the remnant once again. While the nation as a whole broke the covenant, "new wine" (the faithful remnant) was still found among the grapes.

C1—God gives birth to Zion—his covenant fulfillment (66:5–14a)

Chapter 66, verse 2, identifies the "tremblers" mentioned in verse 5. These are the humble and submissive in spirit, those who tremble at God's word. The "hating brothers" in verse 5 refer to non-God-fearing Gentiles who, in their self-centeredness, mock those who love God. These godless individuals speak sarcastically about glorifying God and witnessing the joy of the faithful, but God declares that it is they, the mockers, who will ultimately be put to shame. The passage continues with Zion (representing God's covenant purpose) as a mother giving birth to her child, symbolizing a relationship. The imagery then expands, portraying Zion as both a mother and a garden.

D—Of Israel/Judah, God rejects rebels but rescues his own (65:11–16)

This section opens with a condemnation of Jews who have turned away from God. There is a wordplay here, as God mentions the Canaanite gods—Fortune and Destiny—that the unfaithful Jews have embraced. In contrast, God declares that he will "destine" them for the sword because they did not respond in faith when he called out to them. The passage contrasts the service of God's faithful ones with the rebellion of the faithless.

As the text moves toward its chiastic conclusion, verse 15 says that God will give his servants a new name, a familiar theme in Scripture. A name in the Bible represents more than just an identifier—it reflects character. When Adam named the animals, it was an exercise in discerning their nature, not just assigning a label. Similarly, praying in Jesus's name means praying according to who Jesus is, what he has done, and in line with his purposes. In Revelation, there is a strong emphasis on being given a new name—a new identity, character, and association—as we place our faith and trust in Christ and God (Revelation 2:17b; 3:12; 14:1; 22:4). The conclusion of this faithful covenant with God is his blessing (65:16).

D1—Of nations, God favors the humble but rejects the rebellious (66:2b-4)

Just as the first part of the chiasmus contrasts the faithful and faithless Jews, the second part highlights the same contrast among the Gentiles. Those who tremble at God's word—humble and submissive in spirit—worship God as they should, while the self-serving may imitate religious practices but with ulterior motives. The emphasis here is not on the specific activities performed but on the motivation and spirit behind them. Thus, the passage does not suggest that Gentiles must set up a system of animal sacrifices, but rather it uses figurative language to indicate that Gentiles will act in trust of God. Once again, those who act out of self-interest are condemned.

E—God's people are restored (65:17-66:2a)

The central point of the chiasmus reveals the glory of restoration. First, God declares the creation of a new heaven and a new earth. Verses 17 through 19 in Isaiah parallel much of what we see in Revelation 21:1-4. In Revelation 21:1, John witnesses the new heaven and new earth, which is also foretold in Isaiah 65:17. Additionally, Isaiah 65:17 mentions that past events will be forgotten, corresponding to Revelation 21:1b and 4b. In Isaiah 65:18-19, we read of God creating a Jerusalem filled with joy, where the sound of weeping and crying will no longer be heard. This mirrors Revelation 21:2, where the new Jerusalem descends from heaven, and verse 4, where God wipes away every tear.

The parallel is unmistakable. In Revelation 21, John makes it clear that this new heaven, new earth, and new Jerusalem—this state of no sorrow and no death—comes after Christ's return and the final judgment. It is at this time that God's people realize their ultimate hope, fulfilling God's Zion purpose: to be fully restored in an everlasting covenant relationship with him. Therefore, as we read the verses following Isaiah 65:17–19, we must keep this context in mind. The passage in Isaiah 65:17–66:2 does not describe an earthly kingdom during this present age, which means both premillennialism and postmillennialism fall short[1]; they do not fit within the context provided by the connection with Revelation.

We cannot interpret this as describing a mostly Christianized but still imperfect era. By aligning Isaiah 65:17–19 with Revelation 21:1–4, we recognize this as a time when Christ has already returned, evil has been completely eradicated, hope is fully realized, and the relationship between God and his people is absolutely complete. With this understanding—and only this understanding—we can move forward through the next verses without becoming entangled in misinterpretation.

Immediately, however, we encounter a verse that seems to challenge even the amillennialist view. Verse 20 begins by stating that infants will no longer live only a few days. (This does not present a problem, since Revelation 21:4 tells us that death will be no more.) However, the next clause, which mentions that an old man will no longer fail to live out his days, raises a slight concern with its implication of a limited lifespan. But the real challenge comes in the second half of the verse: "The one who dies at a hundred will be thought a mere child." While living to 100 years may seem a blessing, the mention of death itself is troubling. Furthermore, the following clause—"the one who fails to reach a hundred will be considered accursed"—is difficult to reconcile with the promise in Revelation 21:4 that death will no longer exist. How can there be curses and death in a time when evil has been fully eradicated?

---

1. There are three major views on what is called the "millennium" (the referenced 1,000 years in Revelation 20:1–7. They are called pre-, post-, and amillennialism based on how they are seen in relation to Christ's return. Premillennialism understands a 1,000-year reign after Christ returns, while he reigns on a yet cursed creation. Postmillennialism sees the world improving, becoming Christianized into a golden era prior to Christ's return. Amillennialism understands our current age to be the millennium (with a less-than-literal calculation of the 1,000 years). My view is amillennial, which will become evident in Part 3 of this book as we examine Revelation.

Premillennialists often respond to this by proposing an intermediate stage where Christ returns to establish an earthly kingdom. In this stage, peace, joy, and safety reign, but evil is still present, though temporarily suppressed. However, this idea raises its own set of problems. If someone dies at 100 and is considered young, how will their death not bring sorrow? Revelation 21:4 tells us that God will wipe away all tears. Even when believers pass away today, their deaths are mourned. How could people be cursed during this supposed era of peace? If the so-called kingdom age is no different from our present age, full of cursed individuals, how can it be described as an era of joy and safety? Moreover, why would death exist in this kingdom age if Revelation insists that death has been removed? How could there still be sin and death if the new heaven, new earth, and new Jerusalem have already arrived, as Isaiah 65:17 and Revelation 21:1 suggest?

Postmillennialists face similar challenges. If we claim a postmillennial view, we cannot expect the new heaven, new earth, and new Jerusalem to coexist with sorrow, sin, and death. How can this be, when people are still dying and being cursed? The issues with both premillennialism and postmillennialism are substantial, but is the difficulty with amillennialism truly insurmountable?

I don't think so. To properly interpret Isaiah 65:20, we need to understand its figurative relationship to the preceding verses (65:17–19). Insisting on a literal interpretation leads to ignoring or misapplying related passages. The six verses from 65:20–25 describe events familiar to us in this life, emphasizing those moments of joy and peace. We celebrate the birth of a child and rejoice when that child grows without sickness or death. We take joy in long life and call those who experience it blessed. We find contentment in securing homes and maintaining stable livelihoods. Having food, shelter, and watching our children thrive are blessings we cherish in this life. Peace and safety, symbolized by the image of the wolf and lamb grazing together without violence, are also blessings of life. This passage paints a picture of the joy, peace, and safety that will characterize our eternal relationship with God.

Here's the key: the passage doesn't describe literal scenes but uses expressions of joy, peace, and safety to help us understand how blessed life with God will be. In other words, it takes the familiar joys of this life and projects them into the next. While the circumstances will change, the joy remains constant. As verse 25 concludes, "They will neither harm nor destroy on all my holy mountain."

God closes the passage with a comforting declaration about himself. He is not a local deity dependent on us for his peace, safety, and joy. We cannot provide for him. Instead, he provides for us. He is our Caregiver, Provider, and Father. He made us, and he made all there is. For eternal provision, we can rest securely in faith and hope, confident in our everlasting love relationship with him.

CONCLUSION

There is no need to invent the complex theological frameworks that both premillennialism and postmillennialism require. The greatest (and perhaps only) argument against amillennialism is that it appears pessimistic regarding the influence of the gospel. But as I've argued, this is not the case. Two vital ideas must be emphasized: (1) God does not coerce, and (2) gospel influence will effectively reach all who come to Christ. These points cannot—must not—be understated. God (Father, Son, and Spirit) will not force compliance. The joy, optimism, and glory of the gospel's effectiveness come not from coercion but from genuine, loving engagement. The result is an authentic, everlasting bond, no matter the numbers.

God's purpose, from the beginning, has been to rescue all who will come to him from every age. This is our blessed hope. With the coming of Christ, in whom we find our rest, we enter the Sabbath. The curse will be removed, and creation will be redeemed.

Part 3

God's Retelling of Creation's Story

21

Introducing the Theme (Rev 1)

Jesus, Thou divine Companion,
Help us all to do our best;
Bless in our daily labor,
Lead us to the Sabbath rest.

—Henry Van Dyke; from "Jesus, Thou Divine Companion"

Jesus told him, "I am the way, the truth, and the life.
No one comes to the Father except through Me."

—John 14:6

There's no denying it—understanding the book of Revelation is a challenge. Its difficulty stems not only from its genre, apocalyptic literature—where signs and symbols convey deeper meanings—but also from the fact that even among apocalyptic works, Revelation takes imagery to the extreme. It layers symbolic references upon one another, often without a clear narrative to ground them. As a result, many Christians tend to avoid the book, unwilling to sift through its complex visuals and speculations, waiting instead for heaven's perspective to shine the dark glass clean.

However, I don't believe God would breathe such insight into the present if its only value was reserved for the future. Still, the book is undeniably challenging.

SEVEN KEY PRINCIPLES

By holding fast to these seven key principles,[1] we can keep the broader vision in mind, even as we navigate through the complexities of the details.

Key Principle #1: Revelation is given to reveal.

Confusing imagery can be frustrating. However, the apostle John believed his writing offered revelation (*apokalypsis*). The Greek prefix *apo* means "from" or "out of," and the root *kalypto* means veil, so the book's title refers to the removal of a veil. Though we may at times feel lost in a maze, we must remember the intent of the very first verse—what we are reading is a revelation of Jesus Christ for his servants—us! We can find the right path.

Key Principle #2: Revelation is a book to be seen.

John didn't receive a dictated manuscript, nor was it just a dream he tried to recall the next morning. But, believing the book is inspired, I affirm that God provided revelation to John's imagination. From that, John reveals this figurative story. A literalist who insists on seeing every image as a concrete form—unless explicitly told otherwise—will likely become discouraged trying to force impossible pictures into a literal framework. Yet we don't have to rely solely on genre classification to understand that the book presents symbols. Verse 1 explains that Christ "sent it and *signified* it through his angel to his servant John" (emphasis added). The Greek word used implies that this revelation comes through signs, not literal depictions. While readers' wild interpretations might result in odd conclusions, the next principle should help keep us grounded.

Key Principle #3: Revelation makes sense only in light of the Old Testament.

The signs and symbols in Revelation are not new. Despite their impressive array—beasts, mountains, falling stars, locusts, rivers, trees, trumpets,

---

1. Johnson, *Triumph*, 6–22. Although I am drawing on key principles from Dennis E. Johnson's book, *Triumph of the Lamb*, my view of Revelation differs somewhat from his. Nonetheless, these key principles offer excellent guidelines for our approach.

seals, and more—these symbols all appear in the Old Testament. It's essential, then, to consistently link them to their original meanings unless the text directs otherwise.

Key Principle #4: Numbers count in Revelation.

Nearly every number mentioned in Revelation carries symbolic significance beyond mere counting. Seven is perhaps the most common, always representing fullness or completeness. Threes, tens, sixes, fours, twelves, and even their multiples also carry important symbolic meaning.

Key Principle #5: Revelation is for us—now (and the "us" can include every generation since it was written).

The main purpose of Revelation is not to predict the distant future, nor does it map out a complete prophetic timeline. Instead, God breathed it to comfort and guide his people through the current age of sin, physical curse, and spiritual warfare. The call to remain faithful amid persecution is a constant theme throughout the book.

Key Principle #6: Revelation concerns "what must soon take place."

Verse 1 states that the revelation concerns "what must soon take place." This doesn't mean events will begin immediately but rather that they will unfold quickly once they start. The emphasis on brevity aligns with the purpose of comfort for God's people. The Bible frequently presents persecution and suffering for the faithful as short-lived, especially in Revelation. Long periods are usually associated with joy and fulfillment. For example, the 10 days of Smyrna's persecution in 2:10 contrast with the 1,000 years of reigning with Christ in 20:4 (although neither period is meant to be taken as an exact length of time).

Key Principle #7: The victory belongs to God and to his Christ.

Though the book recounts tribulation, persecution, and suffering, the events inevitably lead to the final and complete blessing—God's victory over the curse, sin, evil, and death, culminating in eternal rest.

REVEALING JESUS

The prologue begins with clear purpose. Right from the start, verse 1 tells us that God wants to reveal Jesus the Christ to his servants. Notice that God is not revealing Jesus as the Son of God, the Word, or the King of kings, but as Christ. "Christ" is the Greek equivalent of the Hebrew "Messiah," emphasizing Jesus's anointed and appointed mission as God's faithful-servant rescuer.[2] God, being all-knowing, understood from the beginning the potential need for rescue. With his grasp of all possibilities, God meticulously planned this rescue from the start, initiating it through the Old Testament covenants with Abraham, Moses, and David. The plan reached its culmination through the virgin birth, the sinless life of the Messiah, his crucifixion, and his resurrection, and it will conclude with Jesus's glorious return.

With God's awareness of all possibilities in mind, it's clear that this final book reveals more than just end-time events. Since the book aims to reveal the Messiah, it encompasses all of Jesus's activity throughout Scripture. This book provides a complete and perfect summation of God's revelation in Jesus the Christ.

Verse 3 offers insight into God's reason for recounting his plan for Jesus's faithful-servant rescue. The verse promises a blessing to those who hear, read, and keep the prophecy.[3] We must constantly remind ourselves of the foundational purpose of creation: God created his image-bearers for an everlasting love relationship. Everything—every thought in Scripture, every divine action—hinges on this central truth. If any interpretation or idea cannot be traced back to this grounding purpose, it should be questioned. Therefore, God's design in revealing Jesus Christ must, like everything else, support our everlasting love relationship with him. The blessing in keeping this prophecy—this revelation of Jesus—comes as we embrace all that God reveals of his rescue and the rescuer, maturing in that love relationship.

The blessing is tied to the declaration that "the time is near!" As believers in and citizens of the kingdom of heaven, we cannot let the world overwhelm our pursuit of God and his truth, goodness, and beauty. We

---

2. The term "God's faithful-servant rescuer" can be understood both as Jesus being God's faithful servant in bringing rescue and as Jesus rescuing those who are faithful servants.

3. Prophecy (Greek *propheteia*) is not mere prediction. It denotes God's revealed purposes.

must remain faithful. The time is now—the need for faithfulness is now. The challenges, persecutions, and tribulations happen now, and therefore, we must hold fast to our faith *now*.

Even though apocalyptic-type figures exist throughout the prologue, the narrative initially anchors us in the literal and easily recognizable world. But the imagery John introduces us to in the descriptions he gives for God, for the Spirit, and for Jesus sets the tone for the book's emphasis. Of course, God is the great three-in-one. And part of that trinitarian outlook means that all three Persons of our one God share their one essence. But in their activity of restoration, they take distinctive roles to accomplish the whole.

These distinct roles are not necessarily eternal characteristics of their Persons but are, nevertheless, specific to each Person's activity in the restoration of God's image-bearers. God's oneness means their essence is the same; each Person has full access to that essence. So, our God is one. But in acting for the cooperative purpose of image-bearer restoration, the activities of each Person of the Godhead are indeed specifically directed. We see this clearly in Jesus, who, in becoming human, temporarily and voluntarily gave up access to certain divine abilities, like omniscience (e.g., Matthew 24:36; Luke 2:52), to demonstrate the human responsibility of trusting in God's guidance (e.g., Matthew 4:1; John 5:19). Even the names "Father" and "Son" reflect role distinctions, though in other aspects, Jesus is even referred to as Father (Isaiah 9:6).

In Revelation 1, John describes the Persons of God in their roles related to restoration. The Father represents the steadfast, immovable surety of the plan—the God who holds it with certainty for all eternity. In perfect truth, goodness, and beauty, he will see the plan through without coercion. This paradox of God's absolute prophetic certainty alongside non-coercive relationship leads to the Holy Spirit's role in building our confidence. The Spirit teaches, admonishes, and turns revelation into wisdom, using the fire of his presence to bring the revelation to light and reveal its quality. This perfect Spirit of God comforts, assuring us through that refining fire, while heaven reveals Jesus to us.

Everything ultimately connects in Jesus. He is God—this we know, proclaim, and sing about. But sometimes, in our enthusiasm, we obscure the importance of his mission. Equally crucial is that Jesus is human! All the descriptors of Jesus in verse 5 focus not on his deity but on his humanity and his role in restoration. In his humanity, he died for us. In his humanity, he rose again. The three descriptions of Jesus in this verse align with his redemptive work. He is the "faithful witness," living his earthly life in dependence on the Father. He is the "firstborn from the dead," having given up his cursed physical body but, because he was sinless, able to reclaim life, free from the curse. Finally, he is the "ruler of the kings of the earth," not in the sense of ruling over earthly kings but in demonstrating true versus false rule. This last title echoes Psalm 89:27, where God says of David, "I will appoint him to be my firstborn, the most exalted of the kings of the earth." Similarly, "most exalted" is the meaning we should understand in Revelation 1:5. By conquering the curse, Jesus reclaimed the dominion God had originally given to humanity in Genesis 1:26–28, which was lost when humanity submitted to its physical essence (Genesis 3:6–19; Romans 1:21–32).

Redemption shines as the purpose of the atonement, and redemption requires a kinsman redeemer. Only a human representative could defeat death and bring about our rescue. Thus, Jesus, in his humanity, assures us that we can be united with God in an everlasting love relationship—the very reason for the rescue and the purpose for creation. This description highlights Jesus the Christ.

The prologue continues to encourage, affirming that Jesus's glory and dominion are forever and that his return is certain. However, this encouragement is for believers alone. As verse 7 suggests, his coming will be both a blessing and a curse—a blessing for those who, by faith, accept him as Lord, but a curse for those who reject him. The verse reveals the love and mercy behind Jesus's return, even for those who pierced him. The "piercers" are not only the few who physically nailed him to the cross or stabbed his side, but also all who, in sharing the same essence, figuratively participated in that act. The "peoples on earth," symbolizing those entrenched in physical-essence worship, will wail in self-pity.

God foretold this blessing-and-curse dichotomy in Genesis 12:3, prophesied it in Zechariah 12:10, and here acknowledges its sad inevitability. This weighs heavily against the belief in universalism. Throughout the New Testament, including Revelation, Christ's return is consistently balanced between joyful redemption and mourning (Matthew 24:29–31; Colossians 3:4–6; 1 Thessalonians 4:13–18; 2 Thessalonians 1:5–10; 2 Peter 3:10–16). The mourning occurs because of those who refuse to embrace Jesus, who pursue their own path, as Peter says, "to their own destruction."

As the section concludes, the Father, Son, and Spirit claim the Old Testament title of Alpha and Omega, the first and the last (Isaiah 44:6)—the one who is, who was, and who is to come, the Almighty!

Verses 1–3 serve as the book's preface, with the first part of verse 4 providing the from-and-to address before continuing through verse 8 with the salutation. In verse 9, the book begins in earnest. Some readers might be tempted to skip introductions to get to the main content, but doing so would miss the purposeful foundation this chapter lays.

Because of the stylistic differences of chapters 1 through 3, readers often treat them as a separate book. However, the keys found in these opening chapters unlock interpretations of the latter parts. While the bulk of the introduction (including chapters 2 and 3) consists of messages to the seven churches, those messages also have an introduction. John tells us in verse 9 that he is our companion in suffering, in the kingdom, and in the endurance that is in Jesus. Notice the mini chiasmus—tribulation, kingdom, and endurance. The first and last ideas—suffering and endurance—are tied together, pointing to the central idea of the kingdom of God, a kingdom unlike the power-driven systems of this world, as Jesus emphasized in John 18:36 and as depicted throughout the Gospels.

John then recounts that he was in the Spirit on the Lord's Day when he heard a voice like a trumpet. The Lord's Day, a term already in use by the late first century when Revelation was written, refers to Sunday.[4] The phrase "in the Spirit," however, may be less familiar. Was John in a trance? Or was he simply worshiping? The point seems less about what John was doing and more about introducing a heavenly message, similar to how Old Testament prophets framed their messages. This pattern repeats frequently, especially in Ezekiel, where the Spirit enters and a loud voice, like rushing waters, announces a message (e.g., Ezekiel 40:1–2; 43:1–5). By setting the scene this way, John makes it clear that what follows is a divine message, though he serves as the prophet-messenger bringing this revelation from God.

John hears a voice commanding him to write to the seven churches. As he turns to see who is speaking, it becomes clear that the appearance of Jesus is as much a part of the revealed vision as the imagery that follows. The act of turning to see connects the image of Jesus (the Redeemer) with the broader vision of redemption found throughout chapters 4–22,

---

4. The earliest record (beside Revelation) of calling Sunday "the Lord's Day" is from Ignatius of Antioch in AD 110 in a letter to the Magnesians, a people located in modern-day Turkey.

as well as with the church messages in chapters 2 and 3. This carryover suggests that the church messages are not meant to be separated from the rest of the book as descriptions of a different era. Rather, the entire vision applies to the entire age. The seven churches, therefore, represent all Christians throughout the interadventual period, but they were also literal churches during that time. As such, the message is directed to them as well as to every generation until Christ returns. Revelation calls all of us to remain faithful, trusting, and hopeful as God gathers his people for redemption through this cursed, evil-spewing world (12:15–17).

Significantly, before John even glimpses Jesus, his eyes are drawn to the seven golden lampstands, symbols of light (revelation) for the vision to come. A few verses later, we learn that the lampstands represent the churches. The number seven signifies completeness, meaning the seven lampstands symbolize the entire people of God. Being made of gold, they also signify great value to their owner. John then sees Jesus standing among these lampstands, reminding us that Jesus—Immanuel, God with us—stands among the churches he treasures.

John describes Jesus as "one like a son of man," echoing the phrase from Daniel 7:13, where a heavenly figure appears in human form—exactly who Jesus is. The imagery continues, emphasizing both priestly and kingly aspects. Jesus wears a long robe with a sash (Leviticus 16:4). His head and hair are white (Daniel 7:9). His eyes burn like fire (reminiscent of the fire that continually burns before God in Leviticus 6:13). His feet shine like bronze—a rare word in Greek, *chalkolibanon*, used only here in Revelation. This appears to be a combination of two root words: *chalkos* (brass) and *libanos* (frankincense). Both substances feature in priestly duties—brass for the tabernacle's laver (Exodus 30:18) and frankincense for burning before the Lord in worship (Exodus 30:7; Leviticus 21:1). These images in the Old Testament represent the priestly function of mediating between the unrighteous congregation and God. In the same way, Jesus, our Redeemer, stands between God and us, bringing us to God—the central focus of the entire book.

As John gazes upon Jesus, like many Old Testament prophets during their visions, he collapses before him (e.g., Ezekiel 43:1–3; Daniel 8:17, 10:7–9). Just as the Old Testament messenger often did (Daniel 10:8–10), Jesus reaches out to touch him, providing strength and encouragement. Jesus tells John not to be afraid, anticipating the purpose of the messages to the churches. Jesus then offers further reassurance, not only to John but to the churches throughout this age: Jesus is the First and the Last, the Living One who was dead but now lives forever, and he holds the keys of death and Hades. These declarations comfort and affirm Jesus's divinity—the same God who declared himself the First and the Last (Isaiah 44:6), whose name, Yahweh, means the "Living One." At the same time, these statements underscore Jesus's role as our human redeemer: he died, rose again, and holds the keys of death and Hades—not as a jailor to lock people in, but as the Redeemer who sets us free.

JESUS REVEALING

As both God and kinsman redeemer, Jesus instructs John to write "what you have seen, what is now, and what will take place later" (1:19). Just like the descriptions in 1:4 and 1:8 ("him who is, and who was, and who is to come"), this threefold instruction encompasses past, present, and future, speaking to Christ's complete redemptive work: (1) John saw Jesus as the redeemer who had already accomplished the atonement sacrifice, (2) John will witness the present struggle in the age of kingdom building, and (3) John will glimpse the future redeemed promised land, cleansed of the curse.

Jesus reveals that the seven stars represent the angels of the churches, and the churches themselves are the lampstands. As we move through chapters 2 and 3, each letter is addressed not to the churches themselves, but to the angel of the church. This raises two important questions: who are these angels, and why are the letters addressed to them rather than directly to the churches?

The Greek word *aggelos*, translated as "angel," means messenger. Some scholars suggest that the "angel" addressed in each letter is not a literal angelic being but rather the collective spirit of that particular church. However, since calling a Christian community a "church" already recognizes its collective unity, adding another layer of representation as an "angel" seems unnecessary. Other scholars propose that the angel might be the pastor of the church, drawing on the idea of a messenger. But this view introduces a hierarchical intermediary among Christ's followers, which doesn't align with New Testament teachings.

Angels, it seems, have a supportive role in relation to humankind. While a detailed study of angels is beyond the scope of this discussion, their purpose appears to be to influence and direct according to God's will. Before the fall, angels were likely under indirect human authority, as humans were tasked with ruling the physical world (Genesis 1:26, 28). When humanity fell into subjugation to the physical realm, the role of angels shifted to providing support and spiritual influence, rather than succumbing to physical corruption. This idea fits the role we see angels play throughout Scripture, including here as helpers of the churches.

A glance back at the Old Testament shows that spiritual understanding was often delivered to prophets through angels. Daniel, from whom John draws much of his imagery, received many of his heavenly messages via angels (Daniel 7:16; 8:13; 8:15–17; 9:21; 10:5, 10). The pattern throughout Scripture is consistent: God delivers his message to an angel (or Christ), who then delivers it to a prophet (or the people). This pattern underscores God's loving care, using angels to communicate with humanity. It may also explain why Lucifer was in Eden—the garden of God's pleasure—assigned to support the newly created image-bearers. However, Lucifer sought to free himself from the human authority that was meant to surpass him in relationship with God.

In this opening chapter, we find angels receiving these messages from God through Christ, with the purpose of delivering them to the churches. This pattern is repeated throughout Revelation. Chapter 1, verse 1, establishes the order: "The revelation from Jesus Christ, which God gave him to show his servants what must soon take place. *He* made it known by sending *his angel* to *his servant John*" (emphasis added). Throughout the book, we continue to see heavenly messages delivered through angels (7:13; 10:8; 11:1; 14:6–9; 17:1; 17:7; 19:9; 21:9; 22:6). Even today, God uses angels to communicate his message to our hearts. Jesus intends these seven messages to awaken the spiritual awareness of his people, and angels, whose very purpose is to serve as messengers, are the ones who deliver them.

22

Encouraging with Reward (Rev 2–3)

God grant that this tired flesh may rest
('Mid many a musing mourner),
While the sermon is preached and the rites are read
In no church where the heart of love is dead,
And the pastor's a pious prig at best,
But in some small nook where God's confessed,—
Some little church round the corner.

—John Chadwick; from "The Little Church round the Corner"

I will declare thy name unto my brethren,
in the midst of the church will I sing praise unto thee.

—Hebrews 2:12 KJV

Revelation 2 opens with the first message to the churches. The structure of these letters, the histories of the actual first-century cities, and the imagery and guidance used within them offer a fascinating study in their own right. Many excellent commentaries provide in-depth analyses on this topic. However, such a detailed review falls outside the scope of this book. Our focus is on connecting Revelation's portrayal of the present age and its eschatological vision to the foundational ideas of Kinship theology. Therefore, I will simply summarize the messages, leaving the finer details to other resources.

EPHESUS

Jesus directs the first letter to the church in Ephesus. In each of these messages, he introduces himself in a way that reflects the particular message for that church. To Ephesus, he reveals himself as the one who holds the seven stars and walks among the lampstands, signifying an Immanuel-like closeness—a heart of love in relationship.

In most of these letters, Jesus begins by commending the church for some admirable activity or attitude. For the Ephesians, he praises their diligence in rooting out false doctrine and teachers. After this commendation, Jesus typically addresses a shortcoming. In Ephesus, they had abandoned their first love. While love for Christ or God comes first, Jesus is likely referring to the love he commanded for his disciples in the Gospel of John (John 13:34)—the "new command" to love one another. Though the Old Testament law was grounded in this same principle (Matthew 22:37–40), Jesus's example revealed the true nature of love, and his atonement made it possible. However, the Ephesians had started to drift away from this communal love.

We see signs of this decline in other passages. In Acts 20, before returning to Jerusalem, Paul stops at Miletus, near Ephesus, to meet with the Ephesian elders. His message to them emphasizes two points: they must guard against "savage wolves" who would "distort the truth" (for which Jesus later commends them) and follow Paul's example of ministering in love. Even then, Paul was so concerned about their waning love that he interrupted his journey to offer this warning. Soon after, Paul was imprisoned in Rome, where he wrote his epistle to the Ephesians, once again addressing their struggle with love.

Paul's letter to the Ephesians focuses on the division between Christian Jews and Gentiles in the church. He reminds them of their unity in Christ—how Christ himself is our peace, breaking down the barrier of hostility between them (Ephesians 2:14). For four chapters, Paul urges them to walk as transformed people, not like the world. He instructs them to cast off "bitterness, rage, anger, brawling, and slander" (4:31) and, in chapter 5, to abandon selfishness in favor of self-giving love. He encourages them to be filled with the Spirit, "speaking to one another with psalms, hymns, and songs from the Spirit. Sing and make music from your heart to the Lord, always giving thanks to God the Father for everything, in the name of our Lord Jesus Christ. Submit to one another out of reverence for Christ" (5:19–21). Power struggles and selfish ambition divide; Paul exhorts all—wives, husbands, children, parents, slaves, and masters—to serve one another for the sake of their community. The Ephesians had forgotten this and had abandoned their first love.

Still concerned about this issue, Paul later wrote his first letter to Timothy, whom he had left as pastor in Ephesus. In chapter 2, he urges the men of the church to pray, lifting holy hands without anger or arguing. This gesture of lifting hands in prayer symbolizes surrender and dependence on God—an attitude that is incompatible with harboring anger and resentment toward members of God's community. Paul similarly encourages the women to demonstrate this attitude, suggesting their adornment should be reflected in good deeds (2:10)—giving of themselves to others.

In the Revelation letter, Jesus also praises the Ephesians for hating the practices of the Nicolaitans, a term derived from the Greek words *nikos* (to conquer) and *laos* (people). It refers to those who seek to rule over others. God did not establish a hierarchy of spiritual authority in his church. We are all invited to boldly approach the throne, with Christ as our sole mediator.

The message to Ephesus, like the others, concludes with a call to listen: "Whoever has ears, let them hear." Jesus uses this same phrase in Matthew 13:9 to urge those who love God to listen to what draws them into deeper relationship. He promises the overcomers the right to eat from the tree of life, which symbolizes eternal relationship with him. We already possess eternal life with God (John 3:16), but the tree of life represents the ultimate fulfillment of creation and redemption—the fullness of everlasting love in relationship with God. As we follow Christ in love, we experience the joy of that relationship.

SMYRNA

In the letter to Smyrna, Jesus introduces himself as "the First and the Last, the One who was dead and came to life." God uses the title "first and last" in Isaiah 44 to instill confidence that he alone is God, and no one else will ever take control. Jesus adopts the title here for the same reason, adding that, though he died, he is now alive. This shows that no worldly power can conquer him. The Smyrnaean Christians needed this message as they faced socio-religious persecution.

Just as unions support workers today, guilds in Smyrna provided similar support to trade workers. However, religion was intertwined with society, and each guild, along with its dues, was dedicated to a particular god. Christians who refused to participate in this pagan worship found it difficult to secure work outside the guilds, which dominated the economy. But the challenge went beyond financial hardship. Smyrna's residents believed that everyone needed to offer worship to their gods and to Caesar for the well-being of the city. Anyone who refused this was seen as a threat to society. As a result, Christians faced persecution on social, economic, and religious levels.

The Jews, on the other hand, enjoyed official recognition as a religious group by Roman decree, which allowed them to establish their own subculture and rely on each other without much interference from the larger society. However, even the Jews mistreated early Christians, most of whom had converted from Judaism. The Jews didn't want Christians (mostly former Jews) to benefit from their official religious status. As a result, Christians were ostracized by both the general community and the Jewish subculture, leaving them isolated in a society that required official religious participation at every turn.

Jesus refers to the Jews as "a synagogue of Satan" (2:9). While they gathered in synagogues (the Greek word for assembly or congregation) to worship God, from God's perspective, their rejection of his redemptive plan opposed his relational purpose. Since Satan leads the opposition to God's plan, Jesus indicates that these Jews, with their counter-purpose, became an assembly of adversaries.

Jesus tells the Smyrnaean Christians not to be afraid, though he does not promise to intervene and rescue them physically. Instead, he encourages them not to fear, despite the suffering they are about to endure. During his earthly ministry, Jesus said, "Do not be afraid of those who kill the body but cannot kill the soul. Rather, be afraid of the One who can destroy both soul and body in hell" (Matthew 10:28). Once again, he emphasizes the hope found in eternal relationship with God. Though physical suffering was imminent, it would be short-lived, symbolically described as 10 days—a brief time in contrast to eternal life.

Those who remain faithful even to the point of physical death will receive the crown of life. Jesus uses a phrase familiar to the Smyrnaeans. The ancient city of Smyrna was situated atop a prominent hill. When Alexander the Great passed through centuries earlier, he left plans to rebuild the city at the waterfront below, making it more accessible for trade. While the newer, lower Smyrna became the center of commerce, the acropolis—the government and public buildings—remained on the hill, which was referred to as the "crown of Smyrna." In contrasting physical life and death with eternal life and death, Jesus urges the Smyrnaeans to let go of the crown of Smyrna and instead pursue the crown of life, which will shield them from the second (spiritual) death.

PERGAMUM

To the church in Pergamum, Jesus presents himself as the one who wields the sharp, double-edged sword. A double-edged sword cuts, divides, and discerns. It calls to mind the "living and active" sword described in Hebrews 4:12, which penetrates soul, spirit, joints, and marrow. This symbol reflects Jesus's complete and profound understanding of human beings as bearers of God's image.

Jesus praises the church in Pergamum for holding firm to their faith in him, even while living in "the place where Satan has his throne." On Pergamum's highest hill stood a temple dedicated to Zeus, the chief god of Greek mythology. But the city was also known for its devotion to Caesar, whom they worshiped as a god. Emperor worship officially began after Augustus's death when the Roman Senate declared him divine. However, the people of Pergamum had already begun worshiping him during his life, erecting a temple in his honor.

Without modern media like the internet, television, or radio, the people knew of Caesar only through stories told by travelers. To them, Caesar seemed godlike—an unseen figure who wielded power over the entire empire, whose goodwill benefited their city, and whose displeasure could bring disaster. So, it wasn't a stretch for the people of Pergamum to add Caesar to their worship of Zeus. Because of this fusion of pagan and imperial worship, Jesus refers to the city as Satan's throne.

Though the Christians in Pergamum remained faithful, Jesus criticizes them for tolerating those who held to the teachings of Balaam and the Nicolaitans. Interestingly, the name "Balaam" in Hebrew mirrors the meaning of the Greek word "Nicolaitans"—both implying the conquering of people. In Numbers 22–24, we find the story of Balaam, a prophet hired by Balak, the king of Moab, to curse the Israelites as they journeyed toward the Promised Land. Initially, Balaam sought God's approval to go with Balak's messengers, but God forbade him. However, after Balak's repeated offers of riches, Balaam persisted with God, and God ultimately granted his petition, though with strict instructions to speak only what God commanded.

So Balaam set out to meet Balak. Along the way, his donkey stopped three times after seeing the imposing Angel of the Lord. Frustrated, Balaam repeatedly whipped the donkey to get it moving until, finally, the donkey turned to Balaam and spoke in protest. At that moment, God opened Balaam's eyes to see the angel. This encounter likely helped ensure that Balaam would stay faithful to God's words when he later blessed Israel instead of cursing them. Naturally, his blessings angered Balak, who withheld the promised reward. Disappointed and empty-handed, Balaam returned home.

While the story seems to end there in Numbers 24, something feels unresolved. Balaam, a seemingly insignificant prophet, had just defied Balak, the king of Moab, who commanded an army. Balak had every reason to be furious—Balaam had done the exact opposite of what he was paid to do. Could such a powerful king have simply shrugged it off and let Balaam leave unscathed? The following chapter in Numbers offers some clues.

In Numbers 25, we learn that the Israelite men began engaging in sexual relationships with Moabite women. Later, they also became involved with Midianite women. These relationships weren't mere casual encounters; they involved intermarriage between the Israelites and these foreign women.

By Numbers 31, we find that a plague had struck the Israelites due to their sin of intermarrying with the Moabites and Midianites, which led them to abandon the worship of God and turn to the false god Baal. Enraged, Moses commanded the Israelites to destroy the Midianites, who had conspired with the Moabites. Though the Israelites carried out the attack, they spared most of the women. Moses was furious again, as he had ordered the women to be killed to prevent their continued influence in leading the Israelites away from God. Later, it is revealed that this plan to lead Israel astray through intermarriage had originated from Balaam's advice. Numbers 31:15–16 records Moses's words: "'Have you allowed all the women to live?' [Moses] asked them. 'They were the ones who followed Balaam's advice and enticed the Israelites to be unfaithful to the Lord in the Peor incident, so that a plague struck the Lord's people.'"

It seems likely that, after Balaam's failure to curse Israel, Balak may have threatened him. In an effort to save himself, Balaam proposed a new strategy: encourage the Moabite and Midianite women to intermarry with the Israelites, leading them away from God and causing divine anger to fall upon them. Balak followed this advice, seeking to "conquer the people" (the meaning of Balaam's name) not through direct conflict, but through a subtle, subversive plan.

In light of this historical background, the message to the church in Pergamum becomes clear. While they hadn't denied their faith—just as Balaam hadn't directly cursed Israel—they allowed corrupting influences to infiltrate their community. By tolerating these teachings, they compromised their relationship with God.

Jesus concludes his message to Pergamum by urging them to listen and promising hidden manna to those who overcome. In the Old Testament, manna was the divine food that sustained the Israelites on their journey to the Promised Land. In John 6:35, Jesus calls himself the bread of life, symbolizing God's provision for spiritual health. The hidden manna in Revelation, in contrast to the feasts of idols, represents the true sustenance God provides to his people in every age.

Along with the hidden manna, Jesus promises a white stone with a new name inscribed on it, known only to its recipient. This white stone has several possible interpretations: (1) it could refer to a judge's use of white stones to signify acquittal in a trial, (2) it may allude to the white stones given to victors in athletic games, granting them access to special privileges, or (3) it could relate to the onyx stones engraved with the names of the tribes of Israel worn by the high priest in the Old Testament.

Each interpretation reinforces a consistent theme of faithfulness and belonging to God. The secrecy of the new name signifies an intimate, personal relationship with him, just as the hidden manna speaks to his ongoing provision and care.

THYATIRA

Christ describes himself to the church in Thyatira as the one with eyes like a fiery flame and feet like fine bronze, highlighting his priestly role. Both fire and bronze held symbolic importance in temple cleansing. The bronze laver stood before the entrance to the Tabernacle and Temple's Holy Place, and the incense altar was located in the Holy Place just before the Holy of Holies. These elements signify washing and refining, both essential for a relationship with God.

Jesus commends the Thyatiran Christians for their love, faith, service, and perseverance. Together, these qualities encompass all the virtues praised in the previous churches. Unlike the Ephesians, they had not lost their first love. Like the Smyrnaeans, they endured hardship, and like the Christians in Pergamum, they remained faithful. No other church after them receives a greater list of commendations. Jesus even notes that they were growing in these virtues.

However, they had a significant problem: they tolerated a woman referred to as Jezebel. This name evokes the Old Testament figure, the wife of King Ahab, who led Israel into pagan worship. The reference here likely signifies a similar form of evil, and the Thyatirans were allowing this sin to persist within their church.

Notice how Jesus addresses this sin. First, he gives them time to repent (2:21). This stands in contrast to how many Christians respond today—often quick to separate and condemn. "God hates sin," we declare, "and so we must hate it too!" But Christ, in line with the ideals of love in his Sermon on the Mount, offers time for repentance. His deepest desire is restoration, not rejection. He loves without limit, and the very existence of a cursed world for thousands of years testifies to God's patient longing for redemption and reconciliation.

For those who refuse to repent, Jesus uses imagery to show his inability to accept sin. The "sickbed" he mentions refers to the same couch (Greek *kline*) used for reclining at meals or bearing invalids. This image conveys that their indulgence in idol feasts leads to spiritual sickness.

It is important to read verse 23 without imposing human emotions of anger or hatred onto it. Literally, Jesus says, "I will kill her children with death." Death here signifies separation from God. Jesus is not speaking of violent punishment, but rather the inevitable outcome of rejecting his gracious love. He cannot sustain those who refuse to embrace his truth, goodness, and beauty (TGB). The apostle James highlights the error of claiming faith while living in opposition to these virtues. Living sinfully leads, over time, to heartache and spiritual decay—it must, by its very nature. Actions matter. We are called to live in truth, goodness, and beauty, relying on Christ in all things. Through this faithfulness, we overcome.

To the overcomers, Jesus promises authority to rule over the nations. This ruling does not refer to governing earthly nations, the unsaved, or any hierarchical system in some future intermediate state prior to the new heavens and earth. Rather the ruling refers to the original rule of the physical world God entrusted to human stewardship (Genesis 1:26,

28). Humanity lost that dominion with the curse, but Jesus, through his sinless life, death, and resurrection, conquered the physical realm. The redemption he achieved includes restoring creation from its curse, and we share in Christ's rule over it.

Jesus also promises the morning star—a star that shines brighter than all others. The morning star contrasts with the darkness of the night just vanquished and with the other stars that have faded from the sky. In Revelation 22:16, Jesus is called the bright morning star. Before his fall, Satan was also referred to as a morning star (Isaiah 14:12). For the Thyatirans, Christ as the morning star represents the hope of the redeemed. Matthew's Gospel recounts the appearance of a morning star (the star in the east) that guided the Magi to the birth of Jesus—Immanuel, God with us. In the same way, the overcomers will experience the birth of eternal life with God.

SARDIS

Sardis has a rich history in more ways than one. The famous King Croesus, ruler of the Lydians in the sixth century BC, lived in Sardis. His immense wealth gave rise to the expression "rich as Croesus," which is still used today. Part of his wealth came from the abundant gold and silver deposits in the region, and another part from Sardis's strategic position along the land route that connected the Greek world with the East (modern-day Middle East).

Fearing the growing power of the Persian Empire in the sixth century, Croesus consulted the Oracle of Delphi, who told him that if he attacked Persia, he would destroy a great empire. Encouraged, Croesus marched on Persia. However, the battle ended in a stalemate, and Croesus returned to Sardis to wait out the winter. King Cyrus of Persia, unwilling to leave Croesus unchecked, pursued him back to Sardis and engaged in battle.

Sardis was built on a hill, guarded on three sides by sheer rock cliffs, making it nearly impossible for Cyrus's army to attack. But according to legend, during a lull in the fighting, a Sardian guard stationed on the back side of the city wall dropped his helmet. To retrieve it, he climbed down a hidden trail along the cliffs. A Persian soldier witnessed this descent, reported it to his commanders, and the Persians used the secret path to launch a surprise attack on the city. As the Oracle had predicted, a great empire was destroyed—Croesus's Lydian Empire, not the Persian.

This historical event illustrates the Sardians' misplaced trust in their wealth and fortified position. Jesus's message to Sardis addresses that same attitude. He appears to them as the one who holds the seven spirits of God and the seven stars, symbolizing his unique role as the only true means of divine access.

Unlike the other churches, the letter to Sardis offers no commendation. Jesus rebukes them, saying they have a reputation for being alive but are actually dead. This likely refers to the city's necropolis (graveyard), which was so prominent that from seven miles away, Sardis appeared to be surrounded by "a thousand hills." Upon closer inspection, travelers realized these hills were burial mounds. This physical reality served as a spiritual metaphor for Sardis's condition: though they seemed alive, they were spiritually dead. Their works, Jesus says, were incomplete—lacking the truth, goodness, and beauty that come from a genuine relationship with God.

Jesus calls them to wake up and repent, warning that he will come like a thief—possibly alluding to the Persian surprise attack. To those who overcome, he promises white garments, symbolizing purity. This purity reflects that while good works flow from a righteous heart, those works alone do not establish a right relationship with God. It is faith and trust in God that make this relationship possible. Jesus also assures them that their names will never be erased from the book of life. Their security is not in themselves, but in their trust in God.

PHILADELPHIA

Attalus II, the second son of Attalus I Soter, king of Pergamum, founded the city of Philadelphia. His older brother, Eumenes, took the throne after their father's death. Attalus II, a skilled military commander, fought alongside the Romans in battle. Impressed by his abilities and loyalty, the Romans offered to help him overthrow his brother and claim the kingship for himself. Attalus refused, earning the nickname *Philadelphus*, meaning "lover of his brother." He embraced the name, founding the city of Philadelphia, which comes from the Greek words *phileo* (love) and *adelphos* (brother). While some reduce *phileo* to a simple brotherly affection, the term speaks of a deep love of heart and passion, distinct from the reasoned nature of *agape*.

Philadelphia, however, lay along a fault line. A powerful earthquake in AD 17 reduced the city to rubble. Tiberius Caesar not only forgave their tribute that year but also financed the city's rebuilding. Yet, the loss of life left the people shaken. Many rebuilt their homes outside the city, hoping to avoid the devastation of future quakes. While the Sardians, as discussed earlier, believed in their invulnerability, the Philadelphians lived with constant insecurity.

To these vulnerable Christians, Jesus reveals himself as the Holy One, the true One, the keeper of the key of David. He opens what no one can shut and shuts what no one can open, a phrase taken from Isaiah 22:22. In that passage, God reprimands Shebna, a court clerk who, during Israel's turmoil, busied himself with building an extravagant tomb. For his arrogance, God declares Shebna would lose his position, replaced by another who would serve as a peg firmly fastened in a wall. Yet, even that peg would eventually loosen and fall, a reminder that no human strength or arrogance could endure. Only trust in God could sustain.

Jesus tells the Philadelphians that he knows they have little strength, but this does not refer to their capacity for endurance, love, or devotion to Christ. In fact, the following phrases affirm that they had kept his word and had not denied his name. Instead, Jesus likely refers to their insecurity in the face of external circumstances. His message reassures them: "I know you. Despite your limited strength, you have kept my word and not denied my name. For that, I will be faithful to you."

Because of their faithfulness, Jesus sets before them an open door, symbolizing their entry into God's embrace. He then rebukes the unbelieving Jews, calling them a synagogue of Satan, emphasizing that the term "Jew" truly applies only to those who are God's people, not simply to those of ethnic descent. These unbelieving Jews sought to exclude Christians who trusted in God's redemptive plan through Jesus, but Jesus, who alone controls access to God, would not allow that. He promises to keep the faithful Christians from (or through) the coming hour of testing—this present age marked by sin and curse.

Finally, Jesus assures the Philadelphians that he is coming quickly. The Bible often portrays tribulation as brief compared to the eternal relationship with God. Jesus promises rewards full of certainty and security—exactly what these earthquake-wary Christians needed. They would become pillars in God's temple. For survivors of quakes, this image of strength and stability would have resonated deeply. Jesus also promises they will bear the name of God, the city of God, and Christ's new name—a flood of relational imagery that assures them of their lasting place in his kingdom.

LAODICEA

Laodicea was a wealthy city, renowned for its production of black wool fabric. It was also a medical hub, famous for developing an eye salve that was sold throughout the Roman Empire and beyond. With the wealth pouring in from trade, Laodicea became a banking and financial center. However, this prosperity led the Laodicean Christians to feel self-sufficient, diminishing their sense of dependency on God. In contrast to the insecurity felt by the Philadelphians, the Laodiceans were overly confident. Though they too experienced the AD 17 earthquake, unlike the Philadelphians, they didn't need Tiberius's help to rebuild. Laodicea's wealth allowed them to restore their city and even assist nearby towns.

Jesus introduces himself to the Laodicean church as the Amen, the Faithful and True Witness, and the Leader of God's creation. These titles emphasize God's steadfastness and stand in stark contrast to the misplaced confidence of the Laodiceans, who trusted in their own security.

Laodicea's geography further illustrates their spiritual condition. To the north, people flocked to the hot springs of Hierapolis for their medicinal properties. To the south, Colossae enjoyed refreshing cold mountain spring water. But Laodicea, situated in between, lacked a clear water source. Jesus draws on this imagery to critique their apathetic Christianity. The city built aqueducts to transport water from five miles away, but by the time it arrived, the water was lukewarm. Its high calcium carbonate content also made it taste so bitter that people wanted to spit it out. Jesus likens this to the Laodiceans' lukewarm faith—neither hot nor cold, but distasteful and ineffective.

Jesus urges them to abandon their complacency. In a direct challenge to their lifestyle, he advises them in verse 18 to trade their earthly riches for the spiritual gold he offers, to exchange their black wool garments for the purity of the white robes he provides, and to seek healing from their spiritual blindness rather than relying on their famous eye salve. Those who respond to his call will sit with him on his throne, just as Christ, through his victory, sits with the Father. This image of reigning with Christ signifies triumph over the curse and embodies a life lived in the community of God, filled with his truth, goodness, and beauty.

CONCLUSION

With the final message to the churches, Revelation's prologue comes to a close. The book of Revelation tells the story of redemption, from its preparation through the atonement and on to its ultimate fulfillment. However, the journey toward that fulfillment is fraught with as much terror as the Israelites faced on their way to the Promised Land. The wilderness of this age is marked by evil, as the world remains cursed until the second coming and reclamation. As a result, struggle defines this interadventual period. Driven by selfish desires and spurred on by spiritual evil, many respond violently to God's truth. Yet, God offers hope and calls his followers to remain faithful.

"This is the story," God declares. "Victory is assured. Redemption is the key to meaning. Hold fast. Keep going. The suffering will be brief, and the glory of eternal love and relationship will be ours. But hold fast." This encouragement, powerfully concentrated in the prologue, sets the tone for the entire book, reinforcing its message of hope and perseverance.

23

Forming God's Restoration Plan (Rev 4–5)

Is there no other way, O God,
Except through sorrow, pain and loss,
To stamp Christ's likeness on my soul,
No other way except the cross?

—Anonymous, from "The Dark Side of Love"

Then I said, "See—it is written about me in the scroll—
I have come to do your will, O God."

—Hebrews 10:7

The sun darkens; colored horses ride out with power; a flood spews from the mouth of a dragon. A beast rises from the sea, its seven heads crowned with 10 horns. A prostitute rides its back, only to be devoured and burned. The beast plunges into a lake of fire before a new heaven and new earth emerge. Revelation abounds with the fantastic, yet nothing that leaps from its pages should astonish us as if newly surprising. The book draws heavily from the Old Testament, referencing 24 of its 39 books. Of the 404 verses in Revelation, 278—nearly 69%—allude to the OT. The prophetic darkening of the sun appears in Joel, horses riding forth in Zechariah, the serpent spewing lies in Genesis, beasts from the sea in Psalms, 10 horns in Daniel, the prostitute metaphor in Ezekiel, and both fire judgment and a new heaven and earth in Isaiah. Nothing in

Revelation compels us to abandon the foundation of Scripture in favor of speculative fantasies.

Still, it makes you wonder, doesn't it? Did John simply pack every Old Testament image he could find into a convoluted, repetitive, plotless jumble? The answer, of course, is no. John tells the restoration story—God's rescue plan drawn from the entire biblical narrative—against the backdrop of a creation burdened by its cursed essence. He recounts real events, infused with an oppressive spiritual darkness, that, if we are not careful, may obscure the rising glory of Christ's kingdom. I say "Christ's" kingdom rather than "God's" because the focus now rests fully on Christ—the Kinsman Redeemer and his redemptive work. Yet, as Paul teaches, at the end, Christ, the man, will hand the kingdom over to God, the Three-in-One, who will then be all in all (1 Corinthians 15:24).

THE SCROLL MOTIF

John presents the familiar story of redemption through vivid imagery, and at times, the figurative language can feel overwhelming. Fortunately, John recognizes this potential issue in his apocalyptic writing, driven by such intense symbolism. To provide cohesion, John uses writing itself—particularly a scroll—as a connecting thread throughout the vision. From the initial command to write on a scroll (1:11), to the repeated commands to record what he sees, to the scroll with seven seals in Revelation 5–8, the little scroll in Revelation 10, and the scroll of life in Revelation 20:12, these writings—whether separate scrolls or one scroll used in multiple ways—bind the parts together, offering a guide for interpretation.

Following the theme of the scroll helps us avoid the misconception that Revelation is simply a collection of disconnected end-time events. It is neither disjointed nor solely focused on the end times. Instead, the book reveals Jesus Christ as the Kinsman Redeemer within God's overarching restoration plan. The scroll functions as a symbol—a testament or title deed to God's creation (a common Old Testament image)—that carries the narrative of the Kinsman Redeemer forward.

Key Principle #3 from chapter 21 reminds us that Revelation's symbolic references make sense only when tied to earlier revelations, particularly from the Old Testament. So we should look there first. In the ancient world, scrolls often served the same purposes as books or documents do today, whether for storytelling, record-keeping, or legal purposes. The Hebrew word for book or scroll is *seper*, and it appears in various contexts:

1. *As a letter*—David sent a letter (missive, note, or instruction) to Joab concerning Uriah in 2 Samuel 11:14–15.

2. *As a proclamation*—Haman, with King Ahasuerus's approval, wrote an edict to the officials of Persia's provinces to destroy the Jews (Esther 3:12–13).

3. *As a historical record*—God instructed Moses to record events as a memorial, such as the defeat of the Amalekites (Exodus 17:14), and also other prophets to write the book of the covenant (Exodus 24:7), the book of the law (Nehemiah 9:3), and even personal pleas for vindication (Job 19:23; Isaiah 34:16).

4. *As a legal document*—Jeremiah used a deed of purchase to demonstrate his faith that God would return his people to their land (Jeremiah 32).

5. *As a genealogical or kingly record*—Examples include the generations of Adam in Genesis 5 and the records of Israel's kings in 2 Chronicles 35:27.

These uses provide important context for the scroll imagery in Revelation. We've already covered the prologue (Revelation 1–3), where Jesus instructs John to write down what he has seen, what is now, and what will happen later. This general record serves as a memorial, comforting the people of God who will endure persecution. But the writing goes beyond this general instruction, as John records specific letters to the seven churches, addressing their unique challenges and blessings in chapters 2 and 3. In this way, the motif of writing shapes the encouragement and hope that Christ offers in the prologue.

I divide Revelation into ten sections, each centered on a distinct theme that is tied to the act of writing, further developing the scroll's symbolic role in God's redemptive narrative. Each section's theme, whether it's a letter, a seal, or a proclamation, is intricately connected to the unfolding story of the scroll and its contents. This symbolic structure is not random but provides a continuous thread that unites the various elements of Revelation, guiding our understanding of God's restoration plan through Jesus Christ. Here's an outline of the sections, each reflecting a distinct aspect of the scroll's ongoing revelation.

- Section 1: Prologue Part 1: Introduction (Revelation 1)—Exhortation of faithfulness to readers

  Writing activity: Command to write what he has seen, what is now, and what will take place later.

- Section 2: Prologue Part 2: Church Letters (Revelation 2–3)—Messages urging faithfulness in this interadvental age

  Writing activity: Written messages to churches

- Section 3: Forming God's Restoration Plan (Revelation 4–5)—Problem of separation to be overcome by the Kinsman Redeemer

  Writing activity: Sealed Scroll—the title deed of redemption

- Section 4: Preparing for Atonement (Revelation 6–7)—The rescue message progressively presented despite the OT's evil environment

  Writing activity: Opening Seals to reveal title deed

- Section 5: Redemption Hope (Revelation 8–11)—Trumpet warnings of broken world while the gathering of the kingdom occurs

  Writing activity: Open Scroll with bitter and sweet elements

- Section 6: Introducing the Interadvental Age (Revelation 12–13)—Satan's attack on the gospel through encouraging subjugation to human essence self-centeredness (as imaged by the sea beast, land beast, and beast image)

  Writing activity: Mark on hand and forehead

- Section 7: Reaping through Wrath (Revelation 14–16)—Focus on the gathering's end amid the revolt to death

  Writing activity: Lamb's name written on foreheads

- Section 8: The Fall of Babylon (Revelation 17–19)—Detail of the rejection of God's TGB source

  Writing activity: Babylon's evil name on the Prostitute's forehead

- Section 9: The Bitter and Sweet End (Revelation 20)—The God-focused reign with Christ; the curse-focused loss of life, humanity, existence

  Writing activity: Read Scroll—names of the people of God

- Section 10: Reign and Rest (Revelation 21–22)—Distinction of reigning with Christ without evil in the realized redemption hope

  Writing activity: Command to write what is "trustworthy and true"

Notice that both the beginning and ending of Revelation (sections 1 and 10) involve commands for John to write. The first section emphasizes faithfulness, and this theme culminates in the final section with the recording of words that are "trustworthy and true" (21:5). This act of writing frames the narrative, reinforcing the scroll as the central symbol of God's redemptive plan. By returning to this theme of writing and recording at key points, Revelation presents a cohesive structure that moves from the initial proclamation to the final affirmation of God's faithfulness.

In sections 3, 5, and 10, actual scrolls appear—one sealed, one open, and one being read. I argue that all these refer to the same scroll. Section 4 continues with the sealed scroll introduced in section 3, as its seven seals are gradually opened. This act symbolizes the preparation for redemption, mirroring the Old Testament's progressive revelation. In section 5, the trumpets sound a warning, proclaiming the truth of God's redemption plan, now opened and held by a mighty angel who reveals atonement, even as the curse lingers. Section 9 presents the scroll as the book of life, from which Christ reads the names of those redeemed. Each of these instances shows how the scroll's imagery structures the narrative, guiding our understanding of God's purpose in the world.

The remaining sections (6–8) depict images of apostasy—worldly self-centeredness, rejection of God and Christ, false religion, and the greed for wealth and power. While no physical scroll appears in these sections, the writing activities still align with the thematic elements at play. These sections reflect the consequences of rejecting God's plan and reinforce the scroll's role as a symbol of God's overarching story, even when the focus shifts away from its physical representation.

While there is a logical progression connecting the sections, they do not strictly follow a chronological order (though they do generally move forward). For example, section 2's letters to the churches span the entire interadvental period, but section 3 shifts focus to the Old Testament's progress toward atonement. Similarly, while the bowl judgments in section 8 describe final judgment, section 9 revisits specific aspects of that destruction.

THE THRONE ROOM

From a door in heaven, Jesus, with the same trumpet-like voice as in 1:10, calls John to witness what must take place "after this." The "this" likely refers to the church letters, which describe this present age. However, the phrasing doesn't suggest that the first thing John sees is the end of the age. Instead, Jesus will reveal the entire pathway leading to the end, presenting the full plan of God in vivid, symbolic imagery that points to the ultimate victory.

The next scene John encounters is the throne room of God. But first, he mentions being "in the spirit," echoing his earlier statement in 1:10. This phrase indicates that what follows are visionary visions rather than literal, physical realities. It makes sense to interpret the imagery as symbolic. We shouldn't assume that God rules from a literal throne in a physical room in a place called heaven. As Jesus told the Samaritan woman, God is Spirit, meaning he is present everywhere. The throne room imagery, therefore, is designed to convey transcendent truths that point beyond the physical realm. Thus, John's ascent to heaven doesn't represent the church being raptured. Throughout Revelation, John acts as a reporter—he is commanded to write, God shows him what to record, and he does so. John isn't one of the images; he's the observer, not a symbol of the church at the end of the age.

John's first mention is the throne, which confirms that the scene is not literal. If you were suddenly in the presence of God, wouldn't your attention immediately go to him, rather than his chair? John begins with the throne for a specific reason: to introduce the theme. In the Bible, thrones often represent authority, control, and governance (as in "the throne of David"). But when referring to God's throne, the focus is typically on judgment (Psalm 9:7; 89:14; Proverbs 20:8; 20:28). This scene emphasizes the necessity of restorative justice due to the broken covenant between God and humanity.

Once the theme is established, John begins to describe God, linking him to the idea of judgment. He sees God as resembling jasper and carnelian (or sardine) stones. Jasper is often white or clear, while carnelian is typically reddish-brown. In this judgment setting, the contrast of white and red stones might symbolize innocence and judgment. In Revelation 2, the white stone promised to the victor could represent innocence, as judges of that time used white stones to signify acquittal. Alternatively, the white could signify God's purity (Revelation 21:11). The red carnelian, often linked to the blood of the gods in ancient cultures and thought to have healing properties, may symbolize God's role as the one who keeps sin—the sickness of creation—at bay.

The imagery of stones in scripture often carries multiple meanings. Another possible connection for God's appearance as jasper and carnelian links to the "breastplate of judgment" in Exodus 28:15, which was worn by the high priest. This breastplate featured twelve gemstones representing the twelve tribes of Israel, arranged in four rows of three. The first stone in the first row is carnelian, and the last stone in the last row is jasper. Associating these stones with God brings to mind his declaration in a judgment passage: "I am the first and I am the last; apart from me, there is no God" (Isaiah 44:6). This same declaration appears in Revelation's prologue, first spoken by God (1:8) and then repeated by Jesus (1:17). Whether through the symbolism of color or title, these stones emphasize God's role as the righteous judge.

Surrounding God's throne is an emerald rainbow. After the flood, the rainbow became a sign of God's tempered judgment. Here, its encircling presence suggests both separation from and a desire to restore a broken relationship. These dual ideas—separation due to sin and a longing for reconciliation—are present in two of God's Trinitarian covenants. In the Covenant of Operational Essence, the persons of God always act according to their unified essence of truth, goodness, and beauty, which separates them from evil. In the Covenant of Creative Purpose, however, God's agreement to create image-bearers for eternal relationship expresses a desire for restoration. These two ideas—separation and reconciliation—are ultimately resolved through the atonement, which John's narrative will soon reveal.

But why an emerald rainbow rather than the typical multi-colored one? The reference to emerald may also relate to the high priest's breastplate. The Greek word for "emerald" is rare in the New Testament, and its Hebrew counterpart appears only a few times in the Old Testament. Two of those references connect to one of the stones on the breastplate. The third stone in the first row is an emerald, corresponding to Levi, the third son of Jacob. Levi's descendants, the priests, didn't inherit land but instead served as mediators between God and his people. This priestly function may be in view here, as God's separation from sin is balanced by his desire for reconciliation. However, if the stones represent the twelve land-inheriting tribes (with Levi replaced by Joseph's sons, Manasseh and Ephraim), the third stone would represent Judah—the tribe from which

Jesus comes. Thus, the emerald rainbow may foreshadow Jesus, the one who will satisfy the judgment curse on creation.

Lightning and thunder issue from the throne, while seven fiery torches—representing the seven spirits of God—block the path to it. Before the throne stretches a "sea of glass, clear as crystal," forming a vast expanse.

The sea of glass symbolizes God's sovereign control and judgment. It serves as a transparent window through which God observes creation's activities. This image of the sea appears earlier in Exodus 24, where Moses, Aaron, Nadab, Abihu, and 70 elders of Israel ascend Mount Sinai. In verse 10, they see the God of Israel, and "under his feet was something like a pavement made of lapis lazuli, as bright blue as the sky." In Exodus, we view heaven from below, looking up through the crystal sea. In Revelation 4, the perspective shifts to God's, with the sea below the throne. This symbolizes God's omniscient gaze—his ability to see and know everything happening in creation, including our fallen condition, which necessitates sovereign judgment.[1]

The scene brims with imagery of judgment and holiness. Holiness, meaning separation, emphasizes that God, in his perfection of truth, goodness, and beauty (TGB), is completely separate from evil. God cannot embrace in loving relationship anyone who does not reciprocate that love grounded in his TGB. Since all have sinned, God's judgment leaves him in solitary holiness. Yet this isn't portrayed as a satisfied God pushing people away in anger. Rather, the scene highlights the deep problem of human sin that God had to address. It appears at the beginning of Revelation to set up the larger narrative, which outlines God's solution to restore that broken relationship.

After this initial description, John introduces two groups of characters to initiate the action: the 24 elders and four living creatures. The living creatures, I believe, are angels.

The Hebrew and Greek words for angel both mean "messenger," which is their primary role (e.g., Gabriel delivering messages to Daniel in Daniel 8–9 and to Mary in Luke 1:28; or an angel appearing to Joseph in Matthew 1:20 with a warning). However, not all angels are messengers.

---

1. Sovereignty is not solely about exercising absolute will. If God's will involves creating free beings for the purpose of fostering genuine love relationships, then the possibility of resistance to his will must exist. However, God's sovereignty remains unshaken, as he permits evil only insofar as it serves the fulfillment of his ultimate purpose: love. Given God's nature, he cannot maintain a relationship with evil unless the potential for love to arise from it is present.

Even the angelic terms "cherubim" and "seraphim" do not necessarily describe who or what they are but rather their function. The Hebrew word "seraphim" means "fiery serpents" and is used in the singular in Numbers 21 to describe the bronze serpent. In Isaiah 6, the term refers to the creatures above God's throne who cry out, "Holy, holy, holy." Isaiah may not be classifying them as "seraphim" but simply describing their brilliant, fiery appearance.

The term "cherubim" is even more elusive in its origin, though some scholars suggest it may come from a Persian word meaning "to hold" or "to guard." This aligns with their primary role of guarding the holy. After the fall, God stationed cherubim at the entrance of the garden of Eden to guard the tree of life. Similarly, the cherubim images on the ark of the covenant guard the sacred space. Thus, the term describes their function—guarding the holy—rather than identifying a distinct class of beings.

These heavenly beings derive their names from their activities—whether delivering messages (angels), guarding the holy (cherubim), or displaying brilliance (seraphim). Therefore, it isn't surprising if John refers to Jesus as a "mighty angel" in Revelation 10 when describing him delivering a message. The term refers to the role, not to classifying Jesus as a created being.

Returning to Revelation 4, the four "living creatures" resemble those described in Ezekiel 1, surrounding God's throne and the crystal sea. The number four, often associated with the earth, suggests that these metaphysical spirit beings act as guardians (like cherubim), preventing the unholiness of the earth from approaching God's holiness. They also echo the seraphim of Isaiah 6, as they too cry out, "Holy, holy, holy." By mirroring both cherubim and seraphim, these creatures are best understood as angels. While there are differences between the creatures in Revelation and those in Ezekiel 1, the imagery is similar. Each creature represents a separate realm of earthly life: a lion (symbolizing wild animals and courage), an ox (representing domesticated animals and strength), a human (indicating intelligence and knowledge), and an eagle (representing birds and swiftness). The eyes all around signify God's omniscience, and their cries of "holy" reinforce the theme of judgment and holiness.

The 24 elders sit on thrones and wear crowns. The number 12, associated with government, is doubled here for emphasis. Their thrones and crowns continue the theme of judgment. With each image of holiness and separation, the problem of humanity's broken relationship with God becomes increasingly prominent.

Despite common interpretations linking the 24 elders with the 12 tribes of Israel (representing the Old Testament) and the 12 apostles (representing the New Testament), simply matching numbers feels unsatisfying. Moreover, it would be strange for John, the apostle, to witness a scene where he himself is represented.

The elders, however, bring to life what the imagery has only suggested. In Israel's ruling system, the Sanhedrin—a council of 70 elders and a leader—was based on the 70 elders and Moses who ascended Mount Sinai in Numbers 11. Although the 70 elders of the Sanhedrin exceed the 24 elders in Revelation 4, a correlation exists. The "lesser Sanhedrin," made up of 23 judges and a leader, was the minimum number required to conduct a criminal trial. It's likely that this lesser Sanhedrin of 24 judges held Jesus's trial before handing him over to Pilate. Interestingly, John, the apostle, was present at that trial, looking into Caiaphas's house (presumably as the unnamed disciple in John 18:15–16). The 24 false judges who condemned Jesus contrast sharply with the 24 heavenly elders who proclaim in song, "You are worthy," in Revelation 5:9.

The imagery of incense (5:8) and singing (5:9) also reflects the priestly and judicial structure of the Old Testament. David organized the Aaronic priests into 24 divisions (1 Chronicles 24:3), and the priestly singers were also divided into 24 groups (1 Chronicles 24:7–18). This priestly idea has much to commend it from a Kinship theology point of view. The role of priests was to represent God to the people and the people to God. The bowls of incense in Revelation 5:8, filled with the prayers of the saints, suggest the elders are acting as priests, presenting these prayers to God in hopes of restoring the broken relationship. This idea leads directly into the activity of Revelation 5.

Chapter 5 opens with God holding a scroll. As mentioned, at this point, the scroll represents the title deed to creation. But the scroll is sealed. A mighty angel (possibly Christ himself) calls out for someone worthy to open the scroll. While Jesus will fulfill this call, recognizing it is Christ who calls for the redeemer should not confuse the presentation. Just as Boaz, the kinsman redeemer, pursued the course of searching for a "closer relative," so Jesus in this scene may be the one calling out for any other who could possibly fulfill the qualifications of opening the redemption scroll.

But his call receives no affirming response. John bursts into tears as the weighty despair sweeps over him. Is God to remain separated in his holiness from all his creation? One of the elders consoles him saying someone has prevailed. That elder, one of the 24, reveals this news because his heavenly governmental council deemed Christ worthy.

Four presentation points qualify the Redeemer: (1) he is from Judah and David (2) he has the seven Spirits of God, (3) he appears as a slaughtered Lamb, and (4) he takes the scroll from the hand of God. Recalling the kinsman redeemer event from the book of Ruth, we should recognize these qualifications. First, the redeemer must be a kinsman, and point (1) shows Jesus as kinsman to humanity while point (2) links him as kinsman to God. Ruth's second qualification required the ability to pay for the redemption, which resolves in point (3) as Jesus presents with the payment price. The final qualification from Ruth is that the kinsman must *want* to redeem as Boaz did. And point (4) reveals that Jesus shares the heart of God who seeks reconciliation by taking the scroll for himself.

When Jesus takes the scroll, a three-part progression of praise begins. First, the elders and living creatures (representing holiness) sing his praise. Then, the entire host of heaven joins in. Finally, all creation joins with heaven in praise.

This progression is not only of those praising the Redeemer but also in what is being said. The first song acknowledges Christ's sacrifice and redemption. The second song declares his worthiness. The final song offers blessing to him forever and ever.

This praise fulfills Christ's claim in Revelation 1:8 as the one "who is, who was, and who is to come." It may also connect to Revelation 1:19, where Jesus instructs John to write what he has seen, what is, and what will take place. The focus of Revelation is not merely on events but on Jesus himself. John, tasked with recording what he has seen, what is, and what is to come, writes of Jesus the Redeemer, who was sacrificed, who is worthy, and who will receive eternal praise.

At first glance, the throne room scene in chapter 5, where God holds the scroll and searches for a redeemer, might appear to take place after the crucifixion and resurrection. Jesus is presented as both the Lion of Judah and the slaughtered Lamb. However, the search for someone worthy points to an earlier moment. Some commentators struggle with the chronology, but these chapters are not intended to represent a specific timeline. Instead, they reveal God's purpose. The scene highlights the problem of creation's separation from God, the need for a redeemer,

Jesus's willingness to redeem, and his qualification to accomplish it. God affirms this plan by releasing the scroll to Jesus. The scene doesn't imply that God was in a panic looking for a redeemer until Jesus stepped up. It shows the entirety of God's plan, which has been in place from the very beginning. Revelation 13:8 even refers to "the Lamb who was slain from the creation of the world." This passage doesn't mark a post-resurrection moment but reveals God's timeless plan to redeem creation from its cursed state.

24

Preparing for Atonement (Rev 6–9)

When darkness long has veil'd my mind,
And smiling day once more appears,
Then, my Redeemer, then I find
The folly of my doubts and fears.

—William Cowper, from "Peace after a Storm"

"Fields will be purchased, the transaction written on a scroll and sealed,
and witnesses will be called on in the land of Benjamin,
in the areas surrounding Jerusalem, and in Judah's cities—the cities of the hill country,
the cities of the Judean foothills, and the cities of the Negev—
because I will restore their fortunes."
This is the Lord's declaration.

—Jeremiah 32:24

Humanity has marched the road to death ever since the fall. But in OT preparation, the Redeemer had been clearing an alternative route, diverging toward life and healing. Mark 5's story of the synagogue leader Jairus paints that picture for us. Jairus had a daughter who was on her deathbed, a picture of humanity that was dying and dead. Jesus went to help. On his way, another woman suffering from a blood disorder reaches out to touch Jesus—just his robe—because she believed the touch would heal her. And it does! Jesus tells her that her faith brought healing. Jesus goes on to Jairus's daughter who had died in the interim. Jesus raises her from the dead.

The story links the two ill females for metaphorical purpose. The woman had the bleeding disease for 12 years, the exact age of Jairus's daughter, and both the girl and the woman are called "daughter" in the passage. Both represent the needs of God's created image bearers: healing and rescue from the control of physical essence.

This diseased woman pictures Israel suffering under the Mosaic Law in its interaction with God even while the Redeemer is on his way to heal the world. Israel, through its sacrificial system, shows the constant issuance of blood, but never becoming well. Thus, Israel needed healing by the Redeemer just as much as the rest of the world, and both the diseased woman and Jairus's daughter, just as Israel and the world, benefit from the redeeming healer Jesus.

As that story in Mark points out the movement of God through OT history toward redemption, so does the image of opening the scroll seals in the section of Revelation we come to now. Sin had separated us from God (Revelation 4). God, desiring to correct the problem so that he can enjoy relationship with his image bearers, sends a Redeemer. That Redeemer willingly accepts his role (Revelation 5). But the title-deed scroll the Redeemer takes up is secured by seven seals. To claim the redemption that the opened scroll would reveal, the Redeemer must break those seven seals. And the plucking open of each seal reveals the condition of the world at that time in preparation for the redemption that Christ will win. With that thought and sequence firmly in mind, let's examine the breaking of those seals in Revelation 6.

BREAKING THE SEALS

The four living creatures (who, as mentioned, are angels guarding the holiness of God from sinful creation) take part in God's preparatory involvement with humanity. Each of the four calls forth a horse and horseman as the first four seals are broken. The activity ties logically to the four living creatures because as guardians they stand at the gate between heaven and earth.

Jesus breaks the first seal in 6:1, and one of the four angels calls for the first horseman and horse—a white one. The rider has a bow and is given a crown. He goes out to conquer. At this point, John sweeps fully into apocalyptic imagery, but let's navigate carefully through the symbolism. Jesus, the Redeemer, is opening the scroll—the heart of God for redemption. White normally represents the pure and good. Therefore, unless there is something specific in the text to counter it (and there is not), the obvious intended meaning of this white horse and horseman with a crown going forth to conquer is that of God's preparatory involvement to ensure victory through his Redeemer. It is the one good image that moves into the darkness of the world following the fall. Throughout the OT, we see God involve himself and reveal himself and his purpose in redemption's plan. Even after the resurrection when Jesus is on the road to Emmaus talking with the two disciples, he takes them back to Moses (the first books of the Bible) to show how he—the Redeemer—was progressively presented throughout OT history.

But into what kind of world does God bring this good and hopeful message? The next three seals and horsemen showcase that world. With the breaking of the second seal, another horse—this one red—comes forward to take peace from the earth. He receives a large sword, and therefore, almost all commentators recognize this red horse and rider as symbolic of war. But notice who wars. This warfare is not of God's making; he doesn't send spiritual conflict to destroy the sin-embracing earth. The horseman was given "power to take peace from the earth and to make *people kill each other.*" The horseman doesn't come to kill; the people kill. Keep that thought in mind as we move to the other horses because we will come back to it.

The next horse, from the breaking of the third seal, is black. The rider carries a set of scales. A voice shouts out a ridiculously inflated price for wheat and barley. That inflated price indicates scarcity and, therefore, famine.

Now let's pause. Did the OT really constantly present famine? While sometimes famine came (during the time Joseph was in Egypt or while armies laid siege to cities), a lack of physical food certainly does not characterize all OT history. The symbol requires more analysis. The "set of scales" translates from the Greek *zygos*. The other five NT verses using that word all translate it as "yoke." For example, Matthew 11:29–30 reads, "Take my *yoke* upon you and learn from me, for I am gentle and humble in heart, and you will find rest for your souls. For my *yoke* is easy and my burden is light." The Greek *zygos* actually does mean yoke (from a root meaning "to join"). It is that wood bar joining a pair of oxen to pull a cart or plow. Such a device gives balance of a sort to the two oxen, but "balance" and especially "weighing scales" do not really indicate the word's meaning. Yet practically every translation of that verse uses "balance" or "scales" (except the Jubilee Bible). The reason for the stretch from "yoke" to "scales" probably relates to the verse's measured amounts of wheat and barley—you have to use something to measure the amounts, so the translators conclude John meant to speak of their balance with scales.

However, "yoke" actually fits better with the passage. As Jesus pointed out in Matthew 11:29-30, the word signifies a *burden*. The yoke was normally a heavy piece of wood, resting on the necks of the oxen and connecting them to something that required strain to move. And even the pulling contrivance that fit over the neck of only a single animal was also called a yoke. Thus, the black horse and rider of the third seal denote not so much a scale as an oppressive burden. The information provided of the costly wheat and barley signifies the difficulty of producing food. Remember what God told Adam after his sin: because of curse, the land would not yield its produce easily (Genesis 3:17-19). Thus, the two negative consequences of the fall described so far with the second and third horse include the destruction of the relationship of human to human (red horse) and the destruction of the relationship of human soul to its human physical essence (black horse).

The fourth horse translates variously as pale, ashen, or green. We more commonly associate pale or ashen color to death, but the Greek there probably translates best as green. The association with death, however, doesn't change. The Greeks linked the pale green look of a person as sickness toward death. And therefore, this horse and rider deliver death through all destructive problems of the world—sword, famine, plague, and wild animals. Like the other two horses of evil, this horse represents the breakdown of relationship—death is the ultimate separation from God caused by our cursed physical essence.

Thus, these three horses and riders (red, black, and pale green) signify the problems of the cursed earth into which the white horse and rider (God's plan for redemption) enter. God did not send these riders in rage, just wanting to destroy everything in sight. In fact, God didn't send them at all. Back in Eden with sin's first entrance, physical creation became cursed. Adam had looked on Eve as she extended that fruit to him and made the conscious choice for her over God because he thought his new-found physical attraction would satisfy his desire for TGB more than relationship with God.[1] So Adam and Eve were the ones who ushered the three evil apocalyptic horses onto the scene. And that thought, that choice, that exchange of "the truth about God for a lie" to worship and serve "created things rather than the Creator" (Romans 1:25) stamped *anathema*—cursed!—on our physical essence.

God intended his image bearers to rule physical creation (Genesis 1:26–28), but with the curse and the departure of God, we instead subjugated our souls to our physical essence and therefore let loose all the horror of a world turned upside down by evil. The first four seals establish that atmosphere of a world gone wrong—yet with God unfailingly interacting to bring about redemption. And his progressive revelation produced two groups: those who embraced the revelation—the God-focused—and those who rejected it—the human- or curse-focused. The cries of each group sound in the breaking of seals five and six.

As the fifth seal is broken, John sees under the altar the souls of the people slaughtered because of their testimony in embrace of God's word. The altar symbolically depicts the separation of body (physical essence) and soul. Sacrifices were brought to the altar specifically to cut open so that the lifeblood (representing the soul) drains from it. The separated lifeblood, collected at the base of the altar, connects through imagery to these souls under the altar who cry out, "How long?" These God-focused souls must endure this disturbing separation from wholeness as they wait for the Messiah's redemption to join with uncursed flesh for fully cleansed communion with God. But God does not merely set them aside in some pathetic state of spiritual longing. We learn in this seal's narrative that God gives them white robes, symbolic of his loving care through this waiting period until their God-focused souls and redeemed essence may function as one again.

Although we read of the God-focused as "the *souls* of those who had been slain because of the word of God and the testimony they had maintained," we should not limit this group to only martyrs whose lives were physically cut short by God-hating enemies. The physical lives of all humans, including all God-focused, are cut short by sin's curse. This seal ties back to seals two, three, and four which portray the violence inherent in all the earth because of our cursed condition. So this group represents the entire congregation of God-focused people who all died

---

1. See my book *The Curse Removed*, chapters 5 and 6.

through their sin-cursed connection to Adam. In representing this entire God-focused group, these altar souls show the hope of God's judgment on sin through redemption so that they may be complete in him. But they are told to wait until others join them, which serves to turn attention back to God's rescue mission in the world.

With the opening of the sixth seal, another group appears. The curse-focused make up this group who reject God and his redemption. The description of immediate events is frightening: violent earthquake, sun turned black, blood moon, stars fall, sky rolls up like a scroll, and mountains and islands move. The curse-focused of the earth cry out for protection—even for death—to avoid this "wrath" of the Lamb (of their own making).

But of course, these violent events are not literal alterations of physical creation. They depict the failing, falling violent doom of the absence of God's TGB. Scripture has used these expressions multiple times before (Job 3, Isaiah 13, Joel 2, Amos 8, Ezekiel 32).

Remember that this first passage of scroll presentation has to do with revelation leading to redemption. And at this forward-looking point, division necessarily takes place. The God-focused will be redeemed. But redemption inescapably causes the separation of the unwilling. When redemption does come at the cross, we see many of these same elements described. In Matthew 27:50–51, Jesus shouts out from the cross and the earth quakes and rocks split. In Luke 23:44–48, darkness comes over the land and people beat their chests. In Luke 23:28–31, on his way to the cross, Jesus warned, "They will begin to say to the mountains, 'Fall on us!' and to the hills, 'Cover us!'"

SEALS' INTERLUDE

Chapter 7 begins an interlude between the sixth and seventh seals; it expands the thoughts of the first six seals. Four angels hold back destructive winds from blowing on the earth, on the sea, and on the trees. Angels (as opposed to demons) follow the instruction of God; therefore, God wants these destructive winds held back from harming the earth. Significantly, this scene suggests that the later destruction we will read of in trumpet blasts and bowls of wrath are *not* caused by God but rather by God no longer holding them back. The winds of destruction are not generated by God but rather are the natural course of a Godless existence that God holds back from enveloping the God-focused—all those who will come to him in relationship. Here then is the purpose for the white horse and rider: God's effective revelation draws OT persons to faith and love.

God seals 144,000 Israelites. The number 12 signifies both government and completeness. Therefore, by counting out 12,000 from each of the 12 tribes, John emphasizes that this group includes all of Israel who are of God's kingdom. But, although 12 tribes are identified, the list appears somewhat odd. Again, Jacob had 12 sons, but normally when mentioning the tribes, because the Levites were designated the tribe of priests (and therefore inherited no land), Joseph's two sons, Ephraim and Manasseh each are counted among the 12 portions of allotted land. However, in this list in Revelation, first, Ephraim is not mentioned, and Joseph is. Second, Levi is also listed, which would have brought the total up to 13, except that the tribe of Dan is left out. Why are Dan and Ephraim left out? The simplest explanation is that both those tribes represented idolatry—a turning away from God—more than any of the others. When the ten northern tribes split from Judah and Benjamin, Jeroboam was made king of the north. The people were confused because God said to worship in Jerusalem, yet Jerusalem was located in the territory of Judah. Jeroboam's fix was to fashion two golden calves and place one in Bethel (the heart of the territory of Ephraim) and one in Dan (a city in the territory of Dan). These two idol worship centers then may have cost those two tribes mention in this Revelation list.

Another interesting aspect of the list pertains to order. No previous biblical listing of tribes places them in the Revelation 7 order. Here, Judah receives top billing, probably because the Redeemer came from its tribe. But the rest of the list does not follow birth order either (although it does end with the two youngest). The list places full brothers together. Remember that Jacob had two wives: Leah and Rachel. In their attempt to gain favor by having more sons, they gave their handmaids to Jacob to bear children. Thus, in the list, the first two—Judah and Reuben—are full brothers from Leah. Next, Gad and Asher are both sons of Zilpah, Leah's maid. We'll skip Naphtali and Manasseh for the moment. Next, Simeon and Levi are sons of Leah. Issachar and Zebulun are also sons of Leah. And Joseph and Benjamin are sons of Rachel. We skipped Naphtali and Manasseh because they are the only two who are not full brothers. Naphtali and Dan were full brothers as sons of Bilhah, Rachel's maid. And Manasseh and Ephraim were full brothers, twin sons of Joseph. But with both Dan and Ephraim excluded, their brothers, Naphtali and Manasseh, are linked instead.

Perhaps no real significance exists with the brotherly groupings except maybe to underscore the fact that God does concern himself with relationship. The whole family and tribe and nation emphasis of Israel was on relationship, and that emphasis was to highlight God's overall purpose for creation and redemption—everlasting love relationship.

Immediately after the listing of this OT grouping of the God-focused, John looks to see a vast multitude from every nation praising the salvation of God. One of the elders asks John who he thinks the multitude is and where they came from. John turns the question back to the elder, and he explains that this multitude came from great tribulation. What is this great tribulation? Again, take care to stay in context. The word could be translated distress or affliction. The turmoil of a sin-encrusted world roiling against God and his revelatory preparation for redemption was tribulation indeed. From the preparation for redemption, predominately revealed through Israel, the rest of the world would learn of Jesus's atonement victory. So the focus turns from those who came to God before Christ's accomplished atonement to those who will come once the whole of God's plan is realized.

Jesus breaks the final seal in the first verse of chapter 8. The emphasis on the shortness of certain time periods in Revelation always signals something that must be endured. Jesus tells Smyrna of "persecution for ten days" in Revelation 2:10, and Satan's release in Revelation 20 is for only "a short time." Here, the seventh seal brings a "silence in heaven for about half an hour"—an incredibly brief moment. This silence occurs at the pivotal transition from the old covenant to the new, marking the moment when God, having taken on corrupted "flesh like ours under sin's domain" (Romans 8:3, HCSB), allowed it to be put to death. The silence reflects the somber mood in heaven as Jesus is crucified, before the hope of resurrection breaks through.

For many churches, Easter week often includes a solemn service on Friday night before a sunrise Sunday service of rejoicing. But Revelation 8's brief silence in heaven does not give way to unrestrained rejoicing. Why that is so is because of the nature of the book. Revelation presents the whole restoration plan, and while Christ's winning of redemption to become Lord of all certainly is the gospel's good news, full realization of that redemption with its restoration must still wait while the gathering completes. And those struggles through this time between the advents of Christ are the subject of the trumpets.

25

Hoping for Redemption (Rev 8–11)

From Seine's cold quays to Ganges' burning stream,
The mortal troupes dance onward in a dream;
They do not see, within the opened sky,
The Angel's sinister trumpet raised on high.

—CHARLES BAUDELAIRE, FROM "THE DANCE OF DEATH"

The voice of the Lord is above the waters.
The God of glory thunders—the Lord, above vast waters.

—PSALM 29:3

EARLY IN REVELATION CHAPTER 8, just before the angels sound their trumpets, another angel mixes the prayers of the saints with incense, and the smoke rises to God. This scene serves as a reminder that God always loves and cares for his people, even in the midst of the torturous trials brought on by our cursed physical state. However, this particular moment marks a shift in God's restoration plan. With atonement accomplished, the preparatory path that led to Jesus's sacrifice comes to a close. As Hebrews states, "By calling this covenant 'new,' he has made the first one obsolete; and what is obsolete and outdated will soon disappear." The obsolete covenant, which centered on Israel as representative of God's people, is now fulfilled.[1]

---

1. Reading Hebrews 8:13 in isolation might give the impression that the "obsolete"

Though Israel's role ended with the victory of Christ's first advent—his life, death, and resurrection—a transition period followed. This apostolic age, lasting about thirty years, practically phased out Israel's representation. Israel was only a shadow of the image-bearing relationship now extended to the whole world through the gospel proclamation that Jesus is Lord. By virtue of his resurrection, the firstfruits of redemption from the curse, God's plan advances toward the redemption of all creation—new bodies, new heaven, and new earth.

Yet, while that forward movement continues, our full redemption remains a future hope. It is delayed because God desires that none should perish but that all should come to repentance. This postponement leaves those who already hold the hope of redemption still grappling with the fleshly conflict of living in a cursed, self-centered world. The tension between glory and groaning is expressed in the angel's offering of incense—the prayers of the saints—and in the casting of fiery coals to the earth.

RALLYING HOPE AMID AN EVIL AGE

Trumpets announce. But they do not always proclaim victory. The purpose for the trumpets sounding here in this interadventral age aligns with the common use of trumpets for rallying the forces throughout the OT (such as with Gideon's trumpet, Saul's trumpet, Joab's trumpet, Israel's trumpet, God's trumpet).

During the apostolic age, the gospel begins its transformative work as the apostles spread the good news throughout the known world. But the trumpet blasts do more than encourage those efforts—they serve as warnings. They forewarn of the ongoing strife encountered even as the message of Jesus's lordship is proclaimed. The trumpets also reveal the simultaneous turning away from God by those focused on the curse, as Paul describes God "giving them over" to their selfish pursuits. Though some destruction accompanies these trumpet blasts, its partial effect—impacting only a third of the earth, sea, waters, and sun—symbolizes

---

or "old" covenant, contrasted with the "new" one, refers to the original Covenant of Life with Adam and Eve. Adam's breaking of that covenant brought about the curse on our physical essence. However, through Christ's atonement—by offering his own body in death and redeeming it to life with God—Jesus established a New Covenant of Life, raising us to newness of life and replacing Adam's failed covenant, which led to death. Yet, the overall context of Hebrews, from opening chapter to this point in chapter 8, consistently contrasts Christ's work with the shadowy image of Israel's Law. Therefore, the "obsolete covenant" here should be understood as a reference to the Mosaic covenant.

God's continued patience as we progress through the gathering period of this interadventual age until the fullness is complete.

The first four trumpets represent the disruption of relationships caused by humanity's focus on the curse. In sequence, harm comes to the earth, sea, waters, and heavenly bodies. These symbolic references correspond to the breakdowns in human relationships with their physical nature, with their national and social groupings, with their psyche (mind), and with God.

With the first trumpet, hail, fire, and blood are hurled from heaven, damaging the land, trees, and grass. The Bible uses the word translated as "hail" only three times, all in Revelation. In its other two uses (Revelation 11:19 and 16:21), hail falls in conjunction with the end of the age, as those focused on the curse lose their connection with physical essence. The Greek word *chalaza* indeed means hailstones, just as we think of them and as used in classical Greek by Homer and others. However, Strong's Concordance suggests the word may also derive from *chalao*, meaning "to lower" or "let down," as in taking down a ship's sail. This "lowering" (or, as Thayer notes, "loosening" or "relaxing") in this context refers to God's loosening his involvement. As with all instances of violence, God is not the cause; instead, violence erupts from the self-serving desires of those focused on the curse when God relaxes his TGB-intending but non-coercive hand.

At the sound of the second trumpet, a mountain is cast into the sea, symbolizing disruption within and between governments[2] and national, ethnic, social, and other self-identified groupings.

The third trumpet blast affects the rivers and springs, beginning with a star called Wormwood (meaning "bitterness") falling from heaven. A falling star often refers to Satan (Isaiah 14:12; Luke 10:18). Here, John introduces Satanic influence, which causes internal harm within the spirits of individuals. Isaiah 14 indicates that pride isolated the king (or Satan), leading to his downfall—losing position, becoming frustrated, and spawning weakness—because truth, goodness, and beauty cannot be achieved through selfishness. The intense thirst, which confuses and distracts, symbolizes Satan's activity in drawing humans away from God. The bitterness of the Wormwood waters represents the confusion of mind and heart that comes with self-absorption.

---

2. Mountains symbolize governments or kingdoms.

The fourth trumpet affects the sun, moon, and stars—symbols in Scripture consistently associated with the consequences of separating from God. In John's other book, his Gospel, he addresses these four ideas of the first four trumpet blasts in the same order, showing how Jesus provides answers for each. First, in John 6, Jesus promises to satisfy the curse on physical creation, which makes life hard to sustain, by declaring, "I am the bread of life." The metaphor of bread and manna relates to Jesus's body—the redeemed, curse-free sustenance we need to live forever (John 6:50–51). Next, as John 6 transitions into chapter 7, Jesus confronts the divisions caused by human groupings based on physical appearance and social conflict (as seen with the second trumpet). Many disciples desert him, prompting Jesus to ask the Twelve, "You do not want to leave too, do you?" Peter responds, "Lord, to whom shall we go? You have the words of eternal life." At the start of John 7, even Jesus's brothers turn against him, and Jesus criticizes the crowds and Pharisees for judging "by mere appearances" with their emphasis on the ethno-religious mark of circumcision. Third, the bitter waters of wormwood (symbolizing confusion from self-absorption) are made sweet by Jesus's promise in John 7: "Let anyone who is thirsty come to me and drink. Whoever believes in me, as Scripture has said, rivers of living water will flow from within them." Finally, the darkened sun, representing separation from God, is cleared as Jesus proclaims in John 8, "I am the light of the world."

The fifth and sixth trumpets, like the fifth and sixth seals, expand the storyline beyond the first four in each series. With the fifth trumpet blast, John sees the fallen star, presumably the same star (Satan) from the third trumpet, receiving the key to a smoky abyss. The continued darkening of the sun emphasizes the absence of God in the demonic forces now at work.

The demons emerging from the abyss appear as locusts. In the Bible, locusts frequently symbolize destructive forces, swarming over crops—the food supply of Israel—and representing invading armies. The torment caused by these locusts, however, is less about physical pain, although they can sting, and more about mental anguish. Imagine being trapped in a swarm of locusts. Waving your arms does nothing to fend them off. Turning right or left offers no escape. Panic sets in as the mental distress intensifies, leaving the victim feeling trapped and out of control.

This trumpet imagery conveys the wild misery that befalls the curse-focused, who, in their pride, reject God's plan and are consequently oppressed on all sides. No matter where they turn, there is no relief. Humanity was made to be fulfilled only in the truth, goodness, and beauty of God. When we push that away, we fall into hopeless despair. As Revelation 9:6 explains, "During those days people will seek death but will not find it; they will long to die, but death will elude them."

The imagery here parallels that of Joel 2:

> Blow the horn in Zion [*reminds of the fifth trumpet blast*];
> Sound the alarm on My holy mountain!
> Let all the residents of the land tremble,
> for the Day of the Lord is coming;
> in fact, it is near—a day of darkness and gloom,
> a day of clouds and dense overcast, [*Rev 9:2 smoke from the abyss*]
> like the dawn spreading over the mountains;
> a great and strong people appears, [*Rev 9:3 the locust/demon horde*]
> such as never existed in ages past
> and never will again in all the generations to come.
> A fire destroys in front of them,
> and behind them a flame devours.
> The land in front of them is like the Garden of Eden,
> but behind them, it is like a desert wasteland;
> there is no escape from them. [*Rev 9:6 swarming, causing despair*]
> Their appearance is like that of horses, [*Rev 9:7 appearance of horses*]
> and they gallop like war horses.
> They bound on the tops of the mountains.
> Their sound is like the sound of chariots, [*Rev 9:9 wings sound like chariots*]
> like the sound of fiery flames consuming stubble,
> like a mighty army deployed for war.

In Joel 2:25, the invading army is figuratively compared to locusts, portraying them as a powerful and overwhelming force. Many commentators mistakenly interpret the description of "hair like women's hair" (Revelation 9:8) in a seductive sense. While sin can indeed seduce, that is not the intended meaning here. Instead, this description highlights the overpowering influence of this demonic army, driving people to despair. The reference to "hair like women's" symbolizes a wildness, as long, loose hair suggests an unrestrained and chaotic presence. A similar description can be found in the pseudepigraphal book *Apocalypse of Zephaniah*, where chapter 4 describes a demonic presence with hair like a woman's:

> Then I walked with the angel of the Lord. I looked before me, and I saw a place there. Thousands of thousands and myriads of myriads of angels entered through it. Their faces were like a

leopard, their tusks being outside their mouths like wild boars. Their eyes were mixed with blood. Their hair was loose like the hair of women, and fiery scourges were in their hands.

Later in *Apocalypse of Zephaniah*, chapter 6 describes Satan himself:

> In that same instant I stood up, and I saw a great angel before me. His hair was spread out like that of lionesses'. His teeth were outside his mouth like a bear. His hair was spread out like women's. His body was like the serpent's when he wished to swallow me. And when I saw him, I was afraid of him so that all the parts of my body were loosened, and I fell upon my face.

The sixth trumpet serves a similar purpose to the fifth, but with a subtle distinction. While the fifth trumpet emphasizes the torment stemming from pursuit of glory apart from God's plan, the sixth trumpet highlights the agonizing search for personal satisfaction at the expense of others. Both represent selfish pursuits, but the fifth trumpet reveals the rejection of a relationship with God, while the sixth illustrates the rejection of relationships with others, as individuals retreat into their own self-serving, siloed interests. The progression from the fifth to the sixth trumpet underscores that without God's TGB as the foundation for life, no other meaningful relationships can exist.

A voice from the altar commands the release of four angels. The fact that this voice is associated with the altar shows that God once again acts in response to the prayers offered there. However, his response is one of release—effectively withdrawing his restraint over the evil angels bound at the Euphrates, a river that historically and metaphorically separated Israel from its enemies: Syria, Assyria, Babylon, and later Parthia.

Notably, when these angels are released, they do not wield swords to kill directly. Instead, their spiritual influence incites humans to turn against one another in warfare—curse-focused people fighting among themselves, symbolizing the breakdown of interpersonal relationships.

The "smoke, fire, and sulfur" symbolize evil and blindness to God's revelation, leading to torment with no hope. These three elements are mentioned together only once elsewhere in Scripture—during the destruction of Sodom and Gomorrah, where smoke, fire, and sulfur marked the collapse of faith, hope, and love.

SWEET AND BITTER SCROLL

John's visions so far have followed a generally chronological sequence. The throne room scenes in chapters 4 and 5 introduce the problem of sin and the separation from God caused by the fall. These chapters also reveal that Jesus is worthy, or qualified, to be the Kinsman Redeemer in God's plan for restoration: he is a close relative, he has the ability, and he has the desire. Chapters 6 and 7 move into the Old Testament era of atonement preparation, as each opened seal reveals either positive or negative elements of that age. The trumpets in chapters 8 and 9 rally the God-focused during the interadventual age, signifying the opened scroll—the title deed of redemption secured through atonement. This rallying is necessary due to the curse that remains on human essence until Christ removes it at his return.

While still within this section of trumpets, John shifts perspective to examine God's plan for the interadventual age from a different angle. Chapter 10 opens with a mighty angel holding an opened scroll. The symbolic description of this figure is significant, leading to the conclusion that this mighty angel is, in fact, Christ, the Kinsman Redeemer. The angel is distinguished from other angels in Revelation in several ways. A cloud surrounds him—an image of God's presence throughout the Old Testament, such as in the cloud during Israel's 40-year wandering (Exodus 13), Ezekiel's vision (Ezekiel 1), and Daniel's prophecy (Daniel 7). A rainbow, the symbol of God's covenant promise to protect the earth while completing his restoration plan, encircles the angel's head. His face shines like the sun, a description used for Jesus in Revelation 1:16 and the Transfiguration in Matthew 17:2, where the Greek wording is identical. His legs are like fiery pillars, echoing the description of Jesus's feet in Revelation 1:15 and recalling the fiery pillar that led Israel in the wilderness (Exodus 13).

The purpose of God's coming in a cloud and fiery pillar during the Exodus was to guide his people, while protecting them, through the desert to the Promised Land. This same purpose aligns with Revelation 10: the mighty angel—Jesus, our Redeemer—comes in a cloud with fiery pillar-like legs to guide John and believers through the journey of this age toward the ultimate Promised Land of the new heaven and new earth. Furthermore, Christ is the Word made flesh, and the Greek word for "angel" means "messenger," which reflects Christ's role as the bearer of God's word. In verse 3, the angel cries out with a loud voice like a roaring lion, another clear reference to Christ as the Lion of the tribe of Judah (Revelation 5:5).

Adding to this symbolism is the fact that this angel is holding the scroll—something only Christ is worthy to do—and swearing an oath concerning the sequence of events to come. Such an oath can be made only by God or Christ, affirming that this mighty angel must indeed be Christ himself.

While holding the scroll, Christ (the mighty angel) places one foot on the land, the other on the sea, and raises his right hand to the sky. In this posture, Christ symbolically reaches out to all of creation, representing human essence, while holding the opened scroll—the title deed of redemption for all creation. He swears an oath by the Creator, declaring that there will be no more delay in claiming his redemption.

Before delving further into the angel's actions, it's important to address the fact that, for the first time, the scroll is referred to as "little." Some commentators suggest that this modifier indicates a different scroll from the one introduced in chapter 5. However, in a book so rich with symbolism, changes in descriptive terms are not meant to distinguish separate items but rather to enhance symbolic meaning. God's restorative judgment on Israel, as shown in the previous chapters, highlights his continual revelation and gathering of the faithful, even amid the evil environment that is being allowed to separate. The Old Testament, especially in Isaiah, repeatedly depicts Israel as separated while God preserves a remnant—a small group of the faithful, capable of true relationship with him. This remnant has always been small in comparison to those in separation for their rejection. Therefore, in Revelation 10, the scroll—representing the God-focused remnant—is fittingly described as "little." These chapters transition us from the promised redemption of the remnant to the larger interadvental environment of evil that surrounds them, and the term "little" aligns with this symbolic flow.

Christ's firm stance on the land, sea, and sky signifies the accomplished fullness of his atonement, and he now stands ready to claim his redemption. In verse 3, Jesus, the mighty angel, roars in victory over creation's curse. Immediately, a chorus of thunders responds. As John prepares to record their message, a voice from heaven instructs him to seal it. Many scholars have overemphasized the mystery surrounding the sealing of the seven thunders. Jesus has just proclaimed the victory of his atonement and his right to redeem creation. The natural response from heaven would be a resounding "YES!"—affirming his victory: "Yes, you have won. Yes, you are King of kings! Reclaim—redeem—all creation. It is yours!" But this response must be sealed, as it pertains to the already-but-not-yet aspect of God's plan.

Consider the example of Boaz. While Boaz redeemed the land, his true motivation and prize was Ruth, not the land itself. The land's redemption was secondary to his love for her. Similarly, God's and Christ's love for us is the driving force behind the plan of redemption. Christ accomplished atonement to redeem us, but the full redemption must wait for the time of calling, witnessing, and drawing in all who would come to receive life.

A tension exists between the redemption already won and the ongoing process of human repentance as hearts awaken to the love of God. Though Jesus secured redemption through his atonement, he delays making full, immediate claim to allow time for the transformation of repentant souls, promising them complete redemption in the future. By offering his already-redeemed body as the resting place for these trusting souls, the wait for full redemption does not prevent us from boldly approaching the throne of grace. In Christ, our forgiven souls can consider these cursed bodies as dead, embracing oneness with his resurrected body. The church, as his body, is not just a metaphor—it is a realized victory. Thus, the angel's oath in verse 6 is the answer to the question, "When?" cried out at the fifth seal. Though the thunders' victorious redemption cry remains sealed (delayed until Christ's second advent), for those who trust in Christ, there is no need to wait any longer to fully embrace God. As Romans 6:4 declares, "We were therefore buried with him through baptism into death, in order that, just as Christ was raised from the dead through the glory of the Father, we too may live a new life." Yet, the sounding of the seventh trumpet at the end of the age will mark the completion of God's redemptive plan, with the arrival of new bodies, a new heaven, and a new earth.

Toward the end of the chapter, a voice from heaven instructs John to eat the scroll—to take its message within and make it his own. Here, John, as the spectator and reporter of the visions, represents us. Though he is the one witnessing the scene, he writes for our sake, so that we, too, may live out this message. Therefore, we are also called to internalize the scroll—God's title deed of redemption.

This scene mirrors Ezekiel 2:8 through 3:3, where Ezekiel ate a scroll bearing a message of judgment. Though the scroll was sweet to the taste, it contained a bitter message of woe and lamentation. This combination of judgment and blessing is always present in God's revelation, as image-bearers respond either with faith or rejection. The judgment is bitter because it reflects God's non-coercive allowance for evil to run its course. Yet, for those who embrace God's revelation, there is blessing—sweetness. In Revelation 10, John also eats the scroll and experiences both its sweetness and bitterness, just as Ezekiel did.

But wait—*John takes the scroll*?! In Revelation 5, only Jesus was worthy to take the scroll! How can John do this? By this point in the story, Jesus has conquered sin and death. John (representing all the faithful who consider themselves redeemed by God's forgiveness and Jesus's atonement) is now able to take the scroll in the righteous status Christ has won. This scene introduces the shared role we have in both redemption and the mission of spreading the message of redemption.

Notice that the mission is to "prophesy again." John represents all believers, so this charge applies to us. We must not focus on John's personal life but instead see that all of God's people are called to prophesy again. The first prophecy refers to that of those who pointed to Christ's coming before his victory. Now, the mission to "prophesy again" applies to us—those living in the aftermath of Christ's victory—who are entrusted with proclaiming the gospel message of our Redeemer King to the world.

WITNESSES TO THE REDEEMER

Revelation 11 expands on the instruction for John (and for us) to "prophesy again," while also offering a high-level view of God's restoration plan through to its completion.

The heavenly voice, which I believe to be God speaking, instructs John to "measure God's sanctuary and the altar, and count those who worship there" (11:1). Throughout the Bible (especially the NT) there are abundant references to God's people as his temple—the sanctuary where God dwells. In the wilderness wanderings, when Israel first became a nation, we read about the exact measurements and design of the tabernacle, the meeting place between God and his image-bearers. That portable tabernacle eventually became Solomon's permanent temple once the Israelites were settled in the land. Even after the Babylonians destroyed it, God supported its reestablishment, indicating his continued commitment to his Zion purpose despite the interference of sin. A detailed measuring, defining, and outlining of a figurative new temple, new land, and new city also fills the final chapters of Ezekiel.

However, God's focus is not on a physical building—the New Testament makes this clear. Rather, his deep concern is for a relationship with us, and this is the true meaning behind the temple imagery. It is all about God being with us.

- 1 Corinthians 3:16–17—Don't you know that *you yourselves are God's temple* and that God's Spirit dwells in your midst? If anyone destroys God's temple, God will destroy that person; for God's temple is sacred, and *you together are that temple.*

- 2 Corinthians 6:14–16—Do not be yoked with unbelievers. For what do righteousness and wickedness have in common? Or what fellowship can light have with darkness? . . . What agreement is there between the temple of God and idols? For *we are the temple of the living God.*

- Ephesians 2:19–22—Consequently, you are no longer foreigners and strangers, but fellow citizens with God's people and also members of his household, built on the foundation of the apostles and prophets, with Christ Jesus himself as the chief cornerstone. *In him the whole building is joined together and rises to become a holy temple in the Lord. And in him you too are being built together to become a dwelling in which God lives by his Spirit.*

- 1 Peter 2:5—You also, like living stones, are being *built into a spiritual house to be a holy priesthood, offering spiritual sacrifices* acceptable to God through Jesus Christ.

The quick, simple conclusion regarding John's instruction to measure in Revelation 11 is that it serves to identify God's people, those who will take part in Christ's redemption and enjoy an everlasting love relationship with God and his community. However, that conclusion alone does not capture the full meaning. The building does not merely symbolize the people of God. While the measuring does identify, it also serves a gathering and protective covenant purpose. Moreover, the command extends beyond measuring the sanctuary to include the altar and the people. Since the people are designated separately, the measurement of the sanctuary must carry additional figurative significance.

The design of the temple separated the outer court from the inner courts. The inner courts included specifically Jewish areas: the court of women, the court of men, the court of priests, the altar, the holy place, and the holy of holies. The outer court was available for Gentiles to worship, as they were not permitted in the inner courts, which were reserved for Jews, considered by many at the time to be the true people of God. While I do not believe God intended this distinction, it was nonetheless a settled fact in the minds of the people.

In my book *The Curse Removed*, I discuss image-based atonement—the idea that salvation addresses our role as image-bearers of God. God exists as three Persons in one essence of truth, goodness, and beauty (TGB). Similarly, humans consist of multiple individual souls within a shared physical essence (matter and energy). Therefore, both aspects of our image—our physical essence and our souls—needed recovery from the fall. God forgives our souls individually of sin as we repent, and through Jesus, God redeems our cursed bodies, the physical essence we share with all creation. While our souls may now be forgiven, our bodies still await Christ's return, when he will redeem all physical essence. In this way, we resemble the temple—our souls are like the inner portion, making us God's people, while our unholy outer bodies await the cleansing of redemption.

In Revelation 11, God commands the measurement of the sanctuary, the altar, and the people—representing the parts that are holy and under God's protection. These correspond to our souls, which are forgiven, cleansed, and secured by God. Meanwhile, verse 2 explains that the outer court is left to be trampled by the nations, symbolizing how our bodies are still subject to the sin-tainted environment caused by the curse.

In the same verses, God connects this human condition (of having a holy inner spirit and an unholy outer body) with a specific period of trampling lasting 42 months. During this time, witnesses will prophesy for 1,260 days. Both time periods translate to three and a half years, which immediately recalls the duration of Jesus's ministry. (John shifts the designation from 42 months to 1,260 days to emphasize the change in perspective from suffering harm to delivering testimony.) Just as Jesus's perfect, sinless spirit remained secure in God while his body—"flesh like ours under sin's domain" (Romans 8:3 HCSB)—was literally trampled to death by the evil of this world, so too does this period reflect the dual condition of believers in the present age.

The mention of the two witnesses in Revelation 11 solidifies the connection between the time period and Jesus. Verses 3 through 13 describe two witnesses whose testimony and lives are marked by both trauma and triumph. According to the Law, two witnesses were required to verify and validate testimony.

Who are these two witnesses? Verses 5 and 6 provide key clues: these witnesses possess (1) power like fire in their words, (2) the ability to close up the sky to prevent rain, (3) the power to turn waters into blood, and (4) the power to strike the earth with plagues. These powers echo Old Testament accounts: Elijah called down fire from heaven (1 Kings 18:38) and, by God's command, shut up the skies from rain (1 Kings 17:1). Moses turned water into blood (Exodus 7:14–21) and brought plagues upon Egypt (Exodus 7–12). Because of these similarities, many commentators believe that the two witnesses in Revelation 11 represent Moses and Elijah. They also appeared together on the Mount of Transfiguration (Matthew 17), representing the Law and the Prophets, which pointed to Christ.

Additionally, similar imagery is found in the dedication of Solomon's temple (2 Chronicles 7:1): "When Solomon finished praying, *fire came down from heaven* and consumed the burnt offering." After the days of celebration, the Lord told Solomon, "I have heard your prayer and have chosen this place for myself as a temple for sacrifices. When I *shut up the heavens so that there is no rain*, or command locusts to devour the land or send a plague among my people, if my people, who are called by my name, will humble themselves and pray and seek my face . . . I will forgive their sin and will heal their land" (2 Chronicles 7:12–14, emphasis added).

Further complicating the identification of the witnesses, Revelation 11:4 describes them as "the two olive trees" and "the two lampstands" that stand before the Lord. This imagery echoes Zechariah 4, where a vision of a lampstand and two olive trees represents Joshua, the high priest, and Zerubbabel, the governor, working together to rebuild the post-exilic temple (Zechariah 4:14).

So, who are these two witnesses? Must we choose between Moses and Elijah or Joshua and Zerubbabel? Revelation 11 seems to draw upon all these figures. The two witnesses reflect the work of Moses, Elijah, Joshua, and Zerubbabel, as well as the temple-building efforts of both Solomon and the post-exilic community. However, all these literal figures and structures serve a figurative purpose, pointing ultimately to Christ. As Jesus explained to his disciples on the road to Emmaus, all the Old Testament scriptures—the people and the events—pointed symbolically to him.

Jesus himself provided symbolic witnesses to his ministry. In John 5:31, he says, "If I testify about myself, my testimony is not true." He goes on to explain that God's words (through the Law and the Prophets) and his works (directed by God) both testify that he is from God. Therefore, the two witnesses are the words and works of God through Christ. Revelation 11 invokes Moses (Law), Elijah (Prophet), Joshua (Priest), and Zerubbabel (King), as they all ultimately point to Christ.

Additionally, the passage specifies that the witnesses' death lasts for three and a half days. Numbers in Revelation carry symbolic meaning, and the three and a half days of death are connected to the 42 months (three and a half years) of trampling described earlier in verse 2. This time period, often associated with our cursed bodily condition, mirrors the three and a half years of Jesus's ministry, which culminated in his death. The witnesses' testimony spans the same period—1,260 days—coinciding with Jesus's mission of presenting God's words and works. The three and a half days of their death also reflect the time from Jesus's arrest to his resurrection and his appearance to the disciples.

Thus, these two witnesses represent the words and works of God that testified through Christ during his earthly life. They followed him to the cross, through his resurrection, and to his ascension. Revelation 11's description aligns directly with the life and ministry of Jesus. These words and works of Christ continue with us, the faithful, as we journey through this interadvental period—trampled in body, but secure in soul.

THE SEVENTH TRUMPET

Revelation 9 concludes with the blast of the sixth trumpet, while chapters 10 and 11 shift perspectives—from preparing for atonement to its realization (especially through the work of the two witnesses) to living out the atonement by prophesying again during the interadventual period. Yet this age will also come to an end, signaled by the seventh trumpet, which announces the final conclusion.

When the seventh trumpet sounds, loud voices in heaven declare that "the kingdom of the world has become the kingdom of our Lord and of his Messiah." But hasn't this already been the case? If the seventh trumpet sounds at the end of the age and only then does the kingdom of the world become Christ's, should we stop proclaiming that Jesus is Lord right now?

This question ties into a long-standing debate among Christians about whether the world consists of one kingdom or two. Some believe that two kingdoms exist—Christ's and Satan's (or sin's)—and that a battle continues throughout this age until Christ conquers and becomes king over all. Others believe that Christ is already reigning over everything, with rebels present but slowly being subdued as evil is gradually pushed out of the world. Both views, however, misunderstand the concept of the kingdom.

Whenever we hear the phrase "the kingdom of God," "the kingdom of Christ," or "the kingdom of heaven," we should immediately recall John 18:36, where Jesus stood before Pilate and declared, "My kingdom is not of this world." Understanding this statement is key to interpreting the use of "kingdom" in Revelation.

With this claim, Jesus made it clear that his aim was not simply to replace those in power. He could not condemn the selfishness and arrogance of human rulers if all he wanted was to take their place. If that were his goal, he would be just as selfish and arrogant. Worshiping God is not right simply because he is stronger and could crush other kings like bugs if they do not obey. Selfishness remains selfishness, regardless of how powerful the person is. Arrogance distorts, whether it comes from someone weaker or stronger. So why would we excuse it in God?

When Jesus told Pilate that his kingdom was not of this world, he meant that he would not be just another ruler subjected to the slavery of human physical essence, which seeks pride and personal gain. Instead, Jesus put to death the selfish master of physical essence and resurrected human essence, restoring it to its rightful subordination to human souls that embrace God's communal spirit of truth, goodness, and beauty.

The transformation of the kingdom in Revelation 11:15 is a death to selfishness and a resurrection to communal life. Yes, Jesus is Lord now, reigning over all, but his lordship is rooted in his victory over physical essence. While the rest of humanity remains enslaved to it, Jesus has conquered it. With his return, he will redeem all physical essence, making all things new—our bodies, the heavens, and the earth. His reign will restore the original dominion of the human soul over physical creation, a dominion that will, as verse 15 proclaims, last forever and ever!

26

Explaining the Current Age (Rev 12–13)

Not only for the past I grieve,
The future fills me with dismay;
Unless Thou hasten to relieve,
I know my heart will fall away.
—Anne Brontë, from "My God! O Let Me Call Thee Mine"

Rebuke the beast in the reeds,
The herd of bulls with the calves of the peoples.
Trample underfoot those with bars of silver.
Scatter the peoples who take pleasure in war.
—Psalm 68:30

REVELATION TELLS THE STORY of redemption, but not merely for curiosity's sake. Both John and Jesus emphasize its purpose: to encourage those of us living in this interadvental age, who have already embraced the glory of atonement but still await the blessed hope of redemption's consummation. We need this encouragement because, although our present age includes many who are part of our God-centered community, the curse of our shared human essence continues to exert a selfish influence. And this influence will persist until God redeems physical creation from the curse, making all things new. Christ necessarily delays this glory because, with his coming redemption, judgment—the ultimate separation chosen by those who are self-focused—also arrives. He cannot redeem all physical creation—giving it a new, unblemished essence—without eliminating the opportunity for those who, as of now, still reject him. Since he desires that none should perish, he waits. He waits as long as any possibility remains for those focused on the curse to open their eyes to his light. Therefore, those of us who already believe need Revelation's encouragement to endure through this curse-laden time.

Thus far, we have explored the curse and the anticipation of God's restoration plan (Revelation 4 and 5), the Old Testament's progressive revelation that paved the way for atonement (Revelation 6 and 7), and the hope of redemption during this dark age of gathering (Revelation 8 through 11). Revelation 12 steps back slightly to refocus on the interadventual age, which the next eight chapters address. It begins by introducing the demonic force behind the evil of the curse. Chapter 12 presents Satan's rebellious assault on both God's restoration plan and those who are God-centered in their souls. His influence further entangles humanity in their desire for and worship of their own physical essence, which, without turning to Christ, ultimately leads to the death of their souls.

THE WOMAN AND THE DRAGON INTRODUCED

John begins chapter 12 by depicting a woman clothed with the sun, moon, and twelve stars. Notably the sign appears "in heaven," positioned deliberately to contrast with the dragon, whose sign also appears in heaven. The positioning indicates the conflict is not a mere earthly skirmish, but one that encompasses the entirety of God's plan. Since the woman gives birth to a male child, widely believed to represent Christ, some interpreters suggest the woman represents Mary. However, this interpretation overlooks the associated imagery. In Genesis 37, Joseph dreams of the sun, moon, and 11 stars bowing down to him. When he shares this dream, his father rebukes him, recognizing immediately that the sun, moon, and stars represent himself, Rachel (Joseph's mother), and Joseph's 11 brothers. We cannot overlook this backdrop in interpreting the sun, moon, and stars in Revelation 12.[1] Given that the Kinsman Redeemer did, in fact, come from Israel, the woman should be understood as symbolizing Israel.

---

1. Some interpretive systems still do manage to ignore the connection. Roman Catholics and the Orthodox usually see the woman as Mary, while historicists often understand the woman to simply represent the Church rather than Israel.

Even so, concluding that the woman represents Israel requires revisiting the lessons learned we discussed about the Israel image earlier in this book. Israel, as a nation, served its illustrative purpose by foreshadowing both Jesus and his spiritual offspring. However, God provided the illustration of Israel during the Old Testament's progressive revelation leading up to the atonement. With this in mind, the woman in Revelation 12 should not simply be equated with the nation of Israel, but more specifically with God's purpose for Israel in the development of his restoration plan. Taken together, this interpretation makes sense: the woman, representing God's image of Israel as a vehicle for restoration, gives birth to the Messiah, the Kinsman Redeemer, who accomplishes atonement for that restoration.

A red dragon appears before the woman. A few verses later (12:9), John applies four names or descriptors to this evil character. First, he is called "dragon," a term rooted in the idea of "looking at," suggesting something that draws attention, fascinates, or mesmerizes the viewer. Next, he is called "old serpent," linking him to the crafty manipulator in the garden of Eden. Then, the name "Devil" literally means one who scatters reason, or in other words, one who deceives. Finally, the Hebrew name "Satan" means adversary. Together, these descriptors reveal that this evil creature is the adversary of God, who mesmerizes God's image-bearers—his prey—to cunningly deceive and lead them away from God's truth, goodness, and beauty.

Although some translations (such as the NIV and HCSB) do not include it, the Greek text plays on the meaning of "dragon" (*to look at*), effectively saying, "*Look*, here is something *to look at* (the dragon)!" The dragon is red, symbolizing war and violence, and has seven heads, ten horns, and seven crowns. The crowns represent authority, the number seven signifies completeness, and the number ten indicates judicial completeness (as seen in the ten plagues, the Ten Commandments, the tithe, etc., in the Old Testament). This imagery portrays Satan's seemingly complete authority over the evil in the world—he is the head or instigator of the attack on God's redemption plan.

Everything presented in chapter 12 so far is symbolic: the woman represents God's Israel plan, the dragon symbolizes Satan, the pregnancy points to the coming of the Redeemer, and the cast-down stars (verse 4) likely represent disobedient angels. The predominance of figurative imagery should caution us against assuming the birth in verse 5 refers to the literal birth of Jesus in the Bethlehem stable. Some commentators, noting that verse 5 quickly mentions the child being caught up to God, suggest that John mentions the Bethlehem birth and then skips over Jesus's earthly life to go directly to his ascension. However, since the woman represents God's redemptive and covenant plan culminating in the birth of the Redeemer, the "birth" in this passage encompasses the entire scope of Jesus's work as Redeemer—his life, death, and resurrection—all that he accomplished during his first advent. Therefore, it makes sense that, after this "birth of atonement," he ascended (as Revelation 12:5 concludes) to the right hand of God, where he intercedes for us (Romans 8:34; Ephesians 1:20; Colossians 3:1; Hebrews 1:3; 8:1; 12:2; 1 Peter 3:22).

The newborn Redeemer is said to "shepherd with a rod of iron" (Revelation 12:5). In this verse, translators often render the Greek verb for "shepherd" as "rule," which may feel overly forceful in this context. Translating the term as "shepherd"—the same word used when Jesus tells Peter to "feed my sheep" (John 21) and when Paul encourages the Ephesian elders to "be shepherds of the church" (Acts 20:28)—is more consistent with the intended imagery. The rod of iron, when paired with shepherding, aligns with the role of a shepherd: not to pummel his own sheep, but rather to defend them against attackers. Through his ministry, death, and resurrection, Jesus demonstrated his "rule" as the Good Shepherd, gathering and protecting his sheep. That guardianship was the purpose of his coming—to remove the curse that kept humanity enslaved to the flesh and separated from God.

THREE AND A HALF YEARS—TIME-PERIOD INTENT

In Revelation 12, the dragon attacks the woman in two separate incidents, but each time God protects her by providing an escape to the "wilderness." The term translated as "wilderness" implies more than a geographic location. It conveys a state of being solitary, desolate, and deprived of aid from others. In this context, it assures that God will faithfully protect his redemptive plan for the faithful remnant of Israel, even though this remnant is rejected by the wider world.

The woman remains in this desolate condition for 1,260 days (verse 6). Later in the passage (verse 14), we again see the dragon attacking, and once more the woman flees to the wilderness, where she is "taken care of" for a time, times, and half a time (that is, a year, two years, and half a year, totaling 1,260 days). This raises several questions: Are these two passages describing the same event or separate ones? What is the significance of the time periods, each covering three and a half years? Why are identical time periods presented using different terminology? And how exactly is the woman being cared for?

This imagery is rooted in the significance of the time period itself. The duration of three and a half years, expressed in various ways, appears repeatedly throughout both the Old and New Testaments. Its first occurrence, which forms the foundation for its later uses, is found in the story of Elijah during the drought recorded in 1 Kings 16–18.

The narrative begins at the end of 1 Kings 16 (verse 29 and following), where we learn that Ahab, the wicked king of Israel's northern kingdom, had ascended the throne. He married Jezebel, a Canaanite woman who worshiped the god Baal. In deference to her, Ahab also began to worship Baal, thereby entrenching Baal worship among the northern tribes of Israel.

Baal, the Canaanite god of the sky, was depicted holding a club in one hand and a lightning bolt in the other. The Israelites worshiped him as the provider of rain for their farming and shepherding, since they lacked irrigation systems like those of the Egyptians, who relied on the Nile, or the Mesopotamian nations, who depended on the Tigris and Euphrates. Baal was also considered a god of fertility, a logical connection since rain was necessary for crops that sustained life. As a result, worshiping nations offered human sacrifices—primarily children—to gain Baal's favor for fertility. For example, the last verse of 1 Kings 16 describes a man sacrificing his children while rebuilding Jericho. When Jericho was destroyed by the Israelites upon entering the Promised Land, Joshua pronounced a curse on anyone who would rebuild the city, declaring that the builder would lose his firstborn and youngest children (Joshua 6:26). Some 500 years later, this curse came true, as the builder deliberately sacrificed his children to gain Baal's favor.

Chapters 17 and 18 of 1 Kings demonstrate how God revealed his authority over the fabricated god Baal. In response to the evil dominion of Baal worship, God sends Elijah to declare a drought—a direct challenge to Baal's supposed control over rain as the god of the sky. The rain does not return until after the dramatic confrontation between Elijah and the prophets of Baal on Mount Carmel (chapter 18). In that account, Elijah challenges Baal's prophets to build an altar and call on Baal to send fire, likely in the form of a lightning bolt, since that was believed to be Baal's signature power. The prophets pray, dance, and plead with Baal to send the bolt, but, being an imaginary god, Baal sends nothing. Elijah then builds his own altar, places a bull sacrifice on it, and drenches the altar with water. After he prays, fire falls from the sky, consuming not only the sacrifice but the altar itself.

This "fire from the sky" was most likely a lightning bolt from an approaching storm over the Mediterranean. The National Weather Service describes such an event as a "bolt from the blue"—a particularly dangerous type of lightning flash that originates from a storm cloud, travels horizontally over long distances (even miles), and then strikes the ground seemingly out of nowhere. A similar incident occurred in 1995 in Melbourne, Florida, when a lightning bolt traveled about 25 miles from a distant storm before striking the ground, appearing to come "out of the blue." In Elijah's case, God appears to have directed such a bolt from the approaching storm in the west to strike Elijah's altar, completely consuming the sacrifice and the altar itself. Immediately afterward, Elijah instructs his servant to look for a cloud in the sky, signaling the end of the drought. After seven trips, the servant finally spots a small cloud, which was the leading edge of the incoming storm. Through this event, God demonstrated that he alone is the true God, controlling both the rain and the storms of the sky.

Between the cessation of rain in 1 Kings 17 and its return in chapter 18, another story unfolds. God directs Elijah to a widow in the city of Zarephath near Sidon. Elijah asks her to make him some bread, but the widow has only a small amount of flour and oil left, which she had planned to use for a final meal for herself and her son before they starved. Elijah tells her to make the bread for him first, assuring her that God would prevent the flour and oil from running out throughout the drought. In faith, she obeys, and, as promised, the flour and oil do not run out for the duration of the drought.

However, during this time, her son becomes ill and dies. The widow complains to Elijah, believing that his presence—bringing the attention of God—had caused God to judge her for a past sin and take her son's life. Elijah prays over the boy, and he is miraculously restored to life.

This incident aligns with the rain stoppage and the lightning from heaven in showcasing God's authority over the three supposed domains of Baal. In addition to controlling rain and lightning, Baal was believed to provide food source and to demand child sacrifices to atone for sin and bring blessing. In reality, however, blessing comes from God—not through the demand of one life for another's sin, but through a relationship of love with him.

In Luke 4:25, Jesus refers to the story of the widow and Elijah, noting that though many widows lived in Israel during Elijah's time, God sent Elijah to this particular widow because of her faith. Similarly, in James 5:17, during a discussion on the power of a righteous person's fervent prayer, James uses Elijah's drought as an example. Both Jesus and James mention that Elijah's drought lasted *three and a half years*.

Thus, the three-and-a-half-year period becomes a biblical standard, evoking the key lessons of Elijah's drought. The curse operates with three characteristic qualities: (1) God allows those focused on the curse to pursue their own destructive choices, (2) the God-focused endure bodily suffering (as seen in Revelation 11:2's "outer court trampled"), and (3) God cares for the souls of the God-focused. These themes from Elijah's three-and-a-half-year drought are echoed in all subsequent references to similar time periods in Scripture.

THREE AND A HALF YEARS—DANIEL REFERENCES

The reference to three and a half years, rooted in the lessons from Elijah's drought, appears three times in the book of Daniel. One of these references is found in Daniel 9, which, in this case, does specify an actual period of time. Verses 26 and 27 describe the final week of the 70 weeks (the last seven years of the 490 prophesied years for Israel), which begins with Jesus's baptism and the start of his ministry. Three and a half years later (midway through this seven-year period), Jesus goes to the cross. The second half of the "week" (another three and a half years) concludes with the call and conversion of Paul, the "apostle to the Gentiles."

The second and third references occur in Daniel 12. The angel concludes the prophecy by speaking of the end of Israel as a nation (at the end of Jesus's first advent) and the end of the age, when final restoration will be accomplished (at Jesus's second advent). The Old Testament often conflates these two events since they represent the bookends of the entire redemptive process. Daniel hears the question: How long until the end? The answer is "for a time, times, and half a time," meaning one year plus two years plus half a year, or three and a half years. It is important to note that the events described from Daniel 9 through 11 span far more than a literal three and a half years. The purpose of the time reference is not to provide a precise duration but to evoke the lessons of Elijah's drought, offering encouragement to the faithful during periods of trial. This time frame emphasizes the three key characteristics of Elijah's drought: (1) God allows those focused on the curse to pursue their own destructive choices, (2) the God-focused suffer physically (as depicted in Revelation 11:2 with the "outer court trampled"), and (3) God cares for the souls of the faithful.

A few verses later in Daniel 12, the angel refers again to a three-and-a-half-year period, this time expressed as 1,290 days. We immediately notice that 1,290 days is 30 days longer than the usual reference of 1,260 days for three and a half years. This difference suggests that the 1,290 days mark a more literal time period, rather than the symbolic span associated with Elijah's story. These 1,290 days likely represent the actual time from the start of Jesus's ministry to the end of the Feast of Unleavened Bread, which occurs seven days after his crucifixion. The period concludes at the end of the feast, rather than at his resurrection, because the Feast of Unleavened Bread symbolized sinlessness (no leaven), which aligns with the goals of the 70 Weeks in Daniel 9:24—to bring rebellion to an end (stop sin and iniquity), and usher in everlasting righteousness.

Interestingly, Daniel 12:12 speaks of a special blessing after day 1,335. This additional 45 days corresponds exactly to the period from the end of the Feast of Unleavened Bread to Pentecost, when the blessing of the Holy Spirit was poured out on all believers.

THREE AND A HALF YEARS—REVELATION REFERENCES

In Revelation, John refers to the three-and-a-half-year period multiple times. As discussed earlier, Revelation 11 speaks of the trampling of the outer court for 42 months, symbolizing the physical suffering of the God-focused, even though their souls are securely protected by God. This same section also mentions the 1,260 days during which the two witnesses testify to the words and works of God through Jesus during his earthly ministry, and figuratively through us until his return.

Returning to Revelation 12, we find two references to this three-and-a-half-year period. First, the woman (representing the faithful remnant of Israel) flees to the wilderness for 1,260 days. John indicates that this period follows immediately after the male shepherd, the leader, is called up to God. Similarly, after Jesus's ascension, the apostles spent the next three and a half years completing the initial (Old Testament) revelation of the redemption plan to the Jews. The dragon's attempt to destroy the woman failed because many believed, and thus, faithful Israel—the woman—was cared for.

Later in Revelation 12, John seems to recount the same event: the dragon again pursues the woman, who flees to the wilderness where she is cared for. This time, however, the period is described as "a time, times, and half a time." John follows Daniel's use of this phrase, extending it to cover the entire interadventual period. This term encompasses the whole span between Christ's first and second advents, during which God lovingly cares for the God-focused, even as they endure suffering in their physical essence while the curse remains in effect. John emphasizes this ongoing period of suffering in verse 17, where he mentions the dragon waging war "against the rest of her offspring"—the people of God throughout this age.

Between these two references to three-and-a-half-year periods in Revelation 12, John recounts the victory of casting the dragon out of heaven. When did this occur? Although Satan lost his place of communion in heaven after contributing to humanity's fall, the Old Testament still records his activity of accusation (such as in Job), where he attempts to accuse both humanity for its sin and God for his perceived lack of judgment. However, God never failed. His plan for overcoming the curse involved both forgiveness and cleansing of the cursed physical essence, which he accomplished through the Redeemer—Jesus—who won redemption by his sinless life, death, and resurrection. The atonement was the pivotal event that changed everything. It demonstrated God's righteousness, both by providing cleansing and by fulfilling his covenant promise to redeem. The atonement shielded the God-focused from Satan's accusations, removing the power of the curse. As a result, Satan's accusations lost their force, and he was cast down from his false stance of self-righteous indignation and accusation against God, fully revealing his vile and devilish nature.

THE BEASTS

The final statement of Revelation 12 likely belongs with verse 1 of chapter 13, as seen in translations like the KJV, NIV, and NASB. The confusion over its placement stems from the ambiguity in the Greek text. In Greek, verbs identify the subject by their form, either first person or third person, without requiring a pronoun. If it is first person, the sentence would read "I [John] stood on the sand of the sea," whereas if it is third person, it would read "He [the dragon] stood on the sand of the sea." The difference in interpretation arises from variations in manuscript traditions. The majority of manuscripts, belonging to the Byzantine family (which produced the KJV), use the first-person verb form, indicating that John stood on the shore. However, earlier manuscripts from the Alexandrian family (which inform most modern translations) use the third-person form, suggesting that the dragon stood on the shore. While textual scholars continue to debate the reasons for these variations, I believe the context provides the clearer answer. Since the dragon is intent on waging war against the faithful remnant of Israel, it makes more sense that the dragon, not John, is depicted standing on the shore, supporting and directing the rise of the evil beast from the sea. John, as the narrator, remains a passive observer, watching and recording the events.

What is the sea from which the beast rises? A few passages offer insight. In Revelation 17, we see a depiction of evil sitting upon a sea, and in verse 15, an angel explains to John, "The waters you saw, where the prostitute sits, are peoples, multitudes, nations, and languages." Thus, the sea represents the sea of humanity. Furthermore, the book of Daniel—on which John frequently draws—describes "four huge beasts" rising from the sea (Daniel 7:3), symbolizing kingdoms or empires of the earth. This confirms that the sea in Revelation 13 also represents humanity as a whole.

The beast is described as having seven heads, ten horns, and ten crowns. This description closely matches that of the dragon in Revelation 12:3, who also has seven heads and ten horns, but seven crowns. The number seven signifies completeness, while the number ten suggests governmental authority. The parallel imagery indicates that the beast, though not identical to Satan, is equally evil and serves as an agent of the dragon.

The beast does not rule over the sea of humanity but rather rises from it. This suggests that the sea, already corrupted, produces the beast. Therefore, the sea should be understood not only as humanity but as humanity's pervasive evil—the curse that drives people toward selfishness and away from the love-based relationship God intended, which is founded on his truth, goodness, and beauty (TGB). The beast's many heads and horns symbolize how thoroughly the curse governs our self-centered ideas, emotions, and desires for power and authority in this world.

Given the beast symbolism of government in Daniel 7 and the later connection in Revelation to Rome, it would be easy to assume this beast represents Rome. However, doing so would overlook the broader connection of the beast to humanity's pervasive evil. These ties illustrate a deeper intent in the drama. Rome's evil is only a part of the universal evil that extends across all eras of the interadvental age, as humanity continues to live under the curse.

In the first half of Revelation 13, this beast appears alone, not yet accompanied by the coming beast from the land, which will later expand the imagery. The dragon stands on the shore, directing the action. His position between sea and land holds interpretive value, as it provides insight whether we look toward the sea or the land. John presents these two beasts to represent different perspectives—distinct both subtly and overtly.

The beast from the sea is given authority for 42 months (13:5b). John's references to the three-and-a-half-year period are fairly consistent. The last use of "42 months" was in Revelation 11:2, referring to the trampling of the outer court (the physical essence of even the God-focused). And that 42-month period covers the entire cursed age until Christ's return (as does the reference to "time, times, and half a time" as well). So the 42-month period in Revelation 13 reflects the entire duration of the curse. During this period, as with all Elijah's three-and-a-half-year episodes, (1) God allows those who embrace the curse to pursue their destructive ways, (2) the God-focused endure physical suffering, and (3) God lovingly preserves the souls of the faithful. In this way, the beast from the sea symbolizes the full impact of the curse on humanity throughout this age.

This beast of human self-worship suffers a fatal wound to one of its heads (13:3), but the wound heals. We need not dwell long on the image of the fatal wound—John has just described the dragon's defeat at the atonement in chapter 12. The healing of the fatal wound refers directly to this—the atonement strikes a blow to human idolatry, particularly in overcoming death. However, in rejecting God (i.e., the wound's healing), the curse continues its evil agenda, as outlined in verses 7 through 10. The beast's destructive activities—chaos and persecution—persist throughout this age, even though the atonement has been accomplished. The beast, embodying humanity's self-centered idolatry and enslavement to its physical desires, brings about physical captivity and death, even for the God-focused. But the perseverance of the saints, mentioned at the end of verse 10, endures through the security of their spirits, which are united with God.

The next beast John introduces, from the land, appears less threatening in form, with only two horns like a ram. This image suggests that individual governments and leaders are not the root of the evil. The sea beast, symbolizing humanity's curse, causes governments to rule by cursed principles. The land beast, therefore, shifts focus to the role of governmental systems in controlling people, showing them as mere products of the overarching curse on humanity's physical essence.

The land beast "exercises all the authority of the first beast on his behalf." John likely had Rome's Caesars in mind, but his writing extends beyond Rome, characterizing kingdoms, nations, and rulers throughout this age. The boasts and blasphemies of the sea beast (13:5–6) are embodied in the land beast, representing governmental evil. By their rule, they compel the worship of physical power, tangible control, earthly conquest, and material reward.

The fire coming down to earth in verse 13 is not a literal event suddenly inserted among all this imagery. Calling down fire from heaven is a wonder because it seems to demonstrate control over physical elements and events. However, God consistently describes the world's seeming control as false and deceptive (2 Thessalonians 2:9; Matthew 24:24). True control over the physical was demonstrated in the death and resurrection of Jesus and will be fully transformative for all creation when he returns.

The image described in verses 14 and 15 closely parallels Nietzsche's concept of the *Übermensch* (the "overman" or "superman" from *Thus Spoke Zarathustra*). Just as Zarathustra claims the *Übermensch*'s will gives life meaning, the image of the beast defines purpose in a similar way. And just as the *Übermensch* targets the earth as his reward, the glory of physical essence becomes the ultimate idol of the beast's aspirations.

Many commentators note that the three creatures—the dragon, the sea beast, and the land beast—form an unholy trinity that mimics God. While this may have been on John's mind, we should treat it as a secondary connection, so as not to miss the main point. Unlike the dragon, who is Satan, the evil represented by the sea beast, the land beast, and the image of the beast (the value system) are not external demonic forces attacking humanity. Instead, they represent humanity's own evil, born from the curse, aimed at self-glorification. This evil involves the idolization of the physical, the self-driven lust for power, prestige, and control, and it resides within all of us because of the curse. It is this very passion, this struggle with the curse, that led Paul to cry out in Romans 7, "What a wretched man I am! Who will rescue me from this body that is subject to death?" Revelation addresses Paul's cry, even as he himself answers it: "Thanks be to God, who delivers me through Jesus Christ our Lord!"

It is dangerously misguided to lapse into complacency, imagining the beast as merely a single, future antichrist world leader—someone external who will lead armies against us. This mindset falsely encourages the belief that Christians must "circle the wagons" to keep out other, supposedly Satan-driven humans. In doing so, we deceive ourselves. There will be no physical swords swung in a climactic battle at Armageddon. The weapons of our warfare are not carnal. The notion of charging into a physical battle to secure a physical reward feeds into the curse, for the beast—the antichrist—is already alive and well, residing in the essence of humanity itself. The only way to combat the beast is to deny it and embrace God's essence. God is our only hope. With his banner of love over us, we can gird ourselves with truth, walk in peace, shield ourselves with faith, and wield the Spirit as our sword in the spiritual battle against the demonic forces that seek to pull us into the curse of our own nature.

Notice that the mark of the beast is placed on the forehead (symbolizing the mind) or on the hand (symbolizing actions), both connected to the physical being and its drive to fulfill self-centered desires. This passage links the concepts of mark, name, and number—all symbolic of identity and ownership. They reveal who you are, where your allegiance lies, and to whom you belong. The mark is not, as some have imagined, a simple and ultimately harmless computer chip implanted under the skin. The true danger lies in the code embedded in one's mind and actions, compelling conformity to the curse—an arrogant reliance on human accomplishment and glory apart from God's truth, goodness, and beauty. The number 666 embodies this identity. Six is the number of humanity and of incompletion (falling short of seven, the number of perfection). Repeated three times—three also being a number of completeness—666 symbolizes complete incompleteness, perfectly characterizing the pride of curse-focused human nature.

27

Reaping through Wrath (Rev 14–16)

While harps unnumbered sound his praise,
In yonder world above;
His saints on earth admire his ways,
And glory in his love.

—John Newton; from "The Refuge, River, and Rock of the Church"

I heard a sound from heaven
like the sound of cascading waters and like the rumbling of loud thunder.
The sound I heard was also like harpists playing on their harps.

—Revelation 14:2

OT SAINTS BENEFIT BY ATONEMENT

In contrast to the Godless, self-seeking satisfaction depicted in Revelation 13, stands the redemption won through Christ's victory over sin, the curse, and death. The 144,000 positioned on Mount Zion in the first verse of chapter 14 represent the "firstfruits" of that triumph. But in what sense are they firstfruits? Who are these firstfruits, and when do they take their stand on Mount Zion?

Elsewhere in the Bible, Jesus is described as the firstfruits. Paul states that Christ became the firstfruits by rising from the dead (1 Corinthians

15:20), securing redemption for us as well. However, this redemption operates in an "already-but-not-yet" framework. The entire age from Christ's first coming to his second presents the cross and resurrection as the victory, Jesus as the firstfruits, Satan's disruption as being defeated, and believers receiving the Spirit as a down payment. At Christ's coming, ending this age, the final defeat of Satan will occur along with the full realization of redemption, a new heaven and earth, eternal judgment, and everlasting peace. Thus, the fulfillment of these two sets of events is divided according to Christ's two advents. We must, therefore, distinguish between the already-assured victory of Christ's atonement, the ongoing process toward its full completion, and that final realization itself.

A time will come when all struggle ceases, peace reigns, and our eternal love relationship with God and the community of believers becomes the only reality. However, progress toward that final end occurs at various points, including with each individual's first turning toward heaven. Through his atonement, Jesus became Lord of all creation, laying the foundation for all the triumphs throughout this age and culminating in his return.

The atonement is victorious because it makes possible a renewed state of life—a love relationship with God based on his essence of truth, goodness, and beauty within our physical essence. Yet even with this understanding, we recognize that while Jesus has already redeemed human essence (physical creation) in himself, he has not yet applied that redemption to all creation to bring about our ultimate union with God.

This moment of atonement won introduces chapter 14. Chapter 12 concluded with the atonement secured, despite the dragon's efforts, and with the dragon setting off to wage war against the saints in this age. Chapter 13 revealed the evil forces at play during this era, and now the beginning of chapter 14 reveals the God-focused as this age unfolds.

The 144,000 first appeared in connection with the sixth seal in Revelation 7, where they represented the redeemed remnant of Old Testament Israel—those who trusted in God for rescue and redemption during the preparatory period leading up to the atonement. Here in Revelation 14, they represent the same group. In Revelation 7:3, we learn that these 144,000 would be sealed on their foreheads, and now in 14:1, we read that the Father's name has been written on their foreheads. This sealing—their identification with the Father—was accomplished through the atonement. While the beast's mark and name are reserved for the curse-focused, these Old Testament saints are marked as belonging to God.

John then hears a combination of sounds from heaven: cascading waters and rumbling thunder (often depicted in the Old Testament as a sign of God's displeasure), along with the sound of harpists playing, a soothing and peaceful melody. These sounds reflect the contrasting images just presented—the beastly, curse-focused figures of Revelation 13 and the redeemed, God-focused figures of Revelation 14.

The 144,000 on Mount Zion sing a "new song," which, in the Old Testament, is always associated with praise (Psalm 33:3, 40:3, 96:1, 98:1, 144:9, 149:1; Isaiah 42:10). No one else can learn this song because it emerges from the redemption experience of those who trusted in God before the Redeemer had actually come. This group is not categorically separate from the believers still to come; the grace by which they are redeemed is the same for all God's family. Rather, the new song highlights their unique experience, offering encouragement to those of this age as we face the beasts of our own era.

John also mentions that the 144,000 "have not been defiled by women" (14:4). This does not imply that marriage or sex is offensive to God. In fact, the Old Testament often depicts Israel as the wife of God. Here, the reference distinguishes the faithful of Israel from the unfaithful adulterers who had gone whoring with the world. The Bible frequently uses sexual purity as a metaphor for faithfulness to God.

John calls the 144,000 "firstfruits," further clarifying their connection to the faithful remnant of Old Testament Israel. While Jesus is the ultimate firstfruits of redemption—having been raised with a glorified body free from the curse—the Old Testament remnant are the firstfruits of those who find their home in Jesus and are presented to God. As Paul writes, the gospel came "first to the Jew, and also to the Greek" (Romans 1:16). No lie is found in them; they are blameless, having received God's forgiveness for their repentant hearts.

ANGEL ANNOUNCEMENTS

Verse 6 marks a shift from looking back at the Old Testament saints to focusing on the present age. Three angels appear "flying high overhead," indicating that their pronouncements provide an overview of this age. The first angel calls on everyone to fear God and give him glory because his judgment has arrived.

Throughout Revelation, and indeed throughout the Bible, the reason for the conflict is clear: physical creation is cursed. The curse began when Adam chose his relationship with Eve over his relationship with God, thereby subjugating his soul to his body and, by extension, to humanity's shared physical essence. This shift in worship—from God to human essence—brought about the curse. At the core of every sin and moral struggle lies this curse, which has separated humankind from God and made a redeemer necessary. As Revelation 14 begins to reveal the events of this interadventual age, we should not expect something entirely new or different. It is the curse-laden physical creation itself that opposes God and dependence on his essence of truth, goodness, and beauty. That is the battle.

When the angel calls on everyone to fear God, it is a call to redirect our attention and worship back to God's essence, away from our own. We are urged to "give him glory." But what is glory? It is the manifestation of worth. Therefore, God's glory is the manifestation of his worth—his essence of TGB. To glorify God means to reflect his worth by proclaiming and living according to his truth, goodness, and beauty. This is precisely how we claim the victory of Christ's atonement—by abandoning dependence on ourselves and glorifying God.

The angel also announces that the time of God's judgment has come. Some interpreters, believing judgment occurs only at the end of time, assume that this Revelation scene has shifted forward to the end of the age, rather than marking the beginning of the interadventual period. However, this interpretation misunderstands the nature of God's judgment.

God's judgment always follows the rejection of his revealed essence. When Israel failed, God judged them. When Assyria committed atrocities, God judged them. The same is true for Egypt, Moab, Edom, and all nations that rejected God's revelation. The Old Testament repeatedly speaks of God's wrath in judgment, but we often misunderstand what judgment is and what wrath entails. As explored in this book (especially chapters 9, 10, and 19), a wrathful, violent attack is not consistent with who God is. The apostle John said that God is love, meaning he acts in love. His wrath is not violent engagement but the allowing of those who reject him to separate from him. For those who separate from God—the source of all truth, goodness, and beauty—all hell breaks loose, literally.

Thus, God's response to rejection is to reveal himself in love and respond accordingly: offering further revelation to those who embrace him and non-coercive release to those who reject him. This is the essence of the angel's proclamation: "Fear God and give him glory, because—if you reject his gospel and the atonement he has secured—he will not coerce you but will allow you to go your self-destructive ways. In that way, the hour of his judgment has come."

The first angel's message concludes by pointing to the heart of the conflict: "Worship him who made the heavens, the earth, the sea, and the springs of water." But why this specific reference to God as Creator? Why not simply say, "Worship God"? The answer lies in the connection to the curse. Adam, along with all who reject God, worshiped the physical world instead of its Creator. The angel proclaims the truth: although creation reveals God's truth, goodness, and beauty, it is not their source. We do witness TGB in heaven, earth, sea, and springs, but only because God is their Creator.

The second angel then declares the fall of Babylon. Many mistakenly rush to interpret this as a future event at the end of the age, reasoning that Babylon still thrives today and must therefore fall at Christ's return for final judgment. However, this interpretation overlooks the ongoing nature of judgment and, more importantly, the victory of Christ's atonement.

Admittedly, Babylon is a complex image in Revelation. We will explore its deeper meaning in chapters 17 and 18, where Babylon is depicted first as a prostitute, collaborating with the beast, who later rejects her. In chapter 18, Babylon is shown as a demonic stronghold, a center of sexual immorality, global commerce, and sorcery deceiving the nations, while a voice from heaven calls God's people to come out of her. So, what does this Babylon represent?

John has already introduced the trio of evil: the sea beast, symbolizing the curse on physical creation; the land beast, representing the corrupt governmental systems born from that curse; and the image of the beast, reflecting the self-glory and control individuals crave in their pride. Though depicted as a trio, these three forms of evil are unified by a single source: the curse that comes from rejecting God and worshiping creation instead.

Babylon, like the beasts, is a manifestation of evil, also rooted in the same underlying curse that gave rise to all human wickedness. The purpose of Babylon's image is to offer yet another perspective on this evil. Babylon represents societal wickedness born from the curse. Just as individuals are steeped in the curse (the sea beast), governed by it (the land beast), and reflect its selfish values (the image of the beast), they unite as a society (Babylon) built upon these cursed principles.

Now, if we understand that Babylon's evil stems from the curse on physical creation, and that Jesus's atonement achieved victory over this curse by his death and resurrection—making him Lord of all creation—then it makes sense that the angel's proclamation of Babylon's fall occurs at the resurrection, at the dawn of the interadventual age. Babylon's attempt to establish truth, goodness, and beauty within a cursed framework collapsed when Christ rose. Babylon continues to fall, stumbling toward its ultimate destruction at Christ's return.

The third angel delivers a warning to those fixated on the curse. This message promises God's wrath for the followers of the beast. The language used in verses 10 and 11—phrases like "God's wrath," "anger," "tormented with fire and sulfur," "the smoke of their torment will rise forever and ever," and "no rest day or night"—often leads to interpretations of unending torture in an eternal hell. However, we must remain consistent with what we have understood so far. The angel's warning applies to the interadventual age, meaning the wrath—like the judgment on Babylon in the second angel's message—occurs in our current age. The torment and unrest are the natural consequences of rejecting God's TGB. As Revelation has consistently used imagery, the fire, smoke, and sulfur are symbolic representations of torment, not literal descriptions.

One cannot insist that this torment extends into eternity as an everlasting reality. We will find further support for this in the final chapters of Revelation. Here, however, the text specifies that it is the smoke, not the torment itself, that rises forever. The smoke is the residue, pointing to the unending nature of the curse's destruction. The torment is not God's punitive retribution but the inevitable state of separation for those who deny God, a condition that cannot be remedied as long as they remain in that denial.

Verses 12 and 13 offer comfort and blessing to those who remain focused on God, persevering through the suffering of this age, despite the violence and torment from those consumed by the curse. The dead in the Lord are blessed because their spirits are clothed with his redeemed body, as they await the ultimate redemption of all physical creation when Christ returns.

REVELATION'S OUTLINE OF THE INTERADVENTAL AGE

Yet again we approach a passage often mistakenly shoved to the end of the age. The scene of verses 14 through 20 (the end of Revelation 14) depicts angels swinging sickles over the earth to harvest people either to relationship with God or to wrath. Premillennialists usually understand the scene to be a rapture-type gathering at Christ's return for both the good and the bad.

But do we really gain a relationship with God only by leaving the earth? And does God's wrath—His non-coercive release of the curse-focused—occur only through a final rapture where they are thrown into a winepress, spilling their blood across 180 miles of earth (verse 20)? I don't think so. We must avoid jumping to conclusions that take the passage out of context.

The angelic messages pertain to this present age: (1) accept God or face the consequences of separating from his TGB here and now, (2) Christ's atonement has triumphed over the cursed physical creation—something society has been unable to accomplish in its selfish pursuit of TGB, and without God's intervention, future attempts will likewise fail, and (3) rejecting God leads to a life of torment, empty and incapable of bringing satisfaction. The reaping scene follows these declarations, demonstrating humanity's response: to either accept or reject God in this age. Remember what Jesus told his disciples in John 4:35-36:

> Don't you have a saying, "It's still four months until harvest"? I tell you, open your eyes and look at the fields! They are ripe for harvest. Even now the one who reaps draws a wage and harvests a crop for eternal life, so that the sower and reaper may be glad together.

In Revelation 14:15, we read, "Take your sickle and reap, because the time to reap has come, for the harvest of the earth is ripe." Why would we disregard Jesus's own words and assume this must point to a rapture at the end of the age? Instead, as Jesus urged, we should open our eyes now.

Our focus here is on Revelation chapters 14 through 16, with the next section covering chapters 17 through 19. Together, these six chapters form a chiasmus. The structure may seem uneven because the first half leading to the center consists of shorter elements—the angelic messages and words of comfort to those focused on God. The second half, extending from the center, covers much larger portions. Yet, we must recognize that John is indeed using a chiastic structure. The first half presents the messages, and the second half illustrates those messages:

    A Angel Message 1: Warning of Judgment (14:6–7)
    —B Angel Message 2: Babylon Fallen (14:8)
    ——C Angel Message 3: Beast Followers Drink Wrath (14:9–11)
    ———D Dead in Christ Blessed (14:12–13)
    ————E Gathering of Good and Bad (14:14–20)
    ———D1 Singing the Song of Moses (15:1–4)
    ——C1 God's Bowls of Wrath (15:5–16:21)
    —B1 Fall of Prostitute Babylon (17:1–18:24)
    A1 Christ, the Word, Rides Forth in Judgment (19:1–21)

The corresponding points of the chiasmus align remarkably well. The first three and last three focus primarily on the curse-driven world, while points D and D1 emphasize the God-focused. The central point, E, applies to both the God-focused and the curse-focused.

In Revelation 15, the D1 point highlights the God-focused, who are depicted singing the Song of Moses—a song of victory, symbolizing their passage through the "Red Sea" tribulations of this age. Notice how the text presents them standing on a sea of glass. In Revelation 4, the sea before the throne was a symbol of a looking glass through which God observed human affairs. Though transparent, the sea represented the curse as an obstacle blocking the relationship between God and his image-bearers. By the time we reach Revelation 21:1, we learn that the sea no longer exists, symbolizing the removal of all barriers between God and humanity. Here in Revelation 15, situated between these two points, the dead in Christ are shown standing on the sea, crossing it through their redemption in Christ.

The final three points of the chiasmus (C1, B1, and A1) mirror the angelic announcements: C—Wrath tormenting the curse-focused, B—Babylon's fall, and A—final judgment. John illustrates the torment caused by rejecting God's revealed truth, goodness, and beauty through the imagery of the bowls of wrath. Revelation 15:5 introduces seven angels, each given a golden bowl filled with wrath. These valuable golden bowls pour out their contents, symbolizing separation. Once emptied, the bowls no longer hold their contents—an image reminiscent of Romans 1, where God gives those entrenched in unbelief over to their self-destructive desires. This theme of separation is further emphasized as the sanctuary fills with smoke (15:8), preventing anyone from entering until the seven "plagues" (or consequences of wrath) are completed. The smoke, representing God's glory (Exodus 40:34–35; 2 Chronicles 5:13; Isaiah 6:4; Ezekiel 10:2–4), emphasizes the spiritual distance between cursed humanity and God throughout this age. Only when Jesus returns to redeem all creation will we, in our resurrected bodies, be able to meet with God face-to-face.[1]

Revelation 15:1 refers to the bowls of wrath as "the seven last plagues," linking them to Jesus as God's ultimate (and final) revelation for humanity's faithful embrace. Rejecting this final revelation leaves no hope for experiencing TGB. Thus, these last plagues represent the final consequences for rejecting Christ. Those who separate from God's grace will face complete destruction when Christ returns, but the bowls also illustrate the ongoing wrath and consequences that persist in this age as it moves toward Christ's return.

The bowl judgments correspond to the seven trumpets and the seven seals of Revelation 6 through 10. This alignment is expected, as the same catastrophe and violence always befall those who turn away from God's life-giving revelation. Let's first examine the seven trumpets and their outcomes:

1. Directed to earth—resulting in 1/3 of all trees and all grass burned
2. Directed to sea—resulting in 1/3 of sea to blood, creatures die, and ships destroyed
3. Directed to rivers and springs—resulting in 1/3 becoming poisonous
4. Directed to sun, moon, and stars—resulting in 1/3 darkening
5. Directed to the curse-focused—resulting in torment for five months
6. Directed to the curse-focused—resulting in 1/3 of humans killed
7. Directed to the kingdom of the world—resulting in it becoming the kingdom of God

---

1. Scripture emphasizes that God meets us in our physical essence (as God met with Adam and Eve in the perfect garden, as God met with the children of Israel in the purified Holy of Holies, etc.), but for that meeting to be true and complete, our essence must be purified. Currently, our essence is not purified, yet God still meets with us—with our forgiven souls—which are 'in Christ,' in his purified, firstfruits, curse-free body. In this way, the entirety of the human condition—both body and soul—is fulfilled in Christ, and we will experience the final restoration of our physical essence when he returns

Now view the seven bowls of wrath:

1. Poured on earth—resulting in painful sores
2. Poured on sea—resulting in all sea to blood and all sea life dead
3. Poured on rivers and springs—resulting in all water to blood
4. Poured on sun—resulting in people being burned from intense heat
5. Poured on Beast—resulting in darkness and torment
6. Poured on Euphrates—resulting in drying it up so armies can cross
7. Poured on air—resulting in cataclysmic destruction

The similarity between the trumpet and bowl judgments should help us grasp the symbolic imagery presented. As mentioned in chapter 25, the trumpet judgments affected only a limited portion (one-third) of creation, focusing on warning while gathering. In contrast, the bowl judgments target only the curse-focused, resulting in total destruction.

The first four bowls depict the breakdown of humanity's relationship with creation. People had made creation their god (Romans 1:25), seeking truth, goodness, and beauty (TGB) from it. But these bowls reveal that no satisfaction can be found in the earth. The fifth bowl is poured out on the beast, representing the delusion of seeking TGB through self-worship apart from God—the true source of TGB. God exposes the darkness and torment of this futile hope, showing again that no satisfaction comes from it. The sixth bowl is poured on the Euphrates, symbolizing the removal of security, just as the sixth trumpet did when the angels of the Euphrates were released to bring war. The violence of war reflects humanity's self-serving aggression against one another. The series culminates in cataclysmic destruction as God, with the seventh bowl, delivers the final and complete release of wrath.

28

Viewing the Fall (Rev 17–19)

Things fall apart; the centre cannot hold;
Mere anarchy is loosed upon the world,
The blood-dimmed tide is loosed, and everywhere
The ceremony of innocence is drowned.
—William Butler Yeats, from "The Second Coming"

And he answered, saying, Babylon has fallen, has fallen.
All the images of her gods have been shattered on the ground.
—Isaiah 21:9b

THE BIBLE FIRST INTRODUCES Babylon as a symbol of humanity's rebellion, where those who rejected God sought to unite in self-glorification. God thwarted their efforts by confusing their language. This story in Genesis 11 reveals much about human nature and God's love. The world had just been consumed by a devastating flood, a result of its own violence and corruption. In the aftermath, God placed his bow in the sky, a sign of his promise to preserve life for the sake of his redemptive plan—a plan rooted in everlasting love. Yet, almost immediately, as Noah's descendants grew into new nations, they reverted to the pre-flood mindset where "every inclination of the human heart was only evil all the time." These early Babylonians, driven by their cursed nature, would have eventually rejected God completely—perhaps all of them. But God, in his infinite wisdom, intervened, preserving the hope of restoration.

From this first story of Babylon, we see the hallmark of its legacy—a society consumed by self-interest. Humanity's fall produced individuals whose spirits are enamored with their own desires. While people may occasionally unite for a common cause, often to overpower others, selfishness inevitably reemerges as the tragic outcome. God's division of the people at Babel was an act of mercy, preventing them from descending into self-destruction. Without God's intervention, this curse-driven trajectory would, and eventually will, lead to their undoing.

Given Babylon's grim origins, its symbolism in Revelation 17 and 18 becomes clear. The prostitute in Revelation 17 bears the name "Babylon" on her forehead, a depiction of unfaithfulness in pursuit of selfish gain. She rides a scarlet beast—undoubtedly the same sea beast from Revelation 13, as both have seven heads and ten horns. Together, they represent the evil of the interadventual age: (1) the beast signifies the curse of creation-worship, which since Adam has alienated humanity from God, and (2) the prostitute represents society's collective efforts to pursue fleshly desires under the curse's influence.

The chapter opens with an angel inviting John to witness the judgment of the prostitute, symbolizing society's godless operation. This prostitute is described as sitting on many waters, which, as in Revelation 13, represent "peoples, multitudes, nations, and languages," as clarified in verse 15.

We then learn that the kings of the earth, along with its people, have committed sexual immorality with the prostitute. In other words, they have rejected God's offer of truth, goodness, and beauty, instead seeking to satisfy their individual lusts through collective societal pursuits. The verse highlights the widespread nature of this evil, as both rulers and commoners eagerly chase after such hollow fulfillment.

The following verses provide further description of the prostitute. John is transported to a desert to observe her—a place symbolizing the world's sinful environment, as seen in the desert of Jesus's temptation and the wilderness the Israelites crossed on their way to the Promised Land.

In verse 5, the prostitute is named Babylon the Great, Mother of Prostitutes. However, this name should not limit our understanding. She represents not just one kingdom, but the collective self-exaltation and curse-driven behavior that dates back to the tower of Babel. We can also connect her to the "great city" in Revelation 7, which is prophetically called Sodom and Egypt, "where also their Lord was crucified." This description does not point to a specific city or kingdom. Although Jesus was crucified in Jerusalem, across the Dead Sea from Sodom and across the Sinai from Egypt, all these places—including Babylon—are embodied in the prostitute, representing curse-driven society as a whole.

Verse 6 notes that John was astonished at the sight of the prostitute. A better translation might be that John *marveled* at her. The Greek word combines amazement with admiration, though John is not seduced by her. Instead, he marvels at the riches, power, esteem, and apparent satisfaction she exudes. Society around us is vast, wealthy, strong, and influential. In his amazement, John may even wonder whether this prostitute could succeed in her pursuits. But immediately, an angel restores clarity to John's thinking. Knowing that the search for TGB apart from God inevitably leads to failure and destruction, the angel proceeds to explain the vision, helping John (and us) see that the prostitute's ambitions are ultimately doomed to fail.

THE BEAST AND ITS HEADS

Verse 8 presents intriguing imagery. It begins with a description of the beast, shifts to how the world perceives it, and then circles back to a similar description. The verse first tells us that the beast "once was, now is not, and yet will come up out of the Abyss and go to its destruction." The phrase "once was" likely refers to the beast's pre-atonement existence. The beast, symbolizing human slavery to and worship of the physical essence, first emerged in Eden. The desire to satisfy the longing for truth, goodness, and beauty within oneself has existed since the fall. The phrase "now is not" then refers to the culmination of God's revelation through the cross and resurrection—in the atonement. Jesus put human essence to death and raised it without the curse, exposing the futility of seeking satisfaction in TGB apart from God.

The verse goes on to say that the beast "will come up out of the Abyss and go to its destruction." The Abyss itself is symbolic; it is not a literal place under lock and key. Rather, it represents the source of pure evil, the direct opposite of God's TGB. In each reference to the Abyss in Revelation (9:1–2, 11; 11:7; and 20:1, 3), the Greek word signifies depth or bottomlessness (it is also used for the sea in Luke 8:31). If you read "source of evil" in place of "Abyss" in these passages, their meaning becomes clearer.

Thus, in Revelation 17:8, the beast, rooted in evil, will ultimately meet its destruction—God remains in control, and God will judge.

The verse closes with a partial repetition of the beast's description but with a slight variation: the beast "once was, now is not, and yet will come." We have already explored the "once was" and "now is not" aspects, but what does it mean that the beast "will come"? Many modern translations interpret this as a future return. For instance, the NIV says, "yet will come," the HCSB and ESV have "is to come," and the NASB reads "will come." However, the Greek does not necessarily imply a future event. The phrase is "*kai pareimi*," which means "and is present," "has arrived," or "is at hand" (indicating nearness). The Textus Receptus, the source of the KJV, has a slight variation but conveys the same idea with the phrase "*kaiper estin*." The KJV, staying closer to the Greek, translates it as "and yet is." I believe the KJV captures the meaning more accurately. The beast "is not" due to Christ's victory at the atonement, but despite this revelation to the world, the beast "yet is," as people continue to deny God's truth and cling to the false belief that they can satisfy their desires for TGB without him.

In the middle of verse 8, we read that these human-centered individuals are "astonished" or "marvel" at the beast. They admire it, convinced that it will bring them fulfillment. But the angel refocuses John's attention, urging him to move beyond marveling at the prostitute and beast. He emphasizes that a mind grounded in wisdom will see things differently. This is not a puzzle for only the wise to solve; rather, the difference lies in perspective. The unwise, curse-focused mindset contrasts with the wise, God-focused one, which embraces God's viewpoint. As Psalm 111:10 and Proverbs 9:10 teach, "The fear of the Lord is the beginning of wisdom." James echoes this idea in his epistle, encouraging the dispersed Christian Jews to shift their mindset away from worldly thinking. He advises them to ask God for wisdom—to see things from God's perspective. Similarly here, the angel calls for clarity, encouraging John to view the beast and the prostitute with divine insight.

The angel then proceeds to explain the imagery, combining elements previously introduced. First, it's important to note that there is only one beast here, unlike the separate sea and land beasts of Revelation 13. The angel's explanation suggests that the concepts behind both beasts are entwined: the beast represents both governments operating under the curse (land beast) and the curse itself (sea beast). While John likely has

Rome in mind to some degree, this reference is only a brief allusion, not meant to limit the broader meaning of the symbolism.

The prostitute is described as sitting on seven mountains. Since Rome is famously known as the city built on seven hills, John likely has Rome partially in mind here. However, in biblical imagery, mountains often symbolize governments or kingdoms. In this passage, the angel immediately connects the mountains to kings. This is where interpretations diverge. Many scholars (and others) argue that the reference to "seven mountains" suggests that the beast represents Rome, and only Rome. According to this view, the heads (or kings) are Roman emperors: the five who "have fallen" would be Julius Caesar (though not technically an emperor, he is often included to make the count), Augustus, Tiberius, Caligula, and Claudius. The king who "is" would be Nero, assuming John wrote Revelation during his reign. The discussion of the seventh and eighth kings becomes less clear. Galba and Otho followed Nero but ruled for only a few months, so they are often overlooked. Vitellius is thought to be the seventh king, despite his brief eight-month reign, and the eighth king is typically seen as the Flavian dynasty, which includes Vespasian, Titus, and Domitian.

However, I see two key issues with this interpretation. First, I believe Revelation was written later than the reign of Nero. Second, identifying the beast with the Flavian dynasty is problematic.[1] Why would the first five heads of the beast be individual emperors, but the eighth head be an entire dynasty? This inconsistency makes it difficult to accept that the beast represents the Flavians as a collective entity.

My interpretation of the seven heads/mountains/kings is that they represent general world governments. Biblically, five major governments that opposed God's people existed before John's time: Egypt, Assyria, Babylon, Medo-Persia, and Greece. The one that "is" during John's time is Rome. This leaves one still to come. In naming these five fallen kingdoms, I do not mean to limit the passage to these alone. Many other evil kingdoms are mentioned in the Bible, and history records dominating kingdoms before John's time in regions like Africa, India, and China. The point, I believe, is that the reference to the five fallen kingdoms is symbolic of all godless governments throughout history. There have always been governments ruled by the curse. There is a government currently ruled by the curse. There will be future governments ruled by the curse.

---

1. Of course, multiple more ideas fill books and the internet concerning identification of the kings and the beast.

VIEWING THE FALL (REV 17-19)   293

This message is framed within the symbolic number seven to signify the totality of all world governments. The seventh king, then, likely represents the governments of the interadvental age.

The Bible refers to the interadvental period—the time between Christ's first and second comings—as the "last days." God's revelation of redemption and restoration had been progressively unfolding since the fall in the garden, culminating in the atonement. Therefore, this entire period, which was future to John, can be understood as one era. In the Old Testament, imagery often pointed to something greater. The nation of Israel symbolized the greater community of all God's people. The Promised Land symbolized the broader inheritance of the whole earth. Likewise, the evil, godless empires of the Old Testament point to the greater collective state of the curse-focused in this interadvental time. With this understanding, the final head/mountain/kingdom can be seen as the godless governmental system of the entire age.

The text also mentions that the beast is an eighth king but belongs to the seven. If we understand the beast as the embodiment of self-worship and the curse, it can be seen as both a king in itself and as entwined in the hearts and minds of all other kings and kingdoms throughout history.

A shift occurs in verse 16. The prostitute, who had been sitting on the beast, symbolizes society's operation supported by the self-serving curse. But in verse 16, the beast and the kings turn against the prostitute. Although the curse binds them together in self-service, no community can truly satisfy the selfish desires of every individual. People may unite in their rebellion against God, but ultimately, self-interest prevails, leading to division as individuals seek to rule for their own benefit, which naturally excludes true community.

This also explains the imagery of sexual immorality to depict the curse-focused. In marriage, sex unites two individuals as one in body, spirit, and psyche. Prostitution, however, represents selfish, pleasure-seeking behavior. Thus, the contrast between sex in marriage and adultery perfectly illustrates the difference between the God-focused and the curse-focused.

The chapter ends with a paradox. While kings seek control, it is the curse-focused kings who want to rule over the people. However, the curse-focused people, represented by the prostitute, always act out of self-interest, giving them an empire of sorts over the kings of the earth.

BABYLON FALLING

In a time when Judah feared Assyria, instead of relying on God, they turned to Babylon for help, hoping it would defeat Assyria and end their oppression. However, Isaiah 21:9b records the prophecy of Babylon's downfall: "Babylon has fallen, has fallen! All the images of its gods lie shattered on the ground!" The shattered gods symbolized Babylon's failure to achieve its purpose.

Revelation 18 also speaks of Babylon's fall, but this time, it's not referring to the literal city. Instead, it represents the symbolic society of the curse-focused, those who worship the physical and reject God. In verse 2, an angel cries out, "Babylon has fallen." The question is, when does this fall occur? In fact, it should be asked, "When did it occur?" Jesus's atoning victory shattered the false gods of Babylon, establishing him as Lord of all. It's important to remember that a "fall" signifies the failure to fulfill a purpose. Adam and Eve fell in the garden when they chose to worship their own essence instead of fulfilling their purpose of worshiping God in relationship with him. Similarly, Jesus said Satan fell like lightning when the disciples, in Jesus's name, exercised authority over demons. In both cases, the fallen were not immediately destroyed—Adam and Eve continued in their fallen state, and Satan remains active today. But the fall indicates a failure of purpose and plan. Babylon has fallen; the curse-focused ideal of physical creation as a satisfying god has failed.

Just like the God-focused, the curse-focused also search for satisfaction in truth, goodness, and beauty (TGB). God created us with this desire for his essence. A relationship with him brings satisfaction because it allows us to experience those qualities in him. However, rejecting that relationship doesn't lessen the desire for TGB. Yet, since God is the source of TGB, the curse-focused are left frustrated in their search. While the God-focused find fulfillment in this pursuit, the curse-focused are left disappointed. This dynamic defines the interadventual period, and Revelation 18 illustrates it.

The spiritual realm also plays a significant role in shaping the curse-focused pursuit of satisfaction. The angel announcing Babylon's fall reveals that it has "become a dwelling place for demons, a haunt for every unclean spirit." Why is this the case? The Great Deceiver, Satan, along with his demons, mirrors what many angels do—they deliver messages. God's angels convey his message of truth, goodness, and beauty (TGB) to those who trust him, while the messages from demons (fallen angels) are filled with deception and false hope.

Babylon's fall was first proclaimed by an angel in Revelation 14:8, where it says that the nations drank the wine of Babylon's (the prostitute's) sexual immorality. This idea is echoed in Revelation 18:3, where the angel again emphasizes that the result is God's wrath—a separation from him, leading to torment and anguish. This theme of impending horror is a focus throughout the chapter.

In chapter 17, the Prostitute seemed to possess allure, wealth, and power. However, in chapter 18, each of these elements crumbles. In verses 9 and 10, the kings of the earth mourn the loss of power. In verses 11 through 17a, the merchants lament the loss of her allure. And in verses 17b through 20, the sailors mourn the loss of wealth. These descriptions are symbolic images of a deeper reality. The true loss being mourned is the endless pursuit of wealth, allure, and power, where people mistakenly believe they will find TGB, only to be met with constant frustration and misery as satisfaction remains elusive.

The chapter concludes in verses 21 through 24 with an angel throwing a millstone into the sea, symbolizing the futility of trying to capture TGB through Babylon's death-driven ways.

ETERNAL GOSPEL ANNOUNCED AND CELEBRATED

Chapter 19 corresponds to the first angelic announcement in Revelation 14:7. That announcement placed the call to fear and worship God around the recognition of the hour of judgment. Similarly, Revelation 19 contains these same elements. It begins with a hallelujah chorus, praising God for his salvation, glory, and power won through the atonement. The praise comes from a "great multitude," likely representing Old Testament saints, as it precedes the introduction of the prostitute's judgment. The victory over the prostitute is declared, with her smoke rising forever. In verse 5, another call to praise follows. This time, the emphasis on the greatness of the "great multitude" in verse 6 appears to include all God's followers from this age, as they now partake in the marriage feast.

Next, heaven opens, and Jesus appears, riding on a white horse (19:11a). This image connects to Revelation 6, when the first seal was opened, revealing a rider on a white horse. In Revelation 6, the scroll—still sealed—represented the plan of redemption, which had yet to be fully revealed during Old Testament history. The opening of the first seal and the rider on the white horse signified God's plan advancing amid the sin that marred creation. Now, in chapter 19, we see the fulfillment of that earlier scene. The Redeemer, Jesus, rides forth on a white horse, symbolizing the completion of redemption. This links the preparation of redemption with its ultimate fulfillment.

Jesus is called Faithful and True (19:11b), fitting names for the one who brings judgment. Earlier in the chapter, the Old Testament redeemed cried out, "His judgments are true and righteous." To be righteous means to be faithful to a covenant, and now, the one who is True and Faithful executes these judgments with perfect righteousness.

He wages war in righteousness (19:11c). While Jesus comes as the Redeemer, we must also consider the other side of redemption. By redeeming, he gathers only those with whom he can have a relationship. This naturally excludes those who reject him; thus, by gathering the God-focused, the curse-focused are simultaneously separated from him.

His eyes are like flames of fire, and he wears many crowns (19:12a). Eyes of fire symbolize perfect judgment—piercing through façades and knowing the heart. No one escapes his gaze. His many crowns confirm his authority to judge.

He also has a name that no one knows except himself (19:12b). This detail should make us pause. Isn't the purpose of a name to identify someone? A name is meant to be known and used by others. So why does the Redeemer have a name that no one knows? What significance does this hold? To understand, we need to reflect on how the Bible treats names, especially the names of God.

We first encounter God in the opening creation scene of Genesis 1, where the Bible introduces him by the name Elohim—a name that conveys power, perfectly suited for the Creator of all things. In this display of divine majesty, God forms stars, the sun, waters, land, and living creatures. However, in the following chapter, and throughout most of Scripture, God is primarily known by another name—Yahweh (or Jehovah). While Yahweh technically means "the one who exists," its use conveys much more than mere existence. It reveals how God exists—specifically, *who* he is. This name reflects God's relational nature, expressed through love. God's defining attribute, the one by which we know him and experience a relationship with him, is love. From eternity past, within the Trinity, God shared this love. Thus, God is, and always has been, a God of love.

The key point is that, in biblical language, a name expresses a person's character. And this connection means that a name can be truly understood only by those who know the person's character. This is evident in how God speaks of himself in Exodus 6:2–3, where he tells Moses, "I am Yahweh. I appeared to Abraham, to Isaac, and to Jacob as El Shaddai [God of power], but by my name Yahweh [the one who exists], I did not make myself fully known to them." To the patriarchs, God revealed himself as El, the God of power, in establishing his promises. But to Moses and the Israelites, God reveals himself as Yahweh, showing not just what he would do, but why—because he is the one who dwells among his people: "I will put my dwelling place among you. . . . I will walk among you" (Leviticus 26:11–12). Throughout the Bible, God's name reflects his desire for a loving relationship, and those who embrace this relationship come to know his name intimately:

> John 17:6 (CSB) I have revealed your name to the people you gave me from the world.

Acts 2:21 And everyone who calls on the name of the Lord will be saved.

> Revelation 2:17 Whoever has ears, let them hear what the Spirit says to the churches. To the one who is victorious, I will give some of the hidden manna. I will also give that person a white stone with a new name written on it, known only to the one who receives it.

In Revelation 19, Christ rides forth to judge those who do not know him. If they do not know him as Redeemer, they do not know his name.

The next six descriptions in Revelation 19 follow a chiastic structure:

A Robe dipped in blood; name is the Word of God
—B Armies of heaven follow him on white horses wearing white linen
——C Sword from mouth to strike nations
——C1 Shepherd with rod of iron
—B1 Treads winepress of God's anger
A1 Robe and thigh with name King of kings and Lord of lords

The robe and name form the outer points of the chiasmus, highlighting that it is from Christ's unique relationship with God that the Redeemer goes forth in judgment. Points B and B1 are connected by their contrast: the faithful are with him, while the unfaithful are trampled. The central points, C and C1, mirror each other in their rejection of the rejecters. The first presents a kingly image, where Christ allows the human-focused to be separated by their rejection of the word of God. In C1, we see a shepherding image, with the shepherd wielding his rod to fend off those who do not belong to the flock.

The scene then shifts to a battle. An angel stands on the sun, symbolizing control over the source of light and life for the world. The angel calls carrion birds—buzzards, vultures, condors—to prepare to feast on the flesh of those who have rejected God. This scene is not meant to be taken literally. The battle occurs throughout this age, and what is depicted here is the aftermath—the birds feasting on the fallen after the battle is over. The finality of judgment comes in the last line of the chapter, which fittingly concludes the human-focused section. The beast is finally defeated, evil comes to an end, and the human-focused have separated from God to their own destruction. Without God, they are lost forever, and judgment (the chosen separation) is complete.

29

Concluding the Bitter and Sweet (Rev 20)

But Death didn't frighten Sister Caroline;
He looked to her like a welcome friend.
And she whispered to us: I'm going home,
And she smiled and closed her eyes.

—James Weldon Johnson, from "Go Down, Death"

Blessed and holy is the one who shares in the first resurrection!
The second death has no power over them.

—Revelation 20:6a

While some sections of Revelation are connected by chronology, the book does not follow a strict timeline. Chapters 4 and 5 logically and chronologically identify the problem of sin and qualify the Redeemer, leading into the removal of the seals in chapters 6 and 7, which represent Old Testament preparation for atonement. This sequence transitions into the trumpet blasts, marking the interadvental period. After the seventh trumpet at the end of chapter 11, however, John shifts his focus, revisiting the interadvental age to provide a more detailed account of evil and judgment. Likewise, while the bowl judgments describe the entire age and culminate in the judgment of Armageddon at the end of chapter 16, chapter 17 backtracks to unveil another aspect of this age, once again addressing judgment in chapter 19. Revelation presents the judgment resulting from the interadvental period three times (at the ends of chapters 11, 16, and 19), each offering a unique perspective. Therefore, it is fitting to return to the theme of atonement at the start of chapter 20, presenting yet another view.

SATAN BOUND

Revelation 20 begins with an angel descending from heaven to seize and bind the Devil. This angel is not able to shackle Satan through greater physical strength or cosmic force. Instead, the angel's power comes from the Creator's spiritual authority—the infinite ability to govern all his creation, including Satan and his angels.[1] Satan is bound for 1,000 years, only to be released for "a short time." But when does this binding and loosing occur?

Satan deceived humanity in the garden of Eden, accused Job before God, and wielded power to influence events surrounding Job's life. His demons even engaged in battle with Gabriel and Michael in Daniel 10. In this present age, he prowls like a roaring lion, seeking to devour (1 Peter 5:8). Revelation 12 shows Satan, the dragon, attacking both before and after the Messiah's atonement. Given Satan's ongoing activity throughout biblical history, the idea that he could ever be bound in a way that prevents him from "deceiving the nations" seems unlikely. This apparent contradiction has given rise to an entire eschatological framework that envisions a future thousand-year period during which Satan will be bound.

However, if the thousand years mentioned at the beginning of Revelation 20 follow chronologically from the battle in chapter 19, the purpose of both the battle and the binding becomes unclear. How, for example, could deception still occur if the beast and the false prophet (the land beast) have already been thrown into the lake of fire (19:20)? If the beasts—symbols of humanity's cursed condition—are gone, redemption for all of physical creation must have been achieved. How, then, could the dragon return to Christ's redeemed creation to deceive after the thousand years? Who is left to be deceived, given that the battle in 19:17–21 involves the universal destruction of evil? With the great battle won, evil

---

1. Satan has never roamed freely because of any lack in the Creator's authority. God permits certain events to unfold, guided by his integrity and love. Rather than coercing, he seeks relationships built on love. It was this same integrity that allowed Satan to remain in heaven, not expelling the accuser until the falsehood of his accusations was fully exposed through the atonement.

vanquished, and Satan imprisoned, why doesn't God simply cast him into the lake of fire? Why does God plan to release him, allowing deception to rise again and leading to yet another army and another battle? What is the purpose of permitting deception after it has been stopped? These questions signal the need for a closer examination of the text.

The angel holding the key to the abyss and a great chain are symbolic elements. God does not need a physical chain to restrain evil. Thus, the binding of Satan is figurative, with the purpose of keeping him from deceiving the nations. Four questions arise from this: (1) When does the binding occur? (2) How did Satan deceive nations before the binding? (3) How does the binding prevent this deception? and (4) Why is he released at the end of this period?

In Matthew 12, Jesus casts out a demon by the Spirit of God, and the Pharisees accuse him of doing so by Satan's power. Jesus responds with a logical point: "If Satan drives out Satan, he is divided against himself.... How can someone enter a strong man's house and steal his possessions unless he first ties up the strong man?" (verses 26 and 29). The logic suggests that in fulfilling God's purpose in this situation, Jesus first "ties up" (or binds) Satan. The binding prevents Satan from obstructing God's work. Importantly, the binding does not stop the strong man from existing, breathing, or acting in other ways—it simply stops him from interfering with the one entering the house to take its goods. Similarly, Satan's binding serves to prevent him from obstructing God's specific plans and purposes.

Jesus came into this cursed world to accomplish God's plan of redemption. With that purpose in mind, he bound Satan—preventing him from interfering with God's redemptive work. Jesus achieved this redemption and, through the apostles and his growing family of believers, intended to bring to God all who would come into his kingdom. Revelation 12 illustrates this figuratively: after the atonement, the dragon (Satan) attempts to destroy the woman (faithful Israel), sending a flood from his mouth to overwhelm her. But the earth helps the woman by swallowing the flood. In this sense, Satan is figuratively bound, unable to destroy God's plan for faithful Israel. The thousand-year period of Satan's binding represents God preventing him from thwarting the ongoing work of building his kingdom during this time.

In the pre-atonement, Old Testament period, God chose the nation of Israel as the means through which his redemption plan would unfold. During this time, Satan deceived the nations, preventing them from worshiping God and expecting God's redemption through Israel, despite the fact that God's "invisible qualities—His eternal power and divine nature—have been clearly seen, being understood from what has been made" (Romans 1:20). With his victory through the atonement, Jesus bound Satan, preventing him from deceiving the nations. This fulfilled the Abrahamic covenant promise that all nations would be blessed, as Jesus brought the gospel to the world. This covenantal fulfillment is God's purpose during this age, and Jesus continues to build his kingdom. While Satan seeks to destroy that kingdom, God restrains him, preventing him from succeeding by keeping him bound.

But once Satan is bound, why would God ever release him? What reason could there be to allow Satan to once again deceive the nations and try to extinguish the gospel? Did Jesus lose control of the chain? Did a crafty demon manage to break the bond with supernatural tools? The only way Satan's deceptive influence could return to dominance over the gospel is if God intentionally releases him—which is precisely what happens at the end of verse 3. God allows this because, at that point, the work of the gospel is complete. As discussed earlier in this book's chapter 10, the age of the gospel will come to an end. Since Christ's resurrection, individuals have waged war within their own hearts. Through his Spirit, God has actively and passionately engaged with the world, using his infinite knowledge of creation and all possibilities to orchestrate circumstances for good and to build the greatest community for an everlasting love relationship. But that relationship begins with faith—the desire for relationship. Those who choose self over God reject his revelation, and God, not wanting any to perish, coordinates all events to provide the greatest possible opportunity for them to come to him.

However, God does not coerce, as love cannot be forced. When individuals reject God's revelation and choose self, their hearts harden. This hardness, when joined with others, causes evil to grow. Eventually, a point is reached when no more opportunities for change remain—when the collective hardness of hearts leaves no space for malleability. When the possibility for repentance is exhausted, God, who knows all possibilities, will release Satan, but without any risk to his kingdom. During that "short time," Satan and his deceptive message will gather and rally the hardened hearts into vast armies, covering the whole earth (20:9a). Deception will seem to have triumphed, as symbolized by the surrounding of "the camp of God's people" (20:9b). But this triumph is fleeting. Christ will return, bringing judgment and redemption (20:9c; 2 Thessalonians 1:7–8).

REIGNING A THOUSAND YEARS

Revelation 20, particularly verses 4 through 6, recounts the events of this age from the perspective of Satan's binding. God intends this message for all of us living between Christ's first advent in victory (verses 1–3) and his final advent in victory (verses 7–9). Verse 4 begins with a vision of thrones and judgment, describing the present age. We are reminded of Jesus's promise to the disciples that they would sit on thrones when he ascended to his. Both Paul and the author of Hebrews affirm that Jesus is now seated with God (Ephesians 1:20; Hebrews 1:3). Likewise, we, too, are seated and reigning with Christ (2 Timothy 2:12; Revelation 1:6). But what does it mean to reign with him? Who are we judging? Who are we instructing? Who recognizes us as authorities? In reality, no one does. But if I'm reigning with Christ, why don't I have anyone under my control?

That's not how it works, and it's not what reigning with Christ means. Whenever we think of reigning with Christ—sitting on thrones, judging the world, or having authority—our minds should immediately return to the Antonia Fortress in Jerusalem, 2,000 years ago, when Jesus stood before Pilate and said, "My kingdom is not of this world" (John 18:36). Understanding this statement is key to understanding what it means to reign in Christ's kingdom.

Christ's kingdom is not of this world and does not follow the power structures of this world. It seeks no control over anyone's thoughts or actions. In Matthew 20:25–28, Jesus told his disciples: "You know that the rulers of the Gentiles [*ethnon*: nations, peoples—the world] lord it over them, and their high officials exercise authority over them. Not so with you. Instead, whoever wants to become great among you must be your servant, and whoever wants to be first must be your slave—just as the Son of Man did not come to be served, but to serve, and to give his life as a ransom for many." For Jesus, reigning does not mean gaining control over others. Love is the hallmark of Christ's kingdom, and love gives; it does not dominate or control.

As image bearers in the kingdom of God and Christ, we reflect his image, shining forth the truth, goodness, and beauty of God. That is what it means to reign, just as Christ reigned and continues to reign. Everything that contrasts with God's truth, goodness, and beauty is exposed as false. Pilate didn't understand Jesus's statement because he expected a king and a kingdom based on the world's notion of power and domination. But Jesus clarified that his kingdom is not like that—it is not of this world or its systems of physical power. Reigning in Jesus's kingdom involves the influence of relational love, not control.

We were created and redeemed to reign with Christ in this present age. In Revelation 20:4, as John describes this age from the beginning, he sees people—Christians, including us—seated on thrones. We reign and judge, but not through physical domination or control. Instead, we reign by reflecting God's truth, goodness, and beauty through love. In this way, we mirror Christ in his reign.

Verse 4 is complex and contains several elements that need clarification, especially since many translations seem to get it wrong. In most English translations, the second statement mentions "beheadings." However, the entire passage (verses 4–7) refers to those who were "beheaded" for their testimony of Jesus, who refused to worship the beast or accept his mark. These individuals came to life and reigned with the Messiah for 1,000 years, a resurrection called the "first resurrection," meaning the second death has no power over them. But hold on—this applies to all believers, not just those who were beheaded. The second death has no power over all who believe. So, is this passage really only about people who were beheaded? What about those who were burned at the stake, killed by the sword, or those who lived their entire lives testifying about Jesus but were not martyred?

The Greek word often translated as "beheaded" does not actually specify the head, nor does it necessarily imply martyrdom, execution, or even death. The word, used only here in the New Testament, literally means "to chop" or "cut off." Most translators assume John is referring to martyrdom and thus interpret it as decapitation. While other Greek texts (like those of Josephus and Plutarch) have used the word this way, the text itself doesn't specify that. Instead, it says those who testified about Jesus were "cut off." The Aramaic Bible in Plain English translates it this way: "And I saw seats, and they sat upon them, and judgment was given to them, and these souls who were *cut off* for the testimony of Yeshua and for the word of God. . . ." [Emphasis added.] In the Septuagint, the word is also used to describe the work of stonecutters and carpenters.

Since this passage speaks of the resurrection conditions that apply to all believers, focusing solely on beheaded martyrs is insufficient. Instead, John is telling us that all who testify of Jesus (the God-focused) are "cut off"—persecuted, ridiculed, or marginalized by the society of the beast.

Therefore, those who reign in Christ's kingdom—those who are "cut off" and who refuse the beast's mark—will come to life (20:4b). In this context, "life" means association with God. Those who come alive in Christ will reign with him throughout this age, whether they are physically alive on earth or with Christ after physical death. They will reign for a thousand years, symbolizing the entirety of this age. All who believe need not fear the second death—the final death reserved for those focused on the curse, who do not come alive during this age.

JUDGMENT AND FIRE

The final scene of chapter 20 (verses 10–15), depicting judgment, is entirely figurative. There is no literal great white throne, no physical scrolls recording every human action, and no actual lake of fire. Yet these elements hold significance because of what they represent. Together, they convey the ultimate destruction—the cessation and disappearance—of all evil.

A great white throne dominates the scene, symbolizing God's authority to judge all of creation that stands in opposition to him. We immediately read that earth and heaven flee from his presence. But why? Are they not part of his creation? Yes, but this physical creation, the essence of humankind, became cursed through human worship of it. The fleeing of earth and heaven highlights that only God is worthy of worship, as his essence—truth, goodness, and beauty—is the sole foundation for a true relationship. Their departure symbolizes the removal of the curse through the Redeemer.

Not all humans appear before God for judgment in this scene. Instead, "the dead" stand before him. The text does not describe the God-focused as "dead"; they are alive (20:4, 6). The books that list the works of the dead represent their failure to live by TGB, in contrast to the book of life. Again, this is figurative—there is no literal book of life. Rather, this book symbolizes the very heart of God. In chapter 5, Jesus takes the book from God's hand, making it his own and sharing God's desire for restored relationship. In chapter 10, the book (God's heart) is opened as Jesus fulfills redemption's plan for the world through his death. And now, in chapter 20, this book, with our names written on his heart, seals our eternal relationship with God.

The sea, Hades, and Death give up their dead, emphasizing that this final event encompasses all those separated from God. All the dead, along with Death itself, are cast into the lake of fire. Verse 10 tells us that Satan, the beast, and the false prophet were already thrown into this lake. The figurative nature of the scene allows abstract concepts—such as the beast, the false prophet, and Death—to join the individuals and angels in the lake of fire. This lake symbolizes the everlasting removal of all who desired separation from God and all that is incompatible with life—relationship with God. Without God's sustaining presence, nothing can continue to exist.

We see this conclusion echoed in the illustrations and pronouncements of destruction throughout Scripture. The chaff in Psalm 1:4 is blown away. The wicked in Psalm 1:6 end in ruin. They are shattered like pottery in Psalm 2:9 and torn apart without rescue in Psalm 50:22. Psalm 69:28 speaks of the wicked being erased from the book of life. Most of the Bible's images of judgment depict destruction, not eternal torment, as the end of evil. For example, Sodom and Gomorrah were destroyed completely; their people did not suffer perpetually. The New Testament similarly uses language that suggests finality in destruction, as seen in Matthew 7:13, John 3:16, 17:12, Acts 8:20, Romans 9:22–23, Philippians 1:28, 3:19, 1 Thessalonians 5:3, 2 Thessalonians 1:9, 2:3, 1 Timothy 6:9, Hebrews 10:39, and 2 Peter 2:1. The New Testament also uses images such as chaff, trees, weeds, and branches being burned up (Matthew 3:12, 7:19, 13:40, John 15:6), a destroyed house (Matthew 7:27), discarded fish (Matthew 13:48), an uprooted plant (Matthew 15:13), and a chopped-down tree (Luke 13:7). Peter emphasizes that Sodom and Gomorrah, reduced to ash and ruin, exemplify the fate of the ungodly. If their destruction was complete, not perpetual torment, should we not consider the punishment of all the ungodly in the same way?

The Bible, especially the New Testament, uses the image of fire as ongoing and unquenchable to emphasize the finality of destruction. For example, in Mark 9:48, when referring to hell's unquenchable fire and undying worms, Mark draws from the final judgment described in Isaiah 66:24: "As they leave, they will see the dead bodies of the men who have rebelled against Me; for their worm will never die, their fire will never go out, and they will be a horror to all mankind." The unquenchable fire is mentioned in the context of completely dead bodies. Clearly, the idea of continuous torture is not in view. Instead, the unquenchable fire symbolizes a judgment that is final and irreversible.

The annihilation—the complete disappearance—of all evil is essential. Creation and life exist by God's intentional creative power, and he sustains everything (Hebrews 1:1–3). Nothing can continue to exist—not even hell—without God's direct and intentional sustaining hand. Ultimate death is separation from God, and anything fully separated from him cannot endure. Revelation 21:4 (HCSB) declares, "Death will no longer exist!" If death no longer exists, then separation from God is no more. God cannot engage in a loveless relationship, and when there is no longer a sustaining purpose for love, everything opposed to God must cease to exist. The image of death consumed in the lake of fire represents this final, ultimate separation.

30

Reigning in Rest (Rev 21–22)

Where never moon shall sway
The stars; but she,
And night, shall be
Drown'd in one endless day.

—Robert Herrick, from "Eternity"

I have installed my king on Zion,
my holy mountain.

—Psalm 2:6

God created humanity for an everlasting love relationship with him. While this relationship became possible through the atonement, its ultimate fulfillment is revealed in Revelation 21. The final two chapters of Revelation emphasize four key ideas: the restoration accomplished (21:1–8), the redeemed described (21:9–27), the rest realized in everlasting life (22:1–5), and the present hope for the swift arrival of that glory (22:6–21).

RESTORATION ACCOMPLISHED

A new heaven and a new earth burst onto the scene, and "burst" is not too dramatic a word. This newness signifies the complete eradication of sin and the removal of the curse that has enslaved us since the fall in the garden. Verse one combines three key elements: the appearance of a new heaven and earth, the passing away of the first heaven and earth, and the absence of the sea.

The transition from the old to the new does not depict cosmic upheaval. The literalist who imagines the destruction of the old universe and the creation of a new one ex nihilo envisions something far beyond even a figurative interpretation. Throughout Scripture, and particularly in Revelation, the emphasis is on redemption, which means restoration, not replacement. The "new" highlights the purity gained, free from the curse. As Paul affirms, "The body that is sown is perishable, it is raised imperishable; it is sown in dishonor, it is raised in glory; it is sown in weakness, it is raised in power; it is sown a natural body, it is raised a spiritual body" (1 Corinthians 15:42b–44a). The old will be reborn, not replaced. Our bodies will be transformed: "For the perishable must clothe itself with the imperishable, and the mortal with immortality" (1 Corinthians 15:52b–53). This transformation is the victory over death, not the concession of the old creation to death's inevitability, but the realization of Christ's triumph in restoration.

One of the central themes of Romans 7 and 8 underscores the distinction between our still-corrupted flesh and our renewed life. Paul expresses anguish over the struggles of his God-centered soul, yearning for freedom from the curse on his flesh. In Romans 8, he declares that our physical essence—creation itself—"waits in eager expectation for the children of God to be revealed (for the creation was subjected to frustration, not by its own choice, but by the will of the one [Adam] who subjected it) in hope that the creation itself will be liberated from its bondage to decay and brought into the freedom and glory of the children of God. We know that the whole creation has been groaning as in the pains of childbirth right up to the present time. Not only so, but we ourselves, who have the firstfruits of the Spirit, groan inwardly as we wait eagerly for our adoption to sonship, the redemption of our bodies" (Romans 8:19–23). Thus, our physical universe will not be dissolved and replaced by redesigned or regenerated matter and energy. Rather, this universe will be gloriously restored to its original, curse-free state.

However, we must recognize that not everything will return to the way it was in Eden. We, who have grown in truth, goodness, and beauty, understand our source in God and our necessity for relationship, and we would not wish to lose that knowledge. We would not desire a regression to Adam and Eve's pre-revelational state, nor a relationship with God that could once again fall. In the new heaven and new earth, there is no tree of the knowledge of good and evil; God has already imparted that knowledge, fully revealed in Jesus. And through his ongoing revelation to us, we are now fully satisfied in TGB. In this new paradise, only the tree of life remains, symbolizing our eternal, unbroken relationship with God (22:2).

Verse 1 also tells us that the sea is no more. In Revelation, we journey from the scene in chapter 4, where God is depicted in judgment, symbolized by thrones, living creatures, and a raging sea. But the Kinsman Redeemer has triumphed, and our names are engraved on his heart. We crossed the sea (15:2). In the victory of chapter 21, the sea is gone! We now have complete access to the full embrace of our God. Death, grief, and pain are no more. We are fully satisfied.

To make this image of satisfaction even more profound, God calls out from the throne with the same words Jesus spoke in the temple (John 7:37–39). He promises springs of living water to quench the thirst of all who are parched. We have thirsted through generations of sin, but with the redeemed creation in place, our thirst is fully quenched. The waters of purification, symbolized by John's baptism and the wedding at Cana, along with the Spirit that secures our adoption (Galatians 3:26–27 and Romans 8:16), come together to complete the satisfaction of this Revelation 21 scene.

REDEEMED DESCRIBED

Beginning in verse 9 of Revelation chapter 21, the focus shifts slightly. The New Jerusalem was introduced earlier in verse 2 as the culmination of God's redemptive plan. However, verse 9 expands on this by offering a fuller description of the redeemed's new state. In verse 2, the city is portrayed as "a bride beautifully dressed for her husband." This image continues in verse 9, where the emphasis is on the city itself representing "the bride, the wife of the Lamb." Pay close attention to this: the New Jerusalem is not merely a place where the redeemed will live; the city, figuratively, is the bride (21:2). The angel tells John, "Come, I will show you the bride, the wife of the Lamb" (21:9), and then reveals "the Holy City, Jerusalem, coming down out of heaven from God" (21:12).

Since the imagery stresses the concept of marriage, we should explore its meaning. The marriage metaphor is deliberately chosen as a symbolic image, representing the oneness in several relationships: (1) within God himself, (2) within the community of believers, and (3) in our union with God. Through this image, God teaches us about his own nature. One key lesson is the idea of using our abilities for the benefit of the whole in relationship. God emphasized this when he created humanity as male and female. He endowed each gender with particular strengths—generally, males with greater physical force and females with greater nurturing capacity. These strengths were given so that each person could wield them in self-denying submission for the good of the whole. In this mutual submission, we glimpse the heart of God.

However, sin entered the world, bringing with it a self-centeredness that distorts the servant-hearted love God intended. Men, instead of using their strength to serve, often dominate others, especially women, for their own gratification. Similarly, women sometimes use their strengths for self-promotion, damaging relationships in the process. To address this selfishness, the law established numerous regulations for Israel to curb such abuses.

Yet even within a sinful world, God calls his people to use their strengths for the good of others, and marriage should still reflect this dynamic of mutual submission. Paul uses marriage as an example of how to "submit to one another" (Ephesians 5:21), as he urges unity among the Gentile and Jewish believers in the Ephesian church. He explains that a husband should give of himself for his wife and for the benefit of their relationship, just as Christ gave himself for the church. Likewise, a wife should give of herself for her husband and for the good of their union. Paul's emphasis is not on authority but on mutual submission, with both partners contributing to the relationship's well-being.

To help distinguish between the concepts of authority over someone and responsibility for someone's care, imagine a king with guards assigned to protect him. The guards have no authority over the king, yet they are responsible for using their skills (training, strength, etc.)—even to the point of sacrificing their lives—to safeguard him. Christ did this for us. In Ephesians 5, Paul calls on husbands to do the same for their wives, just as Christ did for the church. When, for example, a father hands his daughter to the groom in a wedding ceremony, he is not transferring ownership or authority. Rather, he is passing the responsibility of care from one who has given of himself for his daughter to another who is now called to give of himself for his wife, loving her as Christ loved the church. Similarly, the wife submits herself to her husband, but the purpose is not hierarchy—it is the glory of their love relationship. Marriage doesn't require equality in every sense; its beauty lies in self-giving love, where both partners set aside self-focus for the joy of the relationship.

This understanding enhances the excitement of the scene in Revelation 21. The city descends from heaven—not a literal place, but symbolizing the heart of God—like a bride, embodying God's preservation and Christ's life-giving protection. It radiates the truth, goodness, and beauty of God.

To convey this vision, John says the angel "carried me away in the Spirit." This phrase signals a shift from the physical world to a spiritual one. John uses this expression at the beginning of Revelation (1:10) to indicate that what he sees is not earthly. In Revelation 21, the Spirit transports John to a great, high mountain. Throughout Scripture, mountains often represent kingdoms, and here the great, high mountain symbolizes the kingdom of God filling the whole earth, much like the imagery in Nebuchadnezzar's dream in Daniel 2.

It's important to remember that what we read here is a figurative description of God's kingdom, not a literal account of its physical appearance or location. John is using earthly images to communicate spiritual truths. In just a few verses, he describes the city as a cube, 1,400 miles wide, long, and tall. Imagining such a city literally is impractical. Are we to picture it descending to an area that would extend from the Persian Gulf to somewhere near Greece? And what about the 144-cubit-high wall—about 200 feet tall—surrounding a 1,400-mile-high city? It hardly seems appropriate to call the wall "massively high" (21:12) when it's only 0.00003% of the city's height. But we are not meant to envision a physical cubed city. Instead, the description is meant to convey the nature of God's kingdom and the relationship won through Christ.

The wall represents both separation and protection. In Isaiah 60:18, the city's walls are described as salvation and its gates as praise. In Zechariah 2:1–5, we read that the city will have no physical walls, but that God himself will be a wall of fire around it. These different depictions of city walls teach us that God separates us from the sin of this world and brings us into his kingdom of righteousness, where we are protected by him alone.

The gates and their foundations are linked to angels, the tribes of Israel, and the apostles. Gates serve as entry points to a city, and this figurative connection shows that throughout history, God has drawn people into his kingdom through his messengers—angels, Israel, and the apostles—fulfilling Zion's relational purpose.

In verse 15, we see that the city is measured as a cube, resembling the Holy of Holies in the tabernacle and temple, where the Israelites met with God. Just as incense filled the Holy of Holies, so God fills this city—his relational purpose. This signifies that we are in him, and he is in us, as Jesus prayed in John 17:21.

The act of measuring the city carries the same figurative meaning as it does throughout the Bible. In Revelation 11, John measures the sanctuary with a measuring rod, symbolically identifying and defining it. God uses this act of measuring to define those who will have a relationship with him, marking them as his people. Similarly, in Revelation 21, the measurement of the city emphasizes that God has intentionally designed and constructed his people as part of his redemptive plan.

The city's size—12,000 stadia—appears vast. A stadion is about 600 feet, so 12,000 stadia would be approximately 1,400 miles. However, focusing on the literal measurements misses the point. The number 12 signifies judicial or governmental completeness, while the number 1,000 represents a vast quantity (e.g., Psalm 68:17, 90:4, 91:7; Isaiah 30:17; Jeremiah 32:18). Together, the combination of 12 and 1,000 signifies that this city encompasses a vast and complete number, representing God's redemptive purpose.

The materials used in the city's construction are deeply symbolic. The walls are not made of iron or stone, as one might expect for a literal defensive barrier. Instead, they are founded on precious stones. This detail indicates that the walls are not meant to depict physical fortification but rather to represent God's loving protection, grounded in the purity of his truth, goodness, and beauty. The twelve precious stones that form the foundation recall the high priest's breastplate, which bore the names of the tribes of Israel as he entered the Holy of Holies to meet with God. These stones symbolized purity in the relationship between God and his people, and they carry the same meaning here in Revelation 21.

Each gate is made from a single pearl. While it's hard to imagine how a gate could function if made of a large, round pearl, the visual detail isn't the point. We don't need to speculate about where these giant pearls came from. Pearls are formed through irritation, a reminder of the suffering endured by God's people on their journey to his city. This idea, in fact, is central to the message of Revelation.

Verse 22 tells us that no specific temple exists because the entire city serves as a sanctuary where communion with God takes place continuously. Verse 23 adds that the city needs no sun or moon, not to suggest a cosmic disruption but to emphasize a shift in focus—from our physical essence to God's essence. This imagery resonates strongly with Isaiah 24:23: "The moon will be dismayed, the sun ashamed; for the Lord Almighty will reign on Mount Zion and in Jerusalem, and before its elders—with great glory." The glory of the moon and sun, symbols of worldly splendor, will fade as God reigns from the mountain of his fulfilled covenant promise, dwelling with his people in Jerusalem. His essence—truth, goodness, and beauty—manifested through love, will be revealed to all who are wise. In our eternal union with God, our dependence will be on him, not on our perceptions shaped by the physical world. We will see by the light of God's revelation.

Verse 24 echoes this idea. John is not outlining a governmental structure for the new earth. Instead, the nations and kings signify a transformation in how things operate—from selfish interests to the truth, goodness, and beauty of God. The kings bring their actions into the city, where they are transformed into acts of God. Love, expressed through relationship, guides and governs.

The chapter concludes by revealing that the gates of the city never close, even at night. In Scripture, night often represents the end of activity, but in this city, the love and relational activity never cease.

REST REALIZED

The first five verses of Revelation 22 highlight the rest and fulfillment realized through ten symbolic images. The first five of these images remind us of the garden of Eden before sin entered.

A river of living water flows, just as a river once fed Eden. This river comes from God and represents the Spirit, life, and satisfaction. Growing alongside it is the tree of life, described as being on both sides of the river (which could also suggest multiple trees surrounding the river). This tree of life also appeared in Eden, symbolizing life and relationship with God. It produces twelve kinds of fruit—the number representing judicial completion—indicating that God continually provides for all life's needs, year-round, reflecting the never-ending cycle of life. The leaves of the tree provide healing, symbolizing the satisfaction found in God in contrast to the want and despair that characterize the absence of God in an evil environment. This theme culminates in verse 3, where we learn that the curse is finally gone. Ezekiel 47:12 gathers these Old Testament images to describe eternal life in relationship with God: "Fruit trees of all kinds will grow on both banks of the river. Their leaves will not wither, nor will their fruit fail. Every month they will bear fruit, because the water from the sanctuary flows to them. Their fruit will serve for food and their leaves for healing."

Verse 3 continues, "The throne of God and of the Lamb will be in the city, and his servants will serve him." This phrasing emphasizes that God's rule will be unlike worldly rulers who demand service solely for their own benefit. Psalm 89:14 reminds us, "Righteousness and justice are the foundation of your throne; love and faithfulness go before you." God will rule the city with his truth, goodness, and beauty expressed in relational love. Life under God's throne will bring joy and fulfillment for all.

Verses 4 and 5 complete this picture of joy: we will see his face! We will fully know him in relationship. Paul touches on this thought in 1 Corinthians 13 when he speaks of love. He explains that our current understanding of love is limited—like seeing through a dim mirror. But in the New Jerusalem, face to face with God, we will know, understand, express, and receive love in its fullest beauty. God will write his name on our foreheads, symbolizing the care and protection that the head provides to the body. John draws on Paul's head imagery from 1 Corinthians 11 and Ephesians 1 and 5 to underscore again God's TGB provision for us.

Once more, the text reveals the absence of night, which symbolizes the absence of disruption to the full joy of our relationship with God. We will bask in the light of his love without interruption. And we will reign—expressing that love in his truth, goodness, and beauty—forever and ever.

HOPE FOR SOON RETURN

The epilogue of Revelation begins in verse 6 of chapter 22. Many elements of the prologue are mirrored here in the epilogue, reiterating the purpose and assurance of the message. God speaks to and through Jesus, who is the Word—faithful and true. These final words are delivered by an angel to John, who records them for the benefit of all God's people.

At one point, John begins to bow before the angel, but the angel quickly redirects his worship to God. The angel stresses that the message is not his own but God's. This isn't about God reacting with pride over misdirected worship. Rather, true relationship is possible only when grounded in God's truth, goodness, and beauty, which come solely from him. Our lives—our faith, hope, and love—must be anchored in this essence of God to experience the purpose and blessing of relationship with him. We rejoice in this and worship God for who he is.

It's also worth noting that the message delivered by God's angel in verse 6 is the same message John receives from Jesus through Jesus's own angel in verse 16. This connection emphasizes that Jesus is God. However, we cannot overlook his humanity. Though he is divine—as verse 16 tells us, the root (Creator and Giver of life) of David—he is also the offspring of David, qualified to be the human king (Romans 15:12).

Worship continues in verse 17, but with added emphasis on our role as participants. God is worshiped for his TGB, and the Spirit calls out to all image-bearers to come and be satisfied in him. God didn't create us merely to offer praise but to join in the dance of everlasting love. As the bride, we join with the Spirit in calling others to come as we joyfully pursue the kingdom.

I recently came across the thoughts of a Christian theologian who argued in his blog that the church is not the kingdom, and thus pastors should stop urging congregants to help build it. He claimed that the kingdom is purely a gift from God, who builds it alone. According to him, while we can pray for the kingdom and participate in it, we don't contribute to its construction. I believe this writer misunderstands the nature of the kingdom. The kingdom is not just the essence of God as TGB or his rule based on that essence. It is the dynamic interaction between God and those he created. The curse distorted this into the kingdoms of this world, but God's kingdom includes his essence as the foundation of relationship and our active participation in faith, hope, and love. As we join and invite others to join, we not only participate in the kingdom's operation but also in its building. Our involvement does not detract from God as the essential founder, initiator, and sustainer.

Throughout this epilogue, the urgency of the message leaps off the page. The events are said to "soon take place" (22:6), and we are reminded repeatedly that the time is near (22:10). The call to action is clear: "Come! Come!" (22:17). Three times in these final verses, Jesus promises, "I am coming soon!" (22:7, 12, 20). The response of John—and of the entire church—is, "Amen! Come, Lord Jesus!"

Jesus is coming! Blessed are those whose robes have been washed clean—made righteous (faithful to the covenant) through the faithfulness of Jesus. Outside this group, outside the kingdom, are those who remain unrighteous and unfaithful to the covenant. These outsiders are described as liars, murderers, dogs, idolaters, sorcerers, and the sexually immoral. Each of these categories, which are linked to abominations in the Old Testament, directly opposes the image of God:

Liars	oppose	Truth of God
Murderers	oppose	Goodness of God
Dogs	oppose	Beauty of God
Idolators	oppose	Faith of God
Sorcerers	oppose	Hope of God
Sexually Immoral	oppose	Love of God

For those within the kingdom, blessings await: the blessing of the Bright Morning Star (22:16), the blessing of the water of life (22:17), the blessing of God's deliverance (22:20), and the blessing of God's grace (22:21).

The book of Revelation showcases the glory of God's complete redemption story, moving from estrangement from God (chapter 4), through atoning victory (chapter 10), to everlasting love and relationship with him (chapter 22). Along this journey, especially during the gathering of this age, evil swirls around, seeking to harm God's community (chapters 13-19). Christ warns of this ongoing battle and encourages steadfast trust in him (chapters 2 and 3).

Jesus told his disciples that he no longer calls them slaves, because a slave does not know what his master is doing. Instead, he calls them friends, for he has revealed to them everything he heard from the Father (John 15:15). Now, we too—those who have received the full story of God's plan through the revelation of Jesus, believed in it, and placed our hope in it—are embraced as friends of God forever.

Appendix: Kinship Theology

KINSHIP THEOLOGY (KT) OFFERS a transformative lens for understanding God's relationship with humanity and all creation. At its core, KT asserts that every divine action flows from a love relationship—love defined not merely as affection or sentiment, but as the giving of oneself for the benefit of relationship. This foundational perspective reshapes how we view God's essence, humanity's purpose, and the unfolding of God's restorative plan, offering hope and purpose for all creation. KT is not just a theological framework but a relational one that calls us to live in kinship with God and with one another, embodying his love in all things.

KT invites us to a deeper understanding of God's truth, goodness, and beauty—qualities that do more than transform individual lives. These attributes, rooted in relationship, also reshape the bonds that tie us together as God's image bearers. By calling us into kinship with him and each other, KT offers a vision of life as it was always meant to be—marked by divine love and expressed through communal living.

KT'S SEVEN FOUNDATIONAL PRINCIPLES

#1: God's Essence and Activity

KT begins with the assertion that God is one eternal being who exists as truth, goodness, and beauty (TGB), which are perfectly embodied in the three persons of the Trinity. These core qualities are not merely attributes of God; they are the essence of his being. Love, in KT, is God's eternal motivation for all his actions—a love that always seeks relationship. Faith, hope, and love permeate all God's actions, and his essence is perfectly expressed through the Trinity. Every act of God, whether in creation, redemption, or providence, reflects his unwavering commitment to love, inviting humanity into a deep, reciprocal relationship with him.

#2: Creation and Humanity's Purpose

God's creation includes both the heavenly host and humanity, the latter of which is uniquely made in God's image to reflect his essence as they steward the physical world. Humanity's primary purpose is relational: to live in love with God and with one another, manifesting truth, goodness, and beauty in all aspects of life. Our reflection of God's essence is most fully realized through our relationships—with God, with each other, and with creation itself. Thus, our calling is to reflect God's nature in a way that brings harmony to the world, participating in the ongoing act of creation and stewardship.

#3: The Fall—A Relational Breach

The fall of humanity, as described in Genesis, represents not just a moral failure but a relational breach. Adam and Eve's choice to trust in the created world over God resulted in a fractured relationship with their Creator. Sin is more than just disobedience; it is a rupture in the kinship bond that God intended between himself and his image bearers. As a consequence, humanity's essence—its physical nature—was marred, and all physical creation fell under the curse. Yet, despite this breach, God continued to sustain humanity with the hope of eventual restoration, demonstrating his unrelenting love and desire for reconciliation.

#4: Atonement—Redemption through Love

In Kinship Theology, atonement is the means by which God restores the broken relationship between himself and humanity. Through Jesus Christ, God enters into human experience, uniting his divine soul with a fallen, cursed human body. Jesus's perfect life revealed his unblemished soul, and his sacrificial death—though not required for his own soul—fulfilled the curse on human physical essence. In this ultimate act of love, Jesus offered himself to restore humanity to a kinship relationship with God. His resurrection marks the beginning of the renewal of all things, demonstrating the possibility of perfect union with God. Through Christ's atoning work, humanity's essence is restored, and creation itself is brought one step closer to redemption.

#5: Salvation—From Estrangement to Kinship

In Kinship Theology, salvation is not about escaping Hell but about being brought into a restored relationship with God—a transition from estrangement to kinship, from separation to union with the Creator. God elects to restore his image bearers based on faith, a concept known within KT as faith electionism. His mercy and redemption are offered to all sinful humanity, not simply to rescue them from destruction but to draw them into an everlasting love relationship. Although God doesn't coerce, he requires a personal faith expression from the individual, as love cannot be forced. Faith involves trusting that God alone is the source of truth, goodness, and beauty, that he alone rescues from the curse of death, and that he alone offers the hope of everlasting life in union with him. The Holy Spirit plays a vital role in this process, convicting of sin, illuminating God's truth, and empowering believers to live in love as God intended. Through the Spirit, believers are united to God and to one another in the communal expression of truth, goodness, and beauty. Salvation begins and ends with God—through his self-revelation, the atonement of Christ, and the application of its benefits to the believer, all for the sake of love relationship.

#6: Last Things—The Hope of Restoration

The culmination of God's restorative plan includes full redemption—the application of Christ's victory to remove the curse and restore all physical creation to its original and intended place. In this redemption, Christians realize their hope (Romans 8:23b–24a): an everlasting love relationship with God in a renewed creation. This restoration is not merely a physical renewal but the fulfillment of God's purpose to reconcile all things to himself, bringing harmony to creation and deepening the relational bond between God and his image bearers.

Because all physical essence is restored together, the judgment of the wicked (allowing them to follow their desire to be apart from God, which leads to their destruction), the gaining of our new bodies, and the start of the new heavens and earth must all occur simultaneously at the coming of Christ (Titus 2:13). At that moment, love reigns supreme and eternal, as God's image bearers live in eternal kinship with him and with one another in a world redeemed by truth, goodness, and beauty.

#7: Community—Living Out Love

The true manifestation of KT is seen in community. In the kingdom of God, love becomes the central ethic, replacing worldly notions of power and hierarchy. Restored image bearers live out God's essence as a matter of the heart, where love, care, and sacrifice are the guiding principles. KT challenges believers to set aside selfishness for the good of the whole, creating a community marked by reciprocal love and mutual care. This is a vision of unity and fulfillment, where God's love binds believers together, and together they reflect his truth, goodness, and beauty in the world.

CONCLUSION

Kinship Theology offers a powerful vision of God's love that radically transforms how we understand his nature, humanity's purpose, and the plan for redemption. It invites us into a deep, abiding relationship with God—one rooted in love, lived out in community, and ultimately fulfilled in the restoration of all things. Through KT, we are called to live as reflections of God's essence, embodying truth, goodness, and beauty in our relationships with each other and with the world.

Bibliography

Alexander, T. Desmond. *The City of God and the Goal of Creation*. Wheaton: Crossway, 2018.
Anstey, Martin. *The Romance of Bible Chronology*. Vol. 2, *Chronological Tables*. New York: Marshall Brothers, 1913.
Armstrong, Aaron. "What Do We Do with Psalm 137?" *Crosswalk*, July 27, 2017. https://www.crosswalk.com/faith/bible-study/what-do-we-do-with-psalm-137.html.
Beale, G. K. *The Book of Revelation: A Commentary on the Greek Text*. Grand Rapids: Eerdmans, 1999.
———. *A New Testament Biblical Theology: The Unfolding of the Old Testament in the New*. Grand Rapids: Baker Academic, 2011.
Boettner, Loraine. *The Millennium*. Phillipsburg, NJ: Presbyterian and Reformed, 1957.
Boyd, Gregory A. *Cross Vision: How the Crucifixion of Jesus Makes Sense of Old Testament Violence*. Minneapolis: Fortress, 2017.
———. *Is God to Blame?* Downers Grove, IL: InterVarsity, 2003.
———. "Molinism and Open Theism—Part II." *ReKnew*, May 13, 2014. https://reknew.org/2014/05/molinism-and-open-theism-part-ii/.
Bunsen, Christian Karl Josias. *God in History*. Vol. 3. Translated by Susanna Winkworth. London: Longmans, Green, and Co., 1870.
Cachila, J. B. "3 Ways We Water the Gospel Down." *Christian Today*, January 12, 2017. https://www.christiantoday.com/article/3-ways-we-water-the-gospel-down/103788.htm.
Clark, Gordon H. *God's Hammer: The Bible and Its Critics*. Jefferson, MD: The Trinity Foundation, 1982.
Comer, John Mark. "John Mark Comer: The Apprentice." *Outreach Magazine*, January 2, 2024. https://outreachmagazine.com/features/78413-john-mark-comer-the-apprentice.html.
Craig, William Lane. "Is God the Son Begotten in His Divine Nature?" *Reasonable Faith*, March 17, 2024. https://www.reasonablefaith.org/writings/scholarly-writings/christian-doctrines/is-god-the-son-begotten-in-his-divine-nature.
———. *Time and Eternity: Exploring God's Relationship to Time*. Wheaton, IL: Crossway, 2001.
Custer, Stewart. *Does Inspiration Demand Inerrancy?: A Study of the Biblical Doctrine of Inspiration in the Light of Inerrancy*. Nutley, NJ: The Craig Press, 1968.
Feinberg, Charles L. *Millennialism: The Two Major Views*. Chicago: Moody, 1980.
Gregg, Steve. *Revelation: Four Views, Revised & Updated*. Nashville: Thomas Nelson, 2013.

Hart, David Bentley. *That All Shall Be Saved: Heaven, Hell, and Universal Salvation*. New Haven, CT: Yale, 2019.

Hoehner, Harold W. *Ephesians: An Exegetical Commentary*. Grand Rapids: Baker Academic, 2002.

Jersak, Brad. "Nonviolent Identification and the Victory of Christ." In *Stricken by God?*, edited by Brad Jersak and Michael Hardin, 18–53. Grand Rapids: Eerdmans, 2007.

Johnson, Dennis E. *Triumph of the Lamb: A Commentary on Revelation*. Phillipsburg, NJ: P&R, 2001.

Keener, Craig S. *A Commentary on the Gospel of Matthew*. Grand Rapids: Eerdmans, 1999.

Lewis, C. S. *The Four Loves*. New York: HarperCollins, 1960.

——. *Mere Christianity*. New York: HarperCollins, 2001.

MacDonald, Gregory. *The Evangelical Universalist*. Eugene, OR: Cascade Books, 2012.

Mare, Leonard P. "Psalm 137: Exile—Not the Time for Singing the Lord's Song." *Old Testament Essays* 23, no. 1 (2010): 107–119. http://www.scielo.org.za/pdf/ote/v23n1/07.pdf.

Martin, Ernest L. "Chronological Falsehoods." *Associates For Scriptural Knowledge*, March 4, 1998. https://www.askelm.com/prophecy/p980304.htm.

Mason, Mike. *The Mystery of Marriage: Meditations on the Miracle*. Vancouver: Regent College Publishing, 2001.

Moltmann, Jürgen. *The Crucified God: The Cross of Christ As the Foundation and Criticism of Christian Theology*. Minneapolis: Fortress, 1993.

Moreland, J. P., and William Lane Craig. *Philosophical Foundations for a Christian Worldview*. Downers Grove, IL: InterVarsity, 2003.

Neal, Marshall. "Where Is the Lord God of Elijah?" Biblical Viewpoint 17, no. 2 (November 1983): 17–26.

Pentecost, J. Dwight. *Things to Come: A Study in Biblical Eschatology*. Grand Rapids: Zondervan, 1958.

Pink, Arthur W. *The Ability of God: Prayers of the Apostle Paul*. Chicago: Moody, 2000.

Pinnock, Clark H. *Most Moved Mover: A Theology of God's Openness*. Eugene, OR: Wipf & Stock, 2019.

Piper, John. "Rebuilding the Basics: The Centrality of God's Glory." *Desiring God*, November 4, 2009. https://www.desiringgod.org/articles/rebuilding-the-basics-the-centrality-of-gods-glory.

——. "Would God Have Been More Loving Not to Create Anyone?" *Desiring God*, June 22, 2020. https://www.desiringgod.org/interviews/would-god-have-been-more-loving-not-to-create-anyone.

Reymond, Robert L. *A New Systematic Theology of the Christian Faith*. Nashville: Thomas Nelson, 1998.

Sanders, John. *The God Who Risks: A Theology of Divine Providence*. Downers Grove, IL: IVP Academic, 2007.

Scofield, C. I. *What Do the Prophets Say?*. Philadelphia: The Sunday School Times, 1918.

Sproul, R. C. Jr. "Why Doesn't God Save Everybody?" *RC Sproul Jr.*, July 26, 2021. https://rcsprouljr.com/why-doesnt-god-save-everybody/.

Tillich, Paul. "The Word of God." In *Language: An Enquiry into its Meaning and Function*. Edited by Ruth Nanda Anshen. Port Washington, NY: Kennikat, 1971.

Warfield, Benjamin B. "God's Immeasurable Love." New Hope Presbyterian Church. https://www.newhopefairfax.org/images/Warfield__Gods_immeasurable_love.pdf.

Witherington, Ben III, with Darlene Hyatt. *Paul's Letter to the Romans: A Socio-Rhetorical Commentary*. Grand Rapids: Eerdmans, 2004.

Wright, N. T. *Jesus and the Victory of God*. Minneapolis: Fortress, 1996.

www.ingramcontent.com/pod-product-compliance
Lightning Source LLC
Chambersburg PA
CBHW052145300426
44115CB00011B/1527